Atneg

POEMS

FOURTH EDITION

WADSWORTH HANDBOOK AND ANTHOLOGY

C. F. MAIN
Rutgers University

PETER J. SENG
Connecticut College

Wadsworth Publishing Company, Inc.
Belmont, California

English Editor: Randy Cade

Production Editor: Larry Olsen

Printed in the United States of America

1 2 3 4 5 6 7 8 9 10--82 81 80 79 78

Library of Congress Cataloging in Publication Data

Main, Charles Frederick, 1921- ed.
Poems: Wadsworth handbook and anthology.

Includes index.
1. English poetry. 2. American poetry. 3. Poetics.
I. Seng, Peter J. II. Title.
PR1175.M25 1977 808'.1 77-23907
ISBN 0-534-00541-1

Copyrights and Acknowledgments

George Allen & Unwin Ltd.—for "Dread" from *The Collected Works of J. M. Synge*; and for "Because River Fog" from *The Temple*, translation by Arthur Waley.

Atheneum Publishers, Inc.,—for "The Dover Bitch" from *The Hard Hours* by Anthony Hecht, copyright © 1960 by Anthony E. Hecht. Reprinted by permission of Atheneum Publishers. This poem appeared originally in *Transatlantic Review*; and for "Eating Poetry" from *Reasons for Moving*, poems by Mark Strand. Copyright © 1968 by Mark Strand. Reprinted by permission of Atheneum Publishers.

Basic Books, Inc.—for "Down in Dallas" by X. J. Kennedy, from *Of Poetry and Power*; poems occasioned by the Presidency and by the death of John F. Kennedy, edited by Erwin A. Glikes and Paul Schwaber, © 1964 by Basic Books, Inc., Publishers, New York.

Julian Bond—for "Rotation."

Jonathan Cape Ltd.—for "A.E.H." from *A Look Round the Estate* by Kingsley Amis, © 1967 by Kingsley Amis; for "Naming of Parts" from *A Map of Verona* by Henry Reed; for "A Far Cry from Africa" and "In a Green Night" from *In a Green Night;* and for "Star" from *The Gulf and Other Poems* by Derek Walcott.

Charing Cross Music, Inc.—for "Richard Cory" by Paul Simon, © 1966 by Paul Simon. Used with the permission of the publisher.

Chatto & Windus, Ltd.—for "The Horse Chestnut Tree" from *Undercliff* by Richard Eberhart and "The Human Being Is a Lonely Creature" from *Collected Poems 1930–1960* by Richard Eberhart; for "Two Realities" from *Poems* by Aldous Huxley; and for "Arms and the Boy" and "Dulce et Decorum Est" from *Collected Poems,* 1946, 1963 by Wilfred Owen, edited by C. Day Lewis. Reprinted by permission of The Owen Estate and Chatto & Windus Ltd.

Chilmark Press—for "Cock at Sea" from *Grooves in the Wind*, copyright C. A. Trypanis, 1964.

City Lights Books—for "After Yeats" from *Planet News* by Allen Ginsberg, copyright © 1968 by Allen Ginsberg; and for "The Mad Yak" from *Gasoline* by Gregory Corso, copyright © 1958 by Gregory Corso. Both poems reprinted by permission of City Lights Books.

Constable and Company Ltd.—for "Leda and the Swan" by Oliver St. John Gogarty. Also by courtesy of Mr. Oliver D. Gogarty.

The Cresset Press Ltd.—for "The Watch" from *Collected Poems* by Frances Cornford.

Criterion Books, Inc.—for "To Any Member of My Generation" and "To My Mother" from *Collected Poems of George Barker, 1930–1955,* copyright 1957 by George Barker, published by Criterion Books, Inc., 1958.

Waring Cuney—for "The Death Bed" and "No Images" from *The Book of American Negro Poetry*, by permission of Waring Cuney. "The Death Bed" appeared in an anthology entitled *Caroline Dusk* by Countee Cullen, 1927.

Delacorte Press—for "The Chinese Checker Players" from *The Pill Versus the Springhill Mine Disaster* by Richard Brautigan. Copyright © 1968 by Richard Brautigan. A Seymour Lawrence Book/Delacorte Press. Reprinted by permission of the publisher.

J. M. Dent & Sons Ltd.—for "The Donkey" from *The Wild Knight and Other Poems* by G. K. Chesterton; and for "In My Craft or Sullen Art" and "Do Not Go Gentle into That Good Night" from *The Poems of Dylan Thomas,* 1946, 1952. All of these poems by permission of J. M. Dent & Sons, London.

The Dial Press—for "The Snake's Destiny" by Hy Sobiloff from *In the Deepest Aquarium*, copyright © 1959 by Hy Sobiloff, by permission of The Dial Press.

Doubleday & Company, Inc.—for "One Thousand Nine Hundred and Sixty-Eight Winters" by Jaci Earley; for "Twilight" by Paul Engle from the sequence "Harlem Airshaft" in *American Song*, 1934; for "Mushrooms" by Mike Evans from *Holding Your Eight Hands*, edited by E. Lucie-Smith, 1969; for "The Blue-Fly" and "Love without Hope" from *Collected Poems* by Robert Graves, 1955; for "A Sunbather in Late October" by Arthur Gregor; for "Tuskegee" by Leslie Pinckney Hill from *The Poetry of the Negro*, edited by Langston Hughes and Arna Bontemps; for "If," copyright 1910, by Rudyard Kipling and "The Recall," copyright 1909, by Rudyard Kipling from the book *Rudyard Kipling's Verse: Definitive Edition*. Reprinted by permission of The Executors of the Estate of Mrs. George Bambridge and Doubleday & Company, Inc.; and for "Root Cellar" copyright © 1943 by Modern Poetry Association from *Collected Poems* of Theodore Roethke, and "The Waking" from *The Waking: Poems 1933–1953* by Theodore Roethke, copyright 1953 by Theodore Roethke.

Peter Kane Dufault—for "Driving Home," copyright © 1954 by Peter Kane Dufault.

Alan Dugan—for his poems "How We Heard the Name" and "Winter for an Untenable Situation," copyright © 1969 by Alan Dugan. This poem appeared in *Poems 2* published by Yale University Press.

Norma Millay Ellis—for "God's World" from *Renascence and Other Poems* by Edna St. Vincent Millay, copyright 1913, 1941 by Edna St. Vincent Millay; published by Harper & Brothers and reprinted by permission of Norma Millay Ellis.

Faber and Faber Limited—for "In Memory of W. B. Yeats," Musée des Beaux Arts," "O Where Are You Going," and "The Unknown Citizen" from *Collected Shorter Poems 1927–1957* by W. H. Auden; for "The Boston Evening Transcript," "The Love Song of J. Alfred Prufrock," and "Preludes" from *Collected Poems 1901–1962* by T. S. Eliot; and for "Blackie, the Electric Rembrant" and "The Monster" from *My Sad Captains* by Thom Gunn.

Farrar, Straus & Giroux, Inc.—for "Blackie, the Electric Rembrandt" from *Moly and My Sad Captains* by Thom Gunn, copyright © 1961, 1971, 1973 by Thom Gunn; for "The Imaginary Iceberg" from *The Complete Poems* by Elizabeth Bishop, copyright © 1969 by Elizabeth Bishop; for "Plot Improbable, Character Unsympathetic" from *The Scarecrow Christ* by Elder Olson, copyright 1954 by Elder Olson; for "Star" from *Gulf* by Derek Walcott, copyright © 1963, 1964, 1965, 1969, 1970 by Derek Walcott; and for "A Far Cry from Africa" and "In a Green Night" from *Selected Poems* by Derek Walcott, copyright © 1962, 1963, 1964 by Derek Walcott. All of these poems reprinted with permission from Farrar, Straus & Giroux, Inc.

Horace Gregory—for "Come, Lesbia, Let us Live and Love" from *The Poems of Catullus*, translation by Horace Gregory, copyright © 1972 by Horace Gregory. Published by W. W. Norton & Company, Inc. and reprinted by permission of Horace Gregory.

Grove Press, Inc.—for "Icarus" from *Stand Up, Friend, with Me* by Edward Field, copyright © 1963 by Edward Field.

Harcourt Brace Jovanovich, Inc.—for "A. E. H." from *A Look Round the Estate* by Kingsley Amis, copyright © 1962, 1967 by Kingsley Amis; for "To Know the Dark" from *Farming: A Handbook* by Wendell Berry, copyright 1970 by Wendell Berry; for "Boston Evening Transcript," "The Love Song of J. Alfred Prufrock," and "Preludes" from *Collected Poems 1901–1962* by T. S. Eliot, copyright 1936 by Harcourt Brace Jovanovich, Inc.; copyright 1963, 1964 by T. S. Eliot; for "Warhead Wakes" from *Screens and Other Poems* by I. A. Richards, copyright 1959, 1960 by I. A. Richards; for "Death of a Toad" and "Still, Citizen Sparrow" from *Ceremony and Other Poems*, by Richard Wilbur, copyright 1948, 1949, 1950 by Richard Wilbur; and for "Piazza di Spagna" from *Things of This World* by Richard Wilbur, © 1956 by Richard Wilbur. All of these poems reprinted by permission of Harcourt Brace Jovanovich, Inc.

Harper & Row, Publishers, Inc.—for "The Ballad of Edie Barrow" from *In the Mecca* by Gwendolyn Brooks, copyright © 1964, 1965, 1967, 1968 by Gwendolyn Brooks Blakely; for "The Ballad of Rudolph Reed" from *The World of Gwendolyn Brooks* by Gwendolyn Brooks, copyright © 1960 by Gwendolyn Brooks Blakely; for "First Fight. Then Fiddle" from *Selected Poems* by Gwendolyn Brooks, copyright 1949, 1963 by Gwendolyn Brooks Blakely; for "Old Mary," copyright © 1959 by Gwendolyn Brooks Blakely; for three poems from *On These I Stand* by Countee Cullen: "Incident," copyright 1925 by Harper & Row, Publishers, Inc.; renewed 1953 by Ida M. Cullen; for "Protest," copyright 1927 by Harper & Row, Publishers, Inc.; renewed 1953 by Ida M. Cullen; and "Yet Do I Marvel," copyright 1925 by Harper & Row Publishers, Inc.; renewed 1953 by Ida M. Cullen; for "Edge" from *Ariel* by Sylvia Plath, copyright © 1963 by Ted Hughes; for "Prairie Town" by William Stafford, copyright © 1959 by William Stafford and "The Woman at Banff" by William Stafford, copyright © 1961 by William Stafford, both poems from *Traveling through the Dark*, copyright © 1962 by William Stafford; and for "Player Piano" from *The Carpentered Hen and Other Tame Creatures* by John Updike, copyright 1954 by John Updike. This poem originally appeared in *The New Yorker*. All of these poems reprinted by permission of Harper & Row, Publishers, Inc.

Daughter," by John Crowe Ransom, copyright 1924 by Alfred A. Knopf, Inc. and renewed 1952 by John Crowe Ransom; and for "Parting Without a Sequel" by John Crowe Ransom, copyright 1927 by Alfred A. Knopf, Inc. and renewed 1955 by John Crowe Ransom. Both poems from *Selected Poems*, Third Edition, Revised and Enlarged, by John Crowe Ransom. All of these poems are reprinted by permission of Alfred A. Knopf, Inc.

Little, Brown and Company—for "The Private Dining Room" from *Verses from 1929 On* by Ogden Nash, copyright 1951 by Ogden Nash; this poem originally appeared in *The New Yorker*; and for "After Great Pain" from *The Complete Poems of Emily Dickinson*, edited by Thomas H. Johnson, copyright 1929, © 1957 by Mary L. Hampson. These poems reprinted by permission of Little, Brown and Company.

Liveright Publishing Corporation—for "Portrait in Georgia" from *Cane* by Jean Toomer, copyright 1923 by Boni & Liveright; copyright renewed 1951 by Jean Toomer. Reprinted by permission of Liveright Publishing Corporation.

James MacGibbon—for "But Murderous" from *The Best Beast* by Stevie Smith, copyright © 1976 by James MacGibbon, Executor, and reprinted with his permission.

Macmillan Publishing Co., Inc.—for "Epitaph on a Pessimist" and "Transformations" from *Collected Poems* by Thomas Hardy, copyright 1925 by The Macmillan Company, renewed 1953 by Lloyds Bank Ltd.; for three lines from "Poetry" by Marianne Moore, copyright 1935 by Marianne Moore, renewed 1963 by Marianne Moore; for "A Glass of Beer" from *Collected Poems* by James Stephens, copyright 1918 by The Macmillan Company, renewed 1946 by James Stephens; for "Crazy Jane Talks with the Bishop," "Father and Child," and "The Folly of Being Comforted" from *Collected Poems* by William Butler Yeats, copyright 1933 by The Macmillan Company, renewed 1961 by Bertha Georgie Yeats; for "Leda and the Swan" (final version) from *Collected Poems* by William Butler Yeats, copyright 1928 by The Macmillan Company, renewed 1956 by Bertha Georgie Yeats; for "To a Child Dancing in the Wind" from *Collected Poems* by William Butler Yeats, copyright 1916 by The Macmillan Company, renewed 1944 by Bertha Georgie Yeats; for "The Sorrow of Love" (1891 version and final version) from *Collected Poems* by William Butler Yeats, copyright 1906 by The Macmillan Company, renewed 1934 by William Butler Yeats; and for "Adam's Curse" and "Prayer for My Daughter" from *Collected Poems* by William Butler Yeats, copyright 1924 by Macmillan Publishing Co., Inc., renewed 1952 by Bertha Georgie Yeats. All of these poems reprinted by permission of Macmillan Publishing Co., Inc.

The Macmillan Company of Canada Limited—for "By Her Aunt's Grave," "The Convergence of the Twain," "The Darkling Thrush," "During Wind and Rain," "Epitaph on a Pessimist," "Hap," and "Transformations" from *Collected Poems of Thomas Hardy*; for "A Glass of Beer" from *Collected Poems* by James Stephens; for "Apology for Understatement" from *Weep Before God* by John Wain; and for "Adam's Curse" and "A Prayer for My Daughter" from *Collected Poems of W. B. Yeats*, by permission of M. B. Yeats, Miss Anne Yeats, Macmillan London & Basingstoke, and The Macmillan Company of Canada Limited.

Macmillan Services Limited—for "Apology for Understatement" from *Weep Before God* by John Wain. Reprinted by permission of Macmillan, London and Basingstoke, and The Macmillan Company of Canada.

The Marvell Press—for "Ulysses" from *The Minute* by John Holloway and for "Myxomatosis" from *The Less Deceived* by Philip Larkin. Both poems reprinted by permission of The Marvell Press, England.

Robert Mezey—for "A Confession" from *The Door Standing Open* by permission of Robert Mezey and courtesy of Houghton Mifflin Company.

John Murray Ltd.—for "Five O'Clock Shadow" by John Betjeman.

New Directions Publishing Corporation—for "To the Reader" from *The Jacob's Ladder* by Denise Levertov, copyright © 1961 Denise Levertov Goodman; for "Arms and the Boy" and "Dulce et Decorum Est" from *Collected Poems* by Wilfred Owens, copyright Chatto & Windus, Ltd. 1946, © renewed 1963; for "An Easy Decision" from *Collected Poems* by Kenneth Patchen, copyright 1952 by Kenneth Patchen; for "The Bath Tub," "In a Station of the Metro," "Portrait d'une Femme" from *Personae* by Ezra Pound, copyright 1926 by Ezra Pound; for "The Heavy Bear Who Goes with Me" from *In Dreams Begin Responsibilities* by Delmore Schwartz, copyright 1938 by New Directions; for "The Passionate Shepherd to His Love" from *Vaudeville for a Princess* by

Delmore Schwartz, copyright 1950 by New Directions; for "The Boat" from *Selected Poems* by Stevie Smith, copyright © 1962 by Stevie Smith; for "After Work" from *The Back Country* by Gary Snyder, copyright © 1959, 1968 by Gary Snyder; for "The Day" from *The Paradox in the Circle* by Theodore Spencer, copyright 1941 by New Directions; for "Do Not Go Gentle into That Good Night" and "In My Craft or Sullen Art" from *The Poems of Dylan Thomas*, copyright 1946 by New Directions, 1952 by Dylan Thomas; for "Cried the Fox" from *In the Winter of Cities* by Tennessee Williams, copyright 1944, © 1956 by Tennessee Williams; for "The Drunkard," "The Jungle," "Poem," and "The Raper from Passenack" from *Collected Earlier Poems* by William Carlos Williams, copyright 1938 by New Directions; and for "Before Disaster" and "By the Road to the Air-Base" by Yvor Winters from *The Giant Weapon*, copyright 1943 by New Directions. All of these poems reprinted by permission of New Directions Publishing Corporation.

W. W. Norton & Company, Inc.—for "Needs" from *Uplands, New Poems*, by A. R. Ammons, copyright © 1970 by A. R. Ammons; for "The Panther" by Rainer Maria Rilke (translation by Peter J. Seng); for "The Swan" from *Translations from the Poetry of Rainer Maria Rilke* by M. D. Herter Norton, copyright © 1938 by W. W. Norton & Company, Inc., copyright renewed 1966 by M. D. Herter Norton; and for "Two Songs" by Adrienne Rich, reprinted from *Necessities of Life, Poems, 1962–1965* by Adrienne Rich, copyright © 1966 by W. W. Norton & Company, Inc. These poems reprinted by permission of W. W. Norton & Company, Inc.

October House, Inc.—for "Frederick Douglass" from *Selected Poems* by Robert Hayden, copyright © 1966 by Robert Hayden; and for "An Evening of Home Movies" from *Charades & Celebrations* by Constance Urdang, copyright © 1965 by Constance Urdang. These poems reprinted by permission of October House, Inc.

Oxford University Press—for "The Horse Chestnut Tree" and "The Human Being is a Lonely Creature" from *Collected Poems, 1930–1976* by Richard Eberhart, © 1976 by Richard Eberhart; and for "But Murderous" from *Collected Poems of Stevie Smith* by Stevie Smith, © 1937, 1938, 1942, 1950, 1957, 1962, 1971, 1972 by Stevie Smith. This arrangement © by James MacGibbon 1976. These poems reprinted by permission of Oxford University Press, Inc.

Oxford University Press, London—for "At Birth" from *The Owl in the Tree* by Anthony Thwaite, © Oxford University Press, 1963. Reprinted by permission of the publisher.

A. D. Peters—for "Epitaph on the Politician Himself" from *Sonnets and Verse* by Hilaire Belloc, reprinted by permission of A. D. Peters and Company.

Poem—for "California" by Leo Stokesbury. This poem first appeared in *Poem* # 3–4, Huntsville, Alabama.

Random House, Inc.—for "The Fall of Rome," copyright 1947 by W. H. Auden; for "The Unknown Citizen" from *Collected Poems* by W. H. Auden, copyright 1940 and renewed 1968 by W. H. Auden; for "In Memory of W. B. Yeats," copyright 1940 and renewed 1968 by W. H. Auden; for "The Love Feast," copyright 1951 by W. H. Auden; for "Musée des Beaux Arts," copyright 1940 and renewed 1968 by W. H. Auden; for "O Where Are You Going," copyright 1934 and renewed 1962 by W. H. Auden; all from *Collected Shorter Poems 1927–1957* by W. H. Auden; for "Portrait of a King's Mistress, Nude" from *Poems in Praise* by Paul Engle, copyright © 1959 by Paul Engle; for "Thoughts on Capital Punishment" and "The Voyeur" from *Stanyan Street and Other Sorrows* by Rod McKuen, copyright 1954, © 1960 through 1966 by Rod McKuen; and for "The Fly," copyright 1942 by Karl Shapiro, from *Selected Poems* by Karl Shapiro. All of these poems reprinted by permission of Random House, Inc.

Routledge & Kegan Paul Ltd.—for "Gentleman Aged Five before the Mirror" and "When It Comes" from *A Word Carved on a Sill* by John Wain, reprinted by permission of Routledge & Kegan Paul Ltd.

Rutgers University Press—for "Philosopher" from *Of Flesh and Bone* by John Frederick Nims, © 1967 and for "Report" from *Sit Opposite Each Other* by Hollis Summers, © 1970, reprinted by permission of Rutgers University Press.

Charles Scribner's Sons—for "In the Hospital" by George Garrett, copyright © 1957 by George Garrett, from *The Reverend Ghost: Poems* (in *Poets of Today, IV*); for "Fall of Icarus: Breughel" by Joseph Langland (copyright 1951 Accent) from *The Green Town: Poems* (in *Poets of Today, III*); for "RMS Lusitania," copyright © 1957 by Richmond Lattimore, from *Poems from the Decades* by Richmond Lattimore; for "Credo" by Edwin Arlington Robinson from *The Children of the Night* (1897); for "How Annandale Went Out," copyright 1910 by Charles Scribner's Sons and renewed copyright 1938 by Ruth Nivison, and "Miniver Chevy," copyright 1907 by Charles Scribner's Sons, renewal copyright 1935 by Ruth Nivison, both poems from *The Town Down the River* by Edwin Arlington Robinson; for "I Have a Rendezvous with Death" from *Poems* by Alan Seeger, copyright 1916 by Charles Scribner's Sons and renewal copyright 1944 by Elsie Adams Seeger; for "Question" by May Swenson, which first appeared in *Another Animal: Poems*, copyright 1954 by May Swenson, from *To Mix with Time*; and for "The Black Panther" and "The Lion House" by John Hall Wheelock from *The Black Panther*, copyright 1922 by Charles Scribner's Sons and renewal copyright 1950 by John Hall Wheelock. All of these poems reprinted by permission of Charles Scribner's Sons.

Peter Smith, Inc.—for "An Elegy for Five" by Richard P. Blackmur.

The Society of Authors—for "Good creatures, do you love your lives" (A. E. Housman gave no title to this poem, which is usually known by its first line only; however, others have sometimes referred to it as "I Counsel You Beware"), "Eight O'Clock," and "The Night Is Freezing Fast" from *Collected Poems* by A. E. Housman; and for "Loveliest of Trees," "Reveille," "Terence, This Is Stupid Stuff," "To an Athlete Dying Young," "When I Watch the Living Meet," and "With Rue My Heart Is Laden," all from "A Shropshire Lad," Authorized Edition, from *The Collected Poems of A. E. Housman*. These poems are reprinted by permission of The Society of Authors as the literary representative of the Estate of A. E. Housman and Jonathan Cape Ltd., publishers of A. E. Housman's *Collected Poems.*

Gunther Stuhlmann—for "The .38" from *Black Pow-Wow* by Ted Joans, copyright © 1969 by Ted Joans and reprinted by permission of the author's representative, Gunther Stuhlmann.

The Swallow Press Incorporated—for "Epitaph for Someone or Other" from *The Exclusions of a Rhyme,* © 1960 by J. V. Cunningham, by permission of The Swallow Press, Inc., Chicago.

May Swenson—for "The Blindman" from *Half Sun Half Sleep* by May Swenson.

Twayne Publishers, Inc.—for "The Tropic in New York" from *Selected Poems of Claude McKay*, copyright 1953 by Bookman Associates, reprinted by permission of Twayne Publishers, Inc.

The University of Michigan Press—for "At the Crossroads" from *Plans for an Orderly Apocalypse* by Harvey Gross, 1968, by permission of The University of Michigan Press.

The Viking Press—for "The House of God" from *Collected Poems 1930–1965* by A. D. Hope, copyright 1963, 1966 in all countries of the International Copyright Union by A. D. Hope; all rights reserved; for "I hear an army charging upon the land" and "The Twilight Turns from Amethyst" from *Collected Poems* by James Joyce, copyright 1918 by B. W. Huebsch, Inc., renewed 1946 by Nora Joyce; for "True Love at Last" from *The Complete Poems of D. H. Lawrence*, edited by Vivian de Sola Pinto and F. Warren Roberts, copyright © 1964, 1971 by Angelo Ravagli & C. M. Weekley, Executors of the Estate of Frieda Lawrence Ravagli; for "A Choice of Weapons" from *Times Three* by Phyllis McGinley, copyright 1954 by Phyllis McGinley; originally appeared in *The New Yorker*; for "I May, I Might, I Must" from *Complete Poems of Marianne Moore*, copyright © 1967 by Marianne Moore; all rights reserved; and for "Résumé" from *The Portable Dorothy Parker*, copyright 1926, 1954 by Dorothy Parker. All of these poems are reprinted by permission of The Viking Press, Inc.

Jerry Vogel Music Co., Inc.—for "Trees" by Joyce Kilmer, copyright 1913 and renewed 1941 assigned to Jerry Vogel Music Co., Inc., 121 West 45th St., New York, New York 10036. Used by permission of copyright owner. Reproduction prohibited.

Robert Wallace—for "Between Equals" from *Ungainly Things*, © 1968 by Robert Wallace; and for "The Double Play" from *Views from a Ferris Wheel*, © 1965 by Robert Wallace. The poems reprinted by permission of the author.

A. P. Watt & Son—for "Call It a Good Marriage," "Leda," and "Traveller's Curse after Misdirection" from *Collected Poems* by Robert Graves, © 1955, 1965 by Robert Graves, published by Doubleday & Co., Inc. and Cassell & Co., Ltd., by permission of the author; for "If" from *Rewards and Fairies* by Rudyard Kipling and "The Recall" from *The Definitive Edition* of Rudyard Kipling's verse. Reprinted by permission of Macmillan Co. of London & Basingstoke and the Executors of the Estate of the late Mrs. Bambridge; and for "Crazy Jane Talks with the Bishop," "Father and Child," "The Folly of Being Comforted," "Leda and the Swan," "The Sorrow of Love," and "To a Child Dancing in the Wind"; all from *The Collected Poems of W. B. Yeats* by permission of Mr. M. B. Yeats and the Macmillan Company of Canada Ltd.

George Weidenfeld and Nicolson Ltd.—for "The Maltese Goat" from *Exotics*, 1970, by Nigel Dennis, by permission of the publisher.

Wesleyan University Press—for "The Hospital Window" from *Drowning with Others*, copyright © 1962 by James Dickey; poem was first published in *Poetry*; for "Adam's Dream" and "The Unawkward Singers" from *On the Way to the Island*, copyright © 1953, 1957 by David Ferry; several stanzas of "Adam's Dream" appeared originally in *The New Yorker*; for "Mystique" and "Simultaneously" from *Figures of the Human* by David Ignatow, copyright © 1955, 1962 by David Ignatow; for "The Pleasure" from *Rescue the Dead* by David Ignatow, copyright © 1958 by David Ignatow; for "Skinny Poem" from *Cold Water* by Lou Lipsitz, copyright © 1966 by Lou Lipsitz; and for "To the Western World" from *A Dream of Governors* by Louis Simpson, copyright © 1957 by Louis Simpson. All of these poems reprinted by permission of Wesleyan University Press.

Yale University Press—for "Ellie Mae Leaves in a Hurry" from *Lugging Vegetables to Nantucket* by Peter Klappert, copyright © 1971 by Yale University, reprinted by permission of the publisher.

Preface

This fourth edition of *Poems: The Wadsworth Handbook and Anthology* is motivated by the desire to improve rather than replace its immediate predecessor. Thus the book continues to address ordinary, non-literary college students, with the intention of showing them how they can derive interesting and rewarding experiences from poems. Like its earlier versions, it stresses the reading of particular poems, without speculating much on the nature of poetry or the theory of its criticism. This edition also perpetuates the general plan of earlier editions: the two-part division into "Poems for Discussion" and "Poems for Comparison," the ten expository chapters in the first part, the groups of related poems in the second, the appendix on meter. Teachers who have used the book in the past will recognize much that is familiar. But they will also find many changes.

The fourth edition differs from the third in three chief ways: (1) minor revisions have been made throughout to improve emphasis, clarify concepts, and sharpen definitions; (2) some sections—notably Chapter 2 on the words of a poem—have been almost completely rewritten; (3) about forty new poems have been introduced and a corresponding number dropped. The editors hope that these changes, especially in the poems offered, will make the book more useful and attractive to teachers and students. Of course nobody, let alone the present editors, knows enough to decide conclusively that a given poem has outlived its usefulness and should be replaced by another. A decision of this kind, based as it is on guesses and hunches, can be remarkably wrong. Thus Henry Reed's *tour de force* of *double entendre*, "Naming of Parts," was left out of the second and third editions of *Poems* because the editors felt that a poem about a group of army recruits receiving instruction in the nomenclature of the rifle could not possbily interest college students in the seventies. And, if the subject itself did somehow interest them, the innuendo in the poem would offend their allegedly free and open attitudes towards sex. Nothing, apparently, could be further from the facts, if it's safe to trust several teachers who have written to complain that this favorite of their students was missing from *Poems*. "Naming of Parts" has now been restored.

A literature textbook succeeds mainly on the strength of the works it chooses to reprint. *Poems* makes its bid for success by providing a large number and a wide variety of works—too many, in fact, to be studied in the time customarily available for poetry in freshmen and sophomore courses. For every pedagogical point that is made in this book, at least two (and often more) poems are provided as illustrations. This is so that teachers can choose to discuss poems that seem to them most attractive and teachable, and pass over the others. These leftovers will not be wasted, since it's always a good idea to give students access to some poems that won't be discussed in class.

In writing the prose commentary, which is aimed primarily at the students and not at the teachers, the editors have tried throughout to keep in mind George Herbert's promise to his parishioners in his first sermon to them, that he "would not fill their heads with unnecessary notions." The editors have also tried to avoid giving students the impression that a poet writes a poem in order to have it analyzed in textbooks like this one. This is an impression not easily avoided. Successive chapters dealing with diction, imagery, figurative language, sound, and all those literary terms in **bold face**, do tend to imply that poems are meant to be broken down into their elements, and indeed that is what people like English teachers do when they read poetry. Nothing, of course, could be further from the truth. The use of terminology for analysis is meaningful only insofar as it subserves an experience of the entire work. Therefore, to counteract the disintegrating tendencies of Chapters 2–7, the editors provide four chapters that attempt to deal with poems as whole entities: Chapter 1, which an ordinary class can absorb with little or no instruction, Chapter 8 (on tone), Chapter 9 (on form and structure), and Chapter 10 (on judgment). According to this plan, the expository part of the book begins and ends with chapters treating whole poems.

The editors' indebtedness to their students, their colleagues, and their counterparts in other schools, colleges, and universities who have adopted this book over the years is truly too great to be expressed in the customary verbiage of prefatory writing. We thank this immense company of good people, and especially the following reviewers of the third edition, who were most helpful to us when most suspicious of our formulations: Norman Carlson, Western Michigan University; James Culp, Texas Tech University; Gertrude Golladay, University of Texas at Arlington; Judith Kohl, Dutchess Community College; Sharon Pearson, Eastern Illinois University; and Ruth Smith, Hofstra University. Thanks of the editors are due to Connecticut College for modest grants which aided preparation of this fourth edition.

C. F. MAIN
PETER J. SENG

Contents

10 Judging a Poem 323

1
Poems for Discussion

1. Experiencing a Poem

The only thing that can save the world is the reclaiming of the awareness of the world. That's what poetry does. By poetry I mean the imagining of what has been lost and what can be found—the imagining of who we are and the slow realization of it.

Allen Ginsberg

Why do we read poems? For much the same reason that we play games, sing, dance, and tell each other stories. All of these characteristically human activities give us pleasure and yield emotional, physical, and intellectual satisfaction.

If it is true that the desire for pleasurable experience is really what motivates us to read poems and other literary works, then it follows that all literary study should be aimed at increasing our pleasure. That is the aim of this book: to increase the emotional and intellectual satisfaction experienced by readers of poems. If a reader doesn't get pleasure out of a poem, he is unlikely to get much else worth having.

Of course, if you don't understand a poem you won't derive much pleasure from it. And it's also true that many poems are hard to understand. Hence the need for textbooks—like this one—designed to open up poems and make them more accessible to readers. Most of the poems in this first chapter, however, are not difficult and do not require elaborate analysis or annotations. The poems here were chosen to illustrate a few of the many kinds of poems that exist and a few of the many ways in which poems give pleasure to readers.

After Work

The shack and a few trees
float in the blowing fog

I pull out your blouse,
warm my cold hands
        on your breasts.
you laugh and shudder
peeling garlic by the
        hot iron stove.
bring in the axe, the rake,
the wood

we'll lean on the wall
against each other
stew simmering on the fire
as it grows dark
        drinking wine.

Gary Snyder
(1930–   )

What pleasures do we find in Snyder's poem? First, the poem is pleasurable because it describes a scene that we can recognize as possible and familiar, and people with whom we can identify: a man and a woman together in an isolated place, enjoying each other's company. The scene is what we loosely think of as "romantic," although the presence of the hand tools and the smell of garlic in the room are somewhat surprising, since we usually do not associate rakes, axes, and peeling knives with romantic scenes. These unusual things make the description seem realistic and keep it from becoming too mushy. The poet has exercised care and craftsmanship in choosing and arranging all the details so that they create a scene at once desirable and possible. Finally, by putting his woodchopping man and cooking woman in a poem, the poet does not necessarily claim that they ever existed in real life. They may just as well be fictions or creatures of the poet's imagination as real people making love and keeping house in a secluded spot. And the reason we enjoy imaginary characters and scenes is not unconnected with the fact that in our dreams we are all poets who invent scenes, characters, and situations that never existed in real life.

The poem provides, then, the common pleasures of (1) recognition, (2) identification, (3) surprise, (4) imagination, and (5) craftsmanship—not one after the other, but all closely tangled, merged, and mixed together. We experience these pleasures, of course, in our own way and nobody else's. The amount of each kind of pleasure also differs from reader to reader. One reader may derive very little or no pleasure from a particular poem, while another reader may find the same poem very enjoyable. Certainly, nobody is under any obligation to enjoy every poem.

One word of warning: these five kinds of pleasure are not labels to stick on poems: "This is an identification poem," "This is a surprise poem," and so on. The five kinds of pleasure are not meant to provide a classification system for poems. They are isolated from one another in the pages that follow only for the purpose of discussing them further. In the actual experience of reading, all five kinds of pleasure can and frequently do exist in a single poem.

The Pleasures of Recognition

One of the keenest pleasures in reading poems is to come across something that is recognizably true and at the same time accurately expressed. When this shock of recognition occurs, even the most experienced and sophisticated reader has the impulse to write "How true!" or "Right on!" or "Amen" or some such embarrassingly obvious remark in the margin of the poem. Something in the poem immediately strikes home with the reader.

Poems tell us verbally what we already know and have already experienced in a nonverbal way. They confirm our hunches, define our vague feelings, clarify our dim ideas, and reveal the world around us.

Poem

As the cat
climbed over
the top of

the jamcloset
first the right
forefoot

carefully
then the hind
stepped down

into the pit of
the empty
flowerpot

William Carlos Williams
(1883–1963)

Some of the pleasure of this poem comes from recognizing how well Williams has caught in words the experience of a cat climbing over one object and lowering itself into another. The poem is only a single sentence, but by dividing that sentence into twelve lines, the poet suggests in each line the slow, tentative movement of the cat. This imitation of a cat's movement in words is pleasing in itself. Another small pleasure comes when we recognize the rightness of the word *pit,* since to a cat an empty flowerpot would indeed be a deep, pitlike container. And since this poem is not at all ambitious, it is pleasant to see that the poet has given it a modest title, perhaps the most modest title that a poem can have. (When Williams wrote these lines in 1934 the title "Poem" had not become trite from overuse.)

Exercise 1

What pleasures of recognition are available in the following poems?

The Double-Play

In his sea-lit
distance, the pitcher winding
like a clock about to chime comes down with

the ball, hit
sharply, under the artificial
banks of arc lights, bounds like a vanishing string

over the green
to the shortstop magically
scoops to his right whirling above his invisible

shadows
in the dust redirects
its flight to the running poised second baseman

pirouettes
leaping, above the slide, to throw
from mid-air, across the colored tightened interval,

to the leaning-
out first baseman ends the dance
drawing it disappearing into his long brown glove

stretches. What
is too swift for deception
is final, lost, among the loosened figures

jogging off the field
(the pitcher walks), casual
in the space where the poem has happened.

Robert Wallace
(1932–)

Because River-Fog

Because river-fog
Hiding the mountain-base
Has risen,
The autumn mountain looks as though it hung in the sky.

Fukayabu Kiyowara
(c. 1000)
(translated by Arthur Waley)

A Foreign Ruler

He says, *My reign is peace,* so slays
A thousand in the dead of night.
Are you all happy now? he says,
And those he leaves behind cry *quite.*

He swears he will have no contention,
  And sets all nations by the ears;
He shouts aloud, *No intervention!*
  Invades, and drowns them all in tears.

Walter Savage Landor
(1775–1864)

Not Drunk

Not drunk is he, who from the floor
  Can rise alone, and still drink more;
But drunk is he, who prostrate lies,
  Without the power to drink or rise.

Thomas Love Peacock
(1785–1866)

The Chinese Checker Players

When I was six years old
I played Chinese checkers
  with a woman
who was ninety-three years old.
She lived by herself
in an apartment down the hall
  from ours.
We played Chinese checkers
every Monday and Thursday nights.
While we played she usually talked
about her husband
who had been dead for seventy years,
and we drank tea and ate cookies
  and cheated.

Richard Brautigan
(1935–   )

The Pleasures of Identification

Whenever a reader finds himself, his private feelings, or something like his own situation in life depicted in a literary work, he experiences the pleasure of identification. We like to read about ourselves for the same reason that we like to talk about ourselves. All of us are somewhat self-centered and we are gratified when we recognize ourselves on the printed page. "Why, this could be about me," we think. (Is it accurate to say that only a lunatic confuses the real and the imaginary and thinks, "This *is* about me"?)

Father and Child

She hears me strike the board and say
That she is under ban
Of all good men and women,
Being mentioned with a man
That has the worst of all bad names;
And thereupon replies
That his hair is beautiful,
Cold as the March wind his eyes,

William Butler Yeats
(1865–1939)

It would be possible for a father in real life to identify with the father in Yeats's poem, and also for a daughter—at odds with her parents and attracted to a man they disapprove of—to identify with the daughter in the poem. But to limit their identifications to such narrow sympathies would allow the father-reader and the daughter-reader to experience only part of the pleasure that the whole poem affords. A more complete sympathy, an identification with both human characters in the poem, would give more pleasure. After all both characters are "right." The father is not only concerned about his child's respectability in the community; he also feels responsible for her future, and he wants her to make a happy marriage. On the other hand, the daughter is also "right" in her own way: she can't take her father's objections to this man seriously, and she apparently finds him too attractive to give up. Her life and her happiness are at stake, not her father's. And so the reader who sympathizes and identifies with both father and daughter, two people caught in the kind of *impasse* that is so common in human relations, will enjoy the poem much more than a reader who "takes sides."

If a reader who is neither a father nor a daughter can identify with both characters in Yeats's poem, then it follows that the resemblances between the literary work and the reader's personal life don't have to be very close for identification to take place. The reader does not identify with fatherhood or daughterhood as such, but with the capacity of these imagined characters to behave like real people. When we read about persons older or younger than ourselves, or of different race, sex, religion, or nationality, we don't identify with the superficial characteristics of race, age, sex, and so on, but with the humanity that they share with us. The whole matter was neatly summed up long ago by a character in a play by the Roman dramatist Terence: "I am a human being, and so nothing human is alien to me."

At the opposite extreme from Terence's humanist is the person who can identify only with his own kind. When this person reads something, he demands a very close resemblance between the circumstances represented in his reading and the circumstances of his own life. Thus, he limits his choice of works and derives only a narrow sort of pleasure from perusing them.

into another person's thoughts and feelings we are able to take part in another life than our own. We break through the limiting bounds of our own narrow selfhood; we learn and grow by expanding the horizons of our own little worlds.

Exercise 2

In what ways can one identify with the characters and situations depicted in the following poems?

The Drunkard

You drunken
tottering
bum

by Christ
in spite of all
your filth

and sordidness
I envy
you

It is the very face
of love
itself

abandoned
in that powerless
committal

to despair

William Carlos Williams
(1883–1963)

Once in a Saintly Passion

Once in a saintly passion
  I cried with desperate grief,
"O Lord, my heart is black with guile,
  Of sinners I am chief."
Then stooped my guardian angel
  And whispered from behind,
"Vanity, my little man,
  You're nothing of the kind."

James Thomson
(1834–1882)

A Confession

If someone was walking across
your lawn last night, it was me.
While you dreamt of prowlers, I was
prowling down empty lanes, to breathe
the conifer coolness of just
before dawn. Your flowers were closed,
your windows black and withdrawn.

Sometimes I see a square of
yellow light shining through the trees,

and I cross the grass and look in.
Your great body on the bed
is nude and white, and though I'm starved
for love like everyone, the sight
of your black sex leaves me cold.

What would I say to a squad car
if it came on its noiseless tires
and picked me out with its lights, like
a cat or a rabbit? That I
only wanted to see how people
live, not knowing how? That I
haven't had a woman in months?

Therefore I stay out of sight
and do not speak. Or if I speak,
I make small animal sounds
to myself, so as not to wake you.
They were tears full of seed. What
I wanted to do was enter
and bend and touch you on the cheek.

Robert Mezey
(1935–   )

True Love at Last

The handsome and self-absorbed young man
looked at the lovely and self-absorbed girl
and thrilled.

The lovely and self-absorbed girl
looked back at the handsome and self-absorbed young man
and thrilled.

And in that thrill he felt:
Her self-absorption is even as strong as mine.
I must see if I can't break through it
And absorb her in me.

And in that thrill she felt:
His self-absorption is even stronger than mine!
What fun, stronger than mine!
I must see if I can't absorb this Samson of self-absorption.

So they simply adored one another
and in the end
they were both nervous wrecks, because
in self-absorption and self-interest they were equally matched.

D. H. Lawrence
(1885–1930)

Two Sons

Where and to whom
you are married I can only guess
in my piecemeal fashion. I grow old on my bitterness.

On the unique occasion
of your two sudden wedding days
I open some cheap wine, a tin of lobster and mayonnaise.

I sit in an old lady's room
where families used to feast
where the wind blows in like soot from north-northeast.

Both of you monopolized
with no real forwarding address
except for two silly postcards you bothered to send home,

one of them written in grease
as you undid her dress
in Mexico, the other airmailed to Boston from Rome

just before the small ceremony
at the American Church.
Both of you made of my cooking, those suppers of starch

and beef, and with my library,
my medicine, my bath water,
both sinking into small brown pools like muddy otters!

You make a toast for tomorrow
and smash the cup,
letting your false women lap the dish I had to fatten up.

When you come back I'll buy
a wig of yellow hair;
I'll squat in a new red dress; I'll be playing solitaire

on the kitchen floor.
Yes . . . I'll gather myself in
like cut flowers and ask you how you are and where you've been.

Anne Sexton
(1928–1974)

Written in Northampton County Asylum

I am! yet what I am who cares, or knows?
  My friends forsake me like a memory lost.
I am the self-consumer of my woes;
  They rise and vanish, an oblivious host,
Shadows of life, whose very soul is lost.
And yet I am—I live—though I am toss'd

Into the nothingness of scorn and noise,
  Into the living sea of waking dream,
Where there is neither sense of life, nor joys,
  But the huge shipwreck of my own esteem
And all that's dear. Even those I loved the best
Are strange—nay, they are stranger than the rest.

I long for scenes where man has never trod—
  For scenes where woman never smiled or wept—
There to abide with my Creator, God,
  And sleep as I in childhood sweetly slept,
Full of high thoughts, unborn. So let me lie,—
The grass below; above, the vaulted sky.

John Clare
(1793–1864)

The Pleasures of Being Surprised

In contrast with the pleasures of recognition and identification, which arise from our perception of the familiar, the pleasure of being surprised arises from our encounters with the unfamiliar. "How odd," we think when we first come across a new notion or an entirely new way of looking at something, and we react in two possible ways. Either our mind snaps shut, excluding the new experience forever from our consciousness, or our mind remains open, at least long enough to take in the new experience, turn it over, and look at it more closely.

A poetry reader may get a meager sort of pleasure by smugly excluding the new and the unfamiliar, but the process of turning the unfamilar into the familiar is much more pleasurable because it imitates in a small way the whole pattern of human development from infant to adult. For instance, most infants don't care to eat broiled lobster, drink champagne, or perform on the oboe; such tastes and interests develop only gradually as time passes and the infant turns into an adult. But obviously they won't develop at all in a person who automatically rejects new experience, and who finds no pleasure in being surprised. Many grown-up pleasures, including the pleasure of reading poems, are acquired, and they become more satisfying with use.

The Bath Tub

As a bathtub lined with white porcelain,
When the hot water gives out or goes tepid,
So is the slow cooling of our chivalrous passion,
O my much praised but-not-altogether-satisfactory lady.

Ezra Pound
(1885–1972)

What an odd little poem. But a moment's consideration will show that it's as accurate as it is surprising. It brings together two human experiences: falling out of love and sitting in a bath tub so long that the water becomes tepid. What is surprising about the poem is not the separate experiences, which are common enough, but their juxtaposition. Pound has transformed the trite remark "My love is growing cold" into a surprising and interesting comparison between cooling passion and cooling bath water. By mentioning specifically the white porcelain lining of the tub, Pound emphasizes the discomfort of the bather, who is sitting in cold, hard, and wet surroundings that remind him all too forcibly of his unsatisfactory love affair. The poem, which at first struck us as odd, becomes familiar.

The unexpected, then, can be as pleasing as the expected. A reader can come up against a great barrier to his pleasure, however, if he feels that the unexpected is a threat. Suppose that an inexperienced reader should come across a poem beginning

Chieftain Iffucan of Azcan in caftan.

No doubt such a reader would be surprised (for that matter, every reader is somewhat surprised by this opening line the first time he sees it), but it need not threaten him. Strange new words cannot possibly hurt him. Moreover, the poet Wallace Stevens, who wrote the line, is not at all trying to expose the reader's inexperience or lack of ability to understand poems. He is actually having a marvelous time stringing together these surprising words, and he hopes that others will share his pleasure in them and in the whole poem (see page 219). A reader of poems soon gets into the habit of expecting and enjoying the unexpected.

Exercise 3

What surprises are to be found in the following poems?

The Mad Yak

I am watching them churn the last milk
  they'll ever get from me.
They are waiting for me to die;
They want to make buttons out of my bones.
Where are my sisters and brothers?
That tall monk there, loading my uncle,
  he has a new cap.

And that idiot student of his—
  I never saw that muffler before.
Poor uncle, he lets them load him.
How sad he is, how tired!
I wonder what they'll do with his bones?
And that beautiful tail!
How many shoelaces will they make of that!

Gregory Corso
(1930–)

I Think I Could Turn and Live with Animals

I think I could turn and live with animals, they're so placid and self-contain'd,
I stand and look at them long and long.

They do not sweat and whine about their condition,
They do not lie awake in the dark and weep for their sins,
They do not make me sick discussing their duty to God,
Not one is dissatisfied, not one is demented with the mania of owning things,
Not one kneels to another, nor to his kind that lived thousands of years ago,
Not one is respectable or unhappy over the whole earth.

So they show their relations to me and I accept them,
They bring me tokens of myself, they evince them plainly in their possession.

Walt Whitman
(1819–1892)

California

Shouldn't we finally get started?
I mean I think the right time has come.
The wind drops the leaves to the
  ground.
I think we had better get going.
The sunrise, the sunrise has fallen.

The long rows of waves keep on
  coming.
They lap in the rocks by the shore.

I mean it is dusk on the shore.
And the wind kicks the leaves to the
  ground.
All over the black leaves are falling.
Why do we still only stand here?
The time for our starting has come.
Let us go to the boats and launch out;
I think it would be best to run.

What I mean is the sunrise is gone.
Let us run to the boats and start rowing.
The leaves, the leaves keep on falling.
The black leaves have covered the
  beaches.
And why do we still only stand here?
I mean why do we still only stand here?

Leon Stokesbury
(1944–)

One Thousand Nine Hundred & Sixty-Eight Winters

Got up this morning
Feeling good & black
Thinking black thoughts
Did black things
Played all my black records
And minded my own black business
Put on my best black clothes
Walked out my black door
And, Lord have mercy: white snow!

Jaci Earley
(1939–)

Transformations

Portion of this yew
Is a man my grandsire knew,

Bosomed here at its foot:
This branch may be his wife,
A ruddy human life
Now turned to a green shoot.

These grasses must be made
Of her who often prayed,
Last century, for repose;
And the fair girl long ago
Whom I often tried to know
May be entering this rose.

So, they are not underground,
But as nerves and veins abound
In the growths of upper air,
And they feel the sun and rain,
And the energy again
That made them what they were!

Thomas Hardy
(1840–1928)

yew (1): an evergreen tree or shrub commonly found in English cemeteries.

Cells Breathe in the Emptiness

When the flowers turn to husks
And the great trees suddenly die
And rocks and old weasel bones lose
The little life they suddenly had
And the air quells and goes so still
It gives the ears something like the bends,
It is an eerie thing to keep vigil,
The senses racing in the emptiness.

2

From the compost heap
Now arises the sound of the teeth
Of one of those sloppy green cabbageworms
Eating his route through a cabbage,
Now snarling like a petite chainsaw, now droning on . . .

A butterfly blooms on a buttercup,
From the junkpile flames up a junco.

3

How many plants are really very quiet animals?
How many inert molecules are ready to break into Life?

Galway Kinnell
(1927–)

junco (15): a small American finch with conspicuous white tailfeathers.

The Pleasures of the Imagination

From early childhood on, people delight in arrangements of words that describe situations that are impossible, improbable, unverifiable, and simply untrue.

A cat came fiddling out of a barn,
With a pair of bag-pipes under his arm.
All he could sing was "fiddle come fee,
The mouse has married the bumblebee."

A child hearing this nursery rhyme might be pleased by it, but not for a moment would he take it as a factual report. He would know that cats neither fiddle nor play bagpipes—let alone do both at once, while walking out of barns singing about the marriage of two creatures incapable of committing matrimony, especially with one another. Yet this odd mishmash pleases the child just because it is impossible and takes him out of his everyday world, in which animals always behave like animals, and into the world of the poet's imagination, in which anything can happen.

Like children, we also experience the pleasures of the imagination whenever we no longer feel obliged to verify what we are being told and to check it in every detail against reality as we know it. This "poetic faith" was once defined by the poet Coleridge as "the willing suspension of disbelief." That is, when we are confronted with the fictitious and the imaginary, we have to suspend our tendency to disbelieve, and we have to do this willingly and voluntarily. Like all pleasures, the pleasures of the imagination cannot be forced upon us.

Eating Poetry

Ink runs from the corners of my mouth.
There is no happiness like mine.
I have been eating poetry.

The librarian does not believe what she sees.
Her eyes are sad
and she walks with her hands in her dress.

The poems are gone.
The light is dim.
The dogs are on the basement stairs and coming up.

Their eyeballs roll,
their blond legs burn like brush.
The poor librarian begins to stamp her feet and weep.

She does not understand.
When I get on my knees and lick her hand,
she screams.

I am a new man.
I snarl at her and bark.
I romp with joy in the bookish dark.

Mark Strand
(1934–)

Of course, this strange scene takes place in the poet's imagination rather than in a library. And in describing the scene in a poem, the poet doesn't ask us to believe that he *really* chewed poems out of books and devoured them, or that dogs *in fact* came up out of the basement and made a great fuss in a library, or that an *actual* librarian endured all these and more disorders—hand licking, snarling, barking—without calling the police. As a poet, Mark Strand is not like a newspaper reporter, who must stick to the facts. He is, rather, like a painter, who may, if he wishes to create a special effect, paint the sun green and the grass black. Or he is like a composer, who may combine two different sounds to make one never heard before. In short, he is free to create whatever scene his imagination can put together for him.

This poem treats in an imaginative way the positive feelings that can result from reading poems. The poet doesn't use such tired adjectives as "far-out" or "great" or "super" or whatever the current term of approval may be. He doesn't say "Poetry is too much!" "Poetry turns me on!" or "I have a big appetite for verse!" There's no imagination in expressions like these, and no pleasure. Instead, the poet invents a mad, raucous scene that expresses his feelings in an original way.

Sometimes, as in the nursery rhyme and in Strand's poem, the poet's imagination is busy inventing odd, unrealistic scenes and situations. But more often the poet exercises his imagination on the common stuff of human experience: birth and death, love and sex, work and play, the natural and the man-made environment, people's fears, desires, sorrows, joys, likes, dislikes. The poet finds verbal equivalents for these various states and feelings. He must think up the words and then create the right relationships between them that will result in a completed poem. Having the ability to find these happy combinations of words—an ability we call *imagination* for lack of a better term—must be a great source of pleasure and satisfaction to its possessor. A reader of a poem participates in a small way in the pleasure of this creative activity as he experiences a poem.

Exercise 4

What evidence can you find in these poems to indicate that their authors were able to imagine and re-create experience verbally?

The House of God

Morning service! parson preaches;
People all confess their sins;
God's domesticated creatures
Twine and rub against his shins;

Tails erect and whiskers pricking,
Sleeking down their Sunday fur,

Though demure, alive and kicking,
All in unison they purr:

"Lord we praise Thee; hear us Master!
Feed and comfort, stroke and bless!
And not too severely cast a
Glance upon our trespasses:

Yesterday we were not able
To resist that piece of fish
Left upon the kitchen table
While You went to fetch the dish;

Twice this week a scrap with Rover;
Once, at least, we missed a rat;
And we *do* regret, Jehovah,
Having kittens in Your hat!

Sexual noises in the garden,
Smelly patches in the hall—
Hear us, Lord, absolve and pardon;
We are human after all!"

Home at last from work in Heaven,
This is all the rest God gets;
Gladly for one day in seven
He relaxes with His pets.

Looking down He smiles and ponders,
Thinks of something extra nice:
From His beard, O joy, O wonders!
Falls a shower of little mice.

A. D. Hope
(1907–)

An Easy Decision

I had finished my dinner
Gone for a walk
It was fine
Out and I started whistling

It wasn't long before

I met a
Man and his wife riding on
A pony with seven
Kids running along beside them

I said hello and

Went on
Pretty soon I met another
Couple
This time with nineteen
Kids and all of them
Riding on
A big smiling hippopotamus

I invited them home

Kenneth Patchen
(1911–1972)

But Murderous

A mother slew her unborn babe
In a day of recent date
Because she did not wish him to be born in a world
Of murder and war and hate.
"Oh why should I bear a babe from my womb
To be broke in pieces by a hydrogen bomb?"

I say this woman deserves little pity
That she was a fool and a murderess.
Is a child's destiny to be contained by a mind
That signals only a lady in distress?

And why should *human* infancy be so superior
As to be too good to be born in this world?
Did she think it was an angel or a baa-lamb
That lay in her belly furled?

Oh the child is the young of its species
Alike with that noble, vile, curious and fierce

How foolish this poor mother to suppose
Her act told us aught that was not murderous

(As, item, That the arrogance of a half-baked mind
Breeds murder; makes us all unkind.)

Stevie Smith
(1902–1971)

I Wandered Lonely as a Cloud

I wandered lonely as a cloud
That floats on high o'er vales and hills,
When all at once I saw a crowd,

A host, of golden daffodils;
Beside the lake, beneath the trees,
Fluttering and dancing in the breeze.

Continuous as the stars that shine
And twinkle on the milky way,
They stretched in never-ending line
Along the margin of a bay:
Ten thousand saw I at a glance,
Tossing their heads in sprightly dance.

The waves beside them danced; but they
Out-did the sparkling waves in glee:
A poet could not but be gay,
In such a jocund company:
I gazed—and gazed—but little thought
What wealth the show to me had brought:

For oft, when on my couch I lie
In vacant or in pensive mood,
They flash upon that inward eye
Which is the bliss of solitude;
And then my heart with pleasure fills,
And dances with the daffodils.

William Wordsworth
(1770–1850)

An Evening of Home Movies

When Aunt Insomnia came back from the planet Mars
With two hundred color slides, five anecdotes,
Some postcards with pretty views of the universe,

And an extra suitcase filled with souvenirs,
Who could imagine her spin, like a top, through space,
And end over end, besides, in her rayon chemise,

Hand-knitted cardigan, and elasticized hose?
It must have filled the angels with tenderness.
She has travelled faster and farther than you would suppose,

To look at her. Has she forgotten the marvels she saw
(The comets with dragon-tails, the siren-stars,
And earth, that was home, a will-o'-the-wisp below)?

Give thanks for her safe return from wherever she goes.
She has shown us the way. Let us listen and be wise,
Say thank you politely, and treasure the souvenirs.

Constance Urdang
(1927–)

The Witch

I have walked a great while over the snow,
And I am not tall nor strong.
My clothes are wet, and my teeth are set,
And the way was hard and long.
I have wandered over the fruitful earth,
But I never came here before.
Oh, lift me over the threshold, and let me in at the door!

The cutting wind is a cruel foe.
I dare not stand in the blast.
My hands are stone, and my voice a groan,
And the worst of death is past.
I am but a little maiden still,
My little white feet are sore.
Oh, lift me over the threshold, and let me in at the door!

Her voice was the voice that women have,
Who plead for their heart's desire.
She came–she came–and the quivering flame
Sank and died in the fire.
It never was lit again on my hearth
Since I hurried across the floor,
To lift her over the threshold, and let her in at the door.

Mary Coleridge
(1861–1907)

Many Workmen

Many workmen
Built a huge ball of masonry
Upon a mountain-top.
Then they went to the valley below,

And turned to behold their work.
"It is grand," they said;
They loved the thing.

Of a sudden, it moved:
It came upon them swiftly;
It crushed them all to blood.
But some had opportunity to squeal.

Stephen Crane
(1871–1900)

The Pleasures of Craftsmanship

Poets make poems, just as sculptors make statues and composers make songs. Thus, in addition to being a kind of verbal communication between poet and readers, a poem is also a *thing made.* If a poem is well made, it gives us the same sort of pleasure that we get from any product of skilled craftsmanship or from any technically accomplished performance.

It is perhaps worth repeating that good poems are made and don't just happen, although from time to time certain poets have argued that poems should grow naturally, as a tree puts forth leaves, rather than be manufactured consciously, as a carpenter might build a bookcase. Some poets even claim that they find their poems. Yet however a poem comes about, it does not exist before the poet builds it, or grows it, or finds it, and if he wants it to please anybody, he will make it show mastery over the materials of poetry, namely words.

Philosopher

He scowled at the barometer: "Will it rain?"
None heard, with all that pattering on the pane.

John Frederick Nims
(1913–   )

By saying a lot in a little space, Nims shows that he has mastered his craft. He does not waste a word. He allows himself only two lines, and he imposes on himself the further requirement of making the final words in the lines sound alike, or rhyme. Within this circumscribed space he has scored as telling a point against the pedantic, instrument-obsessed, self-absorbed philosopher as if he had written a whole book exposing him.

Of course, economy of expression is only one of many ways in which a poet can demonstrate his skill. A poem that is extravagant in its language can be just as pleasing in its own way as an economical poem. The following poem, for example, is somewhat repetitious, but the repetition—apparently intentional—is one of the ways in which the sound of the poem echoes its subject matter:

The Splendor Falls

The splendor falls on castle walls
And snowy summits old in story:
The long light shakes across the lakes,
And the wild cataract leaps in glory.
Blow, bugle, blow, set the wild echoes flying,
Blow, bugle; answer, echoes, dying, dying, dying.

O hark, O hear! how thin and clear,
And thinner, clearer, farther going!
O sweet and far from cliff and scar
The horns of Elfland faintly blowing!
Blow, let us hear the purple glens replying:
Blow, bugle; answer, echoes, dying, dying, dying.

O love, they die in yon rich sky,
They faint on hill or field or river:
Our echoes roll from soul to soul,
And grow for ever and for ever.
Blow, bugle, blow, set the wild echoes flying,
And answer, echoes, answer, dying, dying, dying.

Alfred, Lord Tennyson
(1809–1892)

cataract (4): waterfall. *scar* (9): side of the mountain.

We enjoy the craftsmanship in a poem whenever we can detect two elements in it: first, that the poet has set up some sort of difficulty that he will overcome in writing the poem; second, that the poet has indeed overcome the self-imposed difficulty. Nims, for instance, permitted himself only a tiny amount of space in which to dispose of the phony philosopher. Tennyson set himself the difficulty of finding verbal equivalents to the sounds of a bugle blown in a romantic landscape. Insofar as both poets succeeded in overcoming their difficulties, they please us with their craftsmanship.

A good poem is not mass-produced; it gives the same sort of pleasure as a handmade object, because it sets its own standards of craftsmanship.

Exercise 5

Consider, in the following poems, what difficulties the poets have set for themselves and how well they have overcome those difficulties.

Rondeau

Jenny kissed me when we met,
  Jumping from the chair she sat in;
Time, you thief, who love to get
  Sweets into your list, put that in!
Say I'm weary, say I'm sad,
  Say that health and wealth have missed me,
Say I'm growing old, but add,
  Jenny kissed me.

Leigh Hunt
(1784–1859)

The Lover to His Lady

My girl, thou gazest much
  Upon the golden skies:
Would I were heaven! I would behold
  Thee then with all mine eyes.

George Turberville
(*c.* 1540–1598)

Epitaph for Someone or Other

Naked I came, naked I leave the scene,
And naked was my pastime in between.

J. V. Cunningham
(1911–   )

Skinny Poem

Skinny
poem,
all
your
ribs

showing
even
without
a
deep
breath

thin
legs
rotted
with
disease.

Live
here!
on
this
page,
barely
making
it,
like
the
mass
of
mankind.

Lou Lipsitz
(1938–)

Player Piano

My stick fingers click with a snicker
And, chuckling, they knuckle the keys;
Light-footed, my steel feelers flicker
And pluck from these keys melodies.

My paper can caper; abandon
Is broadcast by dint of my din,
And no man or band has a hand in
The tones I turn on from within.

At times I'm a jumble of rumbles,
At others I'm light like the moon,
But never my numb plunker fumbles,
Misstrums me, or tries a new tune.

John Updike
(1932–)

Serious Pleasure

Perhaps it sounds like a contradiction in terms to speak of serious pleasure, but the sort of pleasure described in this chapter is indeed serious. The pleasure is serious even if the poem (like many in this chapter) is not. It is serious first in the way that games are serious. Although nothing important will result from either winning or losing most games, playing with people who do not take the game seriously is no fun at all. Golfers who clown on the course or bridge players who constantly prattle are the death of good sport, even when no money has been bet on the outcome of the game. Similarly, a reader who does not seriously focus his attention on the task at hand, which is reading a poem, will neither experience pleasure himself nor communicate any enthusiasm for the poem to other readers.

But the pleasure of reading a poem is serious in another, more important way when the poem itself is serious. Just why this should be is something of a mystery; yet we find that the treatment in art of serious, sad, even depressing or sordid subjects can and does give pleasure. For example, who can think of a more serious subject for literary treatment than death; however, we can read a poem about death and experience all the pleasures described in this chapter, whereas in reading a poem about, say, eating strawberry shortcake (a most pleasurable activity in real life) we may experience only a few of the pleasures. Every day of the year large numbers of people derive great pleasure from watching performances of Shakespeare's tragedies, which depict murders, suicides, disasters and atrocities of all kinds, horribly bad luck, torture, suffering, disappointment, complete failure, and all the other ills that human flesh is heir to. Yet these plays are not depressing; on the contrary, they are highly entertaining.

Exercise 6

Show how each of these poems is capable of communicating pleasure to the "right kind" of reader. And describe the sort of reader who might enjoy each of the poems. Is there any reason why an individual reader could not enjoy all the poems equally?

Dirge in Woods

A wind sways the pines,
And below
Not a breath of wild air;
Still as the mosses that glow
On the flooring and over the lines
Of the roots here and there.

The pine-tree drops its dead;
They are quiet, as under the sea.
Overhead, overhead
Rushes life in a race,
As the clouds the clouds chase;
    And we go,
And we drop like the fruits of the tree,
    Even we,
    Even so.

George Meredith
(1828–1909)

The Ballad of Rudolph Reed

Rudolph Reed was oaken.
His wife was oaken too.
And his two good girls and his good little man
Oakened as they grew.

"I am not hungry for berries.
I am not hungry for bread.
But hungry hungry for a house
Where at night a man in bed

"May never hear the plaster
Stir as if in pain.
May never hear the roaches
Falling like fat rain.

"Where never wife and children need
Go blinking through the gloom.
Where every room of many rooms
Will be full of room.

"Oh my home may have its east or west
Or north or south behind it.
All I know is I shall know it,
And fight for it when I find it."

It was in a street of bitter white
That he made his application.
For Rudolph Reed was oakener
Than others in the nation.

The agent's steep and steady stare
Corroded to a grin.
Why, you black old, tough old hell of a man,
Move your family in!

Nary a grin grinned Rudolph Reed,
Nary a curse cursed he,
But moved in his House. With his dark little wife,
And his dark little children three.

A neighbor would *look,* with a yawning eye
That squeezed into a slit.
But the Rudolph Reeds and the children three
Were too joyous to notice it.

For were they not firm in a home of their own
With windows everywhere
And a beautiful banistered stair
And a front yard for flowers and a back yard for grass?

The first night, a rock, big as two fists.
The second, a rock big as three.
But nary a curse cursed Rudolph Reed.
(Though oaken as man could be.)

The third night, a silvery ring of glass.
Patience ached to endure.
But he looked, and lo! small Mabel's blood
Was staining her gaze so pure.

Then up did rise our Rudolph Reed
And pressed the hand of his wife,
And went to the door with a thirty-four
And a beastly butcher knife.

He ran like a mad thing into the night.
And the words in his mouth were stinking.
By the time he had hurt his first white man
He was no longer thinking.

By the time he had hurt his fourth white man
Rudolph Reed was dead.
His neighbors gathered and kicked his corpse.
"Nigger–" his neighbors said.

Small Mabel whimpered all night long,
For calling herself the cause.
Her oak-eyed mother did no thing
But change the bloody gauze.

Gwendolyn Brooks
(1917–   )

Maltese Goat

A goat can climb anything, but
What it likes best is a
Heap of rubble, stones of all
Sizes, unstable and sliding.
Each neat hoof-hold is
Only for an instant;

Somewhere near the top there's
A sizeable block
Steady enough to allow the
Long lunge forward of
The indiarubber neck, the

Straining upward of
The flexible lips,

The quick nip at the
Fig or the tussock,
The reflective chew in
A lightning zigzag,
The moment's dignity
In a proud eye,
The held poise, the
Taut silhouette.

Dear brother, they say you stink.
Well, so do I. Do you
Recognise me, aspiring one? I
Was born under your sign.

Nigel Dennis
(1912–)

Simultaneously

Simultaneously, five thousand miles apart,
two telephone poles, shaking and roaring
and hissing gas, rose from their emplacements
straight up, leveled off and headed
for each other's land, alerted radar
and ground defense, passed each other
in midair, escorted by worried planes,
and plunged into each other's place,
steaming and silent and standing straight,
sprouting leaves.

David Ignatow
(1914–)

2. *The Words of a Poem*

The power of a poem is derived from an indefinite harmony between what it says and what it is.

Paul Valery

Whatever else a poem may be, it is first of all an arrangement of words—not a collection of words, since *collection* implies either a list or a random assortment—but an ordered arrangement of words. Serious poets select, arrange, and frequently rearrange words until the words say exactly what the poets want them to say. Of course, other writers besides poets can be painstaking with language. The author of a technical manual, for example, must be precise; otherwise people using the manual could cause an explosion or ruin expensive materials. But technical writers are concerned more with language as a means to some other end than with language as an end in itself. The directions in their manuals are aimed at producing results: a smooth-running machine, a perfectly finished product. Usually these satisfactory results can be obtained with any one of several different arrangements of words. There are dozens of ways of telling how to dig a flower bed, or bake biscuits, or form a corporation. Works that give instruction need to be clear, and there are many ways to be clear. But there is only one way of writing a poem like the following:

Rotation

Like plump green floor plans
the pool tables squat
Among fawning mahogany Buddhas with felt heads.
Like clubwomen blessed with adultery
The balls dart to kiss
and tumble erring members into silent oblivion.

Right-angled over the verdant barbered turf
Sharks point long fingers at the multi-colored worlds
and play at percussion
Sounding cheap plastic clicks
in an 8-ball universe built for ivory.

Julian Bond
(1940–)

Title: a kind of pool game.

Bond's description of the game of rotation is vastly different from the way it would be described in a games manual or instruction book. A person could read the poem many times without finding out how many people are supposed to play rotation or what constitutes winning or losing the game. Indeed, such facts are totally irrelevant to the poem, for a poem uses words to present an experience rather than simply to convey information.

In Bond's poem a person (who never mentions himself) is presumably watching or recalling some games of rotation in a pool hall and rendering this experience in words. He is not trying to say what the game *really* is but what it seems like to him. The frozen expressions on the players' faces remind him of Buddha; he compares the behavior of the pool balls somewhat fantastically with club ladies scurrying about, kissing and tumbling. He borrows some of his language from the game. In line 3, for instance, he transfers the word *felt* from the tables to the players' heads. Accomplished players are often called *sharks* (line 8), but here the sharks incongruously bend over green *turf*. In the last line the reader is probably expected to remember the slang expression "behind the 8-ball," describing one who is a habitual loser in both life and pool. And the last word in the poem–ivory–is important for its suggestions of a valuable, solid substance. It contributes to the contrast implied in the last two lines: the world of these players could be ivory, but the poet finds it only cheap plastic. Beyond this interpretation are the larger racial implications of the poem. The poet seems to imply that blacks are left to fend for themselves in "an 8-ball universe" which has been built to work for the benefits of whites (ivory).

To be sure, a poet sometimes conveys information, but in doing so he is only beginning his work. A poet goes beyond giving information by using words and sounds that appeal to the reader's or hearer's feelings; he uses language that is meant to reverberate in one's imagination and memory. He is not like a camera, looking at the world around him merely to record its outward surfaces; his view is rather that of the human eye, which sees not only the outer forms of things but also perceives, through imagination, their inner significance.

Julian Bond's poem *is* a one-of-a-kind arrangement of words that *says* something about the game of rotation. A harmony exists between what the poem is and what it says. In this way a poem like Bond's is different from many other kinds of writing. Such a harmony would not exist, say, in a sociological study of people who frequent pool halls, or in a factual shot-by-shot description that a sports writer might make of a particular game. In prose writings of these kinds, individual words and the order in which they are placed don't have the importance that they have in a poem.

Exercise 7

"Out, Out—"

The buzz saw snarled and rattled in the yard
And made dust and dropped stove-length sticks of wood,
Sweet-scented stuff when the breeze drew across it.
And from there those that lifted eyes could count
Five mountain ranges one behind the other
Under the sunset far into Vermont.
And the saw snarled and rattled, snarled and rattled,
As it ran light, or had to bear a load.
And nothing happened: day was all but done.
Call it a day, I wish they might have said
To please the boy by giving him the half hour
That a boy counts so much when saved from work.
His sister stood beside them in her apron
To tell them "Supper." At the word, the saw,
As if to prove saws knew what supper meant,
Leaped out at the boy's hand, or seemed to leap—
He must have given the hand. However it was,
Neither refused the meeting. But the hand!

The boy's first outcry was a rueful laugh,
As he swung toward them holding up the hand,
Half in appeal, but half as if to keep
The life from spilling. Then the boy saw all—
Since he was old enough to know, big boy
Doing a man's work, though a child at heart—
He saw all spoiled. "Don't let him cut my hand off—
The doctor, when he comes. Don't let him, sister!"
So. But the hand was gone already.
The doctor put him in the dark of ether.
He lay and puffed his lips out with his breath.
And then—the watcher at his pulse took fright.
No one believed. They listened at his heart.
Little—less—nothing!—and that ended it.
No more to build on there. And they, since they
Were not the one dead, turned to their affairs.

Robert Frost
(1875–1963)

Title: See page 81.

According to Frost's biographer Lawrance Thompson, the event that prompted Frost to write this poem was reported in a New Hampshire newspaper, *The Littleton Courier,* for March 31, 1901. A comparison between the poem and the newspaper account that follows it reveals some of the important differences between factual writing in prose and imaginative writing in poetry.

Sad Tragedy at Bethlehem
Raymond Fitzgerald a Victim of Fatal Accident

Raymond Tracy Fitzgerald, one of the twin sons of Michael G. and Margaret Fitzgerald of Bethlehem, died at his home Thursday afternoon, March 24, as a result of an accident by which one of his hands was badly hurt in a sawing machine. The young man was assisting in sawing up some wood in his own dooryard with a sawing machine and accidentally hit the loose pulley, causing the saw to descend upon his hand, cutting and lacerating it badly. Raymond was taken into the house and a physician was immediately summoned, but he died very suddenly from the effects of the shock, which produced heart failure.

1. Many details in the poem could not properly be included in a newspaper story because they are inferences and opinions rather than facts. What are these details? Why does the poem omit certain details that the newspaper account includes?
2. What lines, phrases, and words in the poem hint at the catastrophe to come? Why do you suppose the poet includes the information in lines 4–6 in the poem? Why does he repeat the substance of line 1 in line 7?
3. The appearance of the boy's sister (line 13) is extremely abrupt. Why? Why is *supper* (line 14) in quotation marks?
4. The accident is shocking, but it is not so plainly detailed as to be gruesome. How does Frost avoid gruesome details?
5. Lines 27–33 consist of eight short, factual sentences. What is their effect after the more complicated sentences earlier in the poem?
6. Do the last two lines indicate that the family do not care about the boy? How else can one account for their seeming callousness?
7. Why is the title in quotation marks? Does it remind you of anything?

The Indispensable Dictionary

A reader of a prose work can sometimes skip over unfamiliar words without disaster: a magazine article will still make sense; the plot of a novel will still be clear. But in a short poem every word is important. The loss of a single word may make a poem incomprehensible or distort its meaning. The words skipped in a poem are likely to be its operative words, the ones on which the meaning especially depends.

Hap

If but some vengeful god would call to me
From up the sky, and laugh: "Thou suffering thing,
Know that thy sorrow is my ecstasy,
That thy love's loss is my hate's profiting!"

Then would I bear it, clench myself, and die,
Steeled by the sense of ire unmerited;
Half-eased in that a Powerfuller than I
Had willed and meted me the tears I shed.

But not so. How arrives it joy lies slain,
And why unblooms the best hope ever sown?
—Crass Casualty obstructs the sun and rain,
And dicing Time for gladness casts a moan. . . .
These purblind Doomsters had as readily strown
Blisses about my pilgrimage as pain.

Thomas Hardy
(1840–1928)

Only a reader with a large vocabulary will know all the words in this poem without using his dictionary. Suppose, however, that a reader were so foolhardy as to try to understand the poem without help. At the outset he might absurdly assume that the title is a short form of *happy;* the words *laugh* (line 2) and *joy* (line 9) would seem to support that definition. But obviously the "I" in the poem is not happy, for he says that "joy lies slain" (line 9). To whom, then, does the title apply? It must, surely, apply to the god (line 1) who causes sorrow (line 3). By this time the reader is wallowing in confusion. What he will do with the rest of the poem is better imagined than described, but it seems likely that he will reach some such conclusion as this: "God is happy because man is unhappy." A few minutes with a dictionary would show him how mistaken he is.

Exercise 8

The following poems probably contain several words whose meaning you are not positive of. Before consulting a dictionary, give each of these words the best tentative definition that you can devise. Then, when you have compared your tentative definitions with those in the dictionary, be prepared to explain how you would have misunderstood the poems if you had relied on your own uncorrected impulses to explain the words.

The Maldive Shark

About the Shark, phlegmatical one,
Pale sot of the Maldive sea,

The sleek little pilot-fish, azure and slim,
How alert in attendance be.
From his saw-pit of mouth, from his charnel of maw
They have nothing of harm to dread,
But liquidly glide on his ghastly flank
Or before his Gorgonian head;
Or lurk in the port of serrated teeth
In white triple tiers of glittering gates,
And there find a haven when peril's abroad,
An asylum in jaws of the Fates!
They are friends; and friendly they guide him to prey,
Yet never partake of the treat—
Eyes and brains to the dotard lethargic and dull,
Pale ravener of horrible meat.

Herman Melville
(1819–1891)

Aubade

O, Lady, awake! The azure moon
  Is rippling in the verdant skies,
The owl is warbling his soft tune,
  Awaiting but thy snowy eyes.
The joys of future years are past,
  Tomorrow's hopes are fled away;
Still let us love and even at last
  We shall be happy yesterday.

The early beam of rosy night
  Drives off the ebon moon afar,
Whilst through the murmur of the light
  The huntsman winds his mad guitar.
Then, Lady, wake! My brigantine
  Pants, neighs, and prances to be free;
Tell the creation I am thine,
  To some rich desert fly with me.

Anonymous
(Nineteenth Century)

Parting, without a Sequel

She has finished and sealed the letter
At last, which he so richly has deserved,
With characters venomous and hatefully curved,
And nothing could be better.

But even as she gave it
Saying to the blue-capped functioner of doom,
"Into his hands," she hoped the leering groom
Might somewhere lose and leave it.

Then all the blood
Forsook the face. She was too pale for tears,
Observing the ruin of her younger years.
She went and stood

Under her father's vaunting oak
Who kept his peace in wind and sun, and glistened
Stoical in the rain; to whom she listened
If he spoke.

And now the agitation of the rain
Rasped his sere leaves, and he talked low and gentle
Reproaching the wan daughter by the lintel;
Ceasing and beginning again.

Away went the messenger's bicycle,
His serpent's track went up the hill forever,
And all the time she stood there hot as fever
And cold as any icicle.

John Crowe Ransom
(1888–1974)

Denotation and Connotation

Understanding a poem presupposes knowing the connotation as well as the denotation if its words. **Denotation** is the dictionary meaning of a word. **Connotation** is the shade of meaning words have acquired through association and use. A dictionary defines the word *galleon* as "a sailing vessel of the fifteenth and following centuries, often having three or four decks, and used for commerce." This is the denotation of *galleon*. Among its connotations are "romance," "adventure," "piracy"; it brings to mind the Spanish Main, cutlasses, buccaneers, and pieces of eight. These connotations are part of the total meaning of the word.

In each of these columns the words have similar denotations but different connotations.

Canis familiaris	dame	murder	obese
canine quadruped	miss	slay	bloated
cur	wench	execute	portly
doggy	doll	kill	plump

The words in the first column, for instance, all denote "dog." Yet they carry very different connotations. The first word is associated with zoologists rather than with owners of pets; it would be appropriate in a scientific context. The second might be used by a pretentious or facetious person. The difference in the connotations of the last two can be illustrated by the remarks that two people might make to describe the same event. One might say, "There's a cur in the backyard"; the other, "There's a doggy in the backyard." Although the two remarks denote the same event, they obviously do not "say" the same thing.

Words differ in amount of connotation. Some—like *boy, dog, food, small*—have almost none out of a given context; others—like *atom, rose,* and *heart*—have absorbed so much color from the backgrounds in which they have occurred that by themselves they are rich in connotation. Poets use both kinds. They may choose one word for its precise denotation, another for its complex associations.

Understanding a poem sometimes depends more on a reader's grasping the connotations of its words than on his knowing their denotations. For example, in the following poem much of the man's bitter feelings toward the woman is conveyed by the connotations of the words he uses:

Sonnet 29

Am I failing? For no longer can I cast
A glory round about this head of gold.
Glory she wears, but springing from the mould;
Not like the consecration of the Past!
Is my soul beggared? Something more than earth
I cry for still: I cannot be at peace
In having Love upon a mortal lease.
I cannot take the woman at her worth!
Where is the ancient wealth wherewith I clothed
Our human nakedness, and could endow
With spiritual splendour a white brow
That else had grinned at me the fact I loathed?
A kiss is but a kiss now! and no wave
Of a great flood that whirls me to the sea.
But, as you will! we'll sit contentedly,
And eat our pot of honey on the grave.

George Meredith
(1829–1909)

The word *mould* (line 3) suggests that whatever glory the woman still has for the man is little more than the brightness that springs from the decay of their relationship. In the past her glory was a *consecration* (line 4)—something holy. Now his soul is not merely poor in love for her, but it is *beggared* (line 5). That word suggests complete impoverishment. She is no more than so much clay to him, and he desolately cries out (he does not grieve or weep) for something better (lines 5–6). He cannot rest in a love that he possesses only on a *mortal lease* (lines 6–7); the adjective *mortal* connotes not only a human lease, but also a finite and a fatal lease. *Lease* itself suggests a merely legal arrangement. In line 8 the important word is the basic and physiological *woman:* substituting other words like *the lady, my mistress, my lover* changes the sense of the line completely. In line 10 *nakedness* implies, with its sensual overtones, the sexual relationship.

The word *grinned* (line 12) suggests the grimace of a skull because it appears in the same context with *mould, earth, mortal,* and the final word, *grave.* The horror of the situation culminates in the two final lines of the poem: "we'll sit contentedly"—although there has not been a moment of contentment in the poem—and "eat our pot" (not dish or jar or bowl) of honey on the grave. The poem ends with the earthiest word for interment: not *tomb,* which is dignified and noble; not *sepulchre,* which is ecclesiastical; not *vault* nor *mausoleum,* words that suggest an attempt to preserve what has been lost; but *grave,* which connotes mould, decay, and worms.

Exercise 9

In reading these poems, think of possible reasons why particular words are used rather than words that are roughly synonymous.

Mushrooms

Overnight, very
Whitely, discreetly,
Very quietly

Our toes, our noses
Take hold of the loam.
Acquire the air.

Nobody sees us;
Stops us, betrays us;
The small grains make room.

Soft fists insist on
Heaving the needles,
The leafy bedding,

Even the paving.
Our hammers, our rams,
Earless and eyeless,

Perfectly voiceless,
Widen the crannies,
Shoulder through holes. We

Diet on water,
On crumbs of shadow,
Bland-mannered, asking

Little or nothing.
So many of us!
So many of us!

We are shelves, we are
Tables, we are meek,
We are edible,

Nudgers and shovers
In spite of ourselves.
Our kind multiplies:

We shall by morning
Inherit the earth.
Our foot's in the door.

Sylvia Plath
(1932–1963)

Time

Unfathomable Sea! whose waves are years,
  Ocean of Time, whose waters of deep woe
Are brackish with the salt of human tears!
  Thou shoreless flood, which in thy ebb and flow
Claspest the limits of mortality,
And sick of prey, yet howling on for more,
Vomitest thy wrecks on its inhospitable shore;
Treacherous in calm, and terrible in storm,
    Who shall put forth on thee,
    Unfathomable Sea?

Percy Bysshe Shelley
(1792–1822)

1. What synonyms can you give for the words *unfathomable, woe, brackish, mortality, sick, prey, howling, inhospitable, treacherous, terrible?*

2. Describe as nearly as possible the difference between the synonyms and the words that Shelley uses.

Richard Cory

Whenever Richard Cory went down town,
We people on the pavement looked at him:
He was a gentleman from sole to crown,
Clean favored, and imperially slim.

And he was always quietly arrayed,
And he was always human when he talked;
But still he fluttered pulses when he said,
"Good-morning," and he glittered when he walked.

And he was rich—yes, richer than a king—
And admirably schooled in every grace:
In fine, we thought that he was everything
To make us wish that we were in his place.

So on we worked, and waited for the light,
And went without the meat, and cursed the bread;
And Richard Cory, one calm summer night,
Went home and put a bullet through his head.

Edwin Arlington Robinson
(1869–1935)

in fine (11): in short.

Richard Cory

With Apologies to E. A. Robinson

They say that Richard Cory owns
One half of this old town,
With elliptical connections
To spread his wealth around.
Born into Society,
A banker's only child,
He had everything a man could want:
Power, grace and style.

Refrain:

But I, I work in his factory
And I curse the life I'm livin'
And I curse my poverty
And I wish that I could be
Oh I wish that I could be
Oh I wish that I could be
Richard Cory.

The papers print his picture
Almost everywhere he goes:
Richard Cory at the opera,
Richard Cory at a show
And the rumor of his party
And the orgies on his yacht—
Oh he surely must be happy
With everything he's got. (*Refrain.*)

He really gave to charity,
He had the common touch,
And they were grateful for his patronage
And they thanked him very much,
So my mind was filled with wonder
When the evening headlines read:
"Richard Cory went home last night
And put a bullet through his head." (*Refrain.*)

Paul Simon
(1942–)

1. What words in the two Richard Cory poems are effective primarily because of their connotation?
2. Simon and Garfunkel perform the second poem on their record *Sounds of Silence*. What did they do to Robinson's poem to make it into a popular song?

Diction

Diction is the term commonly applied to the words that a poet or any other writer chooses to use in a literary work. The diction of a poem may be plain, as in most of the poems of Chapter 1 in this book, or it may be fancy, as in Wilde's "The Harlot's House" (page 379). It may be conversational and slangy (Lipsitz's "Skinny Poem," 301), or it may be formal (Emerson's "Days," 385). In choosing a particular word for a particular poem, a careful poet pays close attention to the context the word will have—**context** being, of course, the other words preceding and following that word.

A Remembrance of My Friend Mr. Thomas Morley

Death hath deprived me of my dearest friend;
  My dearest friend is dead and laid in grave.
In grave he rests until the world shall end.
  The world shall end, as end all things must have.
All things must have an end that Nature wrought;
That Nature wrought must unto dust be brought.

John Davies of Hereford
(ca. 1565–1618)

Morley (title) : a musician and composer. *That* (6) : What

Although the diction of this gloomy little poem is quite plain, it is also consistently serious and dignified. An expression like *kicked the bucket* would not fit into the context of the other language because it would be too slangy; at the opposite extreme, *expired* would be too fancy a word for the context. Similarly, Davies could not have said "My dearest friend has croaked" without totally destroying the seriousness of the poem; the context rules out any word with such comic connotations as *croaked*.

Poetic Diction

Critics and poets have long been interested in the relationship between the diction of poetry and the diction of ordinary speech. In some ages they have held that the two dictions resemble each other closely; in others, they have held the opposite view. In the so-called Augustan Age of English poetry (about 1660–1790), for instance, the authors of serious poems avoided words that had acquired "low" or familiar associations from extensive use; in place of these they used fancier or more dignified expressions. Such poets would use words like *swain* for *shepherd, lave* for *wash,* and *scaly brood* for *school of fish.* Some poets of the late eighteenth and early nineteenth centuries protested against such embellished diction. In 1800 Wordsworth asserted that "there neither is, nor can be, any essential difference between the language of prose and metrical composition." He thought that a poem written in "a selection of the language really spoken by men." Consequently, when he wrote about a shepherd, he called him "a shepherd"; sheep he called "sheep." Expressions like "keeper of the fleecy people" he labeled as "poetic diction"—a term that always had a derogatory connotation to him.

But Wordsworth had his own notions of what poetic diction should be; his own diction is no less poetic merely because it differs from the diction of the poets that preceded him. The word *selection* in the passage just quoted ("a selection of the language really spoken by men") implies that Wordsworth did not consider the language of poetry identical with the spoken language. He knew that a good poet selects his words much more carefully than a casual talker ever does. The term **poetic diction,** then, need not be a term of abuse; it may instead refer to the total differences between the language of poetry and the language of common speech at any given time.

In most poems the diction is consistently of one kind, whether formal or conversational. But in every age a few poets have delighted in a mixed kind of diction, putting into their poems words and expressions that do not fit the context and thus seem original and surprising. John Donne, who lived in Shakespeare's time, began a love poem with language appropriate to a back-fence argument: "For God's sake, hold your tongue!" This opening is much more dramatic than that of most love poems. In our own time many poets have astonished and delighted their readers with bold mixtures of kinds of diction.

To the Reader

As you read, a white bear leisurely
pees, dyeing the snow
saffron,

and as you read, many gods
lie among lianas: eyes of obsidian
are watching the generations of leaves,

and as you read
the sea is turning its dark pages,
turning
its dark pages.

Denise Levertov
(1923–)

lianas (5): vines in tropical rain forests. *obsidian* (5): volcanic glass, usually black.

In the context of such elegant, exotic words as *saffron, obsidian,* and *lianas,* the babyish word *pees* is conspicuous, yet somehow right. For one thing, it sounds right, especially after the word *leisurely.* An equally common but more vulgar four-letter word would not sound nearly so right. As for such quasi-medical terms as *urinates* or *micturates,* not to mention such euphemisms as *makes water*—these simply wouldn't do in the poem at all.

T.S. Eliot has said that every age has its own poetic diction. If this is so, perhaps our age demands of some of its poets a mixed diction: at once high and low, rare and common, learned and popular, old and new.

Exercise 10

In one of the three following poems the diction is consistent; in two of them it is a mixture, though it is a different kind of mixture in each. Describe the diction of all three poems.

As Befits a Man

I don't mind dying—
But I'd hate to die all alone!
I want a dozen pretty women
To holler, cry, and moan.

I don't mind dying
But I want my funeral to be fine:
A row of long tall mamas
Fainting, fanning, and crying.

I want a fish-tail hearse
And sixteen fish-tail cars,
A big brass band
And a whole truck load of flowers.

When they let me down,
Down into the clay,
I want the women to holler:
Please don't take him away!
Ow-ooo-oo-o!
Don't take daddy away!

Langston Hughes
(1902–1967)

Heresy for a Class-room

Green willows are for girls to study under
When that green lady, Spring, walks down the street:
Look out the window, Jean, look out and wonder
About their unseen earth-embedded feet.
Under the dark uncolored mouldy clay
Where willow roots are thrust, their life is drawn
Up through the limbs, to burst in bud, and sway
Slow-shaken green festoons above the lawn.

So never doubt that bloom turns into light
As winter into April, or as bloom
Breaks on the barren branches over-night.—
Little enough is learned in any room

With blackboard walls, on afternoons like these,—
O Jean, look out the window at the trees!

Rolfe Humphries
(1894–   )

The Love Feast

In an upper room at midnight
See us gathered on behalf
Of love according to the gospel
Of the radio-phonograph.

Lou is telling Anne what Molly
Said to Mark behind her back;
Jack likes Jill who worships George
Who has the hots for Jack.

Catechumens make their entrance;
Steep enthusiastic eyes
Flicker after tits and baskets;
Someone vomits; someone cries.

Willy cannot bear his father,
Lilian is afraid of kids;
The Love that rules the sun and stars
Permits what He forbids.

Adrian's pleasure-loving dachshund
In a sinner's lap lies curled;
Drunken absent-minded fingers
Pat a sinless world.

Who is Jenny lying to
In her call, Collect, to Rome?
The Love that made her out of nothing
Tells me to go home.

But that Miss Number in the corner
Playing hard to get. . . .
I am sorry I'm not sorry . . .
Make me chaste, Lord, but not yet.

W. H. Auden
(1907–1973)

Title: An allusion to the *agape*, a love feast among primitive Christians which was observed with prayers, songs, scripture-readings. *Catechumens* (9): those enrolled in the earliest stages of instruction in Christian doctrine in the early church. *Love* (15, 23): the Deity. *Make . . . yet* (28): an allusion to the *Confessions* of St. Augustine, Book 8, Chapter 7, "Give me chastity and continency, but do not give it yet."

1. What is the poet's attitude toward the goings-on in this poem? If you think that he approves, why do you suppose he included lines 15–16 and 23–24 in the poem?
2. In what ways is the "I" of the poem—the "speaker"—as much at fault as the others?

A Poet's Freedom

Poets are allowed—and they often take—much greater freedom with language than other writers or speakers. This freedom assumes many forms. Poets are constantly coining new words: *Eastertide,* for example, in Housman's poem on page 371, or *pin-tingling* in Dickey's on page 391. They also revive rare old words: *salamandrine* in Hardy's poem on page 404. And the way they use prepositions without clearly stated referents would cause them to fail freshman English in most colleges.

Poets take great freedoms with the conventional parts of speech; they may use nouns to do the work of adjectives or verbs, or adjectives to do the work of nouns. Shakespeare has his Cleopatra say of Julius Caesar:

> He words me, girls, he words me that I should not
> Be noble to myself.

Here *word,* everywhere else in the English language a noun, becomes a verb.

Poets also takes liberties with syntax, the order of words in a sentence. There are even a few poems consisting entirely of words and phrases rather than of complete sentences. But the most common syntactical liberties are inversions of prose order. "Then would I bear it," writes Thomas Hardy (page 41) rather than "Then I would bear it." Requirements of rhyme and rhythm (see pp. 207ff., 455ff.)

often make it necessary to change the normal order of words, although excessive use of this license, as in the metrical paraphrase of Psalm 23 (page 393), is a defect in a poem. A poet is supposed to be able to control the form of his poem; it should not control him.

Many poets—particularly twentieth-century poets—feel free to leave out of their works all sorts of words that prose writers would put in. Why do they do this? Certainly not because they want to confuse or puzzle their readers; there would be no point in this kind of behavior. Rather, they omit words in order to give the reader the pleasure of supplying those words, or reading the poem carefully and intently enough to be *able* to supply those words. In this way, the reader enters more deeply into the experience of the poem and even becomes a co-creator of the poem.

Reason

Said, Pull her up a bit will you, Mac, I want to unload there.
Said, Pull her up my rear end, first come first serve.
Said, Give her the gun, Bud, he needs a taste of his own bumper.
Then the usher came out and got into the act:

Said, Pull her up, pull her up a bit, we need this space, sir.
Said, For God's sake, is this still a free country or what?
You go back and take care of Gary Cooper's horse
And leave me handle my own car.

Saw them unloading the lame old lady,
Ducked out under the wheel and gave her an elbow,
Said, All you needed to do was just explain;
Reason, Reason is my middle name.

Josephine Miles
(1911–)

Without any kind of introduction, Miles puts us right into the middle of a scene in which people become excited and say rude things to each other. But she tells us only what they say, not who does the saying. The reader must supply all the subjects for the verb *said,* which appears six times, and identify all the persons to whom the pronouns refer.

A careful examination of the clues in the poem suggests that four different people speak:

Line 1 is said by a driver who wants to park his car (no. 1) in front of a theater, in space already partly occupied by another car (no. 2).

Line 2 is said by the illiterate and uncouth driver of car no. 2.

Line 3 is said by a passenger in car no. 1, perhaps the lame old lady of line 9.

Line 5 is said by the theater usher, who has come out to help get the old lady out of car no. 1.

Lines 6–12 are said by car no. 2's driver, who suddenly changes his attitude toward the whole scene.

As for the pronouns, *you* (line 1) apparently refers to driver no. 2; *he* (line 3) to driver no. 2; *we* (line 5) to the usher and driver no. 1; *you* (line 7) to the usher; *them* (line 9) to the usher and driver no. 1.

Two drivers, one usher, and one passenger account for all that is said in the poem except line 4. It's hard to say positively who speaks this line, but it might best be regarded as a sort of stage direction supplied by the poet. Or it could be said by driver no. 2, since the language of "got into the act" resembles his other slangy and cliché-ridden remarks: "my rear end," "still a free country," "reason is my middle name," and so on. But it really doesn't matter who says line 4: the poem is a comedy of misunderstanding, and the omission of speech tags, connective words, and definite pronoun references actually enhances its comic effect.

Exercise 11

What kinds of freedom have poets taken in these poems?

To-day and Thee

The appointed winners in a long-stretch'd game;
The course of Time and nations—Egypt, India, Greece and Rome;
The past entire, with all its heroes, histories, arts, experiments,
Its store of songs, inventions, voyages, teachers, books,
Garner'd for now and thee—To think of it!
The heirdom all converged in thee!

Walt Whitman
(1819–1892)

How Soon Hath Time

How soon hath Time, the subtle thief of youth,
  Stol'n on his wing my three and twentieth year!
  My hasting days fly on with full career,
But my late spring no bud or blossom shew'th.
Perhaps my semblance might deceive the truth,
  That I to manhood am arrived so near,
  And inward ripeness doth much less appear,
That some more timely-happy spirits endu'th.
Yet be it less or more, or soon or slow,
  It shall be still in strictest measure ev'n
    To that same lot, however mean, or high,
  Toward which Time leads me, and the will of Heav'n;
All is, if I have grace to use it so,
    As ever in my great task-Master's eye.

John Milton
(1608–1674)

career (3): speed. *endu'th* (8): provideth, endoweth. *as* (14): as being.

Spring and Fall: To a Young Child

Margaret, are you grieving
Over Goldengrove unleaving?
Leaves, like the things of man, you
With your fresh thoughts care for, can you?
Ah! as the heart grows older
It will come to such sights colder
By and by, nor spare a sigh
Though worlds of wanwood leafmeal lie;
And yet you will weep and know why.
Now no matter, child, the name:
Sorrow's springs are the same.
Nor mouth had, no nor mind, expressed
What heart heard of, ghost guessed:
It is the blight man was born for,
It is Margaret you mourn for.

Gerard Manley Hopkins
(1844–1889)

Goldengrove (2) : a place. *ghost* (13) : spirit. *blight* (14) : see Genesis, Chapter 3.

1. The words *unleaving* (line 2), *wanwood,* and *leafmeal* (line 8) are not to be found in ordinary dictionaries. How, then, could a reader ever be certain of their meaning?
2. Find places in the poem where Hopkins takes liberties with "normal" English word order, and then arrange the words in "normal" order.
3. What word or words are needed to complete the thought of lines 10–11?
4. The poet says that Margaret is actually mourning for Margaret, not for the leaves. What reason does he give for that conclusion?

Paraphrase

Unfamiliar words arranged in unusual ways may make it difficult for a reader to grasp the sense of a poem. One useful way to overcome the difficulty is to write a paraphrase. A **paraphrase** is a word-for-word rendering of a poem, or part of a poem, into clear prose. Although it is seldom necessary to paraphrase a whole poem, here, for purposes of demonstration, is a poem followed by a complete paraphrase.

On My First Daughter

Here lies to each her parent's ruth,
Mary, the daughter of their youth;
Yet all heaven's gifts, being heaven's due,
It makes the father less to rue.
At six months' end she parted hence
With safety of her innocence;
Whose soul heaven's Queen (whose name she bears),
In comfort of her mother's tears,
Hath placed amongst her virgin-train;
Where, while that severed doth remain,
This grave partakes the fleshly birth,
Which cover lightly, gentle earth.

Ben Jonson
(1572–1637)

It is a cause of regret to both her parents that Mary, born to them when they were young, lies dead and buried here. But since her father understands that all of heaven's gifts ultimately belong to heaven, his sadness is lessened. After six months of life she left this world, secure in her sinlessness; the Queen of Heaven, for whom she was named, has placed her soul among the ranks of her attendant virgins in order to comfort the human mother's sorrow. So long as the child's soul remains in heaven separated from her flesh, this grave will hold her body. May the kind earth cover it lightly.

The paraphrase maintains, as far as possible, the person, tense, voice, and mood of the poem. It clarifies elliptical expressions by writing out the idea in full. It disentangles unusual syntax. It provides synonyms for unfamiliar words.

The advantages of such an exercise are almost self-evident. The need to make a paraphrase slows a reader down; it forces him to examine each word, to understand what it means, and then to find a close equivalent. Paraphrasing enforces on an inexperienced reader the kind of close attention that keeps him from racing through a poem at the rapid pace with which he reads most ordinary prose.

The Limitations of Paraphrase

It is imperative to remember that paraphrasing poems is merely an exercise, a device for training a reader to observe care and accuracy. No paraphrase, however exact it may be, is a substitute for, or an equivalent of, the poem itself. A paraphrase is never the poem "in other words." It cannot capture the total meaning or the whole experience of a poem (see Chapter 9). The sense of the words is only one small part of a poem's meaning; other parts are conveyed by sound, rhythm, phrasing, and the very uniqueness of each word used in the poem. These are matters that cannot be paraphrased.

When you change the words of a poem, and the order in which those words occur, the poem itself simply vanishes. For instance, whatever is enjoyable in this sarcastic little poem is totally lost in the paraphrase:

The Georges

George the First was always reckoned
Vile, but viler George the Second;
And what mortal ever heard
Any good of George the Third?
When from earth the Fourth descended
(God be praised!) the Georges ended.

Walter Savage Landor
(1775–1864)

George I has always been regarded as a loathsome person, but George II was actually more despicable. And nobody has ever heard anything favorable said about George III. There have been no more Georges, for which favor we glorify the Deity, since George IV went down to Hell.

Paraphrase is particularly limited as a way of experiencing and understanding a **lyric**, which is the term commonly given to a short, singable or songlike poem expressing feeling.

Hark, Hark! The Lark

Hark, hark! The lark at heaven's gate sings,
  And Phoebus 'gins arise,
His steeds to water at those springs
  On chaliced flowers that lies;
And winking Mary-buds begin
  To ope their golden eyes:
With every thing that pretty is,
  My lady sweet, arise!
    Arise, arise!

William Shakespeare
(1564–1616)

Mary buds (5) : marigolds.

Paraphrasing this admirable lyric is bound to result in foolishness, as the paraphraser becomes involved with the sun god's horses drinking the dew that lies in cup-shaped flowers. Such a paraphrase—if anybody had the brass to undertake it—would be a trivial distraction from the poem rather than a help in appreciating it.

Exercise 12

Write a paraphrase as an aid to understanding any difficult places in the following poems. Point out the differences between your paraphrases and the original passages in the poems.

When I Watch the Living Meet

When I watch the living meet,
  And the moving pageant file
Warm and breathing through the street
  Where I lodge a little while,

If the heats of hate and lust
  In the house of flesh are strong,
Let me mind the house of dust
  Where my sojourn shall be long.

In the nation that is not
  Nothing stands that stood before;
There revenges are forgot,
  And the hater hates no more;

Lovers lying two and two
  Ask not whom they sleep beside,
And the bridegroom all night through
  Never turns him to the bride.

A. E. Housman
(1859–1936)

Protest

I long not now, a little while at least,
For that serene interminable hour
When I shall leave this Barmecidal feast,
With poppy for my everlasting flower;
I long not now for that dim cubicle
Of earth to which my lease will not expire,
Where he who comes a tenant there may dwell
Without a thought of famine, flood, or fire.

Surely that house has quiet to bestow—
Still tongue, spent pulse, heart pumped of its last throb,
The fingers tense and tranquil in a row,
The throat unwelled with any sigh or sob—
But time to live, to love, bear pain and smile,
Oh, we are given such a little while!

Countee Cullen
(1903–1946)

Barmecidal (3): illusory, imaginary. *poppy* (4): opium or forgetfulness.

The Trojan Horse

A horse I am, whom bit,
Rein, rod, nor spur, not fear;
When I my riders bear,
Within my womb, not on my back, they sit.
No streams I drink, nor care for grass nor corn;
Art me a monster wrought,
All nature's works to scorn.
A mother, I was without mother born;
In end all armed my father I forth brought;
What thousand ships, and champions of renown
Could not do free, I captive razed a town.

William Drummond
(1585–1649)

Beginning to Understand a Poem

Our understanding of any given poem grows with successive rereadings and increased experience, both of life and other poems. But everyone has to begin somewhere, and so here are some general hints that may assist in the process:

1. Read the poem aloud, and naturally, several times, making normal pauses for the appropriate punctuation. For advice on reading aloud, see page 227.

2. Make sure that you understand all the words, and that you are aware of the connotations (see p. 43) of the words; use the notes to the poem and a good dictionary.
3. Make sure that you understand how the words fit together to make statements; a prose paraphrase (see p. 44) can test this understanding. Remember that the end of a line in a poem is not necessarily the end of a sentence.
4. Do not hold yourself aloof from the poem; allow it to affect your feelings.
5. Pay careful attention to the whole poem, including the title and the ending; don't make up your mind about the poem until you have taken it *all* in.
6. Don't try to force your own ideas onto the poem; the business of a poem is to be itself. Be certain that you can support your opinions with evidence drawn from the poem.
7. Don't regard this list as exhaustive, and don't regard it as prescribing certain steps that you should take one after the other. Ideally all the activities listed here should go on simultaneously.

3. *The Reader and the Poem*

All works of the mind contain within themselves the image of the reader for whom they are intended.

Jean-Paul Sartre

Like all other writers, poets expect their readers to bring a certain amount of knowledge and experience to their poems. They also expect that what the readers bring will be relevant and will have a genuine connection with the poems being read. The first part of this chapter considers some false conceptions that a reader might impose on poems; the remainder suggests some attitudes and habits of thinking that will assist a reader's understanding.

"Poetic" Subjects

Perhaps the most widespread misconception about poems is the belief that they must be written about "poetic" subjects. According to this view poetic subjects must be pleasant—love, nature, beauty; unpleasant subjects are unpoetic and are therefore unsuited to poems. To trace this circular absurdity to its origin would be neither a profitable nor an easy task. It seems to be related somehow to the stereotyped view of the poet as a pale esthete, so preoccupied with moonlight and rainbows that he never condescends to look at real life. Actually there are no limitations on the suitability of subjects for poems, for there are good poems on almost every conceivable subject. A poet is as free to write about a rusty automobile radiator as about a sunset.

The Fly

O hideous little bat, the size of snot,
With polyhedral eye and shabby clothes,

To populate the stinking cat you walk
The promontory of the dead man's nose,
Climb with the fine leg of a Duncan Phyfe
  The smoking mountains of my food
    And in a comic mood
  In mid-air take to bed a wife.

Riding and riding with your filth of hair
On gluey foot or wing, forever coy,
Hot from the compost and green sweet decay,
Sounding your buzzer like an urchin toy—
You dot all whiteness with diminutive stool,
  In the tight belly of the dead
    Burrow with hungry head
  And inlay maggots like a jewel.

At your approach the great horse stomps and paws
Bringing the hurricane of his heavy tail;
Shod in disease you dare to kiss my hand
Which sweeps against you like an angry flail;
Still you return, return, trusting your wing
  To draw you from the hunter's reach
    That learns to kill to teach
  Disorder to the tinier thing.

My peace is your disaster. For your death
Children like spiders cup their pretty hands
And wives resort to chemistry of war.
In fens of sticky paper and quicksands
You glue yourself to death. Where you are stuck
  You struggle hideously and beg
    You amputate your leg
  Imbedded in the amber muck.

But I, a man, must swat you with my hate,
Slap you across the air and crush your flight,
Must mangle with my shoe and smear your blood,
Expose your little guts pasty and white,
Knock your head sidewise like a drunkard's hat,
  Pin your wings under like a crow's,
    Tear off your flimsy clothes
  And beat you as one beats a rat.

Then like Gargantua I stride among
The corpses strewn like raisins in the dust,

The broken bodies of the narrow dead
That catch the throat with fingers of disgust.
I sweep. One gyrates like a top and falls
  And stunned, stone blind, and deaf
    Buzzes its frightful F
  And dies between three cannibals.

Karl Shapiro
(1913–)

polyhedral (2): having many faces. *Duncan Phyfe* (5): Furniture designed by Phyfe (1768–1854) has elegant spindly legs.

This poem presents some mildly nasty experiences in frank language. It will perhaps never be chanted at a ladies' club luncheon, but it has achieved another kind of success because its observations are comically accurate and because the poet has developed the subject with much imagination, ingenuity, and gusto.

Exercise 13

Study the language in these poems; then explain why certain words must necessarily be gross and harsh if the poet is to express his subject honestly.

Ask Not to Know This Man

Ask not to know this man. If fame should speak
  His name in any metal, it would break.
Two letters were enough the plague to tear
  Out of his grave, and poison every ear.
A parcel of court dirt, a heap and mass
  Of all vice hurled together, there he was:
Proud, false, and treacherous, vindictive, all
  That thought can add, unthankful, the laystall
Of putrid flesh alive! Of blood, the sink!
  And so I leave to stir him, lest he stink.

Ben Jonson
(1572–1637)

name . . . metal (2): that is, inscribed on a metal plate on his tomb. *court dirt* (5): refuse of the court. *laystall* (8): dung heap.

The Pleasure

With broken tooth he clawed it,
with crooked finger held it,
and with naked eyes watched it
as he chewed, hair disheveled,
tie loose, shirt open, socks down—
a bum, greedy, therefore knowing.
How he chewed and how he swallowed
and wiped his lips with the back of his palm,
then spat blood of the raw-veined
brick-red lump meat; and went
looking for more down the side streets
of the market where the trash cans stank,
and came up with chunks greening
at the center and edges, but he chewed
and swallowed and dug for more,
a bum greedy, a bum alive,
a hungry one.

David Ignatow
(1914–)

The .38

I hear the man downstairs slapping the hell out of his stupid wife
again
I hear him push and shove her around the overcrowded room
I hear his wife scream and beg for mercy
I hear him tell her there is no mercy
I hear the blows as they land on her beautiful body
I hear glasses and pots and pans falling
I hear her fleeing from the room
I hear them running up the stairs
I hear her outside my door
I hear him coming toward her outside my door
I hear her banging on my door
I hear him bang her head on my door
I hear him trying to drag her away from my door
I hear her hands desperate on my doorknob
I hear the blows of her head against my door

I hear him drag her down the stairs
I hear her head bounce from step to step
I hear them again in their room
I hear a loud smack across her face (I guess)
I hear her groan—then
I hear the eerie silence
I hear him open the top drawer of his bureau (the .38 lives there)
I hear the fast beat of my heart
I hear the drops of perspiration fall from my brow
I hear him yell I warned you
I hear him say damn you I warned you and now it's too late
I hear the loud report of the thirty eight caliber revolver then
I hear it again and again the Smith and Wesson
I hear the bang bang bang of four death dealing bullets
I hear my heart beat faster and louder—then again
I hear the eerie silence
I hear him walk out of their overcrowded room
I hear him walk up the steps
I hear him come toward my door
I hear his hand on the doorknob
I hear the doorknob click
I hear the door slowly open
I hear him step into my room
I hear the click of the thirty eight before the firing pin hits the
    bullet
I hear the loud blast of the powder exploding in the chamber of
    the .38
I hear the heavy lead nose of the bullet swiftly cutting its way
    through the barrel of the .38
I hear it emerge into space from the .38
I hear the bullet of death flying toward my head the .38
I hear it coming faster than sound the .38
I hear it coming closer to my sweaty forehead the .38
I hear its weird whistle the .38
I hear it give off a steamlike noise when it cuts through my sweat
    the .38
I hear it singe my skin as it enters my head the .38 and
I hear death saying, *Hello, I'm here!*

Ted Joans
(1928–   )

Title: a hand-gun of this caliber. *Smith and Wesson* (28): manufacturers of the gun.

Stock Response and Irrelevant Association

Stock response is a reader's automatic, unthinking reaction to certain words or subjects because of the associations that they have with his natural, conventional feelings. All human beings have certain reservoirs of deep feeling that can be tapped by the appropriate verbal stimulation. It is these feelings that a demagogue seeks to stir with his insincere references to "Old Glory" and "the land of the free, the home of the brave." The "patriotic" orator in Cummings's poem (page 240) is such a demagogue.

It is these reservoirs of natural feelings that a sentimentalist depends on when he refers to "happy hours of carefree childhood," or "little toddlers lisping prayers at father's knee." In the same way, an unskillful poet, unable to prompt fresh or genuine feelings with his verses, may attempt to exploit the natural, ready-made emotions that lie just below the surface in most human beings.

Closely related to stock responses is **irrelevant association,** a reader's reaction to certain words or subjects because of their connections with his personal experiences or prejudices. For example, one reader may respond to the word *lobster* by feeling nauseated; another, by feeling hungry. Thus, an irrelevant association may dispose a reader either favorably or unfavorably toward whatever stimulates it.

Lobsters

Here at the Super Duper, in a glass tank
Supplied by a rill of cold fresh water
Running down a glass washboard at one end
And siphoned off at the other, and so
Perpetually renewed, a herd of lobster
Is made available to the customer
Who may choose whichever one he wants
To carry home and drop into boiling water
And serve with a sauce of melted butter.

Meanwhile, the beauty of strangeness marks
These creatures, who move (when they do)
With a slow, vague wavering of claws,
The somnambulist's effortless clambering
As he crawls over the shell of a dream

Resembling himself. Their velvet colors,
Mud red, bruise purple, cadaver green
Speckled with black, their camouflage at home,
Make them conspicuous here in the strong
Day-imitating light, the incommensurable
Philosophers and at the same time victims
Herded together in the marketplace, asleep
Except for certain tentative gestures
Of their antennae, or their imperial claws
Pegged shut with a whittled stick at the wrist.

We inlanders, buying our needful food,
Pause over these slow, gigantic spiders
That spin not. We pause and are bemused,
And sometimes it happens that a mind sinks down
To the blind abyss in a swirl of sand, goes cold
And archaic in a carapace of horn,
Thinking: There's something underneath the world. . . .

The flame beneath the pot that boils the water.

Howard Nemerov
(1920–)

spin not (27): Matthew vi:28. *carapace* (30): shell of the lobster.

A pro-or-con reaction to lobsters as food is totally irrelevant to this poem, however inevitable it might be as a response to lines 1–19; beginning with line 10, the poet concentrates on lobsters not as food but as strange-looking victims of a fate of which they are ignorant. Only with the conclusion of the poem does its chief significance or theme come home to us: the beholder suddenly completes his own identification with these crustaceans—an identification first suggested, however, as early as line 12. He too is ignorant of the "flame beneath the pot" of his world.

Both stock responses and irrelevant associations are inevitable. No one could entirely rid himself of them, nor would anyone want to. But every reader should be aware of the existence of his own susceptibility to stock responses and his tendency to make irrelevant associations. These reactions are insidious because they require no thought and because they occur automatically. They can prevent a reader from enjoying a poem that he might otherwise enjoy, or encourage a reader to admire a poem that is not worthy of admiration, or even cause a reader to assume that he understands a poem when actually he misunderstands it.

The last-mentioned error is the worst. Suppose, for instance, that a reader of the following poem were the sort of person who automatically feels sympathy for any suffering animal.

The Slaughter-House

Under the big 500-watted lamps, in the huge sawdusted
  government inspected slaughter-house,
head down from hooks and clamps, run on trolleys over
  troughs,
the animals die.
Whatever terror their dull intelligences feel
  or what agony distorts their most protruding eyes
the incommunicable narrow skulls conceal.
  Across the sawdusted floor,
ignorant as children, they see the butcher's slow
  methodical approach
in the bloodied apron, leather cap above, thick square
  shoes below,
struggling to comprehend this unique vision upside
  down,
and then approximate a human scream
  as from the throat slit like a letter
the blood empties, and the windpipe, like a blown valve,
  spurts steam.

But I, sickened equally with the ox and lamb,
  misread my fate,
mistake the butcher's love
  who kills me for the meat I am
to feed a hungry multitude beyond the sliding doors.
  I, too, misjudge the real
purpose of this huge shed I'm herded in: not for my love
  or lovely wool am I here,
but to make some world a meal.
  See, how on the unsubstantial air
I kick, bleating my private woe,
  as upside down my rolling sight

somersaults, and frantically I try to set my world upright;
  too late learning why I'm hung here,
whose nostrils bleed, whose life runs out from eye and ear.

Alfred Hayes
(1911–)

The details in lines 1–9 could easily evoke a reaction of pity and indignation in any tender-hearted reader, who might sincerely but mistakenly assume that the poem is a protest against the wholesale killing of animals. After all, in the unlikely event that such a reader were himself to write a poem about a slaughterhouse, he would loudly denounce its practices, and so he assumes that Alfred Hayes has done the same. The reader might, on the other hand, assume that Hayes is rejoicing in the spectacle that he describes; he would then be so repelled by the poem that he would hardly be able to read it, let alone understand it. In both instances his automatic, unthinking reactions would keep him from seeing what is actually in the poem.

An unbiased reading shows that "The Slaughter-House" is much more concerned with pity for suffering mankind than with pity for animals. The "I" in the poem (line 20) regards himself as a sheep (the very name connotes dumb innocence) hanging upside down in an immense shed, waiting to have his throat slit. Just why he imagines himself in this dreadful predicament is not made explicit. Perhaps his "private woe" (line 30) is a private soldier's woe; perhaps he is about to be slaughtered in a great war that has already turned his life upside down and made a shambles of it. Perhaps he is not actually going to be butchered, but only feels as though he were. At any rate, the poem seeks to evoke pity for a human animal in a world that seems to him like a slaughterhouse, rather than pity for the livestock in a real slaughterhouse.

The details in the poem are likely to automatically repel squeamish readers and automatically attract readers who consider themselves hard-boiled and their view of the world "realistic." The hard-boiled reader may have favorable reactions to such words as *intestines, gore, stainless steel, claw, rape, dung, deceit, torture,* or *debauchery* in a poem; the tender-hearted reader will probably react favorably when he encounters *mother-love, bluebird, rose, twi-*

light, loyal, beautiful, love, patriotism, our Heavenly Father, and so on. Both kinds of readers have ready-made emotional reactions that may easily prevent them from seeing a poem as it actually is.

Exercise 14

Compare the following two poems.

My Mother's Hands

Such beautiful, beautiful hands!
They're neither white nor small;
And you, I know, would scarcely think
That they were fair at all.
I've looked on hands whose form and hue
A sculptor's dream might be;
Yet are those wrinkled, aged hands
Most beautiful to me.

Such beautiful, beautiful hands!
Though heart were weary and sad,
These patient hands kept toiling on,
That the children might be glad;
I always weep, as looking back
To childhood's distant day,
I think how those hands rested not,
When mine were at their play.

Such beautiful, beautiful hands!
They're growing feeble now,
For time and pain have left their mark
On hands, and heart, and brow.
Alas! alas! the nearing time,
And the sad, sad day to me,
When 'neath the daisies, out of sight,
These hands will folded be.

But oh, beyond this shadow land,
Where all is bright and fair,
I know full well these dear old hands
Will palms of victory bear;

Where crystal streams through endless years
  Flow over golden sands,
And where the old grow young again,
  I'll clasp my mother's hands.

Anonymous
(Nineteenth Century)

To My Mother

Most near, most dear, most loved and most far,
Under the window where I often found her
Sitting as huge as Asia, seismic with laughter,
Gin and chicken helpless in her Irish hand,
Irresistible as Rabelais, but most tender for
The lame dogs and hurt birds that surround her,—
She is a procession no one can follow after
But be like a little dog following a brass band.
She will not glance up at the bomber, or condescend
To drop her gin and scuttle to a cellar,
But lean on the mahogany table like a mountain
Whom only faith can move, and so I send
O all my faith, and all my love to tell her
That she will move from mourning into morning.

George Barker
(1913–)

1. What sort of reader might have an automatically favorable response to "My Mother's Hands"? What sort might respond unfavorably? Apply the same questions to "To My Mother."
2. In the latter poem, comment on the connotations of *gin* (lines 4, 10), *Rabelais* (line 5), *mountain* (line 11), *morning* (line 14). What does the poet mean by *mourning* (line 14)?
3. Which of the two mothers is more particularly described and characterized? What traits of this mother are emphasized?
4. Which poem seems to portray almost any mother who has grown old? Can it be said, therefore, that this poem portrays nobody's mother?
5. Are the poems flattering or unflattering to the mothers they describe?
6. Which poem resembles the sort of verse found on greeting cards?

Messages and Morals

Readers who come to every unfamiliar poem expecting it to provide an inspirational message or teach a moral will frequently be disappointed. To be sure, there are many poems—known as **didactic** poems—on moral or religious subjects. A good example is Thomas Carlyle's "Today" on page 385. Another example of a didactic poem, and one that some readers might consider tiresome, is the following bit of Sunday School verse:

Let Me Be

Let me be a little kinder,
Let me be a little blinder
To the faults of those about me—
        Let me praise a little more:
Let me be when I am weary,
Just a little bit more cheery,
Let me serve a little better
        Those that I am striving for.

Let me be a little braver
When temptation bids me waver,
Let me strive a little harder
        To be all that I should be;
Let me be a little meeker
With the brother who is weaker,
Let me think more of my neighbor
        And a little less of me.

Anonymous
(Nineteenth Century)

The sort of reader who enjoys "Let Me Be" should know that there are many, many other poems in the world that are totally indifferent to the aims of edifying readers or improving their conduct. Such poems will be badly misunderstood by whoever attempts to find a message or a moral in them.

Suppose that a hardened message-hunter were to confront this song from *The Tempest:*

Stephano's Sea Chantey

The master, the swabber, the boatswain, and I,
  The gunner, and his mate,
Loved Mall, Meg, and Marian, and Margery,
  But none of us cared for Kate.
  For she had a tongue with a tang,
  Would cry to a sailor "Go hang!"
She loved not the savor of tar nor of pitch;
Yet a tailor might scratch her where'er she did itch.
Then to sea, boys, and let her go hang!

William Shakespeare
(1564–1616)

master (1): commander of a merchant vessel. *mate* (2): the gunner's assistant. *tar, pitch* (7): waterproofing substances used aboard sailing ships; sailors sometimes dressed their queues with them. *tailor* (8): regarded as an unmanly occupation in Shakespeare's day. *scratch . . . itch* (8): have his way with her.

A moralist would be hard put to find messages in this rollicking sea chantey. Desperately catching at straws, he might observe that sailors should not have girls in every port, should show more fidelity, and should keep themselves cleaner. But obviously this song is about none of these things. It is simply a boisterous chantey to be enjoyed on its own terms.

Exercise 15

The following two poems strongly imply messages or morals.

Prospice

Fear death?—to feel the fog in my throat,
  The mist in my face,
When the snows begin, and the blasts denote
  I am nearing the place,
The power of the night, the press of the storm,
  The post of the foe;
Where he stands, the Arch Fear in a visible form,
  Yet the strong man must go:

For the journey is done and the summit attained,
And the barriers fall,
Though a battle's to fight ere the guerdon be gained,
The reward of it all.
I was ever a fighter, so—one fight more,
The best and the last!
I would hate that death bandaged my eyes, and forbore,
And bade me creep past.
No! let me taste the whole of it, fare like my peers,
The heroes of old,
Bear the brunt, in a minute pay glad life's arrears
Of pain, darkness, and cold.
For sudden the worst turns the best to the brave,
The black minute's at end,
And the elements' rage, the fiend-voices that rave,
Shall dwindle, shall blend,
Shall change, shall become first a peace out of pain,
Then a light, then thy breast,
O thou soul of my soul! I shall clasp thee again,
And with God be the rest!

Robert Browning
(1812–1889)

Title: Look Forward. *guerdon* (11): reward. *thou* (27): his wife, Elizabeth Barrett Browning (1806–61).

Crossing the Bar

Sunset and evening star,
And one clear call for me!
And may there be no moaning of the bar,
When I put out to sea.

But such a tide as moving seems asleep,
Too full for sound and foam,
When that which drew from out the boundless deep
Turns again home.

Twilight and evening bell,
And after that the dark!
And may there be no sadness of farewell,
When I embark;

For though from out our bourne of Time and Place
 The flood may bear me far,
I hope to see my Pilot face to face
 When I have crossed the bar.

Alfred, Lord Tennyson
(1809–1892)

1. In your own words, state the moral or message implied by each of these poems.
2. In what ways does each of these poems go beyond being merely a message?

Theme

Most short poems express one chief idea or thought. But since all poems do not contain messages or morals, it is more accurate to refer to the main idea of a poem as its **theme**. A statement of the theme summarizes what the poem is saying. Thus, the theme of "Stephano's Sea Chantey" is what kind of women sailors, and for that matter many other men, like.

It is rare for a poem to contain an explicitly stated theme; rather, themes are usually implied, as in the "Chantey" and in this poem:

A Fascinating Poet's Dream

I am keeping this diary because I am fascinating.
My impacted wisdom teeth are fascinating.
My diet, my sex life, my career, these also are fascinating,
As are my newspaper clippings. Fascinating.
And all in my little book.

Up to now I have stuck to fascinating facts in my book,
Starting at six a.m. when I rise, shave, and write in my book,
And ending at ten-thirty when I retire with Agatha Christie
 and my book;
But starting today I propose to include fascinating dreams in
 my book.

In fact I have just had a smasher
In which I find myself wearing a fascinatingly old-fashioned
six-button book.
Oh little book, oh sweetie, how you adorn me!

Anonymous
(Twentieth Century)

Agatha Christie (2) : a murder mystery, referred to by the name of its author.

The theme of this poem is implicit because the author does not come right out and say what he's getting at. Instead, he implies his main idea—that the "I" in the poem (the speaker) is an egotistical idiot. The poem consists entirely of a list of this character's boring activities, all of which he puts down in his book. In his dream (fascinating to no one but himself) he sees himself wearing the book like a long garment with six buttons. The poem, then, makes an implicit attack on poets whose works consist of nothing but self-indulgent inventories of what they've been doing lately, both in and out of bed. The theme of the poem is the boring egotism of certain kinds of poets.

A reader's ability to express a theme does not depend on his powers as a detective, but on his capacity for making valid generalizations. A theme generalizes what is specific in the poem; it renders concrete details into abstract thoughts. It has something of the same relationship to the poem as the formula *NaCl* has to the product on the dining table. The formula is useful to those who want to understand common salt, but it is in no way a salt substitute. One cannot put the formula on roast beef. Similarly, formulating a theme is an exercise that helps a reader understand and experience the poem, but it is neither a substitute for the poem itself nor the total meaning of the poem (see Chapter 9).

Exercise 16

Study each of these poems to determine whether its theme is explicit or implicit. Express each theme in a sentence.

Composed upon Westminster Bridge

Earth has not anything to show more fair:
Dull would he be of soul who could pass by
A sight so touching in its majesty:
This City now doth, like a garment, wear
The beauty of the morning; silent, bare,
Ships, towers, domes, theatres, and temples lie
Open unto the fields, and to the sky;
All bright and glittering in the smokeless air.
Never did sun more beautifully steep
In his first splendour, valley, rock, or hill;
Ne'er saw I, never felt, a calm so deep!
The river glideth at his own sweet will:
Dear God! the very houses seem asleep;
And all that mighty heart is lying still!

William Wordsworth
(1770–1850)

Westminster Bridge (title): one of the bridges over the Thames in London.

1. Which lines in the poem contain generalizations? Which contain details? What connections can be made between generalizations and details?
2. State as precisely as possible the effect of the scene on the viewer. Does this statement also express the theme of the poem?

A Description of the Morning

Now hardly here and there an Hackney-Coach
Appearing, show'd the Ruddy Morns Approach.
Now Betty from her Masters Bed had flown,
And softly stole to discompose her own.
The Slipshod Prentice from his Masters Door,
Had par'd the Dirt, and Sprinkled round the Floor.
Now Moll had whirl'd her Mop with dex'trous Airs,
Prepar'd to Scrub the Entry and the Stairs.
The Youth with Broomy Stumps began to trace
The Kennel-Edge, where Wheels had worn the Place.

The Smallcoal-Man was heard with Cadence deep,
'Till drown'd in Shriller Notes of Chimney-Sweep,
Duns at his Lordships Gate began to meet,
And Brickdust Moll had Scream'd through half the Street.
The Turnkey now his Flock returning sees,
Duly let out a Nights to Steal for Fees.
The watchful Bailiffs take their silent Stands,
And School-Boys lag with Satchels in their Hands.

Jonathan Swift
(1667–1745)

Broomy stumps (9) : a worn-out broom. *Kennel* (10) : gutter or ditch in a street. *Smallcoal-Man* (11) : peddler of coal. *Duns* (13) : bill collectors. *Moll* (14) : seller of brickdust, used as an abrasive. *Turnkey* (15) : jailer. *Fees* (16) : bills that prisoners had to pay for their keep. *Bailiffs* (17) : officers who arrest debtors.

1. How does the speaker of the poem tell that morning has arrived?
2. Why does Betty (a stock name for a housemaid) "discompose" (line 4) her bed?
3. What is the connotation of *Flock* (line 15)?
4. What do you imagine causes Brickdust Moll to scream? Why can you assume that she screams every morning?
5. Make some general observations on the characters depicted in the poem.
6. Compare Swift's attitude toward the city with Wordsworth's (page 76).

Incident

Once riding in old Baltimore,
  Heart-filled, head-filled with glee,
I saw a Baltimorean
  Keep looking straight at me.

Now I was eight and very small,
  And he was no whit bigger,

And so I smiled, but he poked out
  His tongue and called me, "Nigger."

I saw the whole of Baltimore
  From May until December;
Of all the things that happened there
  That's all that I remember.

Countee Cullen
(1903–1946)

I May, I Might, I Must

If you will tell me why the fen
appears impassable, I then
will tell you why I think that I
can get across it if I try.

Marianne Moore
(1887–1971)

Out of the Night That Covers Me

Out of the night that covers me,
  Black as the Pit from pole to pole,
I thank whatever gods may be
  For my unconquerable soul.

In the fell clutch of circumstance
  I have not winced nor cried aloud.
Under the bludgeonings of chance
  My head is bloody, but unbowed.

Beyond this place of wrath and tears
  Looms but the Horror of the shade,
And yet the menace of the years
  Finds, and shall find, me unafraid.

It matters not how strait the gate,
  How charged with punishments the scroll,
I am the master of my fate:
  I am the captain of my soul.

William Ernest Henley
(1849–1903)

Pit (2): Hell.

The "Hidden Meaning"

Another misconception about poems is that they are puzzles or cryptograms. According to this notion, the poet carefully buries his meaning in the poem, and it is up to the reader to ferret it out. It is easy to see how this idea got started. A beginning reader may arrive at a tentative interpretation of a poem, then hear the "official" interpretation, put forth by a more experienced reader, which turns out to be something else entirely. It is not surprising, then, that when faced with another difficult poem the beginning reader will ask "What is the hidden meaning?"—or worse, will impose on it an irrelevant interpretation of his own.

Some poems are indeed difficult and complicated, and it is the aim of this book to cast light on how such poems are to be understood. But it is a mistake to suppose that good poets deliberately obscure their meanings in an effort to bamboozle the reader. Quite the contrary, most poets strive to make their meanings as clear as possible, while still being faithful to their conception of what a poem should be.

The Reader's Knowledge

As we pointed out at the beginning of this chapter, writers have a right to expect their readers to know certain things. Poets especially have to make this assumption because merely communicating information is seldom their chief aim. In every age they have taken for granted the existence of a reading public well enough informed to understand them. In the seventeenth century, William Drummond did not think it necessary to tell the whole story of the Trojan War when he wrote his riddling poem (page 64); nor, in the twentieth, did George Barker take up valuable space in his poem (page 77) to say that World War II was then going on. Yet a reader who knows nothing about these two wars cannot make much sense of either Drummond's or Barker's poems.

Allusion

A writer makes an allusion when he brings literary or historical material into his work from somewhere outside the work. When Barker mentions the bomber that does not frighten his mother, he is not alluding to the war; the war is going on concurrently with the other events of the poem. But he does make an allusion when he writes that his mother is "like a mountain/Whom only faith can move" because here he paraphrases St. Paul's words, ". . . though I have all faith, so that I could remove mountains." Barker brings these words into the poem from the Bible, where they have a very different context. An **allusion,** then, is an indirect reference, by means of mention or quotation, to something real or fictitious outside the work.

Although there may be several allusions in a given poem, a good poet does not sprinkle his poems with allusions merely to display his vast learning or to make his works seem impressive and confusing to the average reader. He uses allusions because they enable him to say much in a small space. An allusion is functional rather than decorative, but it will not function unless it is recognized. When Frost gave the title "Out, Out" to his poem (page 39), he expected his readers to recall Macbeth's lament for the meaninglessness of life:

> Tomorrow, and tomorrow, and tomorrow
> Creeps in this petty pace from day to day
> To the last syllable of recorded time;
> And all our yesterdays have lighted fools
> The way to dusty death. Out, out, brief candle!
> Life's but a walking shadow, a poor player

That struts and frets his hour upon the stage
And then is heard no more. It is a tale
Told by an idiot, full of sound and fury,
Signifying nothing.

William Shakespeare
(1564–1616)

The title of Frost's poem summons up this familiar passage. The reader who recognizes the allusion perceives that the life of the boy in the poem is an even briefer candle than Macbeth's, that his death is an even more meaningless performance than the poor player's.

Exercise 17

Look at these poems with two questions in mind: What information should a reader possess in order to understand and enjoy each poem? What sort of reader would possess such information?

The Donkey

When fishes flew and forests walked
  And figs grew upon thorn,
Some moment when the moon was blood
  Then surely I was born;

With monstrous head and sickening cry
  And ears like errant wings,
The devil's walking parody
  On all four-footed things.

The tattered outlaw of the earth,
  Of ancient crooked will;
Starve, scourge, deride me: I am dumb,
  I keep my secret still.

Fools! For I also had my hour;
  One far fierce hour and sweet:
There was a shout about my ears,
  And palms before my feet.

Gilbert Keith Chesterton
(1874–1936)

Mock on, Mock on Voltaire, Rousseau

Mock on, Mock on Voltaire, Rousseau:
Mock on, Mock on; 'tis all in vain!
You throw the sand against the wind,
And the wind blows it back again.

And every sand becomes a Gem
Reflected in the beams divine;
Blown back they blind the mocking eye,
But still in Israel's paths they shine.

The Atoms of Democritus
And Newton's Particles of light
Are sands upon the Red sea shore,
Where Israel's tents do shine so bright.

William Blake
(1757–1827)

Down in Dallas

Down in Dallas, down in Dallas
Where the shadow of blood lies black
Lee Oswald nailed Jack Kennedy up
With the nail of a rifle crack.

Every big bright Cadillac stompled its brakes,
Every face in the street fell still,
While the slithering gun like a tooth of sin
Recoiled from the window sill.

In a white chrome room on a table top,
Oh, they tried all a scalpel knows
But they couldn't spell stop to that drop-by-drop
Till it bloomed to a rigid rose.

Down on the altar, down on the altar
Christ is broken to bread and wine
But each asphalt stone where the blood dropped down
Prickled into a cactus spine.

Oh down in Dallas, down in Dallas
Where the wind has to cringe tonight
Lee Oswald nailed Jack Kennedy up
On the cross of a rifle sight.

X. J. Kennedy
(1929–)

Needs

I want something suited to my special needs
I want chrome hubcaps, pin-on attachments
and year round use year after year
I want a workhorse with smooth uniform cut,
dozer blade and snow blade & deluxe steering
wheel
I want something to mow, throw snow, tow
and sow with
I want precision reel blades
I want a console styled dashboard
I want an easy spintype recoil starter
I want combination bevel and spur gears, 14
gauge stamped steel housing and
washable foam element air cleaner
I want a pivoting front axle and extrawide
turf tires
I want an inch of foam rubber inside a vinyl
covering
and especially if it's not too much, if I
can deserve it, even if I can't pay for it
I want to mow while riding.

A. R. Ammons
(1926–)

Naming Of Parts

To-day we have naming of parts. Yesterday,
We had daily cleaning. And to-morrow morning,
We shall have what to do after firing. But to-day,
To-day we have naming of parts. Japonica
Glistens like coral in all of the neighboring gardens,
        And to-day we have naming of parts.

This is the lower sling swivel. And this
Is the upper sling swivel, whose use you will see,
When you are given your slings. And this is the piling swivel,
Which in your case you have not got. The branches
Hold in the gardens their silent, eloquent gestures,
        Which in our case we have not got.

This is the safety-catch, which is always released
With an easy flick of the thumb. And please do not let me
See anyone using his finger. You can do it quite easy
If you have any strength in your thumb. The blossoms
Are fragile and motionless, never letting anyone see
        Any of them using their finger.

And this you can see is the bolt. The purpose of this
Is to open the breech, as you see. We can slide it
Rapidly backwards and forwards: we call this
Easing the spring. And rapidly backwards and forwards
The early bees are assaulting and fumbling the flowers:
        They call it easing the Spring.

They call it easing the Spring: it is perfectly easy
If you have any strength in your thumb: like the bolt,
And the breech, and the cocking-piece, and the point of balance,
Which in our case we have not got; and the almond-blossom
Silent in all of the gardens and the bees going backwards and forwards,
        For to-day we have naming of parts.

Henry Reed
(1914–   )

Blackie, The Electric Rembrandt

We watch through the shop-front while
Blackie draws stars—an equal

concentration on his and
the youngster's faces. The hand

is steady and accurate;
but the boy does not see it

for his eyes follow the point
that touches (quick, dark movement!)

a virginal arm beneath
his rolled sleeve: he holds his breath.

. . . Now that it is finished, he
hands a few bills to Blackie

and leaves with a bandage on
his arm, under which gleam ten

stars, hanging in a blue thick
cluster. Now he is starlike.

Thom Gunn
(1929–   )

The Speaker of a Poem

The relation of an artist to his work is such a complex matter that it cannot be given anything like a full treatment here. Most investigators of the problem believe that individual poets differ greatly in the degree to which they express their own personalities in their first-person poems. Few poets, however, express *merely* their own personalities; even the most subjective poets commonly create an *alter ego,* a second self, to speak for them. Critics, therefore, have adopted the useful term **speaker** to refer them to the voice, other than the poet's, that is heard in a poem. Some poets have a great variety of speakers.

Thus, a reader must beware of regarding every poem as pure autobiography or self-expression. Unlike a poet's birth certificate or his marriage license, his poems are not simply documents; a poet is not under oath to tell the literal truth about himself in his poems. One danger of regarding poems as mere biographical documents is that the reader may substitute interest in the poet's biography for interest in his poems. Then the poems evaporate amidst speculation about the fascinating details of the poet's life. Yet there is also a danger at the opposite extreme: the assumption that biographical data are irrelevant to every poem. There are many poems in which the speaker resembles the poet very closely, and there are a few in which the two are virtually indistinguishable. For a full understanding of such poems, a reader needs some knowledge of the author. Blake's "Mock on, Mock on" (page 89) is much more meaningful to a reader who knows something about the events of Blake's life and the ideas he expresses in his other works than it is to a reader ignorant of this information. However, the reader still must look on the poem as a poem, not as merely another piece of information about Blake.

Dramatic Situations in Poems

A reader can profitably regard this poem, or any other in which one person directly addresses someone else, as a small-scale drama.

Secrecy Protested

Fear not, dear love, that I'll reveal
Those hours of pleasure we two steal.
No eye shall see, nor yet the sun
Descry what thou and I have done;
No ear shall hear our love, but we
Silent as the night will be.
The god of love himself, whose dart
Did first wound mine and then thy heart,
Shall never know that we can tell
What sweets in stolen embraces dwell.
This only means may find it out:
If, when I die, physicians doubt
What caused my death, and, there to view
Of all their judgments which was true,
Rip up my heart—Oh then, I fear,
The world will see thy picture there.

Thomas Carew
(*c.* 1594/5–1639)

There are two actors in this playlet. The one who refers to himself as "I"—in a discussion of the poem he would be called the "speaker"—is a man; he speaks to the woman whom he loves. Here, as in any other drama, there has been some antecedent action: the "hours of pleasure" (line 2) that the lovers have stolen. The scene of the drama is the place where they customarily meet in secret; the time is night. Just before the curtain goes up for line 1 of the poem, the woman has said, in a worried tone, something like this: "I am afraid that people are going to find out about us." This remark, which creates the conflict that a drama always needs, is one that the man cannot let pass without comment, because he wants her to feel confident that he will never betray her as long as he lives. His protestations make up the entire performance; the curtain comes down before the woman replies. The reader never knows whether she continues to be worried or why the lovers must meet secretly.

Notice that this discussion has not mentioned the author of the poem, but has assumed that Carew is writing dramatically rather than autobiographically and that he is not the man speaking in his poem. Since very little is known about Carew's personal life, an autobiographical element in the poem can be neither proved nor disproved. But two things seem certain. First, it would be an error to decide that Carew must have had a secret love affair (probably with a married woman?) just because he wrote a poem about two secret lovers. This view would deny that he had any imagination or ability to invent situations; it would imply that a poet is restricted to writing solely about the events of his own life. Second, even though Carew may have had such a love affair, the reader's knowledge of it would not necessarily increase his understanding and appreciation of the poem. And it might be a positive nuisance if a reader were to regard it as a substitute for directly experiencing the poem.

Carew's poem is an early and rather simple example of a **dramatic monologue:** a poem in which a fictitious or historical character, caught at an important moment in his life, speaks to one or more characters who remain silent. In Carew's monologue the main interest is the situation; in nineteenth- and twentieth-century monologues the main interest is the speaker's character.

Exercise 18

Look up the facts of Browning's life and decide whether any of them are useful in understanding these poems. If you decide that the poems are primarily dramatic, study them by answering these questions:

1. Who is the speaker? To whom does he speak?
2. What is the scene? The time?
3. What has happened immediately before the poem begins?
4. What are the speaker's traits?
5. How is the speaker in the first poem like the one in the second? How do the two speakers differ?

My Last Duchess

Ferrara

That's my last Duchess painted on the wall,
Looking as if she were alive. I call
That piece a wonder, now: Frà Pandolf's hands
Worked busily a day, and there she stands.
Will't please you sit and look at her? I said
"Frà Pandolf" by design, for never read
Strangers like you that pictured countenance,
The depth and passion of its earnest glance,
But to myself they turned (since none puts by
The curtain I have drawn for you, but I)
And seemed as they would ask me, if they durst,
How such a glance came there; so, not the first
Are you to turn and ask thus. Sir, 'twas not
Her husband's presence only, called that spot
Of joy into the Duchess' cheek: perhaps
Frà Pandolf chanced to say, "Her mantle laps
Over my lady's wrist too much," or "Paint
Must never hope to reproduce the faint
Half-flush that dies along her throat": such stuff
Was courtesy, she thought, and cause enough

For calling up that spot of joy. She had
A heart—how shall I say?—too soon made glad,
Too easily impressed: she liked whate'er
She looked on, and her looks went everywhere.
Sir, 'twas all one! My favour at her breast,
The dropping of the daylight in the West,
The bough of cherries some officious fool
Broke in the orchard for her, the white mule
She rode with round the terrace—all and each
Would draw from her alike the approving speech,
Or blush, at least. She thanked men,—good! but thanked
Somehow—I know not how—as if she ranked
My gift of a nine-hundred-years-old name
With anybody's gift. Who'd stoop to blame
This sort of trifling? Even had you skill
In speech—(which I have not)—to make your will
Quite clear to such an one, and say, "Just this
Or that in you disgusts me; here you miss,
Or there exceed the mark"—and if she let
Herself be lessoned so, nor plainly set
Her wits to yours, forsooth, and made excuse,
—E'en then would be some stooping, and I choose
Never to stoop. Oh Sir, she smiled, no doubt,
Whene'er I passed her; but who passed without
Much the same smile? This grew; I gave commands;
Then all smiles stopped together. There she stands
As if alive. Will't please you rise? We'll meet
The company below, then. I repeat,
The Count your master's known munificence
Is ample warrant that no just pretence
Of mine for dowry will be disallowed;
Though his fair daughter's self, as I avowed
At starting, is my object. Nay, we'll go
Together down, sir! Notice Neptune, though,
Taming a sea-horse, thought a rarity,
Which Claus of Innsbruck cast in bronze for me!

Robert Browning
(1812–1889)

Ferrara (subtitle): Italian city where the poem takes place. Its Duke—Alfonso II—is the speaker; he addresses an agent of the Count of Tyrol, who visited Ferrara in 1561 to arrange a marriage between the Count's niece and the Duke. The Duke's "last duchess" has just died. *Frà Pandolf* (3): Brother Pandolf, a fictitious monk-artist. *Claus of Innsbruck* (56): apparently fictitious German metal-founder; the Count of Tyrol lived in Innsbruck.

Confessions

What is he buzzing in my ears?
  "Now that I am come to die,
Do I view the world as a vale of tears?"
  Ah, reverend sir, not I!

What I viewed there once, what I view again
  Where the physic bottles stand
On the table's edge,—is a suburb lane,
  With a wall to my bedside hand.

That lane sloped, much as the bottles do,
  From a house you could descry
O'er the garden-wall; is the curtain blue
  Or green to a healthy eye?

To mine, it serves for the old June weather
  Blue above land and wall;
And that farthest bottle labelled "Ether"
  Is the house o'ertopping all.

At a terrace, somewhere near the stopper,
  There watched for me, one June,
A girl: I know, sir, it's improper,
  My poor mind's out of tune.

Only, there was a way . . . you crept
  Close by the side, to dodge
Eyes in the house, two eyes except:
  They styled their house "The Lodge."

What right had a lounger up their lane?
  But, by creeping very close,
With the good wall's help,—their eyes might strain
  And stretch themselves to Oes,

Yet never catch her and me together,
  As she left the attic, there,
By the rim of the bottle labelled "Ether,"
  And stole from stair to stair,

And stood by the rose-wreathed gate. Alas,
  We loved, sir—used to meet:
How sad and bad and mad it was—
  But then, how it was sweet!

Robert Browning
(1812–1889)

The Reader as Analyzer

Some students who have been asked to analyze poems have responded by quoting Archibald MacLeish, "A poem should not mean/But be" (see page 339); others, perhaps even more knowledgeable, have cited Wordsworth's lines from "The Tables Turned":

Sweet is the lore which Nature brings;
Our meddling intellect
Mis-shapes the beauteous forms of things:—
We murder to dissect.

But such seemingly apt responses quote MacLeish out of context and misinterpret Wordsworth. MacLeish's lines suggest that the total meaning of a poem cannot be separated from the poem itself—that is, cannot be put in *other* words. And Wordsworth is not talking about the analysis of poems but about a scientific approach to the beauties of nature. The reader need have no fears that close study of a poem will spoil it. Indeed, any poem worth reading at all is worth reading closely. Unlike a living organism that dies when it is dissected, a poem cannot be destroyed by analysis. However much it is probed and picked apart, a poem remains intact on the page, ready to be enjoyed even more after it has been understood.

Exercise 19

With the help of the questions read the following poems as carefully as you can.

To the Western World

A siren sang, and Europe turned away
From the high castle and the shepherd's crook.
Three caravels went sailing to Cathay
On the strange ocean, and the captains shook
Their banners out across the Mexique Bay.

And in our early days we did the same.
Remembering our fathers in their wreck
We crossed the sea from Palos where they came
And saw, enormous to the little deck,
A shore in silence waiting for a name.

The treasures of Cathay were never found.
In this America, this wilderness
Where the axe echoes with a lonely sound,
The generations labor to possess
And grave by grave we civilize the ground.

Louis Simpson
(1923–)

caravels (3): Columbus' ships. *Cathay* (3): old name for China. *Palos* (8): the Cape of Palos in Southern Spain, from which Columbus sailed.

1. What was the "siren's song" that turned Europe's attention to the West? What might the "high castle" and "shepherd's crook" have stood for in Europe before 1492?
2. The speaker seems to identify himself with the early explorers who confronted the vast untamed wilderness of a yet-unnamed America. What does he imply by this identification and his statement that "the treasures of Cathay were never found"?
3. What significance do you find in the final line?

Myxomatosis

Caught in the center of a soundless field
While hot inexplicable hours go by
What trap is this? Where were its teeth concealed?
You seem to ask.

I make a sharp reply,
Then clean my stick, I'm glad I can't explain
Just in what jaws you were to suppurate:
You may have thought things would come right again
If you could only keep quite still and wait.

Philip Larkin
(1922–)

Title: An infectious, highly fatal disease of rabbits.

1. Who asks the italicized questions?
2. What happens during the break—represented by the white space in the poem?
3. Myxomatosis has been artificially introduced into England (Larkin's native country) to keep down the rabbit population. How does knowing this fact help you understand the sentence beginning "I'm glad" (lines 5–6) ?

Leave Me, O Love

Leave me, O love which reachest but to dust,
And thou, my mind, aspire to higher things;
Grow rich in that which never taketh rust.
Whatever fades, but fading pleasure brings.

Draw in thy beams, and humble all thy might
To that sweet yoke where lasting freedoms be,
Which breaks the clouds and opens forth the light
That doth both shine and give us sight to see.

O take fast hold, let that light be thy guide
In this small course which birth draws out to death;
And think how evil becometh him to slide,
Who seeketh heaven and comes of heavenly breath.

Then farewell, world, thy uttermost I see;
Eternal love, maintain thy life in me.

Sir Philip Sidney
(1554–1586)

dust (1) : see Genesis ii:7. *rust* (3) : see Matthew vi:19, 20. *yoke* (6) : see Matthew xi:29, 30. *evil becometh* (11) : evilly it suits. *slide* (11) : do wrong. *breath* (12) : see Genesis ii:7.

1. What proof does the poet offer that one kind of love is "higher" than another?
2. To which of the two loves do the "beams" mentioned in line 5 belong? To which does the "yoke" (line 6) belong?
3. Why is the "course" (line 10) described as "small"?

Winter for an Untenable Situation

Outside it is cold. Inside,
although the fire has gone out
and all the furniture is burnt,
it is much warmer. Oh let
the white refrigerator car
of day go by in glacial thunder:
when it gets dark, and when
the branches of the tree outside
look wet because it is so dark
oh we will burn the house itself
for warmth, the wet tree too,
you will burn me, I will burn you,
and when the last brick of the fireplace
has been cracked for its nut of warmth
and the last bone cracked for its coal
and the andirons themselves sucked cold,
we will move on!, remembering
the burning house, the burning tree,
the burning you, the burning me,
the ashes, the brick-dust, the bitter iron,
and the time when we were warm,
and say, "Those were the good old days."

Alan Dugan
(1923–)

1. What is untenable about the situation in which the speaker finds himself?
2. To whom is the poem addressed? How do you know?
3. What does the speaker propose to do to make the situation less untenable? If this is not a practical solution to the problem, what kind of solution is it?

Report

Allow me to speak of the great tits
Of Britain, an area I have visited.

They are plump, aggressive, valiant.
The mother is quick to defend her nest.

In three weeks a pair of tits
Will kill seven thousand insects.

They are glorious acrobats,
Hanging in every conceivable position.

I got my word from *The Birds of Britain*
And a three-week walking trip near London.

Hollis Summers
(1916–)

1. How could a reader misunderstand what this poem is saying? Has the poet been as careful as he possibly could be to avoid being misread?

The Black Panther

There is a panther caged within my breast,
But what his name, there is no breast shall know
Save mine, nor what it is that drives him so,
Backward and forward, in relentless quest—
That silent rage, baffled but unsuppressed,
The soft pad of those stealthy feet that go
Over my body's prison to and fro,
Trying the walls forever without rest.

All day I feed him with my living heart,
But when the night puts forth her dreams and stars,
The inexorable frenzy reawakes:
His wrath is hurled upon the trembling bars,
The eternal passion stretches me apart,
And I lie silent—but my body shakes.

John Hall Wheelock
(1886–)

1. What meaning has the title taken on since Wheelock gave it to this poem in the 1950's? Is this other meaning at all helpful, or is it a hindrance, in reading the poem?

4. Images, Similes, and Metaphors in Poems

> Metaphor creates a new reality, from which the original appears to be unreal.
>
> *Wallace Stevens*

A poet seeks to render an experience as precisely as possible so that it will also become the reader's experience. His passion for exactness is like a mathematician's. But unlike the mathematician, who thinks in abstractions, the poet not only thinks concretely but almost always presents his thoughts in concrete language.

Concreteness

The contrast between abstraction and concreteness is illustrated by this poem:

Love without Hope

Love without hope, as when the young bird-catcher
Swept off his tall hat to the Squire's own daughter,
So let the imprisoned larks escape and fly
Singing about her head, as she rode by.

Robert Graves
(1895–   )

The title and opening words of line 1 use the abstract words *love* and *hope,* which refer to states of mind rather than to tangible objects or visible events. The language of the rest of the poem is concrete: the nouns refer to people and things and the verbs to actions. A dictionary may define *love* as *ardent affection,* and *hope* as *happy expectation,* but such definitions merely substitute one abstraction for another. The poet's approach is to imagine a specific, concrete instance of ardent affection without happy expectation. He imagines a poor young bird-catcher (in the days when there were squires and catching birds to sell them for food was a common occupation of poor young men) who is so struck with love at the sight of the squire's daughter riding past him (all young ladies in this category are strikingly beautiful) that he makes a handsome gesture to express his love. In doing so, the young bird-catcher creates a very pretty scene, and one which we can easily imagine. The bird-catcher's gesture of sweeping off his hat is completely unselfish, since he cannot hope to have his love reciprocated. Yet he doesn't mind losing a whole hatful of larks that he has worked so hard to catch. Thus, without using the abstract word *unselfishness,* the poet has given us a concrete instance of how unselfish true love without hope can be.

The poet who strays too far from the concrete is likely to get twisted up in his own meanings as well as to cause trouble for the reader. Poems made up entirely of abstractions are difficult for the poet to control and for the reader to understand.

Only a Thought

'Twas only a passing thought, my love,
  Only a passing thought,
That came o'er my mind like a ray o' the sun
  In the dimples of waters caught;
And it seemed to me, and I say to thee,
  That sorrow and shame and sin
Might disappear from our happy sphere,
  If we knew but to begin;
If we but knew how to profit
  By wisdom dearly bought:
It was only a passing thought, my love,
  Only a passing thought.

Charles Mackay
(1814–1889)

Except for the comparison in lines 3 and 4 this poem contains nothing concrete—that is, nothing which the reader can touch, taste, hear, smell, or see. Words like *sorrow, shame, sin, happy sphere, profit, wisdom,* and *thought* are abstract; they stand for emotions, conditions, and states of mind that can exist in a different way for each reader. Hence an individual reader can never be sure that his meaning of the terms is the same as Mackay's. In the poem a man seems to be telling a woman that "sorrow and shame and sin" would disappear from "our happy sphere" if we could learn how to make them disappear. But how can he be saying anything so obvious as that? Moreover, doesn't he contradict himself when he calls the world "happy sphere," for how can it be happy if it has all that sorrow? This poem fails, not because it is obvious but because it is too abstract. Unless there is something very definite and concrete in the poet's mind, there will be little or nothing in the reader's.

Exercise 20

Adam's Dream

The sycamores and sidewalks of
His neighborhood were private park
And dark retreat, where he could walk
In congress sweet

With his kind neighbors, sleep and love,
And where their gossip, or nice talk,
Discriminated beast from bird
By proper word:

Adam yawned, and there were cats;
Blinked, and there were antelopes;
Stretched, and everywhere he reached
A mile of meadow bloomed.

He cocked his eye, and fishes leaped
In every brook to praise him;
He rose to walk, and rabbits ran
As couriers to every green
Community to tell of him.

He only glanced at any tree,
Its birds at once began to sing;
He nodded, and the region budded;
He put the bloom on everything.

He was the lord of all the park,
And he was lonely in the dark,
Till Eve came smiling out of his side
To be his bride.

"Sweet rib," he said, astonished at her,
"This is *my* green environ!"
Eve answered no word, but for reply
The wilderness was in her eye.

Adam awoke, the snow had come,
And drifts of daylight covered the park;
And his sweet friends, and their sweet talk,
Were dumb.

David Ferry
(1924–)

congress (4) : a meeting or coming together.

1. The concrete words in the first two stanzas suggest one season, and the concrete words in the final stanza suggest a contrasting season. What has brought about this change in the seasons?
2. Make a list of the verbs describing Adam's actions in stanzas three, four, and five. What natural sequence of events do you detect in them? Explain how these precisely chosen verbs are connected with the events that follow each of them.
3. What is the difference between Adam's *green environ* (line 27) and Eve's *wilderness* (line 29)?

Adam's Curse

We sat together at one summer's end,
That beautiful mild woman, your close friend,
And you and I, and talked of poetry.
I said: "A line will take us hours maybe;
Yet if it does not seem a moment's thought,
Our stitching and unstitching has been naught.

Better go down upon your marrowbones
And scrub a kitchen pavement, or break stones
Like an old pauper, in all kinds of weather;
For to articulate sweet sounds together
Is to work harder than all these, and yet
Be thought an idler by the noisy set
Of bankers, schoolmasters, and clergymen
The martyrs call the world."
                                        And thereupon
That beautiful mild woman for whose sake
There's many a one shall find out all heartache
On finding that her voice is sweet and low
Replied: "To be born woman is to know—
Although they do not talk of it at school—
That we must labor to be beautiful."

I said: "It's certain there is no fine thing
Since Adam's fall but needs much laboring.
There have been lovers who thought love should be
So much compounded of high courtesy
That they would sigh and quote with learned looks
Precedents out of beautiful old books;
Yet now it seems an idle trade enough."

We sat grown quiet at the name of love;
We saw the last embers of daylight die,
And in the trembling blue-green of the sky
A moon, worn as if it had been a shell
Washed by time's waters as they rose and fell
About the stars and broke in days and years.
I had a thought for no one's but your ears:
That you were beautiful, and that I strove
To love you in the old high way of love;
That it had all seemed happy, and yet we'd grown
As weary-hearted as that hollow moon.

William Butler Yeats
(1865–1939)

Title: See Genesis, III:17–19.

1. Yeats's biographers tell us that the "beautiful mild woman" in the poem (line 2) was the actress Maude Gonne, whom Yeats loved passionately but hopelessly. How does this biographical information help the reader understand the poem?

2. The three people in the poem talk about abstract topics—poetry, work, love. How are these topics related to one another? How does the poem make them seem concerte realities rather than vague abstractions?
3. What sort of language is used to describe the moon? What affect does the moon's appearance have on the people?

Images

A concrete detail that appeals to the reader's senses is called an **image.** Although most of the image-making words in any language appeal to sight (and are therefore called visual images), there are also images of touch, sound, taste, and smell. An image may also appeal to the reader's sense of motion: a verb like *escape* in the poem by Graves does so. An image is often a single word, like *birches,* but it can also be a complete sentence, like Shakespeare's "Through the sharp hawthorn blows the cold wind"—a line that appeals simultaneously to the reader's senses of sight, sound, and touch.

These two stanzas from Keats's "The Eve of St. Agnes," in which a man is preparing an exotic midnight snack for a sleeping lady, are frequently used to illustrate all the kinds of images.

> Then by the bed-side, where the faded moon
> Made a dim, silver twilight, soft he set
> A table, and, half-anguish'd, threw thereon
> A cloth of woven crimson, gold, and jet:—
> O for some drowsy Morphean amulet!
> The boisterous, midnight, festive clarion,
> The kettle-drum, and far-heard clarionet,
> Affray his ears, though but in dying tone:—
> The hall door shuts again, and all the noise is gone.
>
> And still she slept an azure-lidded sleep,
> In blanched linen, smooth and lavender'd,
> While he from forth the closet brought a heap
> Of candied apple, quince, and plum, and gourd
> With jellies soother than the creamy curd,
> And lucent syrops, tinct with cinnamon;
> Manna and dates, in argosy transferr'd
> From Fez; and spiced dainties, every one,
> From silken Samarcand to cedar'd Lebanon.

Morphean amulet (5) : charm for inducing sleep. *clarion* (6) : medieval trumpet. *soother* (14) : softer. *lucent* (15) : bright. *tinct* (15) : tinted. *Fez . . . Samarcand . . . Lebanon* (17–18) : place names.

In stanza 1 images of sight and sound predominate. The noise of a celebration going on downstairs (lines 6–9) penetrates the silence of the bedroom, where the man's very motion is soft (line 2) so that he will not awaken the lady. In stanza 2 sight and taste predominate, although *smooth* (line 11) is an image of touch and *spiced* (line 17) one of smell. Few poems have such a rich profusion of images as this excerpt has, and few depend so heavily on the exotic connotations of nouns and adjectives.

The Functions of Imagery

A good poet does not use imagery merely to decorate his poems. He does not ask himself, "How can I dress up my subject so that it will seem fancier than it is?" Rather he asks himself, "How can I make my subject appear to the reader exactly as it appears to me?" Imagery helps him solve his problem, for it enables him to present his subject as it is: as it looks, smells, tastes, feels, and sounds. To the reader imagery is equally important: it provides his imagination with something palpable to seize upon.

The Rhodora: On Being Asked, Whence Is the Flower?

In May, when sea-winds pierced our solitudes,
I found the fresh Rhodora in the woods,
Spreading its leafless blooms in a damp nook,
To please the desert and the sluggish brook.
The purple petals, fallen in the pool,
Made the black water with their beauty gay;
Here might the red-bird come his plumes to cool,
And court the flower that cheapens his array.
Rhodora! if the sages ask thee why
This charm is wasted on the earth and sky,
Tell them, dear, that if eyes were made for seeing,

Then Beauty is its own excuse for being:
Why thou wert there, O rival of the rose!
I never thought to ask, I never knew:
But, in my simple ignorance, suppose
The self-same Power that brought me there brought you.

Ralph Waldo Emerson
(1803–1882)

This poem divides into two distinct parts: lines 1–8, which contain many images, and lines 9–16, which have few. The first part is a kind of demonstration; instead of just saying that the rhodora is beautiful, Emerson exhibits its beauty. In this way he prepares the reader for the second part, which is a statement about beauty in general. The concrete first part presents the subject and supports the abstract conclusion.

Exercise 21

Study the imagery in the following poems and explain how it helps the poet present his subject.

Root Cellar

Nothing would sleep in that cellar, dank as a ditch,
Bulbs broke out of boxes hunting for chinks in the dark,
Shoots dangled and drooped,
Lolling obscenely from mildewed crates,
Hung down long yellow evil necks, like tropical snakes.
And what a congress of stinks!—
Roots ripe as old bait,
Pulpy stems, rank, silo-rich,
Leaf-mold, manure, lime, piled against slippery planks.
Nothing would give up life:
Even the dirt kept breathing a small breath.

Theodore Roethke
(1908–1963)

After Yeats

Now incense fills the air
and delight follows delight,
quiet supper in the carpet room,
music twangling from the Orient to my ear,
old friends rest on bright mattresses,
old paintings on the walls, old poetry
thought anew, laughing at a mystic toy
statue painted gold, tea on the white table.

Allen Ginsberg
(1926–)

Yeats (title) : William Butler Yeats, the poet. See index.

The Eagle

Fragment

He clasps the crag with crooked hands;
Close to the sun in lonely lands,
Ring'd with the azure world, he stands.

The wrinkled sea beneath him crawls;
He watches from his mountain walls,
And like a thunderbolt he falls.

Alfred, Lord Tennyson
(1809–1892)

The Blindman

The blindman placed
a tulip on his tongue for purple's taste.
Cheek to grass, his green

was rough excitement's sheen
of little whips.
In water to his lips

he named the sea blue and white,
the basin of his tears and fallen beads of sight.
He said: This scarf is red;

I feel the vectors to its thread
that dance down from the sun. I know
the seven fragrances of the rainbow.

I have caressed
the orange hair of flames. Pressed
to my ear,

a pomegranate lets me hear
crimson's flute.
Trumpets tell me yellow. Only ebony is mute.

May Swenson
(1919–)

Frog Autumn

Summer grows old, cold-blooded mother.
The insects are scant, skinny.
In these palustral homes we only
Croak and wither.

Mornings dissipate in somnolence.
The sun brightens tardily
Among the pithless reeds. Flies fail us.
The fen sickens.

Frost drops even the spider. Clearly
The genius of plenitude
Houses himself elsewhere. Our folk thin
Lamentably.

Sylvia Plath
(1932–1963)

palustral (3): marshy.

Images, Thoughts and Feelings

It is a common practice for a poet to express his thoughts and feelings through his imagery.

Western Wind

Western wind, when will thou blow,
The small rain down can rain?
Christ, if my love were in my arms
And I in my bed again!

Anonymous
(Sixteenth Century)

The speaker here is a lonely man who longs for two things: the western wind, which will bring a change in the weather, and a reunion with the woman he loves. In its context the appeal to sight, sound, and touch in the image *small rain* (line 2) communicates the idea of relief from a dry spell. The speaker wants a mild spring shower, not a violent storm; he also wants love to renew his life, just as the rain renews nature in the spring. His desire for the woman is expressed in the imagery of lines 3–4. This anonymous poet has used images that convey many ideas—among them loneliness, nature, life, renewal, return, sex, and love.

Exercise 22

Study in the following poems the use of imagery to communicate thoughts and feelings.

Song

The world is full of loss; bring, wind, my love,
  My home is where we make our meeting-place,
  And love whatever I shall touch and read
  Within that face.

Lift, wind, my exile from my eyes;
Peace to look, life to listen and confess,
Freedom to find to find to find
That nakedness.

Muriel Rukeyser
(1913–)

1. Compare this poem with "Western Wind" (page 115). What complications does "Song" introduce into the relationship between the speaker and the absent lover?

Preludes

The winter evening settles down
With smell of steaks in passageways.
Six o'clock.
The burnt-out ends of smoky days.
And now a gusty shower wraps
The grimy scraps
Of withered leaves about your feet
And newspapers from vacant lots;
The showers beat
On broken blinds and chimney-pots,
And at the corner of the street
A lonely cab-horse steams and stamps.
And then the lighting of the lamps.

T. S. Eliot
(1888–1965)

steaks (2): a typical working-class meal when this poem was written.

1. What images in this poem convey an effect of desolation or loneliness? What images suggest a dilapidated neighborhood?
2. What images present the smells, sounds, and sensations of a wintry evening?
3. Compare the use of images in this poem with their use in Swift's "Description of a Morning" (p. 83).

Cock at Sea

The wooden cage was wedged on the ship's prow
Between sails, vomit, chains that groaned all night.
The grey dawn broke, I heard the sick bird crow
Across the bitter water to the light.

The farm was dancing through that jagged cry—
Tall hay-stack, seed-rich field, barn, hedge and tree,
Cocks that could proudly strut, birds that could fly—
And he a captive of the grinding sea.

No answer from that farm, endless the blue,
Endless the waves, the slaps of salty breath.
He crowed again, the day was rising new
To feed the nightmare in the sleep of death.

C. A. Trypanis
(1909–)

Meeting at Night

The gray sea and the long black land;
And the yellow half-moon large and low;
And the startled little waves that leap
In fiery ringlets from their sleep,
As I gain the cove with pushing prow,
And quench its speed i' the slushy sand.

Then a mile of warm sea-scented beach;
Three fields to cross till a farm appears;
A tap at the pane, the quick sharp scratch
And blue spurt of a lighted match,
And a voice less loud, through its joys and fears,
Than the two hearts beating each to each!

Robert Browning
(1812–1889)

Parting at Morning

Round the cape of a sudden came the sea,
And the sun looked over the mountain's rim:
And straight was a path of gold for him,
And the need of a world of men for me.

Robert Browning
(1812–1889)

Bells for John Whiteside's Daughter

There was such speed in her little body,
And such lightness in her footfall,
It is no wonder that her brown study
Astonishes us all.

Her wars were bruited in our high window.
We looked among orchard trees and beyond,
Where she took arms against her shadow,
Or harried unto the pond

The lazy geese, like a snow cloud
Dripping their snow on the green grass,
Tricking and stopping, sleepy and proud,
Who cried in goose, Alas,

For the tireless heart within the little
Lady with rod that made them rise
From their noon apple-dreams, and scuttle
Goose-fashion under the skies!

But now go the bells, and we are ready;
In one house we are sternly stopped
To say we are vexed at her brown study,
Lying so primly propped.

John Crowe Ransom
(1888–)

brown study (3) : reverie. *bruited* (5) : noised loudly. *harried* (8) : chased.

A Noiseless Patient Spider

A noiseless patient spider,
I mark'd where on a little promontory it stood isolated,
Mark'd how to explore the vacant vast surrounding,
It launch'd forth filament, filament, filament, out of itself,
Ever unreeling them, ever tirelessly speeding them.
And you O my soul where you stand,
Surrounded, detached, in measureless oceans of space,
Ceaselessly musing, venturing, throwing, seeking the spheres to
connect them,
Till the bridge you will need be form'd, till the ductile anchor
hold,
Till the gossamer thread you fling catch somewhere, O my soul.

Walt Whitman
(1819–1892)

No Images

She does not know
Her beauty,
She thinks her brown body
Has no glory.

If she could dance
Naked,
Under palm trees.
And see her image in the river
She would know.

But there are no palm trees
On the street,
And dish water gives back no images.

Waring Cuney
(1906–)

Literal and Figurative Statements

As most people know, a poet or any other writer or speaker makes two kinds of statements: literal and figurative. "I am sick";

"Yonder is a mountain"; "The sky is cloudy"—these are literal statements, and they mean exactly what they say. Images usually occur in figurative statements. Figurative statements always have a meaning other than the literal one. Like lies, they depart from literal truth, although not with the intention of deceiving. Thus, a man may say, "I am heartsick," and not be advertising a cardiac condition; "I have mountains of work," and not be preparing to ascend the Alps. He may ask, as King Claudius asks of Hamlet, "How is it that the clouds still hang on you?" without being taken for a weather observer. "The bird is on the wing" is a figurative statement: "the wing is on the bird" is a literal one.

Figurative statements are by no means the exclusive property of poets; they also abound in common talk and writing. Use has even made some of them lose their figurative quality. Thus, shoes have tongues, combs have teeth, needles have eyes—as though these objects were living creatures. Use has made other figurative statements trite ("He is old as the hills"; "She has a baby face"; "He is foxy"). When a student says that his parents "rolled out the red carpet" for him when he arrived home for Christmas vacation, he certainly does not mean that his father and mother painfully laid a long rug down the front walk. A sociologist who writes about the "role" of clergymen in community affairs is not consciously thinking of the theater. Unlike these speakers and writers, the good poet invents new figurative statements. Poets, therefore, are necessary to the welfare of a language because they keep it from becoming stale and exhausted.

Simile and Metaphor

A statement becomes figurative when it contains one of the **figures of language,** or **tropes.** The most common are simile and metaphor. A **simile** uses *like, as,* or *than* to express a resemblance between two essentially unlike entities: "Her hair drooped down her pallid cheeks like seaweed on a clam." Though literally untrue, this comparison creates the desired image of something lank, dank, and dull-colored. It should be observed that not every comparison is figurative: "Her wig, like Jane's, is red" is a literal statement because it compares two entities of the same kind, two wigs.

"John knows Greek better than Jim" is literal; "John can speak Greek as naturally as a pig can squeak" is figurative.

A **metaphor** is a figure of language that omits the comparative term (*like, as, than*) and says or implies that one thing is another thing that it cannot literally be: "All the world's a stage." A simile says that *x* is like *y;* a metaphor, in its explicit form, says that *x* is *y*. This anonymous sixteenth-century song consists of four explicit metaphors.

> April is in my mistress' face,
> And July in her eyes hath place;
> Within her bosom is September,
> But in her heart a cold December.

Here, as in a simile, both terms of the comparisons are explicitly stated: *April–face, July–eyes,* etc.

Implicit Metaphors

In another anonymous song the metaphors are implicit rather than explicit:

> Injurious hours, whilst any joy doth bless me,
> With speedy wings you fly, and so release me.
> But if some sorrow do oppress my heart,
> You creep as if you never meant to part.

When the poet says that the hours have wings (line 2), he is obviously comparing them to a fast-flying bird. This metaphor is an implicit metaphor because one of the comparative terms—*bird*—is implied rather than stated. Similarly, in line 4, the hours are said to creep; here the omitted term is *slow-moving creature.* A metaphor, then, will not necessarily be in the form *x* is *y;* more commonly, the metaphor assumes that *x* is *y* and then goes on to say something about *x* as though it were *y*. These figurative statements contain implicit metaphors: "I will drink life to the lees" (understood explicit metaphor: life is a glass of wine): "She whispered into her husband's long, furry ear" (he is a jackass); "He glittered when he walked" (he was a shiny jewel). In the last example the whole metaphor has been concentrated into the single word *glittered.*

Exercise 23

In the following poems distinguish literal from figurative statements, and identify the similes and metaphors. Classify the metaphors as implicit or explicit.

A Birthday

My heart is like a singing bird
  Whose nest is in a watered shoot;
My heart is like an apple-tree
  Whose boughs are bent with thickset fruit;
My heart is like a rainbow shell
  That paddles in a halcyon sea;
My heart is gladder than all these
  Because my love is come to me.

Raise me a dais of silk and down;
  Hang it with vair and purple dyes;
Carve it in doves and pomegranates,
  And peacocks with a hundred eyes;
Work it in gold and silver grapes,
  In leaves and silver fleurs-de-lys;
Because the birthday of my life
  Is come, my love is come to me.

Christina G. Rossetti
(1830–1894)

halcyon (6): calm, peaceful. *dais* (9): throne. *vair* (10): rare fur.

A Poison Tree

I was angry with my friend:
I told my wrath, my wrath did end.
I was angry with my foe:
I told it not, my wrath did grow.

And I water'd it in fears,
Night and morning with my tears;
And I sunned it with smiles,
And with soft deceitful wiles.

And it grew both day and night,
Till it bore an apple bright;
And my foe beheld it shine,
And he knew that it was mine,

And into my garden stole
When the night had veil'd the pole:
In the morning glad I see
My foe outstretch'd beneath the tree.

William Blake
(1757–1827)

I Taste a Liquor Never Brewed

I taste a liquor never brewed—
From Tankards scooped in Pearl—
Not all the Frankfort Berries
Yield such an Alcohol!

Inebriate of Air—am I—
And Debauchee of Dew—
Reeling—thro endless summer days—
From inns of Molten Blue—

When "Landlords" turn the drunken Bee
Out of the Foxglove's door—
When Butterflies—renounce their "drams"—
I shall but drink the more!

Till Seraphs swing their snowy Hats—
And Saints—to windows run—
To see the little Tippler
From Manzanilla come!

Emily Dickinson
(1830–1886)

Frankfort Berries (3): An earlier version read "Vats upon the Rhine." *Manzanilla* (16): in Cuba; associated with rum. There are two other versions of line 16: "Leaning against the —Sun—" and "Come staggering toward the sun."

Fire and Ice

Some say the world will end in fire,
Some say in ice.
From what I've tasted of desire
I hold with those who favor fire.
But if it had to perish twice,
I think I know enough of hate
To say that for destruction ice
Is also great
And would suffice.

Robert Frost
(1875–1963)

Piazza di Spagna, Early Morning

I can't forget
How she stood at the top of that long marble stair
Amazed, and then with a sleepy pirouette
Went dancing slowly down to the fountain-quieted square;

Nothing upon her face
But some impersonal loneliness,—not then a girl
But as it were a reverie of the place,
A called-for falling glide and whirl;

As when a leaf, petal, or thin chip
Is drawn to the falls of a pool and, circling a moment above it,
Rides on over the lip—
Perfectly beautiful, perfectly ignorant of it.

Richard Wilbur
(1921–)

Title: The Spanish Square in Rome. A vast Baroque stairway descends from the Church of Santa Trinita del Monte on a hill overlooking the piazza to the square below.

Literalism

Literalism—mistaking figurative for literal statements—is a bad and frequently a comic blunder.

On a Horse Who Bit a Clergyman

The steed bit his master;
  How came this to pass?
He heard the good pastor
  Say, "All flesh is grass."

Anonymous
(Eighteenth Century)

All . . . grass (4) : He is quoting from Isaiah xl:26 or I Peter i:24.

In a horse, literalism is probably excusable; in a reader of poems, it is certainly not. A reader with an excessively literal mind will find nothing but nonsensical rubbish in poems. Of course, such a reader has been using similes and metaphors all his life, but he has never stopped to think analytically about them. Learning to analyze figures is the best remedy for literalism.

Analyzing a Figure of Comparison

Every simile and every metaphor consists of two parts: an *x*, or a main entity, and a *y*, or a secondary entity to which the main entity is compared. Simile and explicit metaphor keep the two parts separate; implicit metaphor fuses the two, sometimes into a single word. Analysis of the figure consists first of identifying the two parts and then of explaining the basis on which the comparison is made—that is, the grounds of similarity between the two parts. Sometimes the grounds are stated, as in these lines from *King Lear* (IV, i, 36–37):

> As flies to wanton boys are we to the gods:
> They kill us for their sport.

The two figures (gods are like boys; men are like flies) are followed by a statement of the grounds for the comparison: the gods kill men as heartlessly as reckless boys kill flies.

When the grounds of the comparison are not stated, analysis of the figure must concentrate on the connotation of the second part.

A Red, Red Rose

O, my luve is like a red, red rose,
  That's newly sprung in June.
O, my luve is like the melodie,
  That's sweetly play'd in tune.

As fair art thou, by bonie lass,
  So deep in luve am I,
And I will luve thee still, my dear,
  Till a' the seas gang dry.

Till a' the seas gang dry, my dear,
  And the rocks melt wi' the sun!
And I will luve thee still, my dear,
  While the sands o' life shall run.

And fare thee weel, my only luve,
  And fare thee weel a while!
And I will come again, my luve,
  Tho' it were ten thousand mile!

Robert Burns
(1759–1796)

luve (1): beloved. *bonie:* (5): beautiful. *a'* (8): all. *gang* (8): go. *weel* (13): well.

An analysis of the two similes in stanza 1 supplies all the relevant connotations of *rose* and *melody:*

> The girl is like a rose because she is beautiful in the way a rose is—not just any rose, but a red, red rose. This image suggests something vibrant and startling about her beauty. (A pale pink rose would suggest a fragile beauty and a shy, withdrawn personality.) Since this girl is like a rose that's newly sprung in June, she is the first, not the last rose of summer. She is fresh and young. According to the second simile in the stanza, she is like a melody; she lifts up the lover's heart and pleases him in the same way music does—not just any tune whistled in the street, but a melody that has a kind of simple and artfully artless perfection.

Rather than rambling on in prose about the lady, Burns uses two similes to express, more sharply and precisely than any prosaic inventory could express, both the qualities of the girl and the man's feelings for her. The figures help to communicate the experience because they appeal to the reader's own experience. It is as if the speaker of the poem were saying, "I know this girl and how I feel about her, but you don't. But you *do* know what roses and lovely tunes are like. Well, that's what *she* is like."

In addition to the figures of overstatement (see page 150) in stanzas 2, 3, and 4 of Burns's poem, there is an implicit metaphor in line 12: "sands o' life." Here life is compared to an hourglass in which running sand indicates the passing of time. An analysis of this metaphor, then, would first identify the submerged term, *hourglass,* and then point out that it connotes the passing of time. Burns wants the reader to think of a very long period of time; it would take a long time for the sand to run out in a "lifetime glass," if there were such a thing.

Exercise 24

Analyze the metaphors and similes in these poems.

With Rue My Heart Is Laden

With rue my heart is laden
  For golden friends I had,
For many a rose-lipt maiden
  And many a lightfoot lad.

By brooks too broad for leaping
  The lightfoot boys are laid;
The rose-lipt girls are sleeping
  In fields where roses fade.

A. E. Housman
(1859–1936)

1. What are the possible meanings of *rue* (line 1)?
2. What are the various metaphors implied by *golden* (line 2)?

Fear No More the Heat o' the Sun

Fear no more the heat o' the sun,
  Nor the furious winter's rages;
Thou thy worldly task hast done,
  Home art gone, and ta'en thy wages;
Golden lads and girls all must,
As chimney-sweepers, come to dust.

Fear no more the frown o' the great,
  Thou art past the tyrant's stroke;
Care no more to clothe and eat,
  To thee the reed is as the oak.
The scepter, learning, physic, must
All follow this and come to dust.

Fear no more the lightning flash,
  Nor the all-dreaded thunder-stone;
Fear not slander, censure rash;
  Thou hast finished joy and moan.
All lovers young, all lovers must
Consign to thee and come to dust.

William Shakespeare
(1564–1616)
(*from* Cymbeline)

stone (14): bolt. *consign to* (18): consent to follow your example.

1. In the play two young men address this song to a dead girl. Contrast the attitude toward death here with the attitude in Housman's poem.
2. What are the connotations of *reed* and *oak* (line 10)?

She Walks in Beauty

She walks in Beauty, like the night
  Of cloudless climes and starry skies;
And all that's best of dark and bright
  Meet in her aspect and her eyes:
Thus mellowed to that tender light
  Which Heaven to gaudy day denies.

One shade the more, one ray the less,
  Had half impaired the nameless grace
Which waves in every raven tress,
  Or softly lightens o'er her face;
Where thoughts serenely sweet express,
  How pure, how dear their dwelling-place.

And on that cheek, and o'er that brow,
  So soft, so calm, yet eloquent,
The smiles that win, the tints that glow,
  But tell of days in goodness spent,
A mind at peace with all below,
  A heart whose love is innocent!

George Gordon, Lord Byron
(1788–1824)

1. The description of this lady is based on a contrast. What is the contrast?
2. What connotations of *raven* (line 9) are irrelevant to an understanding of this word in its present context?

Mystique

No man has seen the third hand
that stems from the center,
near the heart. Let either
the right or the left prepare
a dish for the mouth,
or a thing to give,
and the third hand deftly
and unseen will change the object
of our hunger or of our giving.

David Ignatow
(1914–)

1. What common human experience is here described metaphorically?

The Sources of Figurative Language

Poets derive the secondary terms of their figures of comparison from every area of human experience. In the figurative statement "Silence, like a poultice, heals the wounds of sound," the secondary terms come from medicine; in

> To sleep I give my powers away;
> My will is bondsman to the dark . . .

the secondary terms come from legal practice. The metaphors in the following poem are drawn from government, architecture, clothing, and warfare:

Complaint of a Lover Rebuked

Love that liveth and reigneth in my thought,
That built his seat within my captive breast,
Clad in the arms wherein with me he fought,
Oft in my face he doth his banner rest.
She that me taught to love and suffer pain,
My doubtful hope and eke my hot desire
With shamefast cloak to shadow and refrain,
Her smiling grace converteth straight to ire;
And coward love then to the heart apace
Taketh his flight, whereas he lurks and plains
His purpose lost, and dare not show his face.
For my lord's guilt thus faultless bide I pains;
Yet from my lord shall not my foot remove:
Sweet is his death that takes his end by love.

Henry Howard, Earl of Surrey
(*c.* 1517–1547)

eke (6) : also. *plains* (10) : complains.

Campion's song beginning

> There is a garden in her face
> Where roses and white lilies blow . . .

draws on horticulture for its metaphorical images. Nature, religion, business, eating, drinking, objects of every kind, animals, games, studies—all these and many more provide poets with their figures.

Exercise 25

Sonnet 73

That time of year thou mayest in me behold
When yellow leaves, or none, or few, do hang
Upon those boughs which shake against the cold,
Bare ruined choirs, where late the sweet birds sang.
In me thou seest the twilight of such day
As after sunset fadeth in the west,
Which by and by black night doth take away,
Death's second self, that seals up all in rest.
In me thou seest the glowing of such fire
That on the ashes of his youth doth lie,
As the death-bed whereon it must expire,
Consumed with that which it was nourished by.
  This thou perceiv'st, which makes thy love more strong,
  To love that well which thou must leave ere long.

William Shakespeare
(1564–1616)

1. What is the source of the implicit metaphors that run through lines 1–4? Through lines 5–8? Through lines 9–12?
2. What do these metaphors have in common?
3. Do lines 13–14 make a literal or a figurative statement? What is the relationship between these lines and the rest of the poem?

Extended Figures

A single metaphor or simile that runs through several lines, as in Shakespeare's "That time of year," is called an **extended figure;** a figure may even be extended throughout an entire poem. Such a poem is embedded in the dialogue of *Romeo and Juliet,* in the scene in which Romeo, having come uninvited to a masked ball given by the enemies of his family, suddenly sees their daughter and, unaware of who she is, falls in love with her. In disguise he approaches her:

Romeo. If I profane with my unworthiest hand
This holy shrine, the gentle fine is this:
My lips, two blushing pilgrims, ready stand
To smooth that rough touch with a tender kiss.

Juliet. Good pilgrim, you do wrong your hand too much,
Which mannerly devotion shows in this;
For saints have hands that pilgrims' hands do touch,
And palm to palm is holy palmer's kiss.

Romeo. Have not saints lips, and holy palmers too?

Juliet. Ay, pilgrim, lips that they must use in prayer.

Romeo. O, then, dear saint, let lips do what hands do:
They pray; grant thou, lest faith turn to despair.

Juliet. Saints do not move, though grant for prayers' sake.

Romeo. Then move not, while my prayers' effect I take.

The implicit metaphor in these lines likens the meeting of Romeo and Juliet to a pilgrim's approaching the shrine of a saint. All the imagery of the poem, and all its subsidiary metaphors, derive directly from this central comparison. That human love should be spoken of as religious devotion may seem strange, but such language is valid in this poem. The young lovers feel a kind of awe in the presence of each other that is not unlike the devout person's feeling of unworthiness in a holy place.

Exercise 26

On First Looking into Chapman's Homer

Much have I travell'd in the realms of gold,
  And many goodly states and kingdoms seen;
  Round many western islands have I been
Which bards in fealty to Apollo hold.
Oft of one wide expanse had I been told
  That deep-brow'd Homer ruled as his demesne;
  Yet did I never breathe its pure serene
Till I heard Chapman speak out loud and bold:
Then felt I like some watcher of the skies
  When a new planet swims into his ken;
Or like stout Cortez when with eagle eyes
  He star'd at the Pacific—and all his men
Look'd at each other with a wild surmise—
  Silent, upon a peak in Darien.

John Keats
(1795–1821)

Chapman's Homer (title) : the translation of the *Iliad* and the *Odyssey* by George Chapman (1559–1634) . *demesne* (6) : realm. *serene* (7) : landscape or seascape. *Darien* (14) : in Panama.

1. What is being compared with traveling in line 1?
2. What, literally, are the "western islands" (line 3)?
3. How does line 4 help the reader supply the omitted part of the metaphor in lines 1–4?
4. What metaphor extends throughout the poem?
5. What is the connection between the metaphor in lines 9–10 and the extended metaphor?
6. Keats forgot that Balboa (not Cortez) discovered the Pacific. Does this error injure the poem in any way? Why or why not?
7. Why is the "surmise" (line 13) said to be "wild"?

The Lion-House

Always the heavy air,
The dreadful cage, the low
Murmur of voices, where
Some force goes to and fro
In an immense despair.

As though a haunted brain—
With tireless footfalls
The obsession moves again,
Trying the floor, the walls,
Forever, but in vain.

In vain, proud force! A might,
Shrewder than yours, did spin
Around your rage that bright
Prison of steel, wherein
You pace for my delight.

And oh, my heart, what doom,
What warier will, has wrought
The cage, within whose room
Paces your burning thought,
For the delight of Whom?

John Hall Wheelock
(1886–)

1. What do the images in the first three stanzas depict?
2. In the final stanza these images are revealed to be an extended metaphor. What is that metaphor?

The Uses of Figurative Language

First, what does figurative language *not* do? It emphatically does not merely embellish or decorate a thought. A figurative statement is not a more effective or more vivid way of saying something that could be just as well said literally. Compare, for instance, "Shut up!" (an implicit metaphor that likens a human being to a box and thus takes from him all his humanity) and "Stop speaking!" These two commands do not say the same thing; they are not interchangeable. Similarly, the command "Don't butt in!" compares a human being with a goat and is thus not the equivalent of "Don't interfere in my affairs," which makes no comparison at all. What has been said about these colloquial figures applies equally to figures in poems. If figures were merely fancier ways of making literal statements, good poets would have no use for them because a good poet says what he means and nothing else. Figures help him accomplish this purpose.

Suppose that a poet wished to express the feeling of disillusionment. If he were a bad poet, he might scribble some literal doggerel like this:

A thought that once was dear to me
  (How sad is what I say!)
Is not what it appeared to be,
  As I found out today.

These lines are disappointing because they communicate no experience, evoke no images, and actually say very little.

A good poet, in contrast, will find a metaphor to help him say what he has to say.

It Dropped So Low in My Regard

It dropped so low—in my Regard—
I heard it hit the Ground—
And go to pieces on the Stones
At bottom of my Mind—
Yet blamed the Fate that fractured—*less*
Than I reviled Myself,
For entertaining Plated Wares
Upon my Silver Shelf—

Emily Dickinson
(1830–1886)

On the surface this poem is about a mishap or accident: something falls off a shelf and breaks. But the very first line tells the reader that the fall is not a physical or a literal one. The speaker says that the "drop" or "fall" took place in her "Regard"—that is, in her attitude or feelings about something. And the break took place not on the real ground but at the bottom of her "Mind" (line 4). There is nothing strange about this way of speaking, since it is common practice to use the adjectives *high* and *low* when describing one's opinion. "I have a high opinion of her," we say, "but a low one of him." Dickinson has merely made this common but abstract way of speaking into concrete images; she uses the metaphor of a dish falling off a shelf to express the sudden failure of an ideal or the loss of regard that she formerly felt for another person.

The metaphor of the first stanza is extended into the second as the speaker continues to speak of her emotional experience as though it were a physical experience. She holds herself, rather than Fate, responsible for the mishap. She never should have placed such inferior "Plated Wares" (line 7) on the very high shelf where she keeps her sterling silver, the articles of true worth and value.

This poem usefully illustrates a number of the functions that a metaphor can perform. First, it makes the abstract appear to be concrete. Nobody has ever seen or heard an ideal go to pieces in a mind, yet everybody has had accidents with dishes. Thus, the metaphor appeals to the reader's experience and imagination because it creates images lacking in the literal statement "I overvalued something, and now I am disillusioned." Second, a metaphor, if it is successfully developed, can give a poem its structure. It provides the poet with a concise narrative. Third, the metaphor enables the poet to express a judgment without wasting space on such bald exclamations as "How false was my ideal!" The judgment is implicit in the metaphors *go to pieces* (line 3) and *Plated* (line 7). Fourth, the metaphor enables the reader to recreate the speaker's feeling so that he can feel something like it himself. The important word *entertaining* (line 7) tells the reader how the speaker felt before she discovered that her ideal was spurious. Once she entertained (that is, cherished as well as maintained and kept up) the false ideal; now that it has been exposed as worthless, she blames herself. Fate may have brought about the exposure, but only she put the dish (the ideal) high in her cupboard (her mind).

Thus, a metaphor enables a poet to say precisely what he means because (1) it creates images that make abstract statements appear concrete, (2) it gives shape and structure to statements, (3) it conveys judgments, and (4) it communicates feelings.

Exercise 27

Show how the figurative statements in these poems help the poets say precisely what they mean.

The Last Word

Creep into thy narrow bed,
Creep, and let no more be said!
Vain thy onset! all stands fast;
Thou thyself must break at last.

Let the long contention cease!
Geese are swans, and swans are geese.
Let them have it how they will!
Thou art tired; best be still!

They out-talk'd thee, hiss'd thee, tore thee.
Better men fared thus before thee;
Fired their ringing shot and pass'd,
Hotly charged—and broke at last.

Charge once more, then, and be dumb!
Let the victors, when they come,
When the forts of folly fall,
Find thy body by the wall!

Matthew Arnold
(1822–1888)

The Silver Swan

The silver swan, who living had no note,
When death approached, unlocked her silent throat;
Leaning her breast against the reedy shore,
Thus sung her first and last, and sung no more:

"Farewell, all joys! O death, come close mine eyes;
More geese than swans now live, more fools than wise."

Anonymous
(Seventeenth Century)

By the Road to the Air-Base

The calloused grass lies hard
Against the cracking plain:
Life is a grayish stain;
The salt-marsh hems my yard.

Dry dikes rise hill on hill:
In sloughs of tidal slime
Shell-fish deposit lime,
Wild sea-fowl creep at will.

The highway, like a beach,
Turns whiter, shadowy, dry:
Loud, pale against the sky,
The bombing planes hold speech.

Yet fruit grows on the trees;
Here scholars pause to speak;
Through gardens bare and Greek,
I hear my neighbor's bees.

Yvor Winters
(1900–1968)

Easter Wings

Lord, who createdst man in wealth and store,
Though foolishly he lost the same,
Decaying more and more
Till he became
Most poor:
With thee
O let me rise,
As larks, harmoniously,
And sing this day thy victories;
Then shall the fall further the flight in me.

My tender age in sorrow did begin;
And still with sicknesses and shame
Thou didst so punish sin,
That I became
Most thin.
With thee
Let me combine
And feel this day thy victory;
For, if I imp my wing on thine,
Affliction shall advance the flight in me.

George Herbert
(1593–1633)

Driving Home

Nothing. Not even you, Dave, speak
at this speed. We have flattened out
a little toward that radiant
silhouette science talks about:—
mass moving at the speed of light.
Dusk wounds our windshield;
townships divide; the winding creek
unwinds; forest and field
flicker and slant. We have lost weight.
What syllable's not too ponderous
for us—two headlights twinkling
across country—small double star
in its untranquil firmament
of route and suburb. Inkling
of the Immaterial—we mount,
accelerate without effort, pass
through throngs unnoticed . . . . All the same,
we saw a girl step from a car—
calves chiaroscuro; through blurred wood
watched a rotund old gelding plod
his moving pasture . . . . These reclaim
our lost gravity: "Let me out!"
eh, Dave? Observance of the mass
for us. Let angels levitate.

Peter Kane Dufault
(1923–)

To the Senses

When conquering love did first my heart assail,
Unto mine aid I summoned every sense,
Doubting, if that proud tyrant should prevail,
My heart should suffer for mine eyes' offence;
But he with beauty first corrupted sight,
My hearing bribed with her tongue's harmony,
My taste, by her sweet lips drawn with delight,
My smelling won with her breath's spicery;
But when my touching came to play his part
(The king of senses, greater than the rest),
He yields love up the keys unto my heart,
And tells the other how they should be blest;
  And thus by those of whom I hoped for aid,
  To cruel love my soul was first betrayed.

Michael Drayton
(1563–1631)

1. Analyze the extended metaphor.
2. How are the five senses corrupted by the heart's assailant?
3. Why is touch called the king of senses (line 10)?
4. In what way is love cruel (line 14)? Why does the lover think of himself as having been betrayed?

Conceits

A figurative comparison of two strikingly dissimilar entities is called a **conceit.**

Nature's confectioner, the bee
(Whose suckets are moist alchemy,
The still of his refining mold
Minting the garden into gold,
Having rifled all the fields
Of what dainties Flora yields,
Ambitious now to take excise
Of a more fragrant paradise,
At my Fuscara's sleeve arrived
Where all delicious sweets are hived.

In these lines from John Cleveland's "Fuscara" (*c.* 1637) a honeybee is compared to a manufacturer of suckets, or candies (line 1), to an alchemist (line 2), to a coiner of money (lines 3–4), to a thief (line 5), and to a tax collector (line 7). Except for the first and perhaps the second comparison, all these comparisons are conceits. The distance between a bee and a tax collector is so great that the comparison may be considered farfetched. Comparing a girl's sleeve to a beehive (line 10) is also farfetched. Surely the poet wants the reader to admire his cleverness rather than to form an image of this particular dress. Cleveland's lines are cited here because they provide such unmistakable examples of conceits, not because they contain especially effective conceits.

Petrarchan Conceits

Several writers of love poems in sixteenth-century England used stock comparisons that literary historians call **Petrarchan conceits,** after Francesco Petrarch (1304–1374), the Italian poet whom the English poets imitated. In a Petrarchan poem the lover, who is usually the speaker, describes himself as a worshiper of his lady's beauty and virtue. Regardless of what the lady does, the lover suffers. When she is aloof and haughty, he freezes; if she so much as smiles at him, he burns and fries. Sometimes her eyes shoot arrows at him and wound him; then his weeping becomes a shower of rain, and his sighs turn into a windstorm. Petrarchan ladies usually have hair of gold, complexions of lilies and roses, teeth of pearls, necks and breasts of milky whiteness. Their virtue is an impregnable fortress.

Playfully mocking such overused Petrarchan conventions, Shakespeare wrote the following poem.

Sonnet 130

My mistress' eyes are nothing like the sun;
Coral is far more red than her lips' red;
If snow be white, why then her breasts are dun;
If hairs be wires, black wires grow on her head.
I have seen roses damasked, red and white,
But no such roses see I in her cheeks;

And in some perfumes is there more delight
Than in the breath that from my mistress reeks.
I love to hear her speak, yet well I know
That music hath a far more pleasing sound;
I grant I never saw a goddess go;
My mistress, when she walks, treads on the ground.
 And yet, by heaven, I think my love as rare
 As any she belied with false compare.

William Shakespeare
(1564–1616)

damasked (5): mingled red and white. *reeks* (8): is exhaled. *go* (11): walk. *belied . . . compare* (14): lied about with false comparisons.

Yet it would be an error to condemn all Petrarchan conceits merely because some bad poets abused them. The Petrarchan poets who avoided excessively farfetched and hackneyed conceits wrote some fine poems idealizing love and womanhood.

Metaphysical Conceits

The figurative comparisons found in the poems of John Donne (1572–1631) and his imitators are called **metaphysical conceits.** Samuel Johnson described this kind of conceit as "a combination of dissimilar images, or discovery of occult resemblances." A metaphysical conceit is likely to be more unexpected and more original than a Petrarchan conceit. A marriage bed may be compared to a grave, the union of two lovers to an alchemist's mixture, the parting of friends to an eclipse of the sun. "The most heterogeneous ideas are yoked by violence together," said Dr. Johnson, who did not admire these conceits; "nature and art are ransacked for illustrations, comparisons, and allusions." The metaphors of a single poem may be drawn from such difficult studies as theology and astronomy, and from such ordinary activities as commerce and housekeeping. In general the metaphysical poets display more learning in their poems than do the Petrarchans.

Another difference between the metaphysicals and the Petrarchans is that the former do not ordinarily idealize womanhood and love. Instead they attempt to define attitudes toward particular women—and their attitudes are not always respectful. Sometimes the speaker of a metaphysical poem argues ingeniously in defense of an outrageous proposition.

The Flea

Mark but this flea, and mark in this
How little that which thou deniest me is;
It sucked me first, and now sucks thee,
And in this flea our two bloods mingled be.
Thou knowest that this cannot be said
A sin, nor shame, nor loss of maidenhead;
  Yet this enjoys before it woo,
  And pampered swells with one blood made of two,
  And this, alas, is more than we would do.

O stay! Three lives in one flea spare,
Where we almost, yea, more than married are;
This flea is you and I, and this
Our marriage bed and marriage temple is.
Though parents grudge, and you, we're met
And cloistered in these living walls of jet.
  Though use make you apt to kill me,
  Let not to that, self-murder added be,
  And sacrilege, three sins in killing three.

Cruel and sudden! Hast thou since
Purpled thy nail in blood of innocence?
Wherein could this flea guilty be,
Except in that drop which it sucked from thee?
Yet thou triumph'st and saist that thou
Find'st not thyself, nor me, the weaker now.
  'Tis true. Then learn how false, fears be;
  Just so much honor, when thou yield'st to me,
  Will waste, as this flea's death took life from thee.

John Donne
(1572–1631)

This lover's way of persuading his lady to yield to him is certainly unusual; the last thing in the world a "romantic" lover would do would be to compare lovemaking to fleabites. In using this metaphor, the speaker shows that he is cynical about romance and artificial etiquette. He is seeking his own gratification, and he wants to show that he is clever and amusing as well as sexually eager. His metaphor minimizes the importance of what he seeks. In effect what he keeps saying through the metaphor is "What I want of you is just as unimportant as a fleabite."

Donne's "The Flea" represents one extreme in metaphysical poetry; his divine poems represent another. Unlike the Petrarchans, Donne and his followers also wrote passionately ingenious poems on religious subjects.

The Windows

Lord, how can man preach thy eternal word?
  He is a brittle, crazy glass;
Yet in thy temple thou dost him afford
  This glorious and transcendent place,
  To be a window through thy grace.

But when thou dost anneal in glass thy story,
  Making thy life to shine within
The holy preacher's, then the light and glory
  More reverend grows, and more doth win,
  Which else shows waterish, bleak, and thin.

Doctrine and life, colors and light in one,
  When they combine and mingle, bring
A strong regard and awe; but speech alone
  Doth vanish like a flaring thing,
  And in the ear, not conscience, ring.

George Herbert
(1593–1633)

Stanza 1 compares a clergyman to a plain glass window. As a mere man, he is all too imperfect for the holy task assigned to him. He is "brittle" (that is, unstable and insecure) and "crazy" (full of fine cracks and imperfections). He can transmit light (the word of God) only glaringly and imperfectly to his congregation—and only with the help of God's grace. Stanza 2 continues the metaphor by comparing the holy minister—the man who has shaped his life according to God's teachings—to a stained-glass window. His life is a colorfully pictured example of God's doctrine (line 11) because he practices what he preaches. The words of a clergyman in whom God has annealed his story ring in the consciences, not the ears, of his congregation (line 15). Herbert makes the unlikely and artificial comparison of a man to a window seem inevitable and right. The best metaphysical conceits appeal simultaneously to a reader's mental and emotional apparatus—to his mind and heart.

Exercise 28

A Valediction Forbidding Mourning

As virtuous men pass mildly away,
  And whisper to their souls to go,
Whilst some of their sad friends do say,
  The breath goes now, and some say, no:

So let us melt, and make no noise,
  No tear-floods, nor sigh-tempests move;
'Twere profanation of our joys
  To tell the laity our love.

Moving of the earth brings harms and fears;
  Men reckon what it did and meant;
But trepidation of the spheres,
  Though greater far, is innocent.

Dull sublunary lovers' love
  (Whose soul is sense) cannot admit
Absence, because it doth remove
  Those things which elemented it.

But we, by a love so much refined
  That ourselves know not what it is,
Inter-assurèd of the mind,
  Care less, eyes, lips, and hands to miss.

Our two souls, therefore, which are one,
  Though I must go, endure not yet
A breach, but an expansion,
  Like gold to airy thinness beat.

If they be two, they are two so
  As stiff twin compasses are two:
Thy soul, the fixed foot, makes no show
  To move, but doth, if the other do.

And though it in the center sit,
  Yet when the other far doth roam,
It leans and harkens after it,
  And grows erect as that comes home.

Such wilt thou be to me, who must,
  Like the other foot, obliquely run;
Thy firmness makes my circle just,
  And makes me end where I begun.

John Donne
(1572–1631)

trepidation of the spheres (11): precession of the equinoxes.
innocent (12): harmless. *elemented* (16): constituted.

1. To what does the speaker compare the dying of men described in stanza 1? What is the basis of this comparison?
2. Analyze the metaphor implied by *melt* (line 5), *profanation* (line 7), and *laity* (line 8).
3. From what studies are the metaphors in stanza 3 drawn?
4. Should *sublunary* (line 13) be understood figuratively or literally?
5. From what activity is the simile in line 24 drawn?
6. What is the speaker's attitude toward Petrarchan conceits?
7. What kind of compass is referred to in line 26?

Death, Be Not Proud

Death, be not proud, though some have callèd thee
Mighty and dreadful, for thou are not so;
For those whom thou think'st thou dost overthrow

Die not, poor Death, nor yet canst thou kill me.
From rest and sleep, which but thy pictures be,
Much pleasure; then from thee much more must flow,
And soonest our best men with thee do go,
Rest of their bones, and soul's delivery.
Thou art slave to fate, chance, kings, and desperate men,
And dost with poison, war, and sickness dwell,
And poppy or charms can make us sleep as well
And better than thy stroke; why swell'st thou then?
One short sleep past, we wake eternally
And death shall be no more; Death, thou shalt die.

John Donne
(1572–1631)

poppy (11) : drugs, opiates. *charms* (11) : spells, hypnotism.

1. What old proverb or saying lies behind line 7?
2. Why, according to the speaker, should Death not be proud of his accomplishments?
3. Explain why the argument in the poem depends on a belief in immortality.

On Donne's Poetry

With Donne, whose muse on dromedary trots,
Wreathe iron pokers into true-love knots;
Rhyme's sturdy cripple, fancy's maze and clue,
Wit's forge and fire-blast, meaning's press and screw.

Samuel Taylor Coleridge
(1772–1834)

1. Analyze Coleridge's metaphors. What attitudes toward Donne do they imply?
2. Cite examples from Donne's poems that illustrate Coleridge's remarks.

5. *Other Figures in Poems*

The right virtue of the natural reader is the nice ability to tell always when a poem is being figurative and when it is not being figurative.

Robert Frost

Poets have available for their use many different figures of language—over two hundred, in fact, according to the traditional rhetoricians, who identified the various kinds and gave them such formidable labels as *litotes, asyndeton,* and *hendiadys.* Of all these possible figures, the beginning reader of poems will find it useful to know, in addition to simile and metaphor, only six: overstatement, understatement, metonymy, personification, apostrophe, and paradox. Labeling and classifying the various figures is less important, however, than understanding why and how poets use them. The study of figures is not an end in itself but a means for better understanding poems.

Overstatement and Understatement

She Dwelt among the Untrodden Ways

She dwelt among the untrodden ways
  Beside the springs of Dove,
A Maid whom there were none to praise
  And very few to love:

A violet by a mossy stone
  Half hidden from the eye!
—Fair as a star, when only one
  Is shining in the sky.

She lived unknown, and few could know
  When Lucy ceased to be;
But she is in her grave, and, oh,
  The difference to me!

William Wordsworth
(1770–1850)

Dove (2): a stream in the Midlands of England.

Had Wordsworth been writing directly and literally, he might have begun his account of Lucy by saying, "She lived in a very remote place"; but this statement is inexact compared with the first line of the poem. Lucy dwelt in a place so remote that *nobody* walked on the roads: the "ways" were "untrodden." Here, clearly, Wordsworth is exaggerating. A poet makes an **overstatement** (sometimes called **hyperbole**) when he exaggerates, not to deceive the reader but to create a special effect. Wordsworth may have wanted to emphasize, in a single word, how remote and lonely Lucy's dwelling-place was. The last line of the poem, in contrast, is an **understatement,** because it not only says much less than it could have said but less than the occasion warrants. Understatement is effective because of what it leaves unsaid. The effect would have been much less poignant had Wordsworth written "The misery to me!"

Exercise 29

Find examples of overstatement and understatement in these poems, and explain how or why they are used.

Dread

Beside a chapel I'd a room looked down,
Where all the women from the farms and town,
On Holy-days and Sundays used to pass
To marriages, and christenings, and to Mass.

Then I sat lonely watching score and score,
Till I turned jealous of the Lord next door. . . .
Now by this window, where there's none can see,
The Lord God's jealous of yourself and me.

John Millington Synge
(1871–1909)

1. What is happening by the window (line 7)?
2. Why does Synge use overstatement?
3. If you think that the title is inappropriate, suggest a better one.

How Annandale Went Out

"They called it Annandale—and I was there
To flourish, to find words, and to attend:
Liar, physician, hypocrite, and friend,
I watched him; and the sight was not so fair
As one or two that I have seen elsewhere:
An apparatus not for me to mend—
A wreck, with hell between him and the end,
Remained of Annandale; and I was there.

"I knew the ruin as I knew the man;
So put the two together, if you can,
Remembering the worst you know of me.
Now view yourself as I was, on the spot—
With a slight kind of engine. Do you see?
Like this . . . You wouldn't hang me? I thought not."

Edwin Arlington Robinson
(1869–1935)

1. The key to this poem is the proper identification of *slight kind of engine* (line 13). For what word or words is this expression a metaphor?
2. What does *it* (line 1) refer to? Why is *it* used?
3. Why does the speaker repeatedly emphasize that he was there? What does the phrase *on the spot* (line 12) suggest?
4. Characterize the speaker. What is his opinion of himself?

Edge

The woman is perfected.
Her dead

Body wears the smile of accomplishment,
The illusion of a Greek necessity

Flows in the scrolls of her toga,
Her bare

Feet seem to be saying:
We have come so far, it is over.

Each dead child coiled, a white serpent,
One at each little

Pitcher of milk, now empty.
She has folded

Them back into her body as petals
Of a rose close when the garden

Stiffens and odours bleed
From the sweet, deep throats of the night flower.

The moon has nothing to be sad about,
Staring from her hood of bone.

She is used to this sort of thing.
Her blacks crackle and drag.

Sylvia Plath
(1932–1963)

Eight O'Clock

He stood, and heard the steeple
  Sprinkle the quarters on the morning town.
One, two, three, four, to market-place and people
  It tossed them down.

Strapped, noosed, nighing his hour,
  He stood and counted them and cursed his luck;
And then the clock collected in the tower
  Its strength, and struck.

A. E. Housman
(1859–1936)

Epitaph on a Pessimist

I'm Smith of Stoke, aged sixty-odd,
    I've lived without a dame
From youth-time on; and would to God
    My dad had done the same.

Thomas Hardy
(1840–1928)

Mushrooms

Mushrooms grew
Overnight
            like they always did
Only this time
            there was
      nobody
      to
        pick them

Mike Evans
(1941–   )

Metonymy

Metonymy is a figure of language in which a thing is designated not by its own name but by the name of a thing resembling it or closely related to it. Metonymies are very common in everyday speech. "Give me a light," a man says, when he literally means that he wants some fire. "He is addicted to the bottle" is another way of saying that he drinks too much liquor. "I am studying Shakespeare" means that I am studying Shakespeare's plays, not the man himself. (Another example is the use of "Agatha Christie" in "A Fascinating Poet's Dream," p. 81.) In these metonymies a closely related object is substituted for the object itself.

Poets use metonymy to emphasize a significant detail and thereby to suggest something that the literal word does not suggest. For example, when the speaker of the twenty-third psalm (page 393) says of God that "He leadeth me beside the still waters," he reminds his readers of the calming, cleansing, purifying, and life-giving powers of water. This particular effect would be missing had he used such a word as *brook*, or *stream*, or *pond* rather than the metonymy *waters*. Similarly, in Frost's "Out, Out—" (page 39), the injured boy turns toward witnesses of the accident "Half in appeal, but half as if to keep/The *life* from spilling." The metonymy *life* for the literal word *blood* enables Frost to avoid gory detail and to focus the reader's attention on a major point of the poem: a young boy's life spilled out as though it were water.

Exercise 30

Identify the metonymies and discuss their use in these poems.

The Glories of Our Blood and State

The glories of our blood and state
  Are shadows, not substantial things;
There is no armor against fate;
  Death lays his icy hand on kings:
    Scepter and crown
    Must tumble down,
And in the dust be equal made,
With the poor crooked scythe and spade.

Some men with swords may reap the field,
  And plant fresh laurels where they kill;
But their strong nerves at last must yield;
  They tame but one another still:
    Early or late
    They stoop to fate,
And must give up their murmuring breath,
When they, pale captives, creep to death.

The garlands wither on your brow;
Then boast no more your mighty deeds;
Upon death's purple altar now,
See where the victor-victim bleeds:
Your heads must come
To the cold tomb.
Only the actions of the just
Smell sweet and blossom in their dust.

James Shirley
(1596–1666)

blood (1): lineage, family. *state* (1): status, social position.

Old Mary

My last defense
Is the present tense.

It little hurts me now to know
I shall not go

Cathedral-hunting in Spain
Nor cherrying in Michigan or Maine.

Gwendolyn Brooks
(1917–)

Epitaph on Himself

Good friend, for Jesus' sake forbear
To dig the dust enclosed here;
Blest be the man that spares these stones,
And curst be he that moves my bones.

William Shakespeare
(1564–1616)

With You a Part of Me Hath Passed Away

With you a part of me hath passed away;
For in the peopled forest of my mind
A tree made leafless by this wintry wind
Shall never don again its green array.

Chapel and fireside, country road and bay,
Have something of their friendliness resigned;
Another, if I would, I could not find,
And I am grown much older in a day.
But yet I treasure in my memory
Your gift of charity, your mellow ease,
And the dear honour of your amity;
For these once mine, my life is rich with these.
And I scarce know which part may greater be,—
What I keep of you, or you rob from me.

George Santayana
(1863–1952)

Disdain Returned

He that loves a rosy cheek,
  Or a coral lip admires,
Or from star-like eyes doth seek
  Fuel to maintain his fires;
As old Time makes these decay,
So his flames must waste away.

But a smooth and steadfast mind,
  Gentle thoughts and calm desires,
Hearts with equal love combined,
  Kindle never-dying fires.
Where these are not, I despise
Lovely cheeks, or lips, or eyes.

No tears, Celia, now shall win
  My resolved heart to return;
I have searched thy soul within,
  And find nought but pride and scorn;
I have learned thy arts, and now
  Can disdain as much as thou.
Some power, in my revenge, convey
That love to her I cast away.

Thomas Carew
(*c.* 1594/5–1639)

1. How and why does the poet avoid using the word *woman* or one of its synonyms in the first two stanzas?
2. For what experience is *fires* (lines 4, 10) a metonymy? Why has the poet not mentioned the experience directly?
3. Would the poem be improved by lopping off stanza 3? Justify your answer.

A great many metonymies—the *fires* of "Disdain Returned," for example—can also be regarded as metaphors. The label is of no importance, because the various figures of language cannot be separated into exclusive categories. Whether one calls *fires* a metonymy or a metaphor depends on how one looks at the figure. Understanding the functions of figures is more important than giving them tags. Many of the best figures, moreover, escape notice that they *are* figures until they have been carefully examined. And frequently the best figures invite examination from more than one angle.

Personification

Personification is a figure that bestows human traits on something nonhuman. It compares the nonhuman with the human and is thus a kind of metaphor in which one member is always a human being. Animals, objects, natural phenomena, and ideas may be personified. Like metonymy, personification occurs frequently in common speech. "She won't run," a driver says of a stalled car. "Money talks." "Let's get out of this raging storm." In personifying car, money, and storm nobody visualizes them as people. Similarly, while poets do not always expect their readers to visualize their personifications, sometimes they do want such visualization.

Exercise 31

Study the personifications in these poems.

Drinking

The thirsty earth soaks up the rain,
And drinks and gapes for drink again;
The plants suck in the earth, and are

With constant drinking fresh and fair;
The sea itself, which one would think
Should have but little need of drink,
Drinks ten thousand rivers up,
So filled that they o'erflow the cup.
The busy sun—and one would guess
By's drunken fiery face no less—
Drinks up the sea, and when he's done,
The moon and stars drink up the sun:
They drink and dance by their own light
They drink and revel all the night.
Nothing in nature's sober found,
But an eternal health goes round.
Fill up the bowl, then, fill it high!
Fill all the glasses there: for why
Should every creature drink but I?
Why, man of morals, tell me why?

Abraham Cowley
(1618–1667)

1. Which of these personifications are also visual images? Which are not?
2. How would changing the order of the drinkers weaken the poem?
3. Why are there so many overstatements in the poem?
4. What is the main flaw in the argument? Does the flaw increase the reader's enjoyment of the poem? How?

On the Death of Dr. Robert Levet

Condemn'd to hope's delusive mine,
  As on we toil from day to day,
By sudden blasts, or slow decline,
  Our social comforts drop away.

Well tried through many a varying year,
  See Levet to the grave descend;
Officious, innocent, sincere,
  Of ev'ry friendless name the friend.

Yet still he fills affection's eye,
  Obscurely wise, and coarsely kind;
Nor, letter'd arrogance, deny
  Thy praise to merit unrefin'd.

When fainting nature call'd for aid,
  And hov'ring death prepar'd the blow,
His vig'rous remedy display'd
  The power of art without the show.

In misery's darkest caverns known,
  His useful care was ever nigh,
Where hopeless anguish pour'd his groan,
  And lonely want retir'd to die.

No summons mock'd by chill delay,
  No petty gain disdain'd by pride,
The modest wants of ev'ry day
  The toil of ev'ry day supplied.

His virtues walk'd their narrow round,
  Nor made a pause, nor left a void;
And sure th' Eternal Master found
  The single talent well employ'd.

The busy day, the peaceful night,
  Unfelt, uncounted, glided by;
His frame was firm, his powers were bright,
  Tho' now his eightieth year was nigh.

Then with no throbbing fiery pain,
  No cold gradations of decay,
Death broke at once the vital chain,
  And free'd his soul the nearest way.

Samuel Johnson
(1709–1784)

Levet (title): a physician who practiced among the poor of London, lived more or less at Johnson's expense, and died in Johnson's house in 1782. *officious* (7): helpful. *talent* (28): See Matthew xxv:14–30.

1. Who is "condemned" (line 1)? Who is "tried" (line 5)?
2. Why is hope's mine called "delusive" (line 1)?
3. Why are the words *letter'd arrogance* (line 11) set off by commas?
4. What opinion does the poet seem to have of most physicians other than Levet?
5. Show how the figure of personification enables the poet to say much in a small space.

To Autumn

Season of mists and mellow fruitfulness,
Close bosom-friend of the maturing sun;
Conspiring with him how to load and bless
With fruit the vines that round the thatch-eves run;
To bend with apples the moss'd cottage-trees,
And fill all fruit with ripeness to the core;
To swell the gourd, and plump the hazel shells
With a sweet kernel; to set budding more,
And still more, later flowers for the bees,
Until they think warm days will never cease,
For Summer has o'er-brimm'd their clammy cells.

Who hath not seen thee oft amid thy store?
Sometimes whoever seeks abroad may find
Thee sitting careless on a granary floor,
Thy hair soft-lifted by the winnowing wind;
Or on a half-reap'd furrow sound asleep,
Drows'd with the fume of poppies, while thy hook
Spares the next swath and all its twined flowers:
And sometimes like a gleaner thou dost keep
Steady thy laden head across a brook;
Or by a cyder-press, with patient look,
Thou watchest the last oozings hours by hours.

Where are the songs of Spring? Ay, where are they?
Think not of them, thou hast thy music too,—
While barred clouds bloom the soft-dying day,
And touch the stubble-plains with rosy hue;
Then in a wailful choir the small gnats mourn
Among the river sallows, borne aloft
Or sinking as the light wind lives or dies;
And full-grown lambs loud bleat from hilly bourn;
Hedge-crickets sing; and now with treble soft
The red-breast whistles from a garden-croft;
And gathering swallows twitter in the skies.

John Keats
(1795–1821)

1. Where is the first suggestion of personification? As what is Autumn personified? Is the personification effective and appropriate? Does it continue to the end of the poem?

2. Explain these metonymies: *hook* (line 17); *treble* (line 31); *red-breast* (line 32).
3. Does the same kind of imagery predominate in each stanza?
4. Locate every word that relates to time. Then discuss the truth or falsity of these statements: the poem covers the period of a year; the poem covers a period of about three months; the poem covers the period of a day.
5. What words have unpleasant connotations? Why are they in the poem?
6. Where are there suggestions of melancholy? What causes this melancholy?

How Do I Love Thee

How do I love thee? Let me count the ways.
I love thee to the depth and breadth and height
My soul can reach, when feeling out of sight
For the ends of Being and ideal Grace.
I love thee to the level of everyday's
Most quiet need, by sun and candle-light.
I love thee freely, as men strive for Right;
I love thee purely, as they turn from Praise.
I love thee with the passion put to use
In my old griefs, and with my childhood's faith.
I love thee with a love I seemed to lose
With my lost saints—I love thee with the breath,
Smiles, tears, of all my life!—and, if God choose,
I shall but love thee better after death.

Elizabeth Barrett Browning
(1806–1861)

Death Stands above Me

Death stands above me, whispering low
I know not what into my ear:
Of his strange language all I know
Is, there is not a word of fear.

Walter Savage Landor
(1775–1864)

Apostrophe

Apostrophe is a figure in which the absent are addressed as though present, the dead as though living, the inanimate as though animate. In its last-mentioned use it is closely related to personification, for if a poet addresses inanimate things he necessarily personifies them. The root meaning of *apostrophe* is "a turning away." In the last line of "Drinking" (p. 157), the speaker turns away from his course of thought and directly addresses an imaginary man who, he pretends, has been listening to him all along. An apostrophe may come at the very beginning of a poem, as in Blake's "Tyger" (page 188) or any other poem written in the second person. Successful apostrophes add immediacy, excitement, and intensity to a poem. There is nothing, however, more frigid and absurd than an unsuccessful apostrophe. A disaster occurs when a feeble poet embellishes a confused thought with apostrophe and personification.

Stay with me, Poesy! playmate of childhood!
  Friend of my manhood! delight of my youth!
Roamer with me over valley and wildwood,
  Searcher for loveliness, groping for Truth.

Charles Mackay
(1814–1889)

For an effective apostrophe to contrast with this excerpt, see Wordsworth's sonnet addressed to Milton (page 255).

Exercise 32

Adieu, Farewell, Earth's Bliss

Adieu, farewell, earth's bliss!
This world uncertain is;
Fond are life's lustful joys,
Death proves them all but toys,
None from his darts can fly;
I am sick, I must die:
    Lord, have mercy on us!

Rich men, trust not in wealth,
Gold cannot buy you health;
Physic himself must fade;
All things to end are made.
The plague full swift goes by;
I am sick, I must die:
    Lord, have mercy on us!

Beauty is but a flower
Which wrinkles will devour;
Brightness falls from the air,
Queens have died young and fair,
Dust hath closed Helen's eye.
I am sick, I must die:
    Lord, have mercy on us!

Strength stoops unto the grave,
Worms feed on Hector brave,
Swords may not fight with fate;
Earth still holds ope her gate.
Come! come! the bells do cry.
I am sick, I must die:
    Lord, have mercy on us!

Wit with his wantonness
Tasteth death's bitterness;
Hell's executioner
Hath no ears for to hear
What vain art can reply.
I am sick, I must die:
    Lord, have mercy on us!

Haste, therefore, each degree,
To welcome destiny.
Heaven is our heritage,
Earth but a player's stage;
Mount we unto the sky.
I am sick, I must die:
    Lord, have mercy on us!

Thomas Nashe
(1567–1601)

Physic (10): medicine. *Helen* (19): most beautiful of women; her abduction caused the Trojan War. *Hector* (24): bravest of Trojans, in Homer's *Iliad*.

1. Is the last line of each stanza an apostrophe? If it is, how does it differ from the other apostrophes in the poem?
2. Why are the two characters from the Troy legend mentioned?
3. Give the literal equivalents of *gate* (line 25), *hell's executioner* (line 31), *vain art* (line 33), and *degree* (line 36).
4. Would line 17 be improved if it read, as some scholars have said it was meant to be read, "Brightness falls from the hair"? Why or why not?
5. Does the world seem attractive or unattractive to this dying man? Support your answer with details from the poem.

Star

If, in the light of things, you fade
real, yet wanly withdrawn
to our determined and appropriate
distance, like the moon left on
all night among the leaves, may
you invisibly delight this house,
O star, doubly compassionate, who came
too soon for twilight, too late
for dawn, may your faint flame
strive with the worst in us
through chaos
with the passion of
plain day.

Derek Walcott
(1930–)

Paradox

A **paradox** is a statement that seems at first glance to be self-contradictory or opposed to common sense yet is found upon investigation to express a truth. "Make haste slowly" seems to be contradictory advice; a moment's thought about *haste,* however, will show that it is being used here in the sense of long-run progress. The paradox depends on the various possible meanings of *haste* in this context. We can resolve the paradox when we reconcile the apparent contradiction and discover the truth behind it.

A Lame Beggar

"I am unable," yonder beggar cries,
"To stand or move!" If he say true, he lies.

John Donne
(1572–1631)

The paradox of Donne's beggar who simultaneously lies and tells the truth is easily resolved. The word *lies* is a pun, or play on words. A **pun** is an intentional confusion of two words that sound similar but differ in meaning. Many oral riddles are paradoxical because they contain puns; "black and white and red (read) all over," for example, describes a newspaper. "Whether life is worth living or not depends on the liver" is another punning statement. All puns, by the way, are not necessarily contemptible.

Exercise 33

Examine the paradoxes in these poems and resolve them.

The Pulley

When God at first made man,
Having a glass of blessings standing by,
Let us, said he, pour on him all we can.
Let the world's riches, which dispersèd lie,
Contract into a span.

So strength first made a way,
Then beauty flowed, then wisdom, honor, pleasure.
When almost all was out, God made a stay,
Perceiving that alone of all his treasure
Rest in the bottom lay.

For if I should, said he,
Bestow this jewel also on my creature,
He would adore my gifts instead of me,
And rest in nature, not the God of nature:
So both should losers be.

Yet let him keep the rest,
But keep them with repining restlessness.
Let him be rich and weary, that at least
If goodness lead him not, yet weariness
May toss him to my breast.

George Herbert
(1593–1633)

1. Describe the situation in the first stanza.
2. In the Greek myth, Pandora let everything out of the chest except Hope. Here, all good things except one are poured on man. What is left in the glass?
3. Give some synonyms for the first word of line 10.
4. Explain why this particular gift is kept back.
5. Resolve the punning paradox of lines 16–17.
6. What is the significance of the title?

A Choice of Weapons

Sticks and stones are hard on bones.
Aimed with angry art,
Words can sting like anything.
But silence breaks the heart.

Phyllis McGinley
(1905–)

The Day

The day was a year at first
When children ran in the garden;
The day shrank down to a month
When the boys played ball.

The day was a week thereafter
When young men walked in the garden;
The day was itself a day
When love grew tall.

The day shrank down to an hour
When old men limped in the garden;
The day will last forever
When it is nothing at all.

Theodore Spencer
(1902–1949)

To Lucasta, Going to the Wars

Tell me not, sweet, I am unkind,
  That from the nunnery
Of thy chaste breast and quiet mind,
  To war and arms I fly.

True, a new mistress now I chase:
  The first foe in the field;
And with a stronger faith embrace
  A sword, a horse, a shield.

Yet this inconstancy is such
  As you, too, shall adore;
I could not love thee, dear, so much,
  Loved I not honor more.

Richard Lovelace
(1618–*c.* 1658)

1. What is the relationship between the speaker and the listener? What is the occasion?
2. What has the speaker decided to do even before the poem begins?
3. Cite evidence that the listener wants him to do something else.
4. What means does the speaker use to convince the listener?
5. Discuss the language of the poem, using the terms *metaphor, paradox, pun,* and *personification.*

Of Treason

Treason doth never prosper. What's the reason?
For if it prosper, none dare call it treason.

Sir John Harington
(1561–1612)

I Counsel You Beware

Good creatures, do you love your lives
  And have you ears for sense?
Here is a knife like other knives,
  That cost me eighteen pence.

I need but stick it in my heart
  And down will come the sky,
And earth's foundations will depart
  And all you folk will die.

A. E. Housman
(1859–1936)

Batter My Heart, Three-Personed God

Batter my heart, three-personed God, for you
As yet but knock, breathe, shine, and seek to mend;
That I may rise and stand, o'erthrow me, and bend
Your force to break, blow, burn, and make me new.
I, like an usurped town to another due,
Labor to admit you, but oh, to no end;
Reason, your viceroy in me, me should defend,
But is captived, and proves weak or untrue.
Yet dearly I love you, and would be lovèd fain,
But am betrothed unto your enemy;
Divorce me, untie or break that knot again;
Take me to you, imprison me, for I,
Except you enthrall me, never shall be free,
Nor ever chaste, except you ravish me.

John Donne
(1572–1631)

fain (9) : gladly. *enemy* (10) : Satan. *enthrall* (13) : enslave.

Crazy Jane Talks with the Bishop

I met the Bishop on the road
And much said he and I.
"Those breasts are flat and fallen now,
Those veins must soon be dry;
Live in a heavenly mansion
Not in some foul sty."

"Fair and foul are near of kin,
And fair needs foul," I cried.
"My friends are gone, but that's a truth
Nor grave nor bed denied,
Learned in bodily lowliness
And in the heart's pride.

"A woman can be proud and stiff
When on love intent;
But Love has pitched his mansion in
The place of excrement;
For nothing can be sole or whole
That has not been rent."

William Butler Yeats
(1865–1939)

Ambiguity in Poems

A poem communicates an experience that cannot be communicated by ordinary literal language. It does so by means of figurative language, which gives depth and richness to the experience. Some poems are so rich in figurative language that they convey two or even more experiences simultaneously. Since 1930, when William Empson published his *Seven Types of Ambiguity,* the term **ambiguity** has been given to the multiple meanings that a single poem may communicate. The term is perhaps not the best one that might be chosen to describe this phenomenon, because in nonpoetic discourse it denotes two or more incompatible meanings. For instance, the statement "My old uncle has a hearty appetite, and he is very fond of babies" contains the ambiguous word *fond*. In this context the word has two incompatible meanings: "feels affection for" and "likes to eat." The statement is inexact because the old gentleman cannot be fond of babies in both these ways. Ambiguities in prose are either comic or puzzling or both: "This monument was erected to the memory of John Smith, who was shot, as a mark of affection by his brother." "Mr. Jones has just received a letter from Mr. Smith, saying that he will deliver the next annual address." "Lost: a dog belonging to Mr. Brown, who has brass studs on his collar." But as it has come to be applied to poems, the term *ambiguity* denotes multiple meanings that are compatible with one another.

Neither Out Far Nor In Deep

The people along the sand
All turn and look one way.
They turn their back on the land.
They look at the sea all day.

As long as it takes to pass
A ship keeps raising its hull;
The wetter ground like glass
Reflects a standing gull.

The land may vary more;
But wherever the truth may be—
The water comes ashore,
And the people look at the sea.

They cannot look out far.
They cannot look in deep.
But when was that ever a bar
To any watch they keep?

Robert Frost
(1874–1963)

In this poem Frost finds considerable significance in a perfectly natural phenomenon in human behavior. Nearly everyone who has been to the seashore is aware that people usually take up positions on the beach facing the sea. There is certainly not much to be seen out there: an occasional ship passing in the distance, or nearer at hand a seagull reflected in the tidal waves that wash the shore. In fact, the poem implies, the land is more varied (line 9) and hence more interesting. Nevertheless, the people on the beach continue to stare out at the sea. Even the water moves toward the shore (line 11), apparently showing more sense than the people.

The speaker's response to this peculiar situation is ambiguous. Are the people to be condemned for staring at the monotonous sea when they could be observing the more interesting land? Are they mesmerized by the movements of the sea? Does the poet regard their behavior as foolish? "They cannot look out far," he says in line 13—about five miles on a very clear day—nor very deeply into the waters. Why is it, then, that they keep watching? Do they have to stare at the sea? The resolution of these ambiguities is contained in the question that ends the poem. The question implies that man's endeavors to grasp what is beyond his knowledge, his efforts to achieve absolute truths, are bound to end in failure. But the question also implies that such seeming follies are admirable signs of man's indomitable aspirations. In other words, both points of view are true at the same time. The ambiguity allows for multiple simultaneous responses.

At this point two distinctions are necessary. First, the reader must distinguish between an ambiguity that enriches a poem and one that does not. A poem like Mackay's "Only a Thought" (page 106) is ambiguous in a bad sense; it does not communicate even a single definite experience, let alone two experiences. Second, the reader must distinguish between ambiguities that he finds in a poem because he does not thoroughly understand it and ambiguities that are actually in the poem. Making this distinction is not easy. It becomes easier as the reader learns to focus his attention on the poem itself rather than on his own reactions to it. Poems may be ambiguous, but there is no poem so ambiguous that it can mean anything that a particular reader would like it to mean.

Exercise 34

Discuss the contribution made by figurative language to the experiences in these poems.

Each More Melodious Note

Each more melodious note I hear
Brings sad reproach to me,
That I alone afford the ear,
Who would the music be.

Henry David Thoreau
(1817–1862)

At Birth

Come from a distant country,
Bundle of flesh, of blood,
Demanding painful entry,
Expecting little good:
There is no going back
Among those thickets where
Both night and day are black
And blood's the same as air.

Strangely you come to meet us,
Stained, mottled, as if dead:
You bridge the dark hiatus
Through which your body slid
Across a span of muscle,
A breadth my hand can span.
The gorged and brimming vessel
Flows over, and is man.

Dear daughter, as I watched you
Come crumpled from the womb,
And sweating hands had fetched you
Into this world, the room
Opened before your coming
Like water struck from rocks
And echoed with your crying
Your living paradox.

Anthony Thwaite
(1930–   )

To Althea, from Prison

When love with unconfinèd wings
  Hovers within my gates,
And my divine Althea brings
  To whisper at the grates;
When I lie tangled in her hair,
  And fettered to her eye,
The gods that wanton in the air
  Know no such liberty.

When flowing cups run swiftly round
  With no allaying Thames,
Our careless heads with roses bound,
  Our hearts with loyal flames;
When thirsty grief in wine we steep,
  When healths and draughts go free,
Fishes that tipple in the deep
  Know no such liberty.

When, like committed linnets, I
  With shriller throat shall sing
The sweetness, mercy, majesty,
  And glories of my King;
When I shall voice aloud how good
  He is, how great should be,
Enlargèd winds that curl the flood
  Know no such liberty.

Stone walls do not a prison make,
  Nor iron bars a cage;
Minds innocent and quiet take
  That for an hermitage;
If I have freedom in my love,
  And in my soul am free,
Angels alone that soar above
  Enjoy such liberty.

Richard Lovelace
(1618–1658)

King (20): Charles I, in whose cause Lovelace was imprisoned in 1642, just before civil war broke out between the King and the Parliament. *linnets* (17): finches, songbirds.

Still, Citizen Sparrow

Still, citizen sparrow, this vulture which you call
Unnatural, let him but lumber again to air
Over the rotten office, let him bear
The carrion ballast up, and at the tall

Tip of the sky lie cruising. Then you'll see
That no more beautiful bird is in heaven's height,
No wider more placid wings, no watchfuller flight;
He shoulders nature there, the frightfully free,

The naked-headed one. Pardon him, you
Who dart in the orchard aisles, for it is he
Devours death, mocks mutability,
Has heart to make an end, keeps nature new.

Thinking of Noah, childheart, try to forget
How for so many bedlam hours his saw
Soured the song of birds with its wheezy gnaw,
And the slam of his hammer all the day beset

The people's ears. Forget that he could bear
To see the towns like coral under the keel,
And the fields so dismal deep. Try rather to feel
How high and weary it was, on the waters where

He rocked his only world, and everyone's.
Forgive the hero, you who would have died
Gladly with all you knew; he rode that tide
To Ararat; all men are Noah's sons.

Richard Wilbur
(1921–)

They Flee from Me

They flee from me that sometime did me seek,
  With naked foot stalking in my chamber.
I have seen them gentle, tame, and meek,
  That now are wild, and do not remember
  That sometime they put themself in danger
To take bread at my hand; and now they range
Busily seeking with a continual change.

Thanked be fortune, it hath been otherwise
  Twenty times better; but once, in special,
In thin array, after a pleasant guise,
  When her loose gown from her shoulders did fall,
  And she me caught in her arms long and small,
Therewith all sweetly did me kiss,
And softly said, "Dear heart, how like you this?"

It was no dream; I lay broad waking.
  But all is turned thorough my gentleness,
Into a strange fashion of forsaking;
  And I have leave to go of her goodness,
  And she also to use newfangleness.
But since that I so kindly am served,
I would fain know what she hath deserved.

Sir Thomas Wyatt
(1503–1542)

in special (9): especially. *after . . . guise* (10): in a pleasant fashion. *small* (12): slender. *thorough* (16): through. *use newfangleness* (19): search for new experiences. *kindly* (20): naturally; also ironically with modern meaning.

6. Symbolism and Allegory in Poems

The use of symbols has a certain power of emancipation and exhilaration for all men. We seem to be touched by a wand which makes us dance and run about happily, like children.

Ralph Waldo Emerson

Symbols are probably as old as the human race. Prehistoric men scratched the figures of animals on the walls of their caves, apparently hoping to influence the hunt by such magical symbols. Almost all religions have used symbols as visible signs of the invisible. Nations use them as signs of nationhood in flags, emblems, and seals. The commercial world also has its symbols: the red and white striped pole outside a barbershop, the three balls over a pawnbroker's, the dollar sign. Many trademarks, logos, and designs are symbols. Symbolism is more common in real life than it is in literature.

Since symbolism is a relatively rare phenomenon in literature, the reader who has just learned to identify symbols must beware of assuming that every poem contains a hidden symbol that he must discover and then interpret. Reading poems is not solving puzzles. Poets, moreover, do not hide their meaning behind symbols; instead they use symbols to present their meaning. The poem itself will indicate whether or not a given object or event is to be understood symbolically. If a poem contains symbolism, its language will ordinarily be more serious and intense than the language required in a literal treatment of the subject. And, since a reader can seldom be absolutely certain that a particular symbol has a particular significance, he should avoid dogmatism in all his discussions of symbolism.

Symbols in Literature

Literary symbols are best defined functionally—that is, according to how they work. A **literary symbol** is a thing (or an event, person, quality, or relationship) that functions simultaneously in two ways: as itself and as a sign of something outside itself. Hence a literary symbol differs greatly from a symbol like the dollar sign. A dollar sign merely indicates that the number it precedes is to be understood as an amount of money; the sign is not part of the money itself, nor does it have anything more than an arbitrary connection with the money. A literary symbol, in contrast, seems to be part of what it stands for.

An examination of a particular symbol will make the definition clearer. The moon is a symbol in the following poem; in this text every reference to it has been italicized.

Strange Fits of Passion Have I Known

Strange fits of passion have I known:
And I will dare to tell,
But in the Lover's ear alone,
What once to me befell.

When she I loved looked every day
Fresh as a rose in June,
I to her cottage bent my way,
Beneath an *evening-moon.*

Upon the *moon* I fixed my eye,
All over the wide lea;
With quickening pace my horse drew nigh
Those paths so dear to me.

And now we reached the orchard-plot;
And, as we climbed the hill,
The *sinking moon* to Lucy's cot
Came near, and nearer still.

In one of those sweet dreams I slept,
Kind Nature's gentlest boon!
And all the while my eyes I kept
On the *descending moon.*

My horse moved on; hoof after hoof
He raised, and never stopped:
When down behind the cottage roof,
At once, the *bright moon dropped.*

What fond and wayward thoughts will slide
Into a Lover's head!
"O mercy!" to myself I cried,
"If Lucy should be dead!"

William Wordsworth
(1770–1850)

Notice that the moon functions first as a moon and only gradually takes on symbolical significance. A bright object in the sky, it lights the lover on his way as he rides to visit his sweetheart. Along with the hill, the orchard-plot, and the cottage, it is part of the landscape described in the poem. But the moon is also an actor in the drama. At first only an "evening moon" (line 8), it becomes a "sinking moon" (line 15) and a "descending moon" (line 20); then suddenly (line 24) it vanishes. Lucy's cottage, of course, blocks the lover's view of it. But this common-sense explanation never occurs to the lover, who has been gazing at it and thinking of Lucy until she and the moon have merged in his waking dream. The sudden blotting out of the moon's brightness symbolizes to him the death of Lucy. She is the light of his life, and that light may go out as the moon has gone out. The moon, then, functions as a literary symbol: (1) it is literally a moon; (2) it also stands for a possible disaster—the death of Lucy; (3) by suddenly disappearing, it behaves in such a way that it seems to participate in the disaster—that is, it has been identified with Lucy in the lover's mind.

It is useful to make a distinction between two kinds of literary symbols: conventional and nonce.

Conventional Symbols

A **conventional symbol** is an object or an action that has taken on a certain significance through customary association and general agreement. It is a common symbol, both literary and nonliterary. A cross, a flag, a wedding ring, a black mourning band on a coat sleeve—these are all conventional symbols. Similarly, a statue of a blindfolded woman holding scales in one hand and a sword in the other is a conventional symbol of Justice; a playful cherub (Cupid) carrying a bow and arrows symbolizes Love. In literature darkness can conventionally symbolize death; light, wisdom; roses, romantic love. A reader of Tennyson's "Crossing the Bar" (page 80) will understand the speaker's embarkation as his dying; the autumn of Shakespeare's "Sonnet 73" (page 131) inevitably suggests old age; and Shirley's "The Glories of Our Blood and State" (page 154) includes numerous conventional symbols.

The Funeral Rites of the Rose

The Rose was sick and, smiling, died;
And, being to be sanctified,
About the bed there sighing stood
The sweet and flowery sisterhood:
Some hung the head, while some did bring,
To wash her, water from the spring;
Some laid her forth, while others wept,
But all a solemn fast there kept.
The holy sisters, some among,
The sacred dirge and trental sung.
But ah! what sweets smelt everywhere,
As Heaven had spent all perfumes there.
At last, when prayers for the dead
And rites were all accomplishèd,
They, weeping, spread a lawny loom,
And closed her up as in a tomb.

Robert Herrick
(1591–1674)

trental (10): Originally a set of thirty requiem masses; but here used loosely to mean a dirge. *lawny loom* (15): a finely spun pall or shroud.

That this rose is more than a literal flower is clearly indicated by the anthropomorphic language—that is, the language referring to human beings and human events; roses do not smile (line 1), nor are they sanctified (line 2). Although other flowers might be regarded as figuratively weeping (a metaphor for the dew on them) when a rose dies, they certainly do not, even figuratively, fast or sing trentals (lines 8, 10). And it is ludicrous to suppose that they would cover a dead rose with a shroud (line 15). Thus, while the poem talks about flowers, it is signifying—or symbolizing—something more.

The further significance becomes clear when the reader reflects that the rose is a conventional symbol of love, of beauty, and of the beloved person. The poem can accommodate all three of these significations. Herrick may be dramatizing his love for another person, a love that has died and has been buried "as in a tomb." He may be lamenting the death of a beautiful woman, whose passing is regretted by all the "sisterhood" of lovely women whose beauty is equally perishable. He may even be mourning his own sweetheart's untimely death. Literally he is talking about the death of a rose, but he is simultaneously talking about these other things as well.

Exercise 35

Identify and discuss the conventional symbols in these poems.

Sixty-Eighth Birthday

As life runs on, the road grows strange
With faces new, and near the end
The milestones into headstones change,
'Neath every one a friend.

James Russell Lowell
(1819–1891)

To Know the Dark

To go in the dark with a light is to know the light.
To know the dark, go dark. Go without sight,
and find that the dark, too, blooms and sings,
and is traveled by dark feet and dark wings.

Wendell Berry
(1934–)

Credo

I cannot find my way: there is no star
In all the shrouded heavens anywhere;
And there is not a whisper in the air
Of any living voice but one so far
That I can hear it only as a bar
Of lost, imperial music, played when fair
And angel fingers wove, and unaware,
Dead leaves to garlands where no roses are.

No, there is not a glimmer, nor a call,
For one that welcomes, welcomes when he fears,
The black and awful chaos of the night;
For through it all—above, beyond it all—
I know the far-sent message of the years,
I feel the coming glory of the Light.

Edwin Arlington Robinson
(1869–1935)

Up-Hill

Does the road wind up-hill all the way?
  Yes, to the very end.
Will the day's journey take the whole long day?
  From morn to night, my friend.

But is there for the night a resting-place?
  A roof for when the slow, dark hours begin.
May not the darkness hide it from my face?
  You cannot miss that inn.

Shall I meet other wayfarers at night?
  Those who have gone before.
Then must I knock, or call when just in sight?
  They will not keep you standing at that door.

Shall I find comfort, travel-sore and weak?
  Of labour you shall find the sum.
Will there be beds for me and all who seek?
  Yea, beds for all who come.

Christina G. Rossetti
(1830–1894)

The Road Not Taken

Two roads diverged in a yellow wood,
And sorry I could not travel both
And be one traveler, long I stood
And looked down one as far as I could
To where it bent in the undergrowth;

Then took the other, as just as fair,
And having perhaps the better claim,
Because it was grassy and wanted wear;
Though as for that, the passing there
Had worn them really about the same,

And both that morning equally lay
In leaves no step had trodden black.
Oh, I kept the first for another day!
Yet knowing how way leads on to way,
I doubted if I should ever come back.

I shall be telling this with a sigh
Somewhere ages and ages hence:
Two roads diverged in a wood, and I—
I took the one less traveled by,
And that has made all the difference.

Robert Frost
(1874–1963)

Nonce Symbols

A **nonce symbol** is a symbol that the writer invents "for the nonce"—that is, for a particular purpose or occasion. Nonce symbols occur mainly in poems written during the last century and a half. Before that time poets and other writers drew their symbols from the large body of traditional symbolism, especially from the symbolism of Christianity and the rituals of Christian churches. But with the decline of universally accepted religious beliefs and rituals, poets, including Christian poets, began to invent private symbols. This tendency was largely abetted by the so-called Symbolist movement in French poetry from about the middle of the nineteenth century on. The Symbolist poets were interested in expressing intimate, private, often visionary experiences. Some of them used alcohol or drugs to induce hallucinations or to derange their senses, hoping to achieve fresh or heightened sense experiences. To relay these experiences in poems demanded the use of private symbolism.

But even before the Symbolist movement there were poets who used private symbols to express experiences that could not be stated in any other language.

The Sick Rose

O Rose, thou art sick!
The invisible worm
That flies in the night,
In the howling storm,

Has found out thy bed
Of crimson joy:
And his dark secret love
Does thy life destroy.

William Blake
(1757–1827)

If the reader takes the rose in this poem to be a conventional symbol for love or for beauty or for both love and beauty, he still faces the problem of what the worm (line 2) symbolizes. Whatever it is, it is not good. By devoting as much of his poem to the worm as to the sick rose, Blake communicates images of nastiness that are quite different from the pretty images in Herrick's poem on the same subject. The adjective *invisible* (line 2) suggests that the worm comes from the unseen world of evil; real worms do not make "dark secret love" (line 7). The "howling storm" (line 4) suggests a catastrophe far greater than the destruction of a literal rose. Blake's worm seems (*seems* is a very useful word in any discussion of symbolism) to symbolize the unseen forces that destroy love and beauty: materialism, greed, hypocrisy, deceit, prudery, neurosis—the list is endless. The symbol cannot be paraphrased as one particular evil; Blake apparently used a symbol because it enabled him to suggest many kinds of evil.

Identifying and Interpreting Symbols

A symbol can be regarded as a figure that goes two steps beyond a simile and one step beyond a metaphor. "My love is like a star" is a simile; "My love is a star," a metaphor. "My star" could be, in the right context, a symbol for "my love." In a symbol there is little question of comparison; one part of the figure completely replaces the other. Blake would have expressed his thoughts metaphorically rather than symbolically had he said or implied, "Evil is a worm." Instead, he concentrated entirely on the worm. The method of symbolism is to dwell on the subject with such particularity and in such a way that it takes on more than a literal meaning.

The difference between symbols and figures of comparison can be illustrated by contrasting two poems of Rainer Maria Rilke (1875–1926). First, a poem that uses an explicit figure of comparison:

The Swan

This toiling to go through something yet
undone, heavily and as though in bonds,
is like the ungainly gait of the swan.

And dying, this no longer grasping
of that ground on which we daily stand,
like his anxious letting-himself-down—:

into the waters, which receive him smoothly
and which, as though happy and bygone,
draw back underneath him, flow on flow;
while he, infinitely still and sure,
ever more maturely and more royally
and more serenely deigns to draw along.

(*translated by M. D. Herter Norton*)

Here the actions of a swan laboriously waddling across land to the bank of a stream, letting himself down, and then smoothly sailing along are compared with the life of a man: first the struggle through a life to be lived; then the anxiety-ridden dying; then, finally, the masterful serenity of death. The poet has seen the actions of a swan as the metaphorical equivalent of man's life. A symbolical poem would not mention living and dying, but would concentrate on the swan's actions.

The Panther

His vision from the passing by of bars
Has grown so tired that it holds nothing more.
It seems to him there are a thousand bars,
And out beyond those thousand bars no world.

His supple lope and flexibly strong strides,
That always in the smallest circle turn,
Are like a dance of strength around a middle
In which, benumbed, a great will stands.

Just sometimes does the veil upon his eye
Silently rise; then goes an image in,
Goes through the nervous poise of his still limbs,
And ceases, in his heart, to be.

(translated by Peter J. Seng)

Here Rilke concentrates entirely on a restless, caged panther. But he intuits the psychology of the beast in such a way as to suggest that the panther is simultaneously a beast and something more. A caged panther may feel that many bars hold him in; the generalization in line 4, however, is far beyond the mental powers of any animal. Rilke invites the reader to regard the panther as any caged being, caught behind the bars of a limited world and yearning for a greater world beyond, but deadened to that greater world by the years of his captivity. One of the possible interpretations of the symbol might be as follows:

The panther represents man, who is a caged animal in the physical world: he longs for a world of changeless perfection but is trapped in this world which is mutable and stained. His years of captivity to matter and flesh have dulled his vision so that only rarely is he aware of a world outside his cage; in the rare moments when he does have a vision of the changeless perfection of another world, that vision fades when it reaches his practical and human heart. But the numbed longing persists, and whatever he does in his cage-world is simply a dance around a will doomed to frustration.

Exercise 36

Which of the following poems use symbolism? Which do not? Discuss the contribution that symbolism makes to those poems that do employ it.

I Saw a Chapel All of Gold

I saw a chapel all of gold
That none did dare to enter in,
And many weeping stood without,
Weeping, mourning, worshipping.

I saw a serpent rise between
The white pillars of the door,
And he forc'd & forc'd & forc'd;
Down the golden hinges tore,

And along the pavement sweet,
Set with pearls & rubies bright,
All his shining length he drew,
Till upon the altar white

Vomiting his poison out
On the bread & on the wine.
So I turn'd into a sty,
And laid me down among the swine.

William Blake
(1757–1827)

1. What details in this poem suggest that it must have more than a literal meaning?
2. The narrative suggests a defilement of the chapel that leads the speaker to degrade himself. What human experiences can you suggest that would seem to follow this pattern?
3. Point out any conventional symbols in the poem. What interpretations do these symbols suggest?

The Tyger

Tyger! Tyger! burning bright
In the forests of the night,
What immortal hand or eye
Could frame thy fearful symmetry?

In what distant deeps or skies
Burnt the fire of thine eyes?
On what wings dare he aspire?
What the hand dare seize the fire?

And what shoulder, and what art,
Could twist the sinews of thy heart?
And when thy heart began to beat,
What dread hand? and what dread feet?

What the hammer? what the chain?
In what furnace was thy brain?
What the anvil? what dread grasp
Dare its deadly terrors clasp?

When the stars threw down their spears,
And water'd heaven with their tears,
Did he smile his work to see?
Did he who made the Lamb make thee?

Tyger! Tyger! burning bright
In the forests of the night,
What immortal hand or eye,
Dare frame thy fearful symmetry?

William Blake
(1757–1827)

1. Is the speaker's wonder caused solely by the tiger or by something else?
2. Could the tiger symbolize all the things in the world that are cunning, powerful, and rapacious? If so, what could the lamb (line 20) represent?
3. Could the tiger symbolize all the beauty in the world?
4. The Bible compares the devil to a "roaring lion, [that] walketh about, seeking whom he may devour." Is the tiger perhaps meant to be the devil?

5. What is the effect of so many unanswered questions?
6. Does the poem anywhere suggest that the tiger and the lamb are one and the same?
7. What event could be referred to in lines 17–19?
8. Agree or disagree with this statement: "The last stanza is unnecessary because it merely repeats the first."

The Windhover: To Christ Our Lord

I caught this morning morning's minion, king-
  dom of daylight's dauphin, dapple-dawn-drawn Falcon, in his riding
  Of the rolling level underneath him steady air, and striding
High there, how he rung upon the rein of a wimpling wing
In his ecstasy! then off, off forth on swing,
  As a skate's heel sweeps smooth on a bow-bend: the hurl and gliding
  Rebuffed the big wind. My heart in hiding
Stirred for a bird,—the achieve of, the mastery of the thing!

Brute beauty and valour and act, oh, air, pride, plume, here
  Buckle! AND the fire that breaks from thee then, a billion
Times told lovelier, more dangerous, O my chevalier!

  No wonder of it: sheer plod makes plough down sillion
Shine, and blue-bleak embers, ah my dear,
  Fall, gall themselves, and gash gold-vermilion.

Gerard Manley Hopkins
(1844–1889)

Title: a kind of hawk or kestrel. *rung upon the rein* (4) : described a circle, as a horse walking about its trainer. *wimpling* (4) : curving, plaited. *bow-bend* (6) : a bow-shaped figure in skating. *Buckle* (10) : clasp, crumple. *sillion* (12) : furrow.

1. What liberties has the poet taken with syntax and parts of speech?
2. What is the subject of the poem? Study and explain the images in lines 1–7.
3. What indicates that the poem is not merely a description of a bird's flight?
4. Where is the first indication of a connection between the windhover and Christ? What is the connection?
5. Interpret the symbols of the field (lines 12–13) and the fire (lines 13–14).

The Blue-Fly

Five summer days, five summer nights,
The ignorant, loutish, giddy blue-fly
Hung without motion on the cling peach,
Humming occasionally: 'O my love, my fair one!'
    As in the *Canticles.*

Magnified one thousand times, the insect
Looks farcically human; laugh if you will!
Bald head, stage-fairy wings, blear eyes,
A caved-in chest, hairy black mandibles,
    Long spindly thighs.

The crime was detected on the sixth day.
What then could be said or done? By anyone?
It would have been vindictive, mean and what-not
To swat that fly for being a blue-fly,
    For debauch of a peach.

Is it fair, either, to bring a microscope
To bear on the case, even in search of truth?
Nature, doubtless, has some compelling cause
To glut the carriers of her epidemics—
    Nor did the peach complain.

Robert Graves
(1895–)

Canticles (5): the *Song of Solomon* in the Old Testament; a collection of love poetry. *mandibles* (9): mouth-parts.

To a Child Dancing in the Wind

Dance there upon the shore;
What need have you to care
For wind or water's roar?
And tumble out your hair
That the salt drops have wet;
Being young you have not known
The fool's triumph, nor yet
Love lost as soon as won,
Nor the best labourer dead
And all the sheaves to bind.

What need have you to dread
The monstrous crying of the wind?

William Butler Yeats
(1864–1939)

At the Crossroads

They drove the thorny wood beneath my breast;
The priest's hand trembled and he looked away.
I lie and breathe in sour black earth all day,
In porous earth I lie, awake, unblest.

Dry blood still flecks the corners of my mouth.
The green tree holds me fast; my heart is pinned
Where Cain the furious exile tilled and sinned.
I turn and cry the dumb cry of my drouth.

The live world pounds and rumbles overhead.
Along the crossroads where I died and found
My bed in roots and clay, I strain to hear

The grind of wheel on stone, the sudden tear
Of plow or drill, and water underground.
I smell the beating blood on which I fed.

Harvey Gross
(1922–   )

There Was a Lady Loved a Swine

There was a lady loved a swine.
  "Honey," quoth she,
"Pig-hog, wilt thou be mine?"
  "Hoogh," quoth he.

"I'll build thee a silver sty,
  Honey," quoth she,
"And in it thou shalt lie."
  "Hoogh," quoth he.

"Pinned with a silver pin,
"Honey," quoth she,
"That thou may go out and in."
"Hoogh," quoth he.

"Wilt thou have me now,
Honey?" quoth she.
"Speak, or my heart will break!"
"Hoogh," quoth he.

Anonymous
(Seventeenth Century)

Allegory

Allegory is narration or description in which each of the main elements stands for something else that is not mentioned by name. It is seldom used in short poems because it requires more space for development than a short poem affords. Two of the world's most famous poetic allegories—Dante's *Divine Comedy* and Spenser's *Faerie Queene*—are also famous for their length. An allegory usually tells a story that contains one or more other stories; it is like a telegraph wire that transmits several messages simultaneously.

A Rose

A rose, as fair as ever saw the North,
Grew in a little garden all alone;
A sweeter flower did Nature ne'er put forth,
Nor fairer garden yet was never known:
The maidens danced about it morn and noon,
And learnèd bards of it their ditties made;
The nimble fairies by the pale-faced moon
Watered the root and kissed her pretty shade.
But well-a-day!—the gard'ner careless grew;
The maids and fairies both were kept away,
And in a drought the caterpillars threw
Themselves upon the bud and every spray.
God shield the stock! If heaven send no supplies,
The fairest blossom of the garden dies.

William Browne
(1591–1643)

Concealed beneath the surface of Browne's poem there runs another story, each element of which parallels an element in the surface story. A series of equations can be set up between the surface and the submerged narratives: perhaps the rose is a beautiful little girl, an only child on whom her parents and friends dote; the garden (line 2) is her home; the gardener (line 9) is her parents; the caterpillars (line 11) are a disease that strikes her. Certain elements (the other maidens, the fairies, the bards, and heaven) have similar functions in both narratives, and therefore they serve as a link between the two. The submerged narrative might be paraphrased as follows:

> A beautiful child, the fairest ever seen in the north country, lived all alone with her parents. Her radiance was everywhere celebrated: maidens of the village praised it, and poets wrote of it; it seemed as though the fairies themselves visited her by night to cherish her beauty. But as she grew to womanhood, her beauty faded because her parents no longer protected her, and the attendant maids and fairies no longer visited her. In the absence of love she became a prey to disease. But if heaven is gracious, she will recover and will perhaps have a child of her own, who will perpetuate her beauty.

Other allegorical interpretations might be made. The caterpillars, for instance, might stand for evil men who take advantage of the girl after her friends and parents withdraw their protection. But whatever interpretation is made, it must establish a coherent relationship between the surface and what lies under the surface.

Allegory and Symbolism

The method of allegory resembles, but is essentially different from, the method of symbolism. First, allegory is more systematic than symbolism. In the surface narrative of George Orwell's *Animal Farm,* for instance, some domestic animals overthrow the farmer who owns them and set up a new government under the rule of pigs. Every event in this animal revolution systematically parallels an event in Russian history. In an allegory one pattern of characters and events runs alongside another in such a way that a series of equations can be set up between the two patterns. A work could not contain a single allegorical character or event—although it might contain a single symbol. Allegory implies a system of correspondences.

A second difference is that the surface story in an allegory may be read and enjoyed with little awareness of the submerged story. Generations of children have enjoyed the first book of *Gulliver's Travels* without being aware of the political and moral allegory running beneath the surface. A symbolic work, in contrast, means little to a reader unaware of the symbols. Neither Rilke's poem on a panther nor Blake's on a tiger tells an interesting animal story.

Third, the symbolist writer selects objects and events of this world and presents them in such a way that they communicate insights into an unseen world; Blake's real rose and worm stand simultaneously for themselves and for the unseen forces of love and the unseen forces that destroy love. The allegorist, in contrast, invents an imaginary world that reflects the real world. In its crudest form an allegory might tell the story of a knight named Love who is devoured by a dragon named Hate. Unlike worms and roses, knights named Love and dragons named anything exist only in the writer's imagination; the writer invents them to dramatize the opposition between love and hate in the real world. Many allegories contain personified abstractions: Love, Hate, Courage, Rumor. Symbolism concentrates on the concrete, visible world; allegory is likely to be fantastic.

Finally, allegory can sometimes be mechanically interpreted, since it is systematic; symbolism cannot. Once the key to an allegory is known, each element in the submerged story comes to the surface and falls into place. The submerged story can then be paraphrased. A symbol is more elusive; its contents cannot be exhausted by paraphrase.

Despite these differences, the reader should beware of considering allegory and symbolism as mutually exclusive categories. Literary works of any merit cannot be pigeonholed. Probably no writer has ever started to work thinking, "I shall now produce an allegory, and I must carefully avoid all suggestions of symbolism." Writers are more sensible than to place such absurd restrictions upon themselves. Readers, therefore, should regard symbolism and allegory as elements in a work rather than as labels that classify a work. Allegorical and symbolical tendencies may exist in the same work. A work is allegorical insofar as its images fit together to form a coherent pattern of meaning in addition to the surface meaning. It is symbolical insofar as it contains any image that is simultaneously itself and something more significant than itself.

Exercise 37

Discuss the use of allegory and symbolism in these poems.

Excelsior

The shades of night were falling fast,
As through an Alpine village passed
A youth, who bore, 'mid snow and ice,
A banner with the strange device,
    Excelsior!

His brow was sad; his eye beneath,
Flashed like a falchion from its sheath,
And like a silver clarion rung
The accents of that unknown tongue,
    Excelsior!

In happy homes he saw the light
Of household fires gleam warm and bright;
Above, the spectral glaciers shone,
And from his lips escaped a groan,
    Excelsior!

"Try not the Pass!" the old man said;
"Dark lowers the tempest overhead,
The roaring torrent is deep and wide!"
And loud that clarion voice replied,
    Excelsior!

"O stay," the maiden said, "and rest
Thy weary head upon this breast!"
A tear stood in his bright blue eye,
But still he answered, with a sigh,
    Excelsior!

"Beware the pine tree's withered branch!
Beware the awful avalanche!"
This was the peasant's last Good-night;
A voice replied, far up the height,
    Excelsior!

At break of day, as heavenward
The pious monks of Saint Bernard
Uttered the oft-repeated prayer,
A voice cried through the startled air,
    Excelsior!

A traveller, by the faithful hound,
Half-buried in the snow was found,
Still grasping in his hand of ice
That banner with the strange device,
    Excelsior!

There in the twilight cold and gray,
Lifeless, but beautiful, he lay,
And from the sky, serene and far,
A voice fell, like a falling star,
    Excelsior!

Henry Wadsworth Longfellow
(1807–1882)

Title: Higher. *falchion* (7): sword.

Cried the Fox

I run, cried the fox, in circles
narrower, narrower still,
across the desperate hollow,
skirting the frantic hill

and shall till my brush hangs burning
flame at the hunter's door
continue this fatal returning
to places that failed me before!

Then, with his heart breaking nearly,
the lonely, passionate bark
of the fugitive fox rang out clearly
as bells in the frosty dark,

across the desperate hollow,
skirting the frantic hill,
calling the pack to follow
a prey that escaped them still.

Tennessee Williams
(1914–)

Opportunity

This I beheld, or dreamed it in a dream:—
There spread a cloud of dust along a plain;
And underneath the cloud, or in it, raged
A furious battle, and men yelled, and swords
Shocked upon swords and shields. A prince's banner
Wavered, then staggered backward, hemmed by foes.
A craven hung along the battle's edge,
And thought, "Had I a sword of keener steel—
That blue blade that the king's son bears,—but this
Blunt thing—!" he snapt and flung it from his hand,
And lowering crept away and left the field.
Then came the king's son, wounded, sore bestead,
And weaponless, and saw the broken sword,
Hilt-buried in the dry and trodden sand,
And ran and snatched it, and with battle-shout
Lifted afresh he hewed his enemy down,
And saved a great cause that heroic day.

Edward Roland Sill
(1841–1887)

The Tropics in New York

Bananas ripe and green, and ginger-root,
  Cocoa in pods and alligator pears,
And tangerines and mangoes and grapefruit,
  Fit for the highest prize at parish fairs.

Set in the window, bringing memories
  Of fruit-trees laden by low-singing rills,
And dewy dawn, and mystical blue skies
  In benediction over nun-like hills.

My eyes grew dim, and I could no more gaze;
  A wave of longing through my body swept,
And, hungry for the old, familiar ways,
  I turned aside and bowed my head and wept.

Claude McKay
(1890–1948)

The Wayfarer

The wayfarer,
Perceiving the pathway to truth,
Was struck with astonishment.
It was thickly grown with weeds.
"Ha," he said,
"I see that none has passed here
In a long time."
Later he saw that each weed
Was a singular knife.
"Well," he mumbled at last,
"Doubtless there are other roads."

Stephen Crane
(1871–1900)

The Heavy Bear Who Goes with Me

"the withness of the body"

—Whitehead

The heavy bear who goes with me,
A manifold honey to smear his face,
Clumsy and lumbering here and there,
The central ton of every place,
The hungry beating brutish one

In love with candy, anger, and sleep,
Crazy factotum, dishevelling all,
Climbs the building, kicks the football,
Boxes his brother in the hate-ridden city.

Breathing at my side, that heavy animal,
That heavy bear who sleeps with me,
Howls in his sleep for a world of sugar,
A sweetness intimate as the water's clasp,
Howls in his sleep because the tight-rope
Trembles and shows the darkness beneath.
—The strutting show-off is terrified,
Dressed in his dress-suit, bulging his pants,
Trembles to think that his quivering meat
Must finally wince to nothing at all.

That inescapable animal walks with me,
Has followed me since the black womb held,
Moves where I move, distorting my gesture,
A caricature, a swollen shadow,
A stupid clown of the spirit's motive,
Perplexes and affronts with his own darkness,
The secret life of belly and bone,
Opaque, too near, my private, yet unknown,
Stretches to embrace the very dear
With whom I would walk without him near,
Touches her grossly, although a word
Would bare my heart and make me clear,
Stumbles, flounders, and strives to be fed,
Dragging me with him in his mouthing care,
Amid the hundred million of his kind,
The scrimmage of appetite everywhere.

Delmore Schwartz
(1913–1966)

factotum (7): busy-body, jack of all trades.

Question

Body my house
my horse my hound
what will I do
when you are fallen

Where will I sleep
How will I ride
What will I hunt

Where can I go
without my mount
all eager and quick
How will I know
in thicket ahead
is danger or treasure
when Body my good
bright dog is dead

How will it be
to lie in the sky
without roof or door
and wind for an eye

With cloud for shift
how will I hide?

May Swenson
(1919–)

The Horse Chestnut Tree

Boys in sporadic but tenacious droves
Come with sticks, as certainly as Autumn,
To assault the great horse chestnut tree.

There is a law governs their lawlessness.
Desire is in them for a shining amulet
And the best are those that are highest up.

They will not pick them easily from the ground.
With shrill arms they fling to the higher branches,
To hurry the work of nature for their pleasure.

I have seen them trooping down the street
Their pockets stuffed with chestnuts shucked, unshucked.
It is only evening keeps them from their wish.

Sometimes I run out in a kind of rage
To chase the boys away: I catch an arm,
Maybe, and laugh to think of being the lawgiver.

I was once such a young sprout myself
And fingered in my pocket the prize and trophy.
But still I moralize upon the day

And see that we, outlaws on God's property,
Fling out imagination beyond the skies,
Wishing a tangible good from the unknown.

And likewise death will drive us from the scene
With the great flowering world unbroken yet,
Which we held in idea, a little handful.

Richard Eberhart
(1904–   )

Two Realities

A waggon passed with scarlet wheels
  And a yellow body, shining new.
"Splendid!" said I. "How fine it feels
To be alive, when beauty peels
  The grimy husk from life." And you

Said, "Splendid!" and I thought you'd seen
  That waggon blazing down the street;
But I looked and saw that your gaze had been
On a child that was kicking an obscene
  Brown ordure with his feet.

Our souls are elephants, thought I,
  Remote behind a prisoning grill,
With trunks thrust out to peer and pry
And pounce upon reality;
  And each at his own sweet will
Seizes the bun that he likes best
And passes over all the rest.

Aldous Huxley
(1894–1963)

ordure (10): piece of dung.

7. *The Sound of a Poem*

Poetry withers and dries out when it leaves music, or at least imagined music, too far behind. Poets who are not interested in music are, or become, bad poets.

Ezra Pound

Philosophers, scientists, and mathematicians are usually not much concerned with the sounds of the words they use to express their ideas. They communicate their concepts in language that works directly on the mind; they tend to avoid images that might distract the senses or sounds that might stir the feelings. But poets have always been concerned with the reader's sense and feelings. The earliest poems, in fact, were recited rather than read. Poets chanted them from memory or extemporized them on the spot for audiences who could not read. And poems have never lost this early association with the spoken word—with sound.

In all languages there are numerous words whose sounds imitate their meanings. We are aware of certain connections between the sounds and meanings of some words: bees buzz, birds chirp, and rattletrap cars clink, clank, and clunk as they come sputtering down the street. Poets often use such words to convey their experiences as vividly as possible. But there are other uses of sound in poems that are not so obvious: the intricate patterns of rhyme and rhythm as well as the variations that poets play on vowel and consonant sounds to give richness and texture to their poems. A whole book could be written about the various effects of sound in poems, but this chapter will treat only the most basic effects. Once you become aware that you can "read" a poem with your ears as well as your eyes, other effects of sound will become apparent to you. With such awareness you are likely to find your enjoyment of poetry greatly increased.

It is useful to begin by examining the basic patterns of sound in poems, which can be classified under three headings: alliteration, assonance, and rhyme.

Alliteration

Alliteration is the repetition of identical or similar consonantal sounds, usually restricted to words in one line of verse, and usually but not necessarily at the beginning of words: *p*retty *p*ink *p*ills for *p*ale *p*eople. Alliteration does not depend on spelling: *phantom* alliterates with *flower* but not with *pneumonia; cease* with *scissors* but not with *chime.* Colloquial English is strewn with alliterative tags like *might and main, hide nor hair, fit as a fiddle, bold as brass,* and so is advertising of the kind commonly considered "catchy." Since about 1400, however, alliteration has not been an important technical device in English poetry, although before that time it was used as an organizing principle in many poems. *Piers Plowman,* written in the fourteenth century, is typical of the old system of versification according to which a word in the first part of every line alliterates with a word in the second:

> And now is *r*eligion a *r*ider, a *r*oamer by the streets,
> And *l*eader of *l*ove days, and a *l*and buyer.

Since the fourteenth century most poets have used alliteration sparingly, and only for special effects. It can, for instance, underline a contrast, as when Pope writes, "The strength he *g*ains is from the embrace he *g*ives." Or it can emphasize a connection between ideas, as when Dryden begins his poem "To the Memory of Mr. Oldham" with the line "Farewell, too *l*ittle and too *l*ately known." Byron's "Waterloo" describes a soldier who "rushed into the *f*ield, and, *f*oremost *f*ighting, *f*ell." Alliteration in this line helps the words convey to the reader an image of a single, sudden action. When used to create a connection or a contrast between ideas or events, alliteration is a legitimate device, but when used for its own sake it may be tiresome or even laughable. The person who reads a poem primarily for what it says rather than for how it sounds may think that there is an excessive amount of alliteration in this excerpt from *Atalanta in Calydon* by A. C. Swinburne (1837–1909):

> When the hounds of spring are on winter's traces,
>   The mother of months in meadow or plain
> Fills the shadows and windy places
>   With lisp of leaves and ripple of rain. . . .

For winter's rains and ruins are over,
   And all the season of snows and sins;
The days dividing lover and lover,
   The light that loses, the night that wins.

This is ingenious, but it raises a question. Has the poet sacrificed sense for sound? In line 6, for example, winter is said to be a season of sins. Is the word *sins* put in merely for alliterative effect? Here the device seems decorative rather than functional, since it makes little, if any, contribution to the meaning.

Assonance

A second kind of repeated sound is **assonance,** or the repetition of similar or identical vowel sounds: "Thy kingdom c*o*me, thy will be d*o*ne." Assonance, like alliteration, is most effective when restricted to words in one line of verse. The old proverb "A stitch in time saves nine" contains both alliteration and assonance. Other assonant pairs are *each, either; old, mouldy; lady, baby; deep, tree; gaunt, slaughter.* Because assonance depends on sound rather than on spelling, it can be detected only by the ear. Assonance is not used as deliberately and consciously as alliteration, but it has the same functions: to please the ear, to give emphasis, and to point up an antithesis.

Exercise 38

In the following poems, and in Auden's "O Where Are You Going" (page 215), locate all the instances of alliteration and assonance. Then try to explain whether they are decorative or whether they have an additional function.

In Vitam Humanam

The world's a bubble, and the life of man
      Less than a span;
In his conception wretched, and from the womb
      So to the tomb;

Curst from the cradle, and brought up to years
With cares and fears.
Who, then, to frail mortality shall trust
But limns the water, or but writes in dust.

Yet since with sorrow here we live oppressed,
What life is best?
Courts are but only superficial schools
To dandle fools;
The rural parts are turned into a den
Of savage men;
And where's a city from all vice so free
But may be termed the worst of all the three?

Domestic cares afflict the husband's bed
Or pains his head;
Those that live single take it for a curse,
Or do things worse;
Some would have children; those that have them moan
Or wish them gone;
What is it, then, to have or have no wife
But single thraldom or a double strife?

Our own affections still at home to please
Is a disease;
To cross the sea to any foreign soil,
Perils and toil;
Wars with their noise affright us; when they cease
We're worse in peace.
What then remains, but that we still should cry
Not to be born, or being born, to die?

Sir Francis Bacon
(1561–1626)

Title: "Against Human Life." *limns* (8): draws on.

God's Grandeur

The world is charged with the grandeur of God.
It will flame out, like shining from shook foil;
It gathers to a greatness, like the ooze of oil
Crushed. Why do men then now not reck his rod?

Generations have trod, have trod, have trod;
  And all is seared with trade; bleared, smeared with toil;
  And wears man's smudge and shares man's smell: the soil
Is bare now, nor can foot feel, being shod.

And for all this, nature is never spent;
  There lives the dearest freshness deep down things;
And though the last lights off the black West went
  Oh, morning, at the brown brink eastward, springs—
Because the Holy Ghost over the bent
  World broods with warm breast and with ah! bright wings.

Gerard Manley Hopkins
(1844–1889)

foil (2) : gold or silver leaf. *ooze of oil* (3) : from olives being crushed in a press. *reck* (4): give heed to. *Holy Ghost . . . wings* (13–14): Genesis i:2. In Catholic theology, God is held to have created the world through the agency of the Holy Spirit, who also sustains it in existence. In religious paintings and elsewhere, the Holy Spirit is symbolized as a dove.

Rhyme

A third kind of repeated sound is rhyme, perhaps the most commonly known of all the devices a poem may employ—although only a very naïve reader expects every poem to employ it. **Rhyme** can be defined as the repetition of both vowel and consonantal sounds at the ends of words. It is easily distinguished from the other two kinds of repeated sound: while *tool* alliterates with *toad,* and *toad* is assonant with *foam, foam* rhymes with *home.* Rhymes like *home* and *foam* are arbitrarily called **masculine rhymes**—a term that signifies no more than correspondence in sound between stressed syllables. The rhymes in the following bit of doggerel are masculine:

If all be true that I do think,
There are five reasons we should drink:
Good wine, a friend, or being dry,
Or lest we should be by and by,
Or any other reason why.

Henry Aldrich
(1647–1710)

Feminine rhyme is the term given to the correspondence in sound between words of two or more syllables: *mournfully, scornfully; leaping, creeping.*

What is fame? An empty bubble.
Gold? A transient, shining trouble.

James Grainger
(*c.* 1721–1766)

The following epitaph may also be said to employ feminine rhymes because the lines end with the extra unaccented syllable known as a feminine ending (see page 462):

Life is a jest, and all things show it;
I thought so once, but now I know it.

John Gay
(1685–1732)

Although rhyme usually appears at the ends of lines, it may also occur within lines, especially in songs and ballads, and then it is called **internal rhyme.**

I cannot eat but little meat,
  My stomach is not good;
But sure I think that I can drink
  With him that wears a hood.
Though I go bare, take ye no care,
  I am nothing a-cold;
I stuff my skin so full within
  Of jolly good ale and old.

Anonymous
(Sixteenth Century)

Rhyme is capable of many subtle variations. **Rich rhymes** are made up of sounds identical in all respects: *bear, bare.* **Sight rhymes** (sometimes called eye rhymes) are based on correspondence in spelling, as in *dew, sew;* such rhymes as *find, wind* in older poems are now sight rhymes because of pronunciation changes. **Partial rhymes** do not have the correspondence in both vowel and consonant that rhyme proper has. Partial rhyme, which is known by several other names (slant rhyme, pararhyme, consonantal rhyme, near rhyme), makes use of both assonance and alliteration: *dear, dare; fear, rare; actress, mattress.* It is not so important to know the technical names of the different kinds of rhymes as to realize that rhyme does not have to be perfect and that the poet who uses an inexact rhyme has not necessarily made a "mistake."

Exercise 39

Identify the kinds of rhyme in the following poems.

These Are the Days When Birds Come Back

These are the days when Birds come back—
A very few—a Bird or two—
To take a backward look.

These are the days when skies resume
The old—old sophistries of June—
A blue and gold mistake.

Oh fraud that cannot cheat the Bee—
Almost thy plausibility
Induces my belief.

Till ranks of seeds their witness bear—
And softly thro' the altered air
Hurries a timid leaf.

Oh Sacrament of summer days,
Oh last Communion in the Haze—
Permit a child to join.

Thy sacred emblems to partake—
Thy consecrated bread to take
And thine immortal wine!

Emily Dickinson
(1830–1886)

Song

The feathers of the willow
Are half of them grown yellow
  Above the swelling stream;
And ragged are the bushes,
And rusty now the rushes,
  And wild the clouded gleam.

The thistle now is older,
His stalk begins to moulder,
  His head is white as snow;
The branches all are barer,
The linnet's song is rarer,
  The robin pipeth now.

Richard Watson Dixon
(1833–1900)

Charm

The owl is abroad, the bat, and the toad,
  And so is the catamountain;
The ant and the mole sit both in a hole,
  And frog peeps out o' the fountain;
The dogs they do bay, and the timbrels play;
  The spindle is now a-turning;
The moon it is red, and the stars are fled,
  But all the sky is a-burning.

Ben Jonson
(1532–1637)

catamountain (2): wild cat. *timbrels* (5): tambourines.

When a Man Has Married a Wife

When a Man has Married a Wife
he finds out whether
Her Knees and elbows are only
glued together

William Blake
(1757–1827)

The Functions of Rhyme

Down through the centuries poets and critics have debated whether rhyme is necessary or even desirable. The enemies of rhyme have cited Homer, Virgil, and other great Greek and Latin poets who did not use it. They have pointed out that cultivated readers do not respond to crude, jingling sounds, and that the necessity of finding a rhyme can, and often does, force a poet into saying things that he does not wish to say. The first of these arguments would carry weight only in an age that had an exaggerated respect for antiquity. The other two commit the fallacy of arguing against a practice by citing abuses of that practice. Rhyming can, of course, force an unskillful poet into triteness and absurdity, as Pope demonstrates in his *Essay on Criticism.*

Where'er you find "the cooling western breeze,"
In the next line, it "whispers through the trees."
If crystal streams "with pleasing murmurs creep,"
The reader's threaten'd (not in vain) with "sleep."

But the need to find a rhyme can also be a source of inspiration. An epitaph said to be on a tombstone in Leeds, England, provides a trivial but clear-cut example.

Here lies my wife.
Here lies she.
Hallelujah!
Hallelujee!

Needing a rhyme for *she,* this versifier coined a new exclamation that exactly expresses his ecstatic feelings on being released from bondage. The degree of skill that a poet possesses will determine whether rhyme is his servant or his master. A rhyming dictionary may help a would-be poet overcome one of the natural barriers of our language, the relative scarcity of rhyme words in English compared with the large number in, say, Italian. It may help him write verses for greeting cards, but it will never make him a poet because rhyme is only one of the elements in a poem.

A poet who can rhyme easily does, however, have certain advantages over one who cannot. Rhyme pleases most readers because it alternately creates an expectation and satisfies that expectation. The listener hears a sound which experience tells him will soon be repeated with some slight differences. When he hears repeated sound, he is pleased because he is no longer in suspense and because he feels that a difficulty has been overcome. We all enjoy difficulties if they can be quickly overcome, and we all like two sensations that are similar yet slightly different. Rhyme, then, is interesting and pleasing in itself.

A second advantage is the appeal of rhyme to the reader's memory. Most rhymed poems are in meter, and meter is also an aid to memorization. These facts, which hardly need explanation or illustration, account for the prevalence of rhymed folk sayings about the weather and so on, for versified advertisements, and for mnemonic crutches like this one for bad spellers:

I before *e*,
Except after *c;*
Or when sounded as *a,*
As in *neighbor* or *weigh.*

Finally, and most important, end rhyme cooperates with meter in giving shape and unity to a poet's ideas. First, the rhyming word plainly indicates the end of a line, rounding off one of the main structural units of a poem. In this respect a rhymed poem is very different from prose because the lines of the poem stop at an expected time and in an expected way. Prose lines, which obey no such arbitrary rules, lack this kind of shape. Second, the rhymes at the ends of lines are arranged in a pattern that is usually repeated over and over again for the entire length of the poem.

Rhyme Schemes

A pattern of rhymes is known as a **rhyme scheme,** and a group of lines bound together by a rhyme scheme and by metrical devices is called a **stanza.** Here is a stanza from *The Rubáiyát of Omar Khayyám of Naishápúr,* a free translation of a poem by the Persian poet Omar Khayyám (1050–1132) made by Edward Fitzgerald (1809–1883):

A Book of Verses underneath the Bough,
A Jug of Wine, a Loaf of Bread—and Thou
  Beside me singing in the Wilderness—
Oh, Wilderness were Paradise enow!

enow (4): enough.

According to the rhyme scheme adopted here, the last words of lines 1, 2, and 4 rhyme. Rhyme schemes are customarily indicated by italicized small letters—here *a a x a*. Fitzgerald's *Rubáiyát* consists of 101 stanzas rhyming *a a x a*. (All the *a* lines rhyme with one another; the *x* line does not rhyme with anything.) There are, of course, many other possible rhyme schemes and fixed stanzaic forms (see Chapter 9) in English poetry.

Exercise 40

Examine the patterns of sound in the following poems.

On the Late Massacre in Piedmont

Avenge, O Lord, thy slaughtered saints, whose bones
  Lie scattered on the Alpine mountains cold;
  Even them who kept thy truth so pure of old
  When all our fathers worshipped stocks and stones,
Forget not; in thy book record their groans
  Who were thy sheep and in their ancient fold
  Slain by the bloody Piedmontese that rolled
  Mother with infant down the rocks. Their moans

The vales redoubled to the hills, and they
To heaven. Their martyred blood and ashes sow
O'er all the Italian fields where still doth sway
The triple tyrant: that from these may grow
A hundredfold, who having learnt thy way
Early may fly the Babylonian woe.

John Milton
(1608–1674)

Title: In 1655 the Catholic Duke of Savoy sent troops against a Protestant community living in the Piedmont. *stocks* (4): trees. *sheep* (6): John x:11–16. *blood . . . sow* (10): a double allusion to Cadmus, who in Greek mythology sowed dragon's teeth that sprang up as armed men; and to the early Christian saying that "The blood of martyrs is the seed of the Church." *triple tyrant* (12): the Pope, who wears a triple crown. *Babylonian woe* (14): Revelations xviii:2. The Protestants applied this verse to Rome.

1. What are the predominant sounds in Milton's sonnet?
2. What possible connections are there between these sounds and the meaning of the poem?

The Unawkward Singer

Self-praise is a wonderful thing!
It causes all the birds to sing:
The sparrow's brag, thrush's conceit,
They make the whole world cheerly repeat
Cheerly repeat their praise.

For any lark there is no other,
No father, mother, sister, brother,
No sweet wife, nor no dear love;
The dove's the pool in which the dove,
Loving, admires his ways.

Wind out of the swan's throat
His final operatic note:
Impassioned on himself he dies,
Knowing the world is him, is his
By his self-celebration.

Master man cannot so please
Himself with eloquence like these;
Thus clumsily his song is sung,
Thick praise by a thick tongue
For its own limitation.

David Ferry
(1924–)

1. What effects of sound do you notice in Ferry's poem?
2. How do the last two lines contrast in sound with the remainder of the poem?

O Where Are You Going

"O where are you going?" said reader to rider,
"That valley is fatal when furnaces burn,
Yonder's the midden whose odours will madden,
That gap is the grave where the tall return."

"O do you imagine," said fearer to farer,
"That dusk will delay on your path to the pass,
Your diligent looking discover the lacking
Your footsteps feel from granite to grass?"

"O what was that bird," said horror to hearer,
"Did you see that shape in the twisted trees?
Behind you swiftly the figure comes softly,
The spot on your skin is a shocking disease?"

"Out of this house"—said rider to reader,
"Yours never will"—said farer to fearer,
"They're looking for you"—said hearer to horror,
As he left them there, as he left them there.

W. H. Auden
(1907–1973)

Other Repeated Sounds

The repetition of words, phrases, entire lines, or entire groups of lines is another way of using sounds in some kinds of poetry. The recurrence of these elements at regular intervals is known as a **refrain.** Refrains often occur at the ends of stanzas, but there is no rule saying that they must. In every stanza but the last in the following song, which Feste the Jester sings at the end of *Twelfth Night,* the second and fourth lines create a refrain.

Feste's Song

When that I was and a little tiny boy,
With hey, ho, the wind and the rain,
A foolish thing was but a toy,
For the rain it raineth every day.

But when I came to man's estate,
With hey, ho, the wind and the rain,
'Gainst knaves and thieves men shut their gate,
For the rain it raineth every day.

But when I came, alas, to wive,
With hey, ho, the wind and the rain,
By swaggering could I never thrive,
For the rain it raineth every day.

But when I came unto my beds,
With hey, ho, the wind and the rain,
With tosspots still had drunken heads,
For the rain it raineth every day.

A great while ago the world begun,
  With hey, ho, the wind and the rain,
But that's all one, our play is done,
  And we'll strive to please you every day.

William Shakespeare
(1564–1616)

The refrains in this song, as in the poems by Nashe (page 162) and Longfellow (page 195), contribute to the meaning of the poem. Here the "wind and the rain" suggest the hardships that every day come into the singer's life. His indomitable response to these vicissitudes finds its expression in the repeated "hey, ho" that optimistically brushes such affliction aside. Troubles in life, say the refrains, are natural events like wind and rain. However, many of the refrains in older lyrics and ballads (as in modern popular songs) defy rational analysis. Collections of nonsense syllables ("Hey nonny nonny," "Down derry down," "Fa la la") please the tongue and the ear, and nobody expects them to have much connection with the song. Easily learned and easily remembered, such refrains may have been first used in communal singing when the audience joined with the soloist in singing the refrains. Yet despite their slender intellectual content, nonsense refrains can evoke feeling. In merry songs they increase the merriment; in sad songs, they provide contrast.

Not all repeated words, phrases, or sentences in poems are refrains, however. Poets use the device of repetition for rhetorical as well as for musical effect. Like prose writers, they deliberately repeat ideas in order to emphasize them and make them more memorable and persuasive. Repetition can create urgency and intensity, as in the poem by Ted Joans (p. 70) and the one by W. H. Auden (page 215).

Onomatopoeia

One other sound device that remains to be mentioned is **onomatopoeia**—the use of words whose sound suggests their meaning. Onomatopoeic words in English include *bleat, buzz, clink, clank, crash, quack, hiss, rattle, sneeze, snort, squeak,* and so on. Such words obviously do not reproduce an actual sound as a phonograph record does; rather they suggest the actual sounds. A reader will not encounter onomatopoeia very often in poems because its usefulness is strictly limited. Extended onomatopoeic effects, as in Poe's famous "Bells" or Southey's "Cataract of Lodore," are mechanically ingenious, but they are likely to become tiresome upon repeated hearings. Used with restraint, onomatopoeia can help create appropriate images of sound.

In this somewhat less-than-serious poem, the clock's "tick" (itself onomatopoeic) turns into other words that sound like "tick":

The Watch

I wakened on my hot, hard bed,
Upon the pillow lay my head;
Beneath the pillow I could hear
My little watch was ticking clear.
I thought the throbbing of it went
Like my continual discontent.
I thought it said in every tick:
I am so sick, so sick, so sick.
O death, come quick, come quick, come quick,
Come quick, come quick, come quick, come quick!

Frances Cornford
(1886–1960)

Exercise 41

How does sound contribute to meaning in the following poems?

The Human Being Is a Lonely Creature

It is borne in upon me that pain
Is essential. The bones refuse to act.
Recalcitrancy is life's fine flower.
The human being is a lonely creature.

Fear is of the essence. You do not fear?
I say you lie. Fear is the truth of time.
If it is not now, it will come hereafter.
Death is waiting for the human creature.

Praise to harmony and love.
They are best, all else is false.
Yet even in love and harmony
The human being is a lonely creature.

The old sloughed off, the new new-born,
What fate and what high hazards join
As life tries out the soul's enterprise.
Time is waiting for the human creature.

Life is daring all our human stature.
Death looks, and waits for each bright eye.
Love and harmony are our best nurture.
The human being is a lonely creature.

Richard Eberhart
(1904–)

Bantams in Pine Woods

Chieftain Iffucan of Azcan in caftan
Of tan with henna hackles, halt!

Damned universal cock, as if the sun
Was blackamoor to bear your blazing tail.

Fat! Fat! Fat! Fat! I am the personal.
Your world is you. I am my world.

You ten-foot poet among inchlings. Fat!
Begone! An inchling bristles in these pines,

Bristles, and points their Appalachian tangs,
And fears not portly Azcan nor his hoos.

Wallace Stevens
(1879–1955)

Bantams (title): small, noisy fowl with colorful plumage. *Iffucan, Azcan* (1): exotic sounding names, apparently coined by Stevens. The former seems to be the bantam rooster; the latter, perhaps the speaker of lines 1–4 and the owner of the bantams, or perhaps the place where the pine woods is located. *caftan* (1): ankle-length garment of bright silk. *henna* (2): reddish brown. *hackles* (2): neck plumage. *blackamoor* (4): slave. *Fat* (5): Apparently the bantam addresses Azcan at this point. *Inchlings* (7): midgets—the bantams. *Appalachian* (9): mountain. *tangs* (9): tips, points. *hoos* (10): perhaps noises made by Azcan in shooing the birds away.

The Private Dining Room

Miss Rafferty wore taffeta,
Miss Cavendish wore lavender.
We ate pickerel and mackerel
And other lavish provender.
Miss Cavendish was Lalage,
Miss Rafferty was Barbara.
We gobbled pickled mackerel
And broke the candelabara,
Miss Cavendish in lavender,
In taffeta, Miss Rafferty,
The girls in taffeta lavender,
And we, of course, in mufti.

Miss Rafferty wore taffeta,
The taffeta was lavender,
Was lavend, lavender, lavenderest,
As the wine improved the provender.
Miss Cavendish wore lavender,
The lavender was taffeta.
We boggled mackled pickerel,
And bumpers did we quaffeta.
And Lalage wore lavender,
And lavender wore Barbara,
Rafferta taffeta Cavender lavender
Barbara abracadabra.

Miss Rafferty in taffeta
Grew definitely raffisher.
Miss Cavendish in lavender
Grew less and less stand-offisher.
With Lalage and Barbara
We grew a little pickereled,
We ordered Mumm and Roederer
Because the bubbles tickereled.

But lavender and taffeta
Were gone when we were soberer.
I haven't thought for thirty years
Of Lalage and Barbara.

Ogden Nash
(1902–1971)

Lalage (5) : a woman's name, pronounced in three syllables. *mufti* (12) : ordinary clothes. *Mumm and Roederer* (31) : brand names of champagne.

Jabberwocky

'Twas brillig, and the slithy toves
  Did gyre and gimble in the wabe:
All mimsy were the borogoves,
  And the mome raths outgrabe.

"Beware the Jabberwock, my son!
  The jaws that bite, the claws that catch!
Beware the Jubjub bird, and shun
  The frumious Bandersnatch!"

He took his vorpal sword in hand;
  Long time the manxome foe he sought—
So rested he by the Tumtum tree,
  And stood awhile in thought.

And, as in uffish thought he stood,
  The Jabberwock, with eyes of flame,
Came whiffling through the tulgey wood,
  And burbled as it came!

One, two! One, two! And through and through
  The vorpal blade went snicker-snack!
He left it dead, and with its head
  He went galumphing back.

"And hast thou slain the Jabberwock?
  Come to my arms, my beamish boy!
O frabjous day! Callooh; Callay!"
  He chortled in his joy.

'Twas brillig, and the slithy toves
  Did gyre and gimble in the wabe:
All mimsy were the borogoves,
  And the mome raths outgrabe.

Lewis Carroll
(1832–1898)

Euphony and Cacophony

A poet may wish to give the general effect of **euphony,** or pleasant and sweet sound. Euphonious combinations of words can be spoken without sudden changes in the position of the lips, tongue, and jaw, and they are therefore easy to say.

A thing of beauty is a joy for ever:
Its loveliness increases; it will never
Pass into nothingness; but still will keep
A bower quiet for us, and a sleep
Full of sweet dreams, and health, and quiet breathing.

John Keats
(1795–1821)

These lines from *Endymion* almost say themselves. In addition to the end rhymes, partial rhymes mark the caesuras (pauses) in lines 2, 3, 4: *increases, nothingness, us.* This same consonantal sound occurs in *Pass* and *loveliness.* Line 3 has internal rhyme: *still, will.* The long *e* sound of the second rhyme (*keep, sleep*) is repeated in four other words: *increases, sweet, dreams, breathing.* The passage is euphonious because it contains sounds that harmonize.

Certain clusters of consonants are tongue-twisters:

Irks care the crop-full bird? Frets doubt the maw-crammed beast?

This line, from Browning's "Rabbi Ben Ezra," gives the effect of **cacophony:** discord, harshness of sound. Cacophonous lines are not necessarily proof that a poet lacks skill; they can be intentional. In good poems both concord and discord are used functionally.

First Fight. Then Fiddle.

First fight. Then fiddle. Ply the slipping string
With feathery sorcery; muzzle the note
With hurting love; the music that they wrote
Bewitch, bewilder. Qualify to sing
Threadwise. Devise no salt, no hempen thing
For the dear instrument to bear. Devote
The bow to silks and honey. Be remote
A while from malice and from murdering.
But first to arms, to armor. Carry hate
In front of you and harmony behind.
Be deaf to music and to beauty blind.
Win war. Rise bloody, maybe not too late
For having first to civilize a space
Wherein to play your violin with grace.

Gwendolyn Brooks
(1917–)

This poem illustrates some of the ways in which sound devices can be used to make a poem convincing and its ideas acceptable to a reader. Brooks firmly believes that if you want to have a beautiful life, you must be ready to fight for it. "First fight, then fiddle," she says. Expressing the idea in alliterative words makes it seem proverbial, axiomatic, beyond question. Had she written "Struggle before playing the violin," the reader would feel no such firm conviction, no such ready acceptance of her idea.

After this strong start, Brooks continues to use sound devices to help her develop her ideas about "fiddling" (lines 1–8) and "fighting" (9–14). Alliterative pairs and triplets (*slipping, string, sorcery; bewitch, bewilder; malice, murdering*) provide pleasure for the ear and thereby keep the poem from seeming preachy or over-didactic. Such euphonious language gives the effect of exuberance and energy. Perhaps the one place where the poem approaches harshness or cacophony is in the slogan-like command "Win war" (line 12). To be understood, this phrase must be said slowly and deliberately. The closing couplet sums up the connection between fighting and fiddling: you must fight "to civilize a space" (notice that alliteration doesn't depend on spelling) in which to "play your violin"—that is, to live graciously, decently, harmoniously, peacefully.

Exercise 42

Read both of these poems aloud and then contrast the general effect that they make. Identify the devices that contribute to the effect, and decide whether each poem as a whole has an appropriate sound.

The Twilight Turns from Amethyst

The twilight turns from amethyst
  To deep and deeper blue,
The lamp fills with a pale green glow
  The trees of the avenue.

The old piano plays an air,
  Sedate and slow and gay;
She bends upon the yellow keys,
  Her head inclines this way.

Shy thoughts and grave wide eyes and hands
  That wander as they list—
The twilight turns to darker blue
  With lights of amethyst.

James Joyce
(1882–1941)

Twilight

Dusk comes early in the shaft,
An hour before the whistles and the first
Radios have laughed
Enticingly of cigarettes and soup,
And supper cans have burst
Condensed and desiccated food for Jim,
Home from work in time to hear the worst
Tiny tragedies his wife will tell to him
Of gas-pipe leaks and Mrs. Bailey's first.

With sunset, night
Flattens its black face on the windowpane,
Staring and waiting for the moment when
A switch is pulled, to throttle out the light,
To leap against the throats of tired men,
To stretch them on the bed, subdue the brain,
And drag its shapeless body through the house,
Driving its shadows with a dark disdain
Until it rests, triumphant over every part,
And takes a ticking clock for heart.

Paul Engle
(1908–)

shaft (1) : airshaft of a tenement.

Sound and Meaning

The last word on the relationship between sound and meaning is often said to be contained in these lines from *An Essay on Criticism:*

True ease in writing comes from Art, not Chance,
As those move easiest who have learn'd to dance.
'Tis not enough no harshness gives offence;
The sound must seem an echo to the sense.
Soft is the strain when zephyr gently blows,
And the smooth stream in smoother numbers flows;
But when loud surges lash the sounding shore,
The hoarse rough verse should like the torrent roar.
When Ajax strives some rock's vast weight to throw,
The line, too, labours, and the words move slow:
Not so when swift Camilla scours the plain,
Flies o'er th' unbending corn, and skims along the main.

Alexander Pope
(1688–1744)

Ajax (9): an enormous warrior in the *Iliad*. *Camilla* (11): a swift-footed maiden in the *Aeneid*.

Pope's advice to poets is excellent, but his illustrations are not very helpful because they are too obvious; there are few occasions when a poet must match sound and sense as mechanically as they are matched here. Usually they correspond in a way that is much more difficult to explain.

Upon Julia's Clothes

Whenas in silks my Julia goes,
Then, then, methinks, how sweetly flows
That liquefaction of her clothes.

Next, when I cast mine eyes and see
That brave vibration each way free,
O how that glittering taketh me!

Robert Herrick
(1591–1674)

Since Herrick wishes to communicate a pleasant experience, he has chosen euphonious rather than cacophonous sounds. Julia is easy on the eyes; the poem is easy on the ears. Any harshness that might spoil the effect has been excluded from the poem.

All readers should be aware of one particular absurdity that sometimes occurs in discussions of poetic sounds. It goes like this: "Every line of the first stanza of Herrick's 'Julia' contains an *l* sound, the same sound that appears in *lady, lullaby, lily, languor, lawn,* and other lovely and pleasant-sounding words. Therefore the musical smoothness of the poem is caused by the prevalence of the liquid *l* sound." But the liquid *l* sound also occurs in such expressions as "loathsome leaking lavatory," "leather leggings," and "lewd lithographs," and no reader who understands them will maintain that they are especially pleasant and musical. The fact is that words are pleasant according to their meaning as well as according to their sound. If sound alone determined our reactions to words, we should find *coronary thrombosis* as pleasant as *yellow ambrosia.* Since letters and syllables are meaningless unless they are incorporated into words, it is impossible to say that they have any particular effect apart from the words in which they appear. There are no happy vowels, irritable consonants, or sad syllables.

However, something more can be said about the contribution that sound makes to such a poem as Herrick's "Julia." One way to isolate this contribution is to compare a prose paraphrase with the poem:

When my Julia walks about dressed in silk, it seems to me that her clothes flow around her body as though they had turned to liquid. I find her very attractive because she walks so that her dress seems to vibrate and glitter.

This paraphrase hardly does justice to the sense of the poem, let alone to the sound. Lacking rhyme and meter, it does not please the ear as the poem does; it has neither shape nor structure, nor does it convey any of the dramatic excitement of the poem.

Exercise 43

Compare the following poem with Herrick's. Does it say what Herrick's poem says? Is the sound as well adapted to the sense? Does it communicate the same experience?

Herrick's Julia Improved

When all in silk my Julia's dressed,
She flows along, be it confessed,
As if her clothes had deliquesced.

Next, if and when I her behold,
Her oscillations are so bold,
She glistens like a lump of gold.

Reading Aloud

Reading poems aloud can reveal how sound reinforces sense and thereby increases understanding and enjoyment. Here are some suggestions:

1. Always read a poem much more slowly than you would read a prose selection, unless it is simple and self-evident like a jingle, limerick, or song lyric.

2. Read the poem several different ways. For instance, if the poem has a regular meter (see Appendix, p. 000), try reading it first in almost a singsong manner, and then in subsequent readings decrease the emphasis on the accented syllables. A good reading of a poem will enable a person who is not looking at a copy of the poem to understand it and be aware of the meter without being distracted by it.
3. Read naturally; avoid pompous tones and affected speech mannerisms. A great many poems are available on records. You will find it interesting to compare your reading with that of a professional.
4. Look up the pronunciation as well as the meaning of all unfamiliar words. All the words should be given a modern pronunciation (unless, of course, you are reading a Middle English poet like Chaucer), even though you have to sacrifice a rhyme. In Pope's couplet

    Good nature and good sense must ever join;
    To err is human, to forgive divine.

    the words *join* and *divine* are no longer exact rhymes as they were in the eighteenth century. You will occasionally encounter a situation like this when you are reading older poetry, and when you do, you should always give each of the rhyme words its modern pronunciation. Sound is important, but it is less important than sense.

Exercise 44

Show how sound is "an echo of the sense" in these poems.

Portrait of a King's Mistress, Nude

One sinuous wrist is lifted while it shakes
Golden bracelets in the form of snakes.
The black hair rises in a bird-wing hush.
That belly must have burned the painter's brush.
Her slitted eyes measure the mortal distance.
Lips part against the curved jaw's cruel insistence.
Breasts touch the naked sunlight with a kiss.
Arms stroke the crimson cover with a hiss.
The poured-out skin flows on the couch like milk.
The long legs slither through a field of silk.
The small toes curl in sensual indolence.
The bent knees in their waiting lie intense.

Whole body, lithe limb and fanged head alike,
Coil, ready for the rapturous hour to strike.
Tongue trembles, feeling the voluptuous air.
From hinting hand, the white fanged shoulder's stare,
And from the insolent mouth that smiles above,
She drips the lovely venom of her love.

A king was ravished by those charming thighs.
There were no scales before the painter's eyes.

Paul Engle
(1908–)

scales . . . eyes (20): an allusion to Acts ix:18.

A Glass of Beer

The lanky hank of a she in the inn over there
Nearly killed me for asking the loan of a glass of beer;
May the devil grip the whey-faced slut by the hair,
And beat bad manners out of her skin for a year.

That parboiled ape, with the toughest jaw you will see
On virtue's path, and a voice that would rasp the dead,
Came roaring and raging the minute she looked at me,
And threw me out of the house on the back of my head!

If I asked her master he'd give me a cask a day;
But she, with the beer at hand, not a gill would arrange!
May she marry a ghost and bear him a kitten, and may
The High King of Glory permit her to get the mange.

James Stephens
(1882–1950)

Now Sleeps the Crimson Petal

Now sleeps the crimson petal, now the white;
Nor waves the cypress in the palace walk;
Nor winks the gold fin in the porphyry font:
The fire-fly wakens: waken thou with me.

Now droops the milkwhite peacock like a ghost,
And like a ghost she glimmers on to me.

Now lies the Earth all Danaë to the stars,
And all thy heart lies open unto me.

Now slides the silent meteor on, and leaves
A shining furrow, as thy thoughts in me.

Now folds the lily all her sweetness up,
And slips into the bosom of the lake:
So fold thyself, my dearest, thou, and slip
Into my bosom and be lost in me.

Alfred, Lord Tennyson
(1809–1892)

porphyry font (3): a fountain made of a handsome dark red rock.
Danaë (7): She was seduced by Zeus in the form of a shower of golden rain.

A Dirge

Rough wind, that moanest loud
Grief too sad for song;
Wild wind, when sullen cloud
Knells all the night long;
Sad storm, whose tears are vain.
Bare woods, whose branches strain,
Deep caves and dreary main,
Wail, for the world's wrong!

Percy Bysshe Shelley
(1792–1822)

The Jungle

It is not the still weight
of the tree, the
breathless interior of the wood,
tangled with wrist-thick

vines, the flies, reptiles,
the forever fearful monkeys
screaming and running
in the branches—

                    but
a girl waiting,
shy, brown, soft-eyed—
to guide you
            Upstairs, sir.

William Carlos Williams
(1883–1963)

Lucifer in Starlight

On a starred night Prince Lucifer uprose.
Tired of his dark dominion swung the fiend
Above the rolling ball in cloud part screened,
Where sinners hugged their spectre of repose.
Poor prey to his hot fit of pride were those.
And now upon his western wing he leaned,
Now his huge bulk o'er Afric's sands careened,
Now the black planet shadowed Arctic snows.
Soaring through wider zones that pricked his scars
With memory of the old revolt from Awe,
He reached the middle height, and at the stars,
Which are the brain of heaven, he looked, and sank.
Around the ancient track marched, rank on rank,
The army of unalterable law.

George Meredith
(1828–1909)

1. Discuss the effect on the poem of making these changes in its diction: *black hell hole* for *dark dominion* (line 2); *earth* for *ball* (line 3); *kissed their phantom* for *hugged their spectre* (line 4); *bait* for *prey* (line 5); *big devil* for *black planet* (line 8); and *upper skies* for *wider zones* (line 9).
2. How do sound devices help the poet characterize Lucifer and describe his actions?
3. What keeps Lucifer from entering heaven? What sound device does the poet use to emphasize the *one* thing that keeps him out?

The Raper from Passenack

was very kind. When she regained
her wits, he said, It's all right, kid,
I took care of you.

What a mess she was in. Then he added,
You'll never forget me now.
And drove her home.

Only a man who is sick, she said
would do a thing like that.
It must be so.

No one who is not diseased could be
so insanely cruel. He wants to give it
to someone else—

to justify himself. But if I get a
venereal infection out of this
I won't be treated.

I refuse. You'll find me dead in bed
first. Why not? That's
the way she spoke,

I wish I could shoot him. How would
you like to know a murderer?
I may do it.

I'll know by the end of this week.
I wouldn't scream. I bit him
several times

but he was too strong for me.
I can't yet understand it. I don't
faint so easily.

When I came to myself and realized
what had happened all I could do
was to curse

and call him every vile name I could
think of. I was so glad
to be taken home.

I suppose it's my mind—the fear of
infection. I'd rather a million times
have been got pregnant.

But it's the foulness of it can't
be cured. And hatred, hatred of all men
—and disgust.

William Carlos Williams
(1883–1963)

Passenack (title): a place in New Jersey.

Sound as "Music" in Poems

There remains, finally, the subtlest of all effects of sound in poems—the sheer variety of vowel and consonant sounds, and the variegated rhythms, all working together to create the "music" of poems. The word is used by analogy with regular music and should not be confused with the tune of a poem that is sung. A poem that is sung has two kinds of music: the melody to which it is set, and its own rhythms and word sounds. When we speak of the music of poetry we are referring to what you would perceive if a poem were read aloud to you in a language you did not understand.

This overall sound in poems can be analyzed—scansion (analysis of meter) and phonetic transcription are appropriate tools—but it cannot be explained. No skilled poet, for example, ever wrote out a formula for all his rhythmic and sound effects and then proceeded to write a poem that fulfilled the formula. Although, as we have seen, it is possible to create patterns of sound, for the most part the poet must simply trust his ear in creating the overall effects of sound. He must pragmatically test his lines, revising and reshaping them, until they "sound" right to him.

Some poets—notably such fine craftsmen as Tennyson, Gerard Manley Hopkins, and Dylan Thomas—appear to have been keenly concerned with the sheer sound of their poems. Other poets are apt to be more conceptual in their approach to writing poems, preferring clarity of meaning to fullness of sound.

Perhaps the best way of illustrating these two approaches to sound is to contrast a poem that is dominated by effects of sound with another in which the music is deliberately muted.

In My Craft or Sullen Art

In my craft or sullen art
Exercised in the still night
When only the moon rages
And the lovers lie abed
With all their griefs in their arms,
I labour by singing light
Not for ambition or bread
Or the strut and trade of charms
On the ivory stages
But for the common wages
Of their most secret heart.

Not for the proud man apart
From the raging moon I write
On these spindrift pages
Not for the towering dead
With their nightingales and psalms
But for the lovers, their arms
Round the griefs of the ages,
Who pay no praise or wages
Nor heed my craft or art.

Dylan Thomas
(1914–1953)

The Boston Evening Transcript

The readers of the *Boston Evening Transcript*
Sway in the wind like a field of ripe corn.

When evening quickens faintly in the street,
Wakening the appetites of life in some
And to others bringing the *Boston Evening Transcript,*

I mount the steps and ring the bell, turning
Wearily, as one would turn to nod good-bye to Rochefoucauld,
If the street were time and he at the end of the street,
And I say, "Cousin Harriet, here is the *Boston Evening Transcript.*"

T. S. Eliot
(1888–1965)

Title: a now defunct Boston newspaper much read by rich and socially prominent people. *Rochefoucauld* (7): Francois de Marsillac, Duc de la Rochefoucald (1613–1680), author of cynical maxims based on a philosophy of enlightened self-interest.

When these poems are read aloud, the reader becomes aware of the sonorities of Thomas's poem, filled as it is with variegated vowel sounds, alliteration, and assonance, compared to the lack of these devices in Eliot's poem. The presence or lack of such devices of sound in a poem does not mark it as either good or bad, however. Thomas sought richness of sound as appropriate to his subject matter. Eliot, who has elsewhere written poems filled with sound, here chooses to ignore this device. The lack of sound devices may be his way of conveying his weariness and boredom with the upper classes of Boston, whose drab lives seem to circulate around nothing more than the news and social columns of the *Boston Evening Transcript.*

8. The Tone of a Poem

the same thing may be said for all of us, that we
do not admire
what we cannot understand.

Marianne Moore

In everyday conversation we do not rely on words alone to express our ideas and feelings; we also use facial expression, gestures, and tone of voice to convey nuances of meaning. People can sound ironic, sarcastic, bemused, outraged, malicious—the list can be extended to the whole range of human attitudes. "That's great!" means one thing when a father compliments his daughter for making good grades; it means something very different when he says it to a daughter who has just dented the fender of his car. Failure to understand the tone of what is said often results in failure to understand the meaning of what is said.

Tone in Literature

The word **tone** in literary discussion is borrowed from the expression *tone of voice*. Tone is the manner in which a poet makes his poem reflect his attitude toward his subject and toward his readers. Since printed poems lack the intonations of spoken words, readers must learn to "hear" their tone with the mind's ear. Tone cannot be heard in a particular place, as rhymes are heard at the ends of lines; rather, it pervades the whole poem. Neither can readers be certain that a poem will have the tone that they themselves would associate with a given subject. And—to make matters more complicated—tone can change within a poem, even within a short poem.

The three following poems have very different tones.

I Travelled among Unknown Men

I travelled among unknown men,
  In lands beyond the sea;
Nor, England! did I know till then
  What love I bore to thee.

'Tis past, that melancholy dream!
  Nor will I quit thy shore
A second time; for still I seem
  To love thee more and more.

Among thy mountains did I feel
  The joy of my desire;
And she I cherished turned her wheel
  Beside an English fire.

Thy mornings showed, thy nights concealed,
  The bowers where Lucy played;
And thine too is the last green field
  That Lucy's eyes surveyed.

William Wordsworth
(1770–1850)

Traveller's Curse after Misdirection

(from the Welsh)

May they stumble, stage by stage
On an endless pilgrimage,
Dawn and dusk, mile after mile,
At each and every step, a stile;
At each and every step withal
May they catch their feet and fall;
At each and every fall they take
May a bone within them break;
And may the bone that breaks within
Not be, for variation's sake,
Now rib, now thigh, now arm, now shin,
But always, without fail THE NECK.

Robert Graves
(1895–   )

Résumé

Razors pain you;
Rivers are damp;
Acids stain you;
And drugs cause cramp.
Guns aren't lawful;
Nooses give;
Gas smells awful;
You might as well live.

Dorothy Parker
(1893–1967)

Wordsworth's poem makes a simple statement of the patriotic love the speaker feels for his native country, both for itself and for its associations as the home of his beloved Lucy. The words of the poem are exactly proportioned to the experience and feelings that the poet is expressing. Thus, we can say that the tone of this poem is straightforward, sober, and serious.

In the other two poems, it is the disproportion between the words and the experience or feeling that reveals their tones. Grave's poem has an angry, frustrated, and comically vindictive tone. We sense that the speaker is not entirely serious, because the punishment so far exceeds the crime, and we enjoy the malevolence of the poem because we too have often been given faulty directions.

Dorothy Parker's verse is unserious in tone, because no would-be suicide could ever be dissuaded from the act by the flimsy arguments advanced here. The poem has also a mocking tone, because it is clearly directed against those who wallow in self-pity and threaten to kill themselves but always find reasons not to carry out their threats.

The two latter poems are examples of **light verse:** poems appealing primarily to a reader's sense of humor rather than to his mind and heart. Since light verse can be as skillfully written as serious poetry, there is always a danger that a beginning reader will treat it seriously and search for symbols and hidden significance. Attention to tone can prevent this error. Good light verse is polished, not profound.

Verbal Irony

Arms and the Boy

Let the boy try along this bayonet-blade
How cold steel is, and keen with hunger of blood;
Blue with all malice, like a madman's flash;
And thinly drawn with famishing for flesh.

Lend him to stroke these blind, blunt bullet-heads
Which long to nuzzle in the hearts of lads,
Or give him cartridges of fine zinc teeth,
Sharp with the sharpness of grief and death.

For his teeth seem for laughing round an apple.
There lurk no claws behind his fingers supple;
And God will grow no talons at his heels,
Nor antlers through the thickness of his curls.

Wilfred Owen
(1893–1918)

At first glance this poem seems to be fanatically militaristic. Let a young boy handle firearms, the speaker advises; make him familiar with bayonet blades, bullet heads, and cartridges. But does the speaker sincerely mean what he says? Does he really want the parents of young boys to take his advice literally? The images which describe the weapons suggest that he does not. These images personify the weapons, make them malicious and hungry for blood. They are images that a hater of war would use, not a lover of war. There is, then, a contradiction between what the speaker says literally and the way in which he says it—a contradiction that the third stanza resolves: God will not turn the boy into a monster with fangs, claws, talons, and horns, but man can do so by giving him arms and making him a soldier. If stanza 3 describes what happens when the boy is given arms, stanzas 1 and 2 must be ironical in tone.

A poem or any other work of literature contains **verbal irony** when it makes statements that mean the opposite of what they seem to mean on the surface. Failure to detect irony will cause a reader to understand just the opposite of what is intended—a very serious error indeed. There is, unfortunately, no magic formula for detecting verbal irony. If one existed, it would destroy the pleasure felt by an alert reader when he discovers that a writer is not saying what he means. This discovery always creates a bond between reader and writer something like the bond connecting two people who share a private joke. Recognition of verbal irony depends on the reader's mental alertness, his close attention to the words of a poem, and his quickness in responding to certain signals. Among these signals are inconsistencies like those in "Arms and the Boy," overstatement, and understatement (see Chapter 5).

Verbal irony must be carefully distinguished from mere **sarcasm.** According to *Webster's New Collegiate Dictionary,* the word *sarcasm* means "a keen or bitter taunt; a cutting gibe or rebuke." There is nothing ironical in such ordinary sarcasms as "Drop dead!" They say exactly what they mean. Everybody "gets" sarcasm, but irony can easily be misunderstood.

On Proclus's Great Nose

Thy nose no man can wipe, Proclus, unless
He have a hand as big as Hercules.
When thou dost sneeze, the sound thou dost not hear:
Thy nose is so far distant from thine ear.

Anonymous
(Seventeenth Century)

While these unkind lines exaggerate the size of Proclus's nose, they say essentially what they mean: the nose is immense. In contrast, an ironical poem on a large nose would claim that it was actually a small nose!

Exercise 45

Analyze the following poems. Determine which of them employ verbal irony.

A Short Song of Congratulation

Long-expected one and twenty
Ling'ring year at last is flown,
Pomp and Pleasure, Pride and Plenty
Great Sir John, are all your own.

Loosen'd from the Minor's tether,
Free to mortgage or to sell,
Wild as wind, and light as feather
Bid the slaves of thrift farewell.

Call the Bettys, Kates, and Jennys
Ev'ry name that laughs at Care,
Lavish of your Grandsire's guineas,
Show the Spirit of an heir.

All that prey on vice and folly
Joy to see their quarry fly,
Here the Gamester light and jolly
There the Lender grave and sly.

Wealth, Sir John, was made to wander,
Let it wander as it will;
See the Jocky, see the Pander,
Bid them come, and take their fill.

When the bonny Blade carouses,
Pockets full, and Spirits high,
What are acres? What are houses?
Only dirt, or wet or dry.

If the Guardian or the Mother
Tell the woes of wilful waste,
Scorn their counsel and their pother,
You can hang or drown at last.

Samuel Johnson
(1709–1784)

pother (27): fuss.

1. Why is the year called "ling'ring" (line 2)?
2. If a *tether* is a rope or chain that prevents an animal from ranging beyond a set radius, what is a "Minor's tether" (line 5)?
3. What has Sir John done to deserve the epithet *great* (line 4)?
4. Who are the women in line 9?
5. How can you tell that the speaker does not approve of the gamester (line 15), the jockey, and the pander (line 19)?

The Latest Decalogue

Thou shalt have one God only; who
Would be at the expense of two?
No graven images may be
Worshipped, except the currency:
Swear not at all; for, for thy curse
Thine enemy is none the worse;
At church on Sunday to attend
Will serve to keep the world thy friend:
Honour thy parents; that is, all
From whom advancement may befall:
Thou shalt not kill; but needst not strive
Officiously to keep alive:
Do not adultery commit;
Advantage rarely comes of it:
Thou shalt not steal; an empty feat,
When it's so lucrative to cheat:
Bear not false witness; let the lie
Have time on its own wings to fly:
Thou shalt not covet; but tradition
Approves all forms of competition.
The sum of all is, thou shalt love,
If any body, God above:
At any rate shall never labour
More than thyself to love thy neighbour.

Arthur Hugh Clough
(1819–1861)

to keep alive (12): to keep another man alive.

1. Why is biblical language used?
2. What does *two* (line 2) refer to? *all* (line 9)?
3. What are *graven images* (line 3)?
4. Explain the difference between the two parts of each couplet.
5. Locate every word associated with money. Why are there so many? What is the speaker's attitude toward money?
6. Is the speaker ridiculing the Ten Commandments? Explain your answer.
7. Most editors omit the last four lines. Does this omission improve the poem?

Call It a Good Marriage

Call it a good marriage—
For no one ever questioned
Her warmth, his masculinity,
Their interlocking views;
Except one stray graphologist
Who frowned in speculation
At her h's and her s's,
His p's and w's.

Though few would still subscribe
To the monogamic axiom
That strife below the hip-bones
Need not estrange the heart,
Call it a good marriage:
More drew those two together,
Despite a lack of children,
Than pulled them apart.

Call it a good marriage:
They never fought in public,
They acted circumspectly
And faced the world with pride;
Thus the hazards of their love-bed
Were none of our damned business—
Till as jurymen we sat on
Two deaths by suicide.

Robert Graves
(1895–   )

monogamic axiom (10): the conventional wisdom that a husband and wife should be mutually faithful and that a happy sex life is not essential to a good marriage. *jurymen* (23): coroner's jurors inquiring into the cause of the deaths.

1. In what ways is the meaning of the word *good* (line 1) somewhat changed by the time the reader reaches the last word in the poem?

Limericks

There were three young women of Birmingham,
And I know a sad story concerning 'em:
They stuck needles and pins
In the reverend shins
Of the Bishop engaged in confirming 'em.

A lady there was of Antigua,
Who said to her spouse, "What a pig you are!"
He answered, "My queen,
Is it manners you mean,
Or do you refer to my figure?"

There was a young girl of Lahore,
With the same shape behind as before.
As no one knew where
To offer a chair,
She had to sit down on the floor.

Cosmo Monkhouse
(1840–1901)

Other Kinds of Irony

According to H. W. Fowler's *A Dictionary of Modern English Usage,* irony always presupposes a double audience. One audience perceives only the surface meaning; the other, more acute, sees beyond the surface to a deeper meaning. In verbal irony the more perceptive audience grasps the surface meaning *and* the deeper intent, which is just the opposite of the surface meaning. Irony results from the clash of these two meanings. The same double effect is present in **irony of situation**: here the variation exists between what should be and what is, or between what is expected to happen, and what does in fact happen.

By Her Aunt's Grave

"Sixpence a week," says the girl to her lover,
"Aunt used to bring me, for she could confide
In me alone, she vowed. 'Twas to cover
The cost of her headstone when she died.
And that was a year ago last June;
I've not yet fixed it. But I must soon."

"And where is the money now, my dear?"
"O, snug in my purse . . . Aunt was *so* slow
In saving it—eighty weeks, or near." . . .
"Let's spend it," he hints. "For she won't know.
There's a dance to-night at the Load of Hay."
She passively nods. And they go that way.

Thomas Hardy
(1840–1928)

This situation is ironical because it is the opposite of what the aunt expected. The money that she had slowly saved for her tombstone is now going to be spent at a dance hall. Hardy does not explicitly condemn any of the three people: the short-sighted aunt, the weak niece, the insensitive young man. The poet implies the irony merely by setting up the contrasting situation.

Irony of character is a device in which a discrepancy exists between what a character seems to be and what he is:

Miniver Cheevy

Miniver Cheevy, child of scorn,
  Grew lean while he assailed the seasons;
He wept that he was ever born,
  And he had reasons.

Miniver loved the days of old
  When swords were bright and steeds were prancing;
The visions of a warrior bold
  Would set him dancing.

Miniver sighed for what was not,
  And dreamed, and rested from his labors;
He dreamed of Thebes and Camelot,
  And Priam's neighbors.

Miniver mourned the ripe renown
  That made so many a name so fragrant;
He mourned Romance, now on the town,
  And Art, a vagrant.

Miniver loved the Medici,
  Albeit he had never seen one;
He would have sinned incessantly
  Could he have been one.

Miniver cursed the commonplace
  And eyed a khaki suit with loathing;
He missed the mediæval grace
  Of iron clothing.

Miniver scorned the gold he sought,
  But sore annoyed was he without it;
Miniver thought, and thought, and thought,
  And thought about it.

Miniver Cheevy, born too late,
  Scratched his head and kept on thinking;
Miniver coughed, and called it fate,
  And kept on drinking.

Edwin Arlington Robinson
(1869–1935)

on the town (15): impoverished.

Miniver is not what he seems to be. He thinks that he would have been happy and successful had he lived in the glorious past rather than in the dull present. Of course he is deluded: his sickness, his laziness, and his addiction to drink would make him a miserable failure in any age. Robinson uses verbal irony throughout the poem to convey his complex feelings about Miniver. He finds Miniver contemptible, pitiful, and ludicrous all at the same time and for the same reasons. Without irony, these contradictory feelings could not be expressed simultaneously.

A poet may employ irony of character by making the character the speaker (see "My last Duchess," page 95). In such first-person poems irony of character is present whenever there is a discrepancy between what the character says about himself and what the poet wants the reader to think about him.

Exercise 46

Identify and discuss the kinds of irony in these poems.

Yet Do I Marvel

I doubt not God is good, well-meaning, kind,
And did He stoop to quibble could tell why
The little buried mole continues blind,
Why flesh that mirrors Him must some day die,
Make plain the reason tortured Tantalus
Is baited by the fickle fruit, declare
If merely brute caprice dooms Sisyphus
To struggle up a never-ending stair.
Inscrutable His ways are, and immune
To catechism by a mind too strewn
With petty cares to slightly understand
What awful brain compels His awful hand.
Yet do I marvel at this curious thing:
To make a poet black, and bid him sing!

Countee Cullen
(1903–1946)

Tantalus (5): a character in Greek myth who was punished in Hades by hunger and thirst; food and drink receded at his approach.
Sisyphus (7): a mythological figure who was condemned in Hades to roll a stone uphill only to have it roll down again.

Song

Go and catch a falling star,
  Get with child a mandrake root,
Tell me where all past years are,
  Or who cleft the devil's foot,
Teach me to hear mermaids singing,

Or to keep off envy's stinging,
    And find
    What wind
Serves to advance an honest mind.

If thou beest born to strange sights,
  Things invisible to see,
Ride ten thousand days and nights,
  Till age snow white hairs on thee.
Thou, when thou return'st, wilt tell me
All strange wonders that befell thee,
    And swear
    No where
Lives a woman true and fair.

If thou find'st one, let me know:
  Such a pilgrimage were sweet;
Yet do not; I would not go,
  Though at next door we might meet.
Though she were true when you met her,
And last till you write your letter,
    Yet she
    Will be
False, ere I come, to two or three.

John Donne
(1572–1631)

mandrake root (2): said to be forked, like the lower part of a human body.

How We Heard the Name

The river brought down
dead horses, dead men
and military debris,

indicative of war
or official acts upstream,
but it went by, it all
goes by, that is the thing
about the river. Then
a soldier on a log
went by. He seemed drunk
and we asked him Why
had he and this junk
come down to us so
from the past upstream.
"Friends," he said, "the great
Battle of Granicus
has just been won
by all of the Greeks except
the Lacedaemonians and
myself: this is a joke
between me and a man
named Alexander, whom
all of you ba-bas
will hear of as a god."

Alan Dugan
(1923–)

river (1): The Granicus, site of the battle in 334 B.C. between Alexander the Great and Darius. Alexander's 30,000 men routed the Persian army which numbered 600,000, after which Alexander went on to conquer Asia Minor. *by . . . Lacedaemonians* (18–19): Alexander left an inscription that he had won the battle without the help of the Lacedaemonian Greeks.

Satire

Satire is a kind of writing that holds up wickedness, vice, and folly to ridicule with the purpose of seeking its amendment. Instead of setting an ideal before the reader, the satirist sets up the opposite of an ideal and then invites the reader to join him in ridiculing it. Satirists sometimes make a direct attack on vice and folly, as Jonson does in "Ask Not to Know This Man" (page 69); but more commonly they attack indirectly by means of irony.

On an Old Woman

Mycilla dyes her locks 'tis said,
 But 'tis a foul aspersion;
She buys them black. They therefore need
 No subsequent immersion.

William Cowper
(1731–1800)

This satirical epigram, which Cowper paraphrased from an ancient Greek original, pretends to defend an old woman while actually attacking her. The epigram is therefore an example of indirect satire. Mycilla is not satirized because she is old and gray but because she doesn't want to appear old and gray. Her fault is vanity—not old age. An old, deformed, or hideous person is not a proper butt for satire unless that person pretends to be young, sound, and beautiful; a lame man is ordinarily immune to satire unless he claims to be a high jumper or an agile dancer. Kings, presidents, and other conspicuous persons are automatically butts of satire because of their prominence. Not all satire, of course, is personal. Customs, institutions, and organizations may also be objects of satire.

Exercise 47

Which of the following poems have a satirical tone and which do not? What evidence do you find in the poems for your judgments?

A Far Cry from Africa

A wind is ruffling the tawny pelt
Of Africa. Kikuyu, quick as flies,
Batten upon the bloodstreams of the veldt.
Corpses are scattered through a paradise.
Only the worm, colonel of carrion, cries:
"Waste no compassion on these separate dead!"
Statistics justify and scholars seize
The salients of colonial policy.

What is that to the white child hacked in bed?
To savages, expendable as Jews?
Threshed out by beaters, the long rushes break
In a white dust of ibises whose cries
Have wheeled since civilization's dawn
From the parched river or beast-teeming plain.
The violence of beast on beast is read
As natural law, but upright man
Seeks his divinity by inflicting pain.
Delirious as these worried beasts, his wars
Dance to the tightened carcass of a drum,
While he calls courage still that native dread
Of the white peace contracted by the dead.
Again brutish necessity wipes its hands
Upon the napkin of a dirty cause, again
A waste of our compassion, as with Spain,
The gorilla wrestles with the superman.
I who am poisoned with the blood of both,
Where shall I turn, divided to the vein?
I who have cursed
The drunken officer of British rule, how choose
Between this Africa and the English tongue I love?
Betray them both, or give back what they give?
How can I face such slaughter and be cool?
How can I turn from Africa and live?

Derek Walcott
(1930–   )

Kikuyu (2): native tribesmen of Kenya, a former British colony in Africa. *Batten* (3): feed voraciously. *veldt* (3): grassland. *salients* (8): conspicuous features. *What . . . Jews* (9–10): referring to the slaughter of innocents on both sides during the Kikuyu wars for independence (1953) and to Hitler's policy of genocide against the Jews before and during World War II. *Spain* (24): referring to the Spanish Civil War (1936–1939).

1. In what ways is this poem more than just a protest against the colonialist policies of Western nations in Africa?
2. What is the dilemma in which the speaker finds himself?
3. What do the references to the slaughter of the Jews in Hitler's Germany (line 10) and the Spanish Civil War (line 24) suggest about the events described in the poem?

The Unknown Citizen

(To JS/07/M/378 This Marble Monument Is Erected by the State)

He was found by the Bureau of Statistics to be
One against whom there was no official complaint,
And all the reports on his conduct agree
That, in the modern sense of an old-fashioned word, he was a saint,
For in everything he did he served the Greater Community.
Except for the War till the day he retired
He worked in a factory and never got fired,
But satisfied his employers, Fudge Motors Inc.
Yet he wasn't a scab or odd in his views,
For his Union reports that he paid his dues,
(Our report on his Union shows it was sound)
And our Social Psychology workers found
That he was popular with his mates and liked a drink.
The Press are convinced that he bought a paper every day
And that his reactions to advertisements were normal in every way.
Policies taken out in his name prove that he was fully insured,
And his Health-card shows he was once in hospital but left it cured.
Both Producers Research and High-Grade Living declare
He was fully sensible to the advantages of the Installment Plan
And had everything necessary to the Modern Man,
A phonograph, a radio, a car and a frigidaire.
Our researchers into Public Opinion are content
That he held the proper opinions for the time of year;
When there was peace, he was for peace; when there was war, he went.
He was married and added five children to the population,
Which our Eugenist says was the right number for a parent of his generation,
And our teachers report that he never interfered with their education
Was he free? Was he happy? The question is absurd:
Had anything been wrong, we should certainly have heard.

W. H. Auden
(1907–1973)

The Woman at Banff

While she was talking a bear happened along, violating
every garbage can. Shaking its loose, Churchillian,
V for victory suit, it ripped up and ate
a greasy "Bears Are Dangerous!" sign.

While she was talking the trees above signalled—
"Few," and the rock back of them—"Cold."
And while she was talking a moose—huge, black—
swam that river and faded off winterward,

Up toward the Saskatchewan.

William Stafford
(1914–)

Churchillian . . . suit (2–3) : During World War II, Winston Churchill sometimes wore a baggy-looking jump suit when he was giving his famous "V-for-Victory" salute.

London

I wander thro' each charter'd street,
Near where the charter'd Thames does flow,
And mark in every face I meet
Marks of weakness, marks of woe.

In every cry of every Man,
In every Infant's cry of fear,
In every voice, in every ban,
The mind-forg'd manacles I hear.

How the Chimney-sweeper's cry
Every black'ning Church appalls;
And the hapless Soldier's sigh
Runs in blood down Palace walls.

But most thro' midnight streets I hear
How the youthful Harlot's curse
Blasts the new born Infant's tear,
And blights with plagues the Marriage hearse.

William Blake
(1757–1827)

1. In an earlier version of the poem Blake used the adjective *dirty* rather than *charter'd* (line 2), a word that connotes legal restrictions of some sort. Is the earlier adjective preferable? Does the metaphor implied by *charter'd* occur elsewhere in the poem?

2. What is the effect of the repetition and parallel structure?
3. Why does Blake associate the chimney sweeper with the church? The soldier with the palace? What is the soldier's complaint?
4. Why does Blake mention a "youthful" (line 14) harlot rather than an old one?
5. *Blasts* (line 15) and *blights* (line 16) are metaphors drawn from gardening. Explain their appropriateness.

Peter

Peter hath lost his purse, but will conceal it
Lest she that stole it to his shame reveal it.

Anonymous
(Seventeenth Century)

1. What is the thief's other occupation besides stealing?

London, 1802

Milton! thou shouldst be living at this hour:
England hath need of thee: she is a fen
Of stagnant waters: altar, sword, and pen,
Fireside, the heroic wealth of hall and bower,
Have forfeited their ancient English dower
Of inward happiness. We are selfish men;
Oh! raise us up, return to us again;
And give us manners, virtue, freedom, power.
Thy soul was like a Star, and dwelt apart;
Thou hadst a voice whose sound was like the sea:
Pure as the naked heavens, majestic, free,
So didst thou travel on life's common way,
In cheerful godliness; and yet thy heart
The lowliest duties on herself did lay.

William Wordsworth
(1770–1850)

Milton (1): Wordsworth is thinking of John Milton not only as the great epic poet, but also as the great champion of freedom and as the undersecretary of state for the Commonwealth.

1. Find some figures of language that reveal Wordsworth's attitude toward contemporary England and toward Milton. Identify the other figures and show how they are used.
2. Compare Wordsworth's description of the contemporary scene with Blake's in "London."

On the Death of a Late Famous General

His Grace! impossible! what, dead!
Of old age too, and in his bed!
And could that mighty warrior fall?
And so inglorious, after all!
Well, since he's gone, no matter how,
The last loud trump must wake him now;
And, trust me, as the noise grows stronger,
He'd wish to sleep a little longer.
And could he be indeed so old
As by the newspapers we're told?
Threescore, I think, is pretty high;
'Twas time in conscience he should die.
This world he cumbered long enough;
He burnt his candle to the snuff;
And that's the reason, some folks think,
He left behind so great a stink.
Behold his funeral appears,
Nor widow's sighs nor orphan's tears,
Wont at such times each heart to pierce,
Attend the progress of his hearse.
But what of that? his friends may say
He had those honours in his day.
True to his profit and his pride,
He made them weep before he died.
  Come hither, all ye empty things,
Ye bubbles raised by breath of kings,
Who float upon the tide of state,
Come hither, and behold your fate!
Let pride be taught by this rebuke
How very mean a thing's a duke;
From all his ill-got honours flung,
Turn'd to that dirt from whence he sprung.

Jonathan Swift
(1667–1745)

General (Title) : John Churchill, first Duke of Marlborough, a great military hero who became a petty politician. *Grace* (1) : title given to a duke. *trump* (6) : the trumpet signalling the end of the world and the Last Judgment. *snuff* (14) : the end of the wick.

1. What are the implications of lines 7 and 8?
2. What is the difference between the *widow* and *orphan* of line 18 and the widows and orphans referred to in line 24?
3. What double meaning is involved in the use of the word *dirt* in line 32 rather than *dust*?

Portrait in Georgia

Hair—braided chestnut,
    coiled like a lyncher's rope,
Eyes—fagots,
Lips—old scars, or the first red blisters,
Breath—the last sweet scent of cane,
And her slim body, white as the ash
    of black flesh after flame.

Jean Toomer
(1894–1967)

Epitaph on the Politician

Here richly, with ridiculous display,
The Politician's corpse was laid away.
While all of his acquaintance sneered and slanged
I wept: for I had longed to see him hanged.

Hilaire Belloc
(1870–1953)

slanged (3): used abusive language.

1. What is the speaker's motive in reporting the conduct of the dead man's friends?
2. What is ironical about the speaker's situation?

Irony versus Sentimentality

Satirists are not the only kinds of poets who may employ an ironical tone. Irony, in one form or another, is likely to be a device of any poet who wishes to suggest more than he says directly, or who wishes to avoid oversimplifying human experience.

To Hear an Oriole Sing

To hear an Oriole sing
May be a common thing—
Or only a divine.

It is not of the Bird
Who sings the same, unheard,
As unto Crowd—

The Fashion of the Ear
Attireth that it hear.
In Dun, or fair—

So whether it be Rune,
Or whether it be none
Is of within.

The "Tune is in the Tree—"
The Skeptic—showeth me—
"No Sir! In Thee!"

Emily Dickinson
(1830–1886)

The opening lines present a problem. Is the oriole's song a common thing or a divine thing? The remainder of the poem suggests that the answer to this question depends on the listener to the song. Whether it is divine (*rune*) or not depends on the inner response (the *within*) of the listener. To the speaker of the poem, the song is divine—but only divine. The word *only* (line 3) is ironical because it is unexpected; we should expect *only* to be applied to common rather than to divine things. Its use here implies the paradox that what is natural is more uncommon than what is divine. Irony has enabled the poet to be as hard-minded as the skeptic with whom she is arguing, and to express her sense of wonder without becoming sentimental.

Sentimentality is the evocation of a greater amount of feeling or emotion than is justified by the subject. It must not be confused with *sentiment,* which is merely another name for feeling or emotion, and which does not have the negative connotations of *sentimentality.* (Some students confuse these two nouns because the adjective *sentimental* seems to be derived from both. *Sentimental* goes with *sentimentality,* not with *sentiment.*) The poet who adopts a sentimental tone becomes more tearful or more ecstatic over his subject than it deserves. The sentimentalist is addicted to worn-out baby shoes, gray-haired mothers, and small animals—subjects certain to evoke an automatic response in a particular kind of reader. But sentimentality is not so much a matter of subject as it is a matter of treatment.

Thoughts on Capital Punishment

There ought to be capital punishment for cars
that run over rabbits and drive into dogs
and commit the unspeakable, unpardonable crime
of killing a kitty cat still in his prime.

Purgatory, at the very least
should await the driver
driving over a beast.

Those hurrying headlights coming out of the dark
that scatter the scampering squirrels in the park
should await the best jury that one might compose
of fatherless chipmunks and husbandless does.

And then found guilty, after too fair a trial
should be caged in a cage with a hyena's smile
or maybe an elephant with an elephant gun
should shoot out his eyes when the verdict is done.

There ought to be something, something that's fair
to avenge Mrs. Badger as she waits in her lair
for her husband who lies with his guts spilling out
cause he didn't know what automobiles are about.

Hell on the highway, at the very least
should await the driver
driving over a beast.

Who kills a man kills a bit of himself
But a cat too is an extension of God.

Rod McKuen
(1933–)

The chief defect of this poem is its sentimentality; the feelings it expresses are wholly disproportionate to the subject matter. No person with decent feelings, of course, takes pleasure in the deaths of animals on the road; and if it is our own pet that is killed we may be genuinely grieved. But to call such accidents unspeakable, unpardonable crimes seems rather excessive. Unfortunately there is no evidence that the speaker's maudlin language is redeemed by irony. "Kitty cat" is baby talk; and chipmunks with fathers, does with husbands, and Mrs. Badger and her husband belong to the world of children's animal stories. Such sentimentality also yields failures in logic. Would the crime be more pardonable if the kitty cat were not in its prime? Are the cars or the drivers who steer them to be punished? A little reflection leads us to the conclusion that there are worse evils in this world than the accidental deaths of animals on the road.

Wit

When Emily Dickinson (page 258) calls the oriole's song "only divine," she is being witty in a serious way. Her tone is playful and clever, yet the poem is perfectly serious and sincere. Only a naïve reader would assume that because the poem is not long-faced and solemn, it is trivial. Serious poems as well as light verse may employ wit, or intellectual cleverness. The reader must determine whether a poem with a witty tone is serious or jocose.

In literary history, the term *wit* is used in a special sense. As applied to the writings of Donne, Herbert, Marvell, and other seventeenth-century English poets, **wit** signifies the ability to perceive and to express the complexities of experience. The poetry of wit contains metaphysical conceits (see page 142), paradoxes (see page 164), and irony.

The Mistress

An age in her embraces passed,
  Would seem a winter's day,
Where life and light, with envious haste,
  Are torn and snatched away.

But, oh! how slowly minutes roll,
  When absent from her eyes,
That feed my love, which is my soul;
  It languishes and dies.

For then no more a soul but shade,
  It mournfully does move,
And haunts my breast, by absence made
  The living tomb of love.

You wiser men despise me not,
  Whose love-sick fancy raves
On shades of souls, and Heaven knows what:
  Short ages live in graves.

Whene'er those wounding eyes, so full
  Of sweetness, you did see,
Had you not been profoundly dull,
  You had gone mad like me.

Nor censure us, you who perceive
  My best belov'd and me
Sigh and lament, complain and grieve;
  You think we disagree.

Alas! 'tis sacred jealousy,
  Love raised to an extreme,
The only proof 'twixt her and me,
  We love, and do not dream.

Fantastic fancies fondly move,
And in frail joys believe,
Taking false pleasure for true love;
But pain can ne'er deceive.

Kind jealous doubts, tormenting fears,
And anxious cares, when past,
Prove our heart's treasure fixed and dear,
And make us blest at last.

John Wilmot, Earl of Rochester
(1647–1680)

Here a lover tells what his love means to him. He begins, surprisingly enough, by saying that a very long period of time spent in his lady's arms would be like a single winter's day. At first glance this comparison seems paradoxical, for how can lovemaking resemble winter? Lines 3 and 4 resolve the paradox; the lover is thinking of the shortness of a winter's day and of the intensity with which people who want "light and life" have to live in cold weather. He cannot spend an age with his mistress; the time that he can spend with her is much too short, like the time that the sun stays out in winter. He therefore is envious of time, and he takes his pleasures violently. Upon examination, then, the comparison does not seem farfetched, but it does require the reader to think rather than simply to form mental pictures. Many of the images in poems of serious wit cannot be visualized.

In stanzas 2 and 3 the lover explains what happens when he is away from the lady. In a very bold metaphor he says that his love is his soul—bold because a man's soul is his most precious possession, immaterial and immortal. Unless fed by the lady's eyes (an image that cannot be visualized), the soul dies and haunts the lover's breast, which paradoxically becomes a "living tomb" (line 12). The witty metaphor that extends through these two stanzas enables the lover to give the highest possible praises to his mistress.

Stanzas 4 and 5 show that the lover is aware of his excesses. He addresses some imaginary auditors, some men "wiser" than he, who may despise and mock him because he has said that his love is his soul. To defend himself, he says, "Short ages live in graves" (line 16): a cryptic remark, which may imply that his dead soul will revive shortly, when he sees the lady again. He must be ironical when he calls these listeners wise, because he later calls them "profoundly dull" (line 19) for not sharing his madness. Moreover, they do not understand the relationship between the lovers; they assume that the lovers disagree when they "sigh and lament, complain and grieve" (line 23).

In the last three stanzas the lover explains the nature of that relationship. Actually the two lovers are agreeing rather than disagreeing. They inflict pain on each other because pain is more real than pleasure. Without the pangs of "sacred jealousy" (line 25), their love would be so pleasant that it would seem a dream. Pleasure is deceptive; pain, on the other hand, "can ne'er deceive" (line 32). True love, he asserts, causes pain, and true lovers welcome that pain. This truth about love is profoundly paradoxical. The paradox was earlier suggested in the image of the winter's day, and it is finally resolved in the last stanza. Doubts and fears past, the lovers become "blest" (line 36), more "blest" than they would have been if they had never doubted and feared. They know that their love is "fixed" (line 35)—that is, firm—because it can survive such turmoil. The word *blest* ordinarily appears in a religious context; it reminds the reader that the lover has earlier spoken of his love as his soul and has called his jealousy sacred. Love, in short, is a kind of religion because it provides ultimate realities. Without love, life would not be real.

The tone of this poem is very different from the tone of a love poem like "A Red, Red Rose" by Robert Burns (see page 126). Both poems are hyperbolical, but Burns's hyperbolical figures appeal primarily to the reader's senses, Rochester's to both the intellect and the senses. Burns does not surprise the reader with witty paradoxes; his lover sings. Rochester's lover argues and explains, because he is more interested in defining the psychological state of being in love than in commending the beauty of his lady. Instead of addressing the lady, he addresses a public made up of dull men who cannot understand the religion of love. Hence his tone becomes satirical when he thinks of his public, intense and tender when he thinks of his mistress. The tone of Burns's lyric does not shift in this way. Rochester makes many more demands on the reader because the experience he is communicating is more complex than Burns's. The devices of serious wit enable him to communicate that experience.

Mock-Heroic

A poem with a **mock-heroic** tone uses lofty language and learned allusions to elevate a trivial subject. Mock-heroic poems seem funny to readers who can perceive the contrast between an insignificant subject and a pompous treatment. In the following poem, a subject that would seem tragic to Rod McKuen is treated so elaborately that it becomes comic:

Ode

On The Death of a Favorite Cat,
Drowned in a Tub of Goldfishes

'Twas on a lofty vase's side,
Where China's gayest art had dyed
  The azure flowers that blow,
Demurest of the tabby kind,
The pensive Selima, reclined,
  Glazed on the lake below.

Her conscious tail her joy declared;
The fair round face, the snowy beard,
  The velvet of her paws,
Her coat, that with the tortoise vies,
Her ears of jet, and emerald eyes,
  She saw; and purred applause.

Still had she gazed; but 'midst the tide
Two angel forms were seen to glide,
  The genii of the stream:
Their scaly armor's Tyrian hue
Through richest purple to the view
  Betrayed a golden gleam.

The hapless nymph with wonder saw:
A whisker first and then a claw,
  With many an ardent wish,
She stretched in vain to reach the prize.
What female heart can gold despise?
  What cat's averse to fish?

Presumptuous maid! with looks intent
Again she stretched, again she bent,
  Nor knew the gulf between.
(Malignant Fate sat by and smiled)
The slippery verge her feet beguiled,
  She tumbled headlong in.

Eight times emerging from the flood
She mewed to every watery god,
  Some speedy aid to send.
No dolphin came, no Nereid stirred;
Nor cruel Tom, nor Susan heard;
  A favorite has no friend!

From hence, ye beauties, undeceived,
Know, one false step is ne'er retrieved,
  And be with caution bold.
Not all that tempts your wandering eyes
And heedless hearts, is lawful prize;
  Nor all that glisters, gold.

Thomas Gray
(1716–1771)

blow (3) : bloom. *genii* (15) : guardian spirits. *Tyrian* (16) : in antiquity, a rich reddish purple. *dolphin* (34) : in classical mythology, a dolphin rescued the singer Arion when he fell overboard. *Nereid* (34) : water nymph.

Burlesque

As applied to literature, **burlesque** refers to the deliberate debasement of important matters for comic or satirical purposes. Thus, it is the exact opposite of mock-heroic. In 1774 the great German writer Goethe published a novel, *The Sorrows of Young Werther,* a tragic tale of hopeless and unrequited love that had a strong influence on the Romantic poets. The following poem, written during the next century, burlesqued the theme of the novel.

Sorrows of Werther

Werther had a love for Charlotte
  Such as words could never utter;
Would you know how first he met her?
  She was cutting bread and butter.

Charlotte was a married lady,
  And a moral man was Werther,
And, for all the wealth of Indies,
  Would do nothing for to hurt her.

So he sighed and pined and ogled,
  And his passion boiled and bubbled,
Till he blew his silly brains out,
  And no more was by it troubled.

Charlotte, having seen his body
  Borne before her on a shutter,
Like a well-conducted person,
  Went on cutting bread and butter.

William Makepeace Thackeray
(1811–1863)

Parody

Parody is the imitation of an author's language and style for comic or satiric purposes. To perceive parody, a reader must be acquainted with the original work or works being parodied. The two following poems should be compared with poems actually written by Housman or Wordsworth. There are several in this book (pages 25, 63, 83, 294, 300, and 346). Which parody seems the more successful, and why?

A.E.H.

Flame the westward skies adorning
Leaves no like on holt or hill;
Sounds of battle joined at morning
Wane and wander and are still.

Past the standards rent and muddied,
Past the careless heaps of slain,
Stalks a redcoat who, unbloodied,
Weeps with fury, not from pain.

Wounded lads, when to renew them
Death and surgeons cross the shade,
Still their cries, hug darkness to them;
All at last in sleep are laid.

All save one, who nightlong curses
Wounds imagined more than seen,
Who in level tones rehearses
What the fact of wounds must mean.

Kingsley Amis
(1922–)

He Lived amidst th' Untrodden Ways

He lived amidst th' untrodden ways
  To Rydal Lake that lead;
A bard whom there were none to praise,
  And very few to read.

Behind a cloud his mystic sense,
  Deep hidden, who can spy?
Bright as the night when not a star
  Is shining in the sky.

Unread his works—his "Milk White Doe"
  With dust is dark and dim;
It's still in Longman's shop, and oh!
  The difference to him!

Hartley Coleridge
(1796–1849)

Rydal Lake (2) : near Wordsworth's final home. *Milk White Doe* (9) : *The White Doe of Rylstone,* a long poem by Wordsworth. *Longman's shop* (11) : English publisher.

Exercise 48

Discuss the tone of these poems. Remember that all the elements in a poem contribute to its tone. Comment on any shifts of tone that you discover within a poem.

I Hear an Army

I hear an army charging upon the land,
  And the thunder of horses plunging, foam about their knees:
Arrogant, in black armor, behind them stand,
  Disdaining the reins, with fluttering whips, the charioteers.

They cry unto the night their battle-name:
  I moan in sleep when I hear afar their whirling laughter.
They cleave the gloom of dreams, a blinding flame,
  Clanging, clanging upon the heart as upon an anvil.

They come shaking in triumph their long, green hair:
  They come out of the sea and run shouting by the shore.
My heart, have you no wisdom thus to despair?
  My love, my love, my love, why have you left me alone?

James Joyce
(1882–1941)

Portrait d'une Femme

Your mind and you are our Sargasso Sea,
London has swept about you this score years
And bright ships left you this or that in fee:
Ideas, old gossip, oddments of all things,
Strange spars of knowledge and dimmed wares of price.
Great minds have sought you—lacking someone else.
You have been second always. Tragical?
No. You preferred it to the usual thing:
One dull man, dulling and uxorious,
One average mind—with one thought less, each year.
Oh, you are patient, I have seen you sit
Hours, where something might have floated up.
And now you pay one. Yes, you richly pay.
You are a person of some interest, one comes to you
And takes strange gain away:
Trophies fished up; some curious suggestion;
Fact that leads nowhere; and a tale or two,
Pregnant with mandrakes, or with something else
That might prove useful and yet never proves,
That never fits a corner or shows use,

Or finds its hour upon the loom of days:
The tarnished, gaudy, wonderful old work;
Idols and ambergris and rare inlays,
These are your riches, your great store; and yet
For all this sea-hoard of deciduous things,
Strange woods half-sodden, and new brighter stuff:
In the slow float of differing light and deep,
No! there is nothing! in the whole and all,
Nothing that's quite your own.
                    Yet this is you.

Ezra Pound
(1885–1972)

Title: "Portrait of a Lady." *Sargasso Sea* (1): a tract of calm water in the North Atlantic, full of vegetation. *uxorious* (9): excessively fond of a wife.

Mr. Z

Taught early that his mother's skin was the sign of error,
He dressed and spoke the perfect part of honor;
Won scholarships, attended the best schools,
Disclaimed kinship with jazz and spirituals;
Chose prudent, raceless views for each situation,
Or when he could not cleanly skirt dissension,
Faced up to the dilemma, firmly seized
Whatever ground was Anglo-Saxonized.

In diet, too, his practice was exemplary:
Of pork in its profane forms he was wary;
Expert in vintage wines, sauces and salads,
His palate shrank from cornbread, yams and collards.

He was as careful whom he chose to kiss:
His bride had somewhere lost her Jewishness,
But kept her blue eyes; an Episcopalian
Prelate proclaimed them matched chameleon.
Choosing the right addresses, here, abroad,
They shunned those places where they might be barred;
Even less anxious to be asked to dine
Where hosts catered to kosher accent or exotic skin.

And so he climbed, unclogged by ethnic weights,
An airborne plant, flourishing without roots.
Not one false note was struck—until he died:
His subtly grieving widow could have flayed
The obit writers, ringing crude changes on a clumsy phrase:
"One of the most distinguished members of his race."

M. Carl Holman
(1919–)

obit (25): obituary.

Snow

In the gloom of whiteness,
In the great silence of snow,
A child was sighing
And bitterly saying: "Oh,
They have killed a white bird up there on her nest,
The down is fluttering from her breast!"
And still it fell through that dusky brightness
On the child crying for the bird of the snow.

Edward Thomas
(1878–1917)

Prairie Town

There was a river under First and Main;
the salt mines honeycombed farther down.
A wealth of sun and wind ever so strong
converged on that home town, long gone.

At the north edge there were the sandhills.
I used to stare for hours at prairie dogs,
which had their town, and folded their little paws
to stare beyond their fence where I was.

River rolling in secret, salt mines with care
holding your crystals and stillness, north prairie—
what kind of trip can I make, with what old friend,
ever to find a town so widely rich again?

Pioneers, for whom history was walking through dead grass,
and the main things that happened were miles and the time of day—
you built that town, and I have let it pass.
Little folded paws, judge me: I came away.

William Stafford
(1914–)

The Recall

I am the land of their fathers.
In me the virtue stays.
I will bring back my children,
After certain days.

Under their feet in the grasses
My clinging magic runs.
They shall return as strangers.
They shall remain as sons.

Over their heads in the branches
Of their new-bought, ancient trees,
I weave an incantation
And draw them to my knees.

Scent of smoke in the evening,
Smell of rain in the night—
The hours, the days and the seasons,
Order their souls aright,

Till I make plain the meaning
Of all my thousand years—
Till I fill their hearts with knowledge,
While I fill their eyes with tears.

Rudyard Kipling
(1865–1936)

9. The Whole Poem

> A poem is that species of composition, which is opposed to works of science, by proposing for its immediate object pleasure, not truth; and from all other species (having this object in common with it) it is discriminated by proposing to itself such delight from the *whole* as is compatible with a distinct gratification from each component part.
>
> *Samuel Taylor Coleridge*

Like other works of art or finished creations, poems exist within definite limits. They have a beginning and an end, and what happens between those limits does not happen accidentally. A poem is not a random assemblage of images and sounds, just as a piece of music is not a collection of noises. In a good poem all the elements—diction, images, ideas, figures, rhythm, sound—are so organized that they make up a unified whole. The whole poem is something different, something more significant, than the sum of its parts, just as a house is much more than a confused heap of bricks, boards, glass, nails, and so on.

External Form

To give the poetic materials external shape, a poet may use one of the **fixed forms,** which are combinations of lines that have been long established in English and American poetry. The following are some of the most common of these fixed forms. The technical terms used here, such as **iambic pentameter,** are described in Appendix A.

Blank verse: unrhymed iambic pentameter lines (Frost, "Out, Out—").

Couplets: lines rhyming *a a b b c c* , and so on. They are **closed** when the thought within the two lines is complete (Swift, "A Description of the Morning"), **open** when the thought runs past the two rhymed lines (Browning, "My Last Duchess"). Closed iambic pentameter couplets are called **heroic couplets**.

Stanzas: successive groups of the same number of lines held together by meter and rhyme scheme, printed as a unit and separated by a space from similar units in a poem. Some poems are broken into **verse paragraphs** (Arnold, "Dover Beach"), which are units of thought of varying length.

The most common stanzas (couplets are occasionally printed as stanzas) are these:

Triplets or tercets: three lines rhyming *a a a* followed by three rhyming *b b b,* and so on (Tennyson, "The Eagle"). Triplets are sometimes inserted among couplets (Hopkins, "Spring and Fall").

Terza rima: a series of iambic pentameter lines rhyming *a b a* followed by three rhyming *b c b,* and then three rhyming *c d c,* and so on (Shelley, "Ode to the West Wind").

Quatrains: stanzas of four lines with a fixed pattern of rhyme and meter. There are numerous arrangements possible, but the most common are pentameter rhyming *a b a b* (Robinson, "Richard Cory"), *a b b a* (Wilbur, "Still, Citizen Sparrow"), or *a a b b* (Belloc, "Epitaph on the Politician"); tetrameter rhyming *a b a b* (Swift, "The Progress of Beauty"), *a b b a* (Tennyson, *In Memoriam*), or *a a b b* (Housman, "To an Athlete Dying Young"); and alternating tetrameter and trimeter lines rhyming *a b a b* (Wordsworth, "Strange Fits of Passion Have I Known"). The last-mentioned arrangement comprises one of the quatrains called **ballad quatrains,** from their frequent use in folk ballads (page 283); a ballad quatrain may also rhyme *x a x a* (Keats, "La Belle Dame Sans Merci"), the symbol *x* indicating a nonrhyming line. Less common, probably because of their singsong effect, are **trimeter** and **dimeter quatrains** (Frost, "Neither Out Far nor in Deep" and "Dust of Snow").

Longer stanzas, of which there are a great variety, are analyzed and described in the same way as quatrains, by determining (1) the kind and number of feet in a line—all the lines will not necessarily be of equal length; (2) the number of lines in the stanza; and (3) the rhyme scheme. Three of the longer stanzaic forms have names: **rhyme royal**—seven iambic pentameter lines rhyming *a b a b b c c*—a form used by Chaucer in *Troilus and Criseyde* and by Shakespeare in *Lucrece;* **ottava rima**—eight iambic pentameter lines rhyming *a b a b a b c c*—used by Byron in *Don Juan;* and the **Spenserian stanza**—nine lines, eight of them iambic pentameter and the ninth an alexandrine, rhyming *a b a b b c b c c*—used by Spenser in *The Faerie Queene* and by Keats in "The Eve of St. Agnes." In addition to the fixed stanzaic forms, there are also fixed forms for entire poems. By far the most important of these is the sonnet, which is treated below.

Knowing the names of the fixed forms and being able to describe them accurately will not necessarily increase a reader's understanding or enjoyment of poems. This knowledge is primarily useful in the way that any technical nomenclature is useful: it is a short-cut way of speaking about the external forms of poems.

Exercise 49

Describe the stanzaic form in each of these poems:

1. Rochester, "The Mistress" (page 261).
2. Wyatt, "They Flee from Me," (page 174).
3. Donne, "Song" (page 249).
4. Keats, "To Autumn" (page 160).

Some Complex Forms

There are also in English poetry a number of complex fixed forms that are held together by prescribed rhyme schemes. The **sonnet,** by far the most important of these, is discussed below. Three others—like the sonnet, first brought to perfection in the Romance languages and then adapted to English—have some importance in English poetry: the villanelle, the triolet, and the rondel. In French and Italian, which abound in rhyme words, these forms are not very difficult to handle. But in English, which is relatively deficient in rhyme words, the successful use of these forms has always been more or less a stunt.

The **villanelle** is a poem composed of tercets (usually five) and a final quatrain in which the first and third lines of the initial tercet are alternatively repeated as the final lines of the tercets which follow, and come together as a couplet in the final quatrain. The tercets are rhymed *a b a,* and the quatrain *a b a a.* The following variation on the form by a modern poet illustrates the pleasant repetition of sound in a villanelle.

Gentleman Aged Five before the Mirror

It tells you what you do but never why,
Your image in the glass that watches you:
You cannot catch it napping if you try.

It can be counted on to laugh or cry,
Make faces, dance, do anything you do;
It tells you what you do but never why.

It is no use to tell the glass a lie;
It answers just as if your words were true.
You cannot catch it napping if you try.

Suppose you cross your heart and hope to die,
It silently replies *I hope so too.*
It tells you what you do but never why.

They say there is a mirror in the sky,
That looks not only at you but right through;
You cannot catch it napping if you try.

And yet, it seems, that mirror is too high
For you to see however tall you grew,
And so you still know What but never Why.

You cannot see that mirror till you die.
Till then this one will keep you still in view.
You cannot catch it napping if you try.
It tells you what you do but never why.

John Wain
(1925–)

The regularly recurring rhymes and repetitions of the villanelle create a kind of artificial music in the poem that makes it especially suitable for light and airy subjects. But it has been successfully used for grave and serious subjects like Dylan Thomas's "Do Not Go Gentle into That Good Night" (page 278).

A **triolet** is a lyric, usually playful, of eight lines and two rhymes, with the first line repeated as the fourth, and the first and second lines repeated at the end of the poem.

Easy Is the Triolet

Easy is the triolet,
If you really learn to make it!
Once a neat refrain you get,
Easy is the triolet.
As you see!—I pay my debt
With another rhyme. Deuce take it,
Easy is the triolet,
If you really learn to make it.

William Ernest Henley
(1849–1903)

Closely related to the triolet is the rondel. Usually a poem of thirteen lines and three stanzas, the **rondel** also uses only two rhymes; its first two lines are repeated at the end of the second stanza, and one of them at the end of the third.

The Wanderer

Love comes back to his vacant dwelling,—
The old, old Love that we knew of yore!
We see him stand by the open door,
With his great eyes sad, and his bosom swelling.

He makes as though in our arms repelling,
He fain would lie as he lay before;—
Love comes back to his vacant dwelling,—
The old, old Love that we knew of yore!

Ah, who shall help us from over-spelling
That sweet forgotten, forbidden lore!
E'en as we doubt in our heart once more,
With a rush of tears to our eyelids welling,
Love comes back to his vacant dwelling.

Austin Dobson
(1840–1921)

Exercise 50

In what interesting ways is the villanelle form used in these poems?

Ellie Mae Leaves in a Hurry

There's some who say she put death up her dress
and some who say they saw her pour it down.
It's not the sort of thing you want to press

so we just assumed she planned on leaving town
and gave her money for the first express.
She had some family up in Puget Sound.

Well we are married men. We've got interests.
You can't take children out like cats to drown.
It's not the sort of thing you want to press.

We didn't know she'd go and pour death down,
though most of us had heard of her distress.
We just assumed she planned on leaving town.

There's some of us who put death up her dress
but she had family up in Puget Sound.
We gave her money for the first express.

Well we are married men. We've got interests.
Though most of us had heard of her distress.
You can't take children out like cats to drown,
it's just the sort of news that gets around.

Peter Klappert
(1942–)

Do Not Go Gentle into That Good Night

Do not go gentle into that good night,
Old age should burn and rave at close of day;
Rage, rage against the dying of the light.

Though wise men at their end know dark is right,
Because their words had forked no lightning they
Do not go gentle into that good night.

Good men, the last wave by, crying how bright
Their frail deeds might have danced in a green bay,
Rage, rage against the dying of the light.

Wild men who caught and sang the sun in flight,
And learn, too late, they grieved it on its way,
Do not go gentle into that good night.

Grave men, near death, who see with blinding sight
Blind eyes could blaze like meteors and be gay,
Rage, rage against the dying of the light.

And you, my father, there on the sad height,
Curse, bless, me now with your fierce tears, I pray.
Do not go gentle into that good night.
Rage, rage against the dying of the light.

Dylan Thomas
(1914–1953)

The Waking

I wake to sleep, and take my waking slow.
I feel my fate in what I cannot fear.
I learn by going where I have to go.

We think by feeling. What is there to know?
I hear my being dance from ear to ear.
I wake to sleep, and take my waking slow.

Of those so close beside me, which are you?
God bless the Ground! I shall walk softly there,
And learn by going where I have to go.

Light takes the Trees; but who can tell us how?
The lowly worm climbs up a winding stair;
I wake to sleep, and take my waking slow.

Great Nature has another thing to do
To you and me; so take the lively air,
And, lovely, learn by going where to go.

This shaking keeps me steady. I should know.
What falls away is always. And is near.
I wake to sleep, and take my waking slow.
I learn by going where I have to go.

Theodore Roethke
(1908–1963)

Internal Structure

Structure is the arrangement of materials within the poem. The distinction between form (the external frame, so to speak, that holds the materials) and structure (the ordering of the materials within the frame) can be illustrated by this poem:

Epitaph Intended for Sir Isaac Newton

Nature, and Nature's Laws lay hid in Night.
God said, Let Newton be! and All was Light.

Alexander Pope
(1688–1744)

In form this poem is a single heroic couplet. Its structure might be described as chronological, or narrative, for the materials within the couplet are arranged according to a time sequence: the pre-Newtonian darkness, the coming of Newton, the post-Newtonian light.

You Beat Your Pate

You beat your Pate, and fancy Wit will come:
Knock as you please, there's no body at home.

Alexander Pope
(1688–1744)

This poem has the same form as the "Epitaph," but a different structure. Line 1 presents a situation; line 2, an explanatory comment.

On the Funeral of a Rich Miser

What num'rous lights this wretch's corpse attend,
Who, in his lifetime, saved a candle's end!

Anonymous
(Eighteenth Century)

Still in couplet form, this poem has a third kind of structure: an ironical contrast between lines 1 and 2.

Pope's poem on Newton, as the title indicates, is a **verse epitaph:** a label given to a brief poem on a dead person, either real or fictitious. Verse epitaphs are not necessarily suitable for inscription on tombstones, nor are they invariably serious (see Belloc's "Epitaph on the Politician"; Gay's "Life is a jest"). There are no fixed forms or tones for the epitaph or for the **verse epigram,** which is a brief poem usually ending with a witty point (Donne's "A Lame Beggar"; Pope's "You Beat Your Pate"). Succinct expression is valued in an epigram; in a good one, every successive detail makes an advance toward the final point.

The three little poems in couplets illustrate the fact that there are many more kinds of inner structure than there are of outer form. The latter can be and have often been tabulated in literary handbooks; the former cannot be reduced to systems because each poem has its own inner structure, its own way of relating the parts to the whole poem. With each new poem, therefore, the reader must discover the structure anew.

One of the most efficient means for laying bare the structure of a poem is to ask and answer this question: "What are its main parts, and what is the relationship of the parts to one another?" Many poems have two main parts.

The Fall of Rome

The piers are pummelled by the waves;
In a lonely field the rain
Lashes an abandoned train;
Outlaws fill the mountain caves.

Fantastic grow the evening gowns;
Agents of the Fisc pursue
Absconding tax-defaulters through
The sewers of provincial towns.

Private rites of magic send
The temple prostitutes to sleep;
All the literati keep
An imaginary friend.

Cerebrotonic Cato may
Extoll the Ancient Disciplines,
But the muscle-bound Marines
Mutiny for food and pay.

Caesar's double-bed is warm
As an unimportant clerk
Writes I DO NOT LIKE MY WORK
On a pink official form.

Unendowed with wealth or pity,
Little birds with scarlet legs,
Sitting on their speckled eggs,
Eye each flu-infected city.

Altogether elsewhere, vast
Herds of reindeer move across
Miles and miles of golden moss,
Silently and very fast.

W. H. Auden
(1907–1973)

Fisc (6): "Fiscal Agency," a British equivalent of "Internal Revenue Service." *prostitutes* (10): The state religion of ancient Rome maintained in the temples prostitutes whose duty it was to solace the worshipers as part of the religious (especially fertility) rites. *literati* (11): poets and writers in general. *Cerebrotonic* (13): "brain-bound." *Cato* (13): Stoic philosopher.

Stanzas 1 through 5 contain a rapid succession of specific details drawn from one aspect or another of what is known as civilization: trains, evening gowns, taxes, Marines, temples, double beds, and so on. In contrast, the main details of stanzas 6 and 7 do not come from the world of man, but from nature: birds, eggs, reindeer, moss. The poem apparently has two main parts that are contrasted with each other; it juxtaposes civilization and nature.

Having identified the parts, a reader should next examine their interconnections. In this poem the two parts are first set against each other in stanza 1: waves (part of nature) pummel the piers (man-made): rain lashes the train. The words *pummelled* and *lashes* suggest active hostility. As for the outlaws, nature seems already to have triumphed over them: they are living like animals in caves. The train, however, has not necessarily been abandoned because of rainstorms. It is more likely meant as a symbol of failure within the system; perhaps a bureaucrat, like the clerk in line 19, was malingering when he should have done something to keep the train running. The train might also be a symbol for the social bonds that should unite people with each other—bonds that have become lax in this society. But perhaps the most interesting thing about the train is that it appears in a poem with this title. Auden could, of course, be thinking of an army supply train, but the word inevitably reminds us also of railroad trains.

The train, along with such other details as the "Fisc" (line 6) and the "Marines" (line 15), suggests that Auden is concerned with something less specific than the historical phenomenon of Rome's fall. The most famous dead civilization, Rome, is a convenient symbol of all decaying civilizations. Auden mixes ancient and modern instances that suggest excess and disintegration. The government is floundering, perhaps because the ruler overindulges in sex (line 17), perhaps because the ruling classes have too many mad parties (line 5), perhaps because the citizens have good reasons not to pay taxes (lines 6–8). It is impossible to differentiate the instances that cause disintegration from those that are its effects. Morale is low in the armed forces (lines 15–16) and the church (lines 9–10), those two great bulwarks of the state. Some intellectuals, like Cato, preach the traditional virtues to deaf ears (lines 13–14); others are so out of touch with their fellow men that all their personal relations are imaginary (lines 11–12). The ordinary people are bored by their work, which seems to them meaningless red tape (lines 18–20). But meantime the winds and the waters, the birds and the animals, go on as though nothing were happening. They have no stake in civilization. The scarlet-legged birds (lines 22–24) could not be less concerned; the fast-moving reindeer are "altogether elsewhere" (lines 25–28).

Although Auden avoids overt moralizing, it is not difficult to detect where his sympathies lie, and they do not lie with this civilization. There is an important change in tone after stanza 6. Stanzas 1–6 are frivolously but desperately contemptuous; stanza 7 is repectful. The vast expanse of golden moss has no sewers and no flu-infected cities. It is quiet and beautiful. Auden has arranged his material in such a way that his meaning is clear.

In a successful poem the inner structure subtly harmonizes with the outer form. The interaction between the two can perhaps best be studied in the sonnet, where it is dramatically clear—if the sonnet is a good one.

The Sonnet

Formally considered, a **sonnet** contains fourteen iambic pentameter lines rhyming according to one of two general schemes. The **Italian** (or **Petrarchan**) sonnet has an octave (eight lines) rhyming *a b b a a b b a* followed by a sestet (six lines) usually rhyming *c d e c d e*. The **English** (or **Shakespearean**) sonnet has three quatrains usually rhyming *a b a b c d c d e f e f* followed by a couplet rhyming *g g*. Both kinds of sonnet provide opportunities for breaks or turns in the thought: the Italian, after line 8; the English, after line 12. Each quatrain of an English sonnet usually develops different aspects of a single thought.

Tuskegee

Wherefore this busy labor without rest?
Is it an idle dream to which we cling,
Here where a thousand dusky toilers sing
Unto the world their hope? "Build we our best
By hand and thought," they cry, "although unblessed."
So the great engines throb, and anvils ring,
And so the thought is wedded to the thing;
But what shall be the end, and what the test?
Dear God, we dare not answer, we can see
Not many steps ahead, but this we know—
If all our toilsome building is in vain,

Availing not to set our manhood free,
If envious hate roots out the seed we sow,
The South will wear eternally a stain.

Leslie Pinckney Hill
(1880–1960)

This is a successful Italian sonnet because its inner structure corresponds at each point with its outer form. The octave states the problem with three specific questions: what is the significance of all the thought, labor, and expended energies of liberated blacks in the South? Why should they struggle to build their best when "their hope" may prove to be merely an "idle dream"? What goal, what "test" shall prove it all to have been worthwhile? The octave of the poem seems almost like the comments of a detached observer; but in the sestet the speaker of the poem identifies himself with the toiling blacks by means of the insistent first-person "we." The sestet does not resolve the problem raised in the octave; instead it comments on it. If the blacks' struggle to achieve equality and "manhood" (line 12) is frustrated by racial hatred, the South will be perpetually dishonored.

Sonnet 30

When to the sessions of sweet silent thought
I summon up remembrance of things past,
I sigh the lack of many a thing I sought,
And with old woes new wail my dear time's waste.
Then can I drown an eye, unused to flow,
For precious friends hid in death's dateless night,
And weep afresh love's long-since cancelled woe,
And moan the expense of many a vanished sight.
Then can I grieve at grievances foregone,
And heavily from woe to woe tell o'er
The sad account of fore-bemoaned moan,
Which I new pay as if not paid before.
  But if the while I think on thee, dear friend,
  All losses are restored, and sorrows end.

William Shakespeare
(1564–1616)

In this representative English sonnet each shift in rhyme scheme signals a new development of the thought. The first quatrain states the subject in general terms: the sadness of "things past" (line 2). The second (lines 5–8) amplifies the subject with specific details: dead friends, lost loves, vanished sights. The third, which runs parallel with the second (see lines 5 and 9), is also general like the first, but is somewhat more intense. The main break in thought occurs after line 12, when the speaker suddenly remembers and directly addresses a dear friend who is still living. The final incisive couplet is balanced against the preceding twelve lines in such a way that it seems to solve the problem completely. The break, however, does not seem unduly abrupt because the couplet continues a legal-business metaphor that has run through the three quatrains: *sessions* (line 1), *summon* (line 2), *expense* (line 8), *tell* (line 10, in the sense of "count"), *account* (line 11), *pay* (line 12), and *losses* (line 14). This extended metaphor is an important element in the structure of the poem.

Few of the thousands of sonnets in existence adhere as closely to the theoretically fixed forms as do these two by Hill and Shakespeare. In practice poets take all sorts of interesting liberties with the rhyme schemes and with the position of the turn. Even so, the sonnet is a difficult and challenging kind of poem to write because its complex outer form requires a supporting inner structure of thought.

Exercise 51

In addition to the sonnets below, this book contains many others in which the correspondence between structure and form can be profitably studied: Keats, "On First Looking into Chapman's Homer"; Meredith, "Lucifer in Starlight"; Humphries, "Heresy for a Classroom," MacLeish, "The End of the World"; Hopkins, "The Windhover"; and Shakespeare, "Sonnet 116."

Sonnet

Bright star! would I were steadfast as thou art—
  Not in lone splendour hung aloft the night
And watching, with eternal lids apart,

Like nature's patient, sleepless Eremite,
The moving waters at their priestlike task
Of pure ablution round earth's human shores,
Or gazing on the new soft fallen mask
Of snow upon the mountains and the moors—
No—yet still steadfast, still unchangeable,
Pillow'd upon my fair love's ripening breast,
To feel for ever its soft fall and swell,
Awake for ever in a sweet unrest,
Still, still to hear her tender-taken breath,
And so live ever—or else swoon to death.

John Keats
(1795–1821)

Eremite (4): hermit.

1. In what respects does the speaker wish to resemble the star? To differ from it?
2. Is this an English or an Italian sonnet? Where does the main turn in thought come?
3. Explain the metaphors implied by *eternal lids* (line 3) and *priestlike* (line 5).
4. Resolve the paradox implied by *sweet unrest* (line 12).
5. Describe the tone. Is it lewd? Sentimental?

On His Blindness

When I consider how my light is spent
Ere half my days in this dark world and wide,
And that one talent which is death to hide
Lodged with me useless, though my soul more bent
To serve therewith my Maker, and present
My true account, lest he returning chide;
"Doth God exact day-labor, light denied?"
I fondly ask. But Patience, to prevent
That murmur, soon replies: "God doth not need
Either man's work or his own gifts. Who best
Bear his mild yoke, they serve him best. His state

Is kingly: thousands at his bidding speed
And post o'er land and ocean without rest;
They also serve who only stand and wait."

John Milton
(1608–1674)

talent (3): See Matthew xxv: 14–30.

1. What problems in interpretation would face a reader who lacked the clues provided in the title? (This is not an artificial question: Milton left the sonnet untitled, and "On His Blindness" has been furnished by his editors.)
2. The opening lines are somewhat difficult syntactically. Point out the ending of the adverbial clause beginning with *When* (line 1).
3. Which of the two main kinds of sonnet is this one? What liberty has the poet taken with the form? Does the inner structure justify taking that liberty?
4. For what is *yoke* (line 11) a metaphor?
5. Explain the pun in *talent* (line 3).
6. *Thousands* (line 12) refers to God's angels. To what does Milton liken God in lines 11–13?
7. Would line 14 be improved if *sit* were substituted for *stand?* How would this substitution alter the theme?

Since There's No Help

Since there's no help, come let us kiss and part.
Nay, I have done; you get no more of me.
And I am glad, yea, glad with all my heart
That thus so cleanly I myself can free.
Shake hands forever, cancel all our vows,
And when we meet at any time again,
Be it not seen in either of our brows
That we one jot of former love retain.
Now at the last gasp of love's latest breath,
When, his pulse failing, passion speechless lies,
When faith is kneeling by his bed of death,
And innocence is closing up his eyes,

Now if thou wouldst, when all have given him over,
From death to life thou mightst him yet recover.

Michael Drayton
(1563–1631)

1. Who is the speaker of this poem? Whom is he speaking to? What sort of person is he?
2. For what is *brows* (line 7) a metonymy?
3. Is the lover dying? To whom does *him* (line 14) refer?
4. Describe the tone. Is it consistent throughout?

Development

Unlike some other kinds of art, a poem is not static; thus, it is convenient to think of its structure as something that moves and changes—something that develops. **Development** is the means by which a poem reveals itself—the means by which it moves from its beginning to its end. There are four main types of development: narrative, descriptive, argumentative, and expository. Within these main types there are as many subtypes as there are poems, because every individual poem develops in its own way. If a reader is to experience a whole poem, he must be aware of how and where it is moving.

Narrative Development

A poem whose details are organized chronologically has a **narrative development** (Frost, "Out, Out—"; Blake, "A Poison Tree"). Such a poem tells a story, and it may have all or some of the features of plotted fiction: a **rising action** (in which a conflict develops), a **climax** (in which the conflict takes a decisive turn), and a **falling action** (in which the conflict reaches a conclusion).

The most obvious examples of narrative progression occur in **folk** or **popular ballads** ("The Three Ravens"), which are anonymous narrative songs handed down orally from one generation to the next. Rarely, however, do folk ballads tell a completely developed story; they frequently begin at or near the climax, or they move spasmodically by leaping over some events and lingering on others, so that the modern reader has to use his imagination to fill in details that are apparently missing. Both folk ballads and their imitations, called **art** or **literary ballads** (Keats, "La Belle Dame sans Merci"), commonly have one or more of these features: stanzaic form; repetition of one kind or another, as in a refrain or in parallel structure of sentences; stories about violent, horrible, or supernatural events ("La Belle Dame sans Merci"). Humor, except for the grimmest kind of irony and understatement, is missing from most ballads. Frequently the ballad story is related dramatically, by means of a dialogue between two speakers ("The Twa Corbies"). The reader of such a ballad, like the reader of a dramatic monologue, must piece together the story from what a speaker says.

Exercise 52

The Draft Horse

With a lantern that wouldn't burn
In too frail a buggy we drove
Behind too heavy a horse
Through a pitch-dark limitless grove.

And a man came out of the trees
And took our horse by the head
And reaching back to his ribs
Deliberately stabbed him dead.

The ponderous beast went down
With a crack of a broken shaft.
And the night drew through the trees
In one long invidious draft.

The most unquestioning pair
That ever accepted fate
And the least disposed to ascribe
Any more than we had to hate,

We assumed that the man himself
Or someone he had to obey
Wanted us to get down
And walk the rest of the way.

Robert Frost
(1875–1963)

The Monster

I left my room at last, I walked
The streets of that decaying town,
I took the turn I had renounced
Where the carved cherub crumbled down.

Eager as to a granted wish
I hurried to the cul de sac.
Forestalled by whom? Before the house
I saw an unmoved waiting back.

How had she never vainly mentioned
This lover, too, unsatisfied?
Did she dismiss one every night?
I walked up slowly to his side.

Those eyes glazed like her windowpane,
That wide mouth ugly with despair,
Those arms held tight against the haunches,
Poised, but heavily staying there:

At once I knew him, gloating over
A grief defined and realized,
And living only for its sake.
It was myself I recognized.

I could not watch her window now,
Standing before this man of mine,
The constant one I had created
Lest the pure feeling should decline.

What if I were within the house,
Happier than the fact had been
—Would he, then, still be gazing here,
The man who never can get in?

Or would I, leaving at the dawn
A suppler love than he could guess,
Find him awake on my small bed,
Demanding still some bitterness?

Thom Gunn
(1929–   )

cul de sac (6): dead end.

The Ballad of Edie Barrow

I fell in love with a Gentile boy.
All creamy-and-golden fair.
He looked deep and long in my long black eyes.
And he played with my long black hair.
He took me away to his summertime house.
He was wondrous wealthy, was he.
And there in the hot black drapes of night
he whispered, "Good lovers are we."
Close was our flesh through the winking hours,
closely and sweetly entwined.
Love did not guess in the tight-packed dark
it was flesh of varying kind.
Scarletly back when the hateful sun
came bragging across the town.
And I could have killed the gentle Gentile
who waited to strap him down.
He will wed her come fall, come falling of fall.
And she will be queen of his rest.
I shall be queen of his summerhouse storm.
A hungry tooth in my breast.

Gwendolyn Brooks
(1917–   )

Descriptive Development

Descriptive development is an arrangement of pictorial details. Although there are descriptive passages in many poems, there are few purely descriptive poems because of the nature of poetry. Poetry is a temporal rather than a spatial art, and when it tries to compete with such a spatial art as painting the result is rather thin.

Symphony in Yellow

An omnibus across the bridge
  Crawls like a yellow butterfly,
  And, here and there, a passer-by
Shows like a little restless midge.

Big barges full of yellow hay
  Are moved against the shadowy wharf,
  And, like a yellow silken scarf,
The thick fog hangs along the quay.

The yellow leaves begin to fade
  And flutter from the Temple elms,
  And at my feet the pale green Thames
Lies like a rod of rippled jade.

Oscar Wilde
(1854–1900)

Temple (10): district in London.

Unlike a painter, Wilde cannot present his picture all at once with each detail in its place; he has to present his details piecemeal—one at a time. To overcome this difficulty, which is inherent in all word-paintings, Wilde has chosen a title that suggests a musical rather than a pictorial analogy. He has selected and presented details from the landscape that blend harmoniously to give a dominant impression of greenish yellowness. Each successive detail contributes to that impression. Had Wilde gone on piling up yellow details through several more quatrains, he would have forfeited his readers' interest.

In most poems descriptive development is used in conjunction with another kind of development. In Keats's "To Autumn," for instance, there is a good deal of description, but the presence of narrative and expository progressions makes the poem more interesting than it would be if it were a mere series of autumnal vignettes.

Argumentative Development

When a poet advances a proposition and then presents reasons in defense of it, he uses **argumentative development.** Donne's famous sonnet beginning "Death, be not proud" consists of a series of reasons why death should not be proud; his "Valediction Forbidding Mourning" similarly gives reasons why true lovers need not be sad when they are temporarily separated. Few poems, however, have only an argumentative progression because a person who merely wants to present an argument can do so more convincingly in prose than in verse.

Terence, This Is Stupid Stuff

'Terence, this is stupid stuff:
You eat your victuals fast enough;
There can't be much amiss, 'tis clear,
To see the rate you drink your beer.
But, oh, good Lord, the verse you make,
It gives a chap the belly-ache.
The cow, the old cow, she is dead;
It sleeps well, the horned head:
We poor lads, 'tis our turn now
To hear such tunes as killed the cow.
Pretty friendship 'tis to rhyme
Your friends to death before their time
Moping melancholy mad.
Come, pipe a tune to dance to, lad.'

Why, if 'tis dancing you would be,
There's brisker pipes than poetry.
Say, for what were hop-yards meant,
Or why was Burton built on Trent?
Oh many a peer of England brews,
Livelier liquor than the Muse,
And malt does more than Milton can
To justify God's ways to man.
Ale, man, ale's the stuff to drink
For fellows whom it hurts to think:
Look into the pewter pot
To see the world as the world's not.
And faith, 'tis pleasant till 'tis past:
The mischief is that 'twill not last.
Oh I have been to Ludlow fair
And left my necktie God knows where,
And carried half-way home, or near,
Pints and quarts of Ludlow beer:
Then the world seemed none so bad,
And I myself a sterling lad;
And down in lovely muck I've lain,
Happy till I woke again.
Then I saw the morning sky:
Heigho, the tale was all a lie;
The world, it was the old world yet,
I was I, my things were wet,
And nothing now remained to do
But begin the game anew.

Therefore, since the world has still
Much good, but much less good than ill,
And while the sun and moon endure
Luck's a chance, but trouble's sure,
I'd face it as a wise man would,
And train for ill and not for good.
'Tis true, the stuff I bring for sale
Is not so brisk a brew as ale;
Out of a stem that scored the hand
I wrung it in a weary land.
But take it: if the smack is sour,
The better for the embittered hour;
It should do good to heart and head
When your soul is in my soul's stead;

And I will friend you, if I may,
In the dark and cloudy day.

There was a king reigned in the East:
There, when kings will sit to feast,
They get their fill before they think
With poisoned meat and poisoned drink.
He gathered all that springs to birth
From the many-venomed earth;
First a little, thence to more,
He sampled all her killing store;
And easy, smiling, seasoned sound,
Sate the king when healths went round.
They put arsenic in his meat
And stared aghast to watch him eat;
They poured strychnine in his cup
And shook to see him drink it up:
They shook, they stared as white's their shirt:
Them it was their poison hurt.
—I tell the tale that I heard told.
Mithridates, he died old.

A. E. Housman
(1859–1936)

this (1): the poems of "Terence" (Housman's playful name for himself?). *Burton* (18): English brewery town on the River Trent. *Milton* (21): The stated purpose of *Paradise Lost* is "to justify the ways of God to men." *Ludlow* (29): English town in Shropshire. *king* (59): Mithridates, king of Pontus (132–63 B.C.).

The poem has two main parts, each containing an argument. In the first part (lines 1–14) somebody advises Terence—whose poems, like Housman's (see pages 118, 370) are apparently somewhat morbid—to write about happier subjects. Terence then replies (lines 15–76). He argues first that beer is a better escape from life's troubles than poetry. Then he points out that escape by way of beer is at best temporary. Since life is what it is, trouble cannot be permanently avoided. And since trouble must be faced, poetry can help a man face it, especially if the poetry has a sour taste (line 53). Terence's conclusions follow logically from his premises. To clinch his argument that bitterness is desirable in poems, he concludes with an anecdote about Mithridates, who became venom-proof by eating a little poison every day.

Any arrangement by means of which a poet sets forth or exposes his ideas and feelings is **expository development.** Thus broadly defined, a development of this kind must exist in every good poem.

At the beginning of Thom Gunn's "The Monster," the reader does not know who the monster is; at the end, he recognizes that the monster is the lover's "double," or alter ego, that insists on suffering and perhaps even enjoys suffering. Such a discovery occurs in every poem, or some such question is answered. The attitude of the lover in Drayton's "Since There's No Help" is not evident when the sonnet opens; it becomes evident as the poem progresses. Every poem raises and answers some sort of question. One kind of expository development, then, is a movement from ignorance at the beginning of the poem to knowledge at the end. If a poem expresses a feeling, that feeling will be less vague at the end than at the beginning; if it expresses an idea, the idea will be clearer; if it describes a scene, the scene will be more vivid in the reader's mind.

There are many ways by which a poem may move from ignorance to knowledge or from vagueness to precision. The following poem accomplishes the movement by supporting a generalization with specific details.

Sonnet 66

Tired with all these, for restful death I cry:
As to behold desert a beggar born,
And needy nothing trimmed in jollity,
And purest faith unhappily forsworn,
And gilded honor shamefully misplaced,
And maiden virtue rudely strumpeted,
And right perfection wrongfully disgraced,
And strength by limping sway disabled,
And art made tongue-tied by authority,
And folly, doctor-like, controlling skill,
And simple truth miscalled simplicity,
And captive good attending captain ill:
  Tired with all these, from these would I be gone,
  Save that to die, I leave my love alone.

William Shakespeare
(1564–1616)

Contrast (Keats's sonnet beginning "Bright star!") and comparison (any poem with an extended metaphor) are other common expository devices. A succession of precise images (Swift's "Description of the Morning") helps to make the subject of a poem clear and memorable.

Another general kind of expository development causes a poem to become more emotionally profound as it proceeds from beginning to end. This sort of development is best studied in the **lyric** (see p. 62), a term originally applied to poems that were sung to the accompaniment of a lyre but now applied to any short poem expressing personal thoughts and feelings rather than public events (see Herrick, "To Blossoms"; Byron, "She Walks in Beauty"; Roethke, "The Waking"; and many other poems in this book). A lyric is ordinarily stanzaic and euphonious; its speaker is not necessarily the poet.

Mother, I Cannot Mind My Wheel

Mother, I cannot mind my wheel;
  My fingers ache, my lips are dry:
Oh! if you felt the pain I feel!
  But Oh, who ever felt as I?

No longer could I doubt him true;
  All other men may use deceit:
He always said my eyes were blue,
  And often swore my lips were sweet.

Walter Savage Landor
(1775–1864)

wheel (1): spinning wheel.

In this lyric, which Landor adapted from a fragment by Sappho (a Greek lyric poet), a girl complains to her mother. There is a kind of false emotional climax at line 4. At this point the girl's feelings seem to be deepest, but the reader is not yet emotionally involved because he needs more information. The reader's response is greater at line 8 than at line 4. Although the poem has no narrative development, it does imply a story: a man has flattered the girl, gained her confidence, probably seduced her, and then certainly abandoned her.

The poem has two expository developments that function concurrently: as the reader becomes more mentally aware—that is, as his mind takes in what has happened—he becomes more emotionally involved.

Unlike a sentimentalist, who would pump emotion into the poem, Landor avoids any overt expression of feeling in the second quatrain. Here the girl is meditating aloud, remembering what has happened. "No longer could I doubt him true," she says, to justify herself for having given in to him. The irony in "All other men may use deceit" increases the pathos. This man was obviously a deceiver; if he had been faithful, the girl would now be happy. The word *swore* (line 8) suggests an oath to be faithful. It is ironical because it is modified by *often:* for a faithful person one oath is enough. The man often swore that her lips were sweet. He apparently knew very well just how sweet they were. By letting the situation speak for itself, so that the reader must share in creating the experience, Landor increases the emotional impact of the poem. He arranges the details in such a way that they make a progressively greater appeal to the heart.

The ode and the elegy, two varieties of lyric, ordinarily have more complex patterns of thought and feeling than those in a relatively simple song like Landor's, and they are ordinarily longer than "song" lyrics. Down through the ages the term **ode** has been applied to poems in many different forms, but most poems so designated have a serious tone and treat lofty subjects (Keats, "Ode on a Grecian Urn"). The term **elegy,** originally designating a poem in a particular Latin or Greek meter, now is given to poems of contemplative tone that treat death in general or mourn a dead person (Gray, "Elegy Written in a Country Church-Yard"; Milton, "Lycidas").

Exercise 53

Study the ways in which thought and feeling are developed in these poems.

Frederick Douglass

When it is finally ours, this freedom, this liberty, this beautiful
and terrible thing, needful to man as air,
usable as earth; when it belongs at last to all,

when it is truly instinct, brain matter, diastole, systole,
reflex action; when it is finally won; when it is more
than the gaudy mumbo jumbo of politicians:
this man, this Douglass, this former slave, this Negro
beaten to his knees, exiled, visioning a world
where none is lonely, none hunted, alien,
this man, superb in love and logic, this man
shall be remembered. Oh, not with statues' rhetoric,
not with legends and poems and wreaths of bronze alone,
but with the lives grown out of his life, the lives
fleshing his dream of the beautiful, needful thing.

Robert Hayden
(1913–   )

Title: *c.* 1817–1891, early Black leader of antislavery movement.

1. In what sense can freedom be called a "terrible thing"? "Needful to man as air"? "Usable as earth"?
2. The language of this poem indicates its three-step development. What are these steps?
3. The poet appears to believe that freedom will not be won until it is "instinct . . . reflex action" (lines 4 and 5). Why?

Reveille

Wake: the silver dusk returning
  Up the beach of darkness brims,
And the ship of sunrise burning
  Strands upon the eastern rims.

Wake: the vaulted shadow shatters,
  Trampled to the floor it spanned,
And the tent of night in tatters
  Straws the sky-pavilioned land.

Up, lad, up, 'tis late for lying:
  Hear the drums of morning play;
Hark, the empty highways crying
  "Who'll beyond the hills away?"

Towns and countries woo together,
  Forelands beacon, belfries call;
Never lad that trod on leather
  Lived to feast his heart with all.

Up, lad: thews that lie and cumber
  Sunlit pallets never thrive;
Morns abed and daylight slumber
  Were not meant for man alive.

Clay lies still, but blood's a rover;
  Breath's a ware that will not keep.
Up, lad: when the journey's over
  There'll be time enough to sleep.

A. E. Housman
(1859–1936)

Title: a morning signal ordering soldiers to arise. *thews* (17) : muscle and sinews. *cumber* (17) : burden. *pallets* (18) : beds.

1. What kind of progression is found in the first two stanzas?
2. The poem gives reasons why the soldier should get up. Describe the order in which these reasons are arranged. What kinds of progression are involved here?

Apology for Understatement

Forgive me that I pitch your praise too low.
Such reticence my reverence demands,
For silence falls with laying on of hands.

Forgive me that my words come thin and slow.
This could not be a time for eloquence,
For silence falls with healing of the sense.

We only utter what we lightly know.
And it is rather that my love knows me.
It is that your perfection set me free.

Verse is dressed up that has nowhere to go.
You took away my glibness with my fear.
Forgive me that I stand in silence here.

It is not words could pay you what I owe.

John Wain
(1925–)

laying . . . hands (3) : an act of consecration.

1. For what kind of behavior is the speaker apologizing?
2. What reasons does the speaker give for the behavior?
3. Explain whether the speaker wants to be forgiven or to be understood by the listener.
4. Does the poem merely reinforce the trite old proverb "still waters run deep," or is it saying something more? At what point in the poem does the reader become aware that the speaker is paying compliments to the listener?

Between Equals

A dragonfly blue as the June Atlantic
slim as its horizon
came over the dunes:

helicoptering off and on
a grass beside my chair
not demanding money, nor love.

Nor did I want anything (money, love).
A small event.
He stayed. And went.

Robert Wallace
(1932–)

The Death Bed

All the time they were praying
He watched the shadow of a tree
Flicker on the wall.

There is no need of prayer,
He said,
No need at all.

The kin-folk thought it strange
That he should ask them from a dying bed.
But they left all in a row
And it seemed to ease him
To see them go.

There were some who kept on praying
In a room across the hall
And some who listened to the breeze
That made the shadows waver
On the wall.

He tried his nerve
On a song he knew
And made an empty note
That might have come
From a bird's harsh throat.

And all the time it worried him
That they were in there praying,
And all the time he wondered
What it was they could be saying.

Waring Cuney
(1906–)

Ode to the West Wind

1

O wild West Wind, thou breath of Autumn's being,
Thou, from whose unseen presence the leaves dead
Are driven, like ghosts from an enchanter fleeing,

Yellow, and black, and pale, and hectic red,
Pestilence-stricken multitudes: O thou,
Who chariotest to their dark wintry bed

The wingèd seeds, where they lie cold and low,
Each like a corpse within its grave, until
Thine azure sister of the Spring shall blow

Her clarion o'er the dreaming earth, and fill
(Driving sweet buds like flocks to feed in air)
With living hues and odours plain and hill:

Wild Spirit, which art moving everywhere;
Destroyer and preserver; hear, oh, hear!

2

Thou on whose stream, 'mid the steep sky's commotion,
Loose clouds like earth's decaying leaves are shed,
Shook from the tangled boughs of Heaven and Ocean,

Angels of rain and lightning: there are spread
On the blue surface of thine airy surge,
Like the bright hair uplifted from the head

Of some fierce Mænad, even from the dim verge
Of the horizon to the zenith's height
The locks of the approaching storm. Thou dirge

Of the dying Year, to which this closing night
Will be the dome of a vast sepulchre,
Vaulted with all thy congregated might

Of vapours, from whose solid atmosphere
Black rain, and fire, and hail will burst: oh, hear!

3

Thou who didst waken from his summer dreams
The blue Mediterranean, where he lay,
Lulled by the coil of his crystàlline streams,

Besides a pumice isle in Baiæ's bay,
And saw in sleep old palaces and towers
Quivering within the wave's intenser day,

All overgrown with azure moss and flowers
So sweet, the sense faints picturing them! Thou
For whose path the Atlantic's level powers

Cleave themselves into chasms, while far below
The sea-blooms and the oozy woods which wear
The sapless foliage of the ocean, know

Thy voice, and suddenly grow gray with fear,
And tremble and despoil themselves: oh, hear!

4

If I were a dead leaf thou mightest bear;
If I were a swift cloud to fly with thee;
A wave to pant beneath thy power, and share

The impulse of thy strength, only less free
Than thou, O uncontrollable! If even
I were as in my boyhood, and could be

The comrade of thy wanderings over Heaven,
As then, when to outstrip thy skiey speed
Scarce seemed a vision; I would ne'er have striven

As thus with thee in prayer in my sore need.
Oh, lift me as a wave, a leaf, a cloud!
I fall upon the thorns of life! I bleed!

A heavy weight of hours has chained and bowed
One too like thee: tameless, and swift, and proud.

5

Make me thy lyre, even as the forest is:
What if my leaves are falling like its own!
The tumult of thy mighty harmonies

Will take from both a deep, autumnal tone,
Sweet though in sadness. Be thou, Spirit fierce,
My spirit! Be thou me, impetuous one!

Drive my dead thoughts over the universe
Like withered leaves to quicken a new birth!
And, by the incantation of this verse,

Scatter, as from an unextinguished hearth
Ashes and sparks, my words among mankind!
Be through my lips to unawakened Earth

The trumpet of a prophecy! O Wind,
If winter comes, can Spring be far behind?

Percy Bysshe Shelley
(1792–1822)

Maenad (21): In classical mythology the Maenads were the wildly drunken or possessed women who served the god of wine, Dionysus.
Baiæ (32): village near Naples, Italy.

1. Where does the first sentence in the poem end? The second? The third? Comment on the effect produced.
2. How can the wind be both "destroyer and preserver" (line 14)?
3. The scene is different in each of the first three sections. Where and what is the wind blowing in section 1? Where and what in 2? In 3?
4. Analyze these implicit metaphors: *boughs* (line 17); *dirge* (line 23); *sleep* (line 33). Are there extended metaphors?
5. Into what two main parts may the poem be divided? How are the parts related?
6. What is the speaker's sore need (line 52)? Does he wish that his troubles were gone with the wind, or does he have some other need?
7. Explain why it is necessary to understand sections 1–4 in order to know the full import of these words in section 5: *leaves* (line 58); *universe* (line 63); *new birth* (line 64).
8. What is the speaker's prophecy (line 69)?
9. What is the full answer to the question with which the ode ends? Could this ode be regarded as propaganda for a revolution? Can any good come from the scattered sparks of a fire (lines 66–67)?

Call for the Robin-Redbreast

Call for the robin-redbreast and the wren,
Since o'er shady groves they hover,
And with leaves and flowers do cover
The friendless bodies of unburied men.
  Call unto his funeral dole
  The ant, the field mouse, and the mole,
To rear him hillocks that shall keep him warm,
And, when gay tombs are robbed, sustain no harm;
But keep the wolf far thence, that's foe to men,
For with his nails he'll dig them up again.

John Webster
(*c.* 1580–1625)

Conventions and Traditions

Poems, like all other forms of art, have their **conventions**—artificial and sometimes unrealistic devices that are accepted by common agreement between the artist and his public. In the movies, for instance, the passage of time is sometimes indicated by a series of rapidly flashed pictures of newspaper headlines and easily recognized events. The audience may spend only a minute looking at the pictures, yet it agrees to accept that minute as equivalent to twenty-five years in the hero's life. Among the conventions of poems are rhyme, meter, fixed forms, symbols—in fact, any of the devices that make poems different from ordinary discourse. One kind of poem—necessarily excluded from this book because of its length—which makes elaborate use of conventions is the **epic:** a narrative poem of heroic action, such as Homer's *Iliad* and *Odyssey,* Virgil's *Aeneid,* Milton's *Paradise Lost.* Although the epic tells a story, it begins by convention in the middle; it employs extended similes, invokes the Muses, contains lists of things, traces the characters' genealogies, shows supernatural beings interfering in the affairs of men, depicts games, and so on.

A poem that uses conventions similar to those in other poems is said to be written in a **tradition**. Among the many traditions are the Petrarchan (see page 141) and the metaphysical (page 142). A theme may also be traditional; there are, for instance, hundreds of poems on the *carpe diem* ("seize the day") theme (Marvell, "To His Coy Mistress"). The **pastoral tradition,** which is found in both prose and verse, can baffle a reader unless he recognizes it. The author of a work in the pastoral tradition depicts his characters as shepherds, who may fall in love with shepherdesses (Marlowe, "The Passionate Shepherd"), or who may lament a death (Milton, "Lycidas"—a pastoral elegy). The term *pastoral* is sometimes applied to any poem with a rural setting or to any poem that idealizes the simple life.

The Meaning of a Whole Poem

"What does this poem mean?" is a highly ambiguous question, because the answer depends mainly on how one defines *mean*. Some definitions of *mean* are more useful than others. For instance, one not very useful definition is "mean in prose." Then the question becomes "What would this poem mean if it were written in prose?" and the answer is a prose paraphrase of the poem. This answer is unsatisfactory because translating the words of the poem into other words completely changes the poem. "Poetry," says Robert Frost, "is what gets lost in translation." A more useful definition of *mean* is "say about its subject." The answer to the question "What does this poem say about its subject?" is a statement of the theme. Yet the theme is not equivalent to the total meaning of the poem, because it is only one element. No one would read with any interest a book merely listing the themes of poems; one might as well read a book of rhyme schemes. Perhaps the best definition of *mean* is one that makes the question ask, "What does the poem say about its subject and how does it say it?" The answer to this question is a discussion of both the how (the manner) and the what (the matter) of the whole poem. Unlike the paraphrase, the discussion is not offered as a substitute for the poem. In the poem manner and matter are fused. The discussion separates them only for purposes of study.

There are two chief ways in which the discussion of a poem can go wrong. First, beginning readers are likely to concentrate more on the matter than on the manner of a poem. A reader who ignores tone, fails to recognize figurative statements, pays no heed to the connotation of words—who uses only the mental equipment he uses on the sports pages of a tabloid—will inevitably misinterpret a poem. Such a reader is ignoring the manner of the poem. Second, a reader who seizes on a part of the poem and allows that part unduly to influence his view of the whole will also misinterpret it. A discussion must accord with the whole poem.

Students are often surprised to discover that authorities on poetry, even expert critics, offer different interpretations of the same poem. As a result of this discovery they are tempted to conclude that a poem has any meaning that an individual reader may find in it. Told that his interpretation of a poem is wrong, a student may ask, "If a poem can have a number of meanings, who is to say which is the right one?"

This is a fair question, and it deserves an honest answer. First, no poem has a single "correct" interpretation in the way that a problem in arithmetic has a single right answer. The interpretations of different readers will differ as their individual sensibilities do. An interpretation will reflect the depth and breadth of the reader's experience, both in literature and in life. But the fact that a poem does not have a single "right" interpretation does not mean that it cannot be given a wrong one, or that a wrong one cannot be labeled as such. Who is to say what is wrong and what is right? The poem itself.

Exercise 54

This exercise is intended to demonstrate that a wrong interpretation can be revealed simply by using the poem itself as a test of that interpretation.

The Folly of Being Comforted

One that is ever kind said yesterday:
"Your well-beloved's hair has threads of grey,
And little shadows come about her eyes;
Time can but make it easier to be wise
Though now it seems impossible, and so
All that you need is patience.'

Heart cries, 'No,
I have not a crumb of comfort, not a grain.
Time can but make her beauty over again:
Because of that great nobleness of hers
The fire that stirs about her, when she stirs,
Burns but more clearly. O she had not these ways
When all the wild summer was in her gaze."

O heart! O heart! if she'd but turn her head,
You'd know the folly of being comforted.

William Butler Yeats
(1865–1939)

1. Frame in your own mind an interpretation of this poem by answering these questions:
   a. What is the motive of the "ever kind" person who makes the remarks in lines 2–6? What does he mean by *wise* (line 4)?
   b. What does the main speaker think of the advice he is given?
   c. What is the relationship between the speaker and the woman?
2. A distinguished critic has annotated this poem as follows:

   "The final couplet—in which the poet's rationalization that his beloved is really more beautiful now that she is older, is suddenly and devastatingly shattered by the physical reality—has an almost epigrammatic quality."

   So far as you can judge from this note, what does his interpretation of the poem seem to be? How does it compare with yours?
3. Read the following interpretation, and then read the poem again:

Since the title of Yeat's poem is "The Folly of Being Comforted," the speaker of the poem must be in need of comfort. Why? There seems to be two possibilities: either he needs to be comforted because he loves a woman who doesn't love him, or he needs to be comforted because the woman he loves is growing old and unattractive. On the basis of lines 2–3, we might decide that the speaker needs to be comforted because of the latter reason. But there are difficulties with this decision. If the woman's aging is what disturbs the speaker, "one who is ever kind" would neither be kind nor comforting to the speaker by telling him that time will make the woman older, greyer, and more wrinkled. It isn't the woman's aging, then, that bothers the speaker.

The other possible cause for the speaker's unhappiness is that his love is unreturned by the woman. In this case, the advice of the "ever kind" friend makes sense. "Your beloved is growing older," the friend says; "time will take its toll, and if you only have patience, your love for her will end."

To this advice, however well meant, the speaker's "heart" can only answer, "No!" The heart has reasons the mind knows nothing of. The heart refuses to take any consolation from the fact that its beloved is aging; the passing of time "can but make her beauty over again"–that is, re-create it and on a higher level. Because of her "nobleness" her beauty becomes more incandescent with age; her autumnal beauty is even more ravishing than the beauty of her youth, "When all the wild summer was in her gaze." Let her but "turn her head," and the poet becomes aware of the "fire that stirs about her when she stirs." She has merely to turn her face to him and the poet has shattering proof that the aging of the woman he loves will bring no end to the pangs of his unrequited love. She turns her head, he sees the effects of time, but these changes in her appearance make no difference. The fire "burns but more clearly." Thus the "folly" of being comforted, of taking idle comfort from the kind words of a friend. The proffered consolation is no consolation at all.

4. Have you changed your mind about what the poem means? In what ways?

The Whole Work of a Poet

People who habitually listen to music can identify the work of certain composers and performers even when the piece being played is totally new and unfamiliar to them. "That must be Beethoven," they say; or "That must be Charlie Parker." And the same is true of poetry. All great poets—and most good ones—put an unmistakable stamp of authorship on their works. Their stamp permeates the poem, and in its own way it is just as obvious as the poet's name at the beginning or end of the poem. Thus, an experienced reader of poetry could never confuse Whitman with Tennyson, or Donne with Allen Ginsberg, or Milton with Wallace Stevens, or Frost with Keats, because each of these poets speaks with a voice as immediately recognizable as a friend's voice on the telephone. The friend may be saying something that you've never heard him say before, but you know almost automatically that he and nobody else is the person speaking.

Each poem—however complete it may be in itself—is in reality only part of a whole body of work, and the more familiar a reader becomes with the whole body, the more understandable and enjoyable he will find the individual parts. With experience, a reader becomes familiar with the ways in which a particular poet handles the elements of his art: his images, figures, metrical devices, private symbols. Thus, when a person reads a tenth poem by, say, William Blake, he will find it much more accessible than the first Blake poem that he reads. One poem sheds light on all the others and provides a commentary on all the others.

As a general rule, advanced students of literature do not study poems piecemeal; instead, they study a number of poems by one poet, and then a number of poems by another. Although this kind of study is beyond the scope of a book designed for less advanced students, a small start can be made here by looking at a number of poems by a single poet. Robert Herrick is an appropriate choice, since most of his poems are short, and since the best ones have certain characteristics that mark them as Herrick's own.

Robert Herrick (1591–1674) came from a family of London goldsmiths, and before he went to Cambridge to study for the ministry, he worked for a time as an apprentice in his uncle's shop. Perhaps this early experience accounts for Herrick's lifelong fascination with the small and the beautiful. Gold is a precious substance, and the worker in gold must make a little of it go a long way. Herrick does with words what the goldsmith does with metal. He is at once economical and lavish. Elsewhere in this book there are several of his highly polished and bejeweled and shiny little poems: "Upon Julia's Clothes" (page 226); "To the Virgins, to Make Much of Time" (page 413); "The Funeral Rites of the Rose" (page 180); and others. These titles suggest that Herrick's world is full of beautiful girls and flowers, and indeed it is.

But it's not a sentimental or saccharine world, because Herrick has a strong dislike of mawkishness:

Upon Julia Weeping

She by the river sat, and sitting there,
She wept, and made it deeper by a tear.

Certainly Julia is crying, but the poet regards this allegedly sad spectacle from some distance and with considerable irony: the river rises only by the amount of water in one tear. It is hardly a flood and so not really very sad.

Upon the Loss of His Mistresses

I have lost, and lately, these
Many dainty mistresses:
Stately Julia, prime of all;
Sapho next, a principal;
Smooth Anthea, for a skin
White and heaven-like crystalline;
Sweet Electra; and the choice
Myrha, for the lute and voice;
Next Corinna, for her wit,
And the graceful use of it;
With Perilla. All are gone;
Only Herrick's left alone
For to number sorrow by
Their departures hence, and die.

Mistress (title): In the seventeenth century, this word did not necessarily imply a sexual relationship.

A man who loses this many charming young girl friends would appear to be either very inattentive or very unattractive. And the final line might suggest that he is also a defeatist. But in Herrick's world, the girls are entirely imaginary, artificial, and invented. They are just as pretty as, but no more real than, porcelain figures. To demand realism and "sincerity" of this sort of poetry would be like wanting a diamond ring to be useful as well as beautiful.

Herrick's work is often lightly ironic, almost always technically accomplished, and sometimes innocently erotic:

Her Legs

Fain would I kiss my Julia's dainty leg,
Which is as white and hairless as an egg.

And Herrick can be sensuous in a fanciful way:

Her Bed

See'st thou that cloud, as silver clear,
Plump, soft, and swelling everywhere?
'Tis Julia's bed, and she sleeps there.

But Herrick is not always concerned with decorative subjects; he also has a strong earthy strain which he expresses in little comic poems about disgusting subjects, like ugly people with dirty habits:

The Custard

For the second course, last night, a custard came
To the board so hot as none could touch the same:
Furze three or four times with his cheeks did blow
Upon the custard, and thus coolèd so.
It seemed by this time to admit the touch;
But none could eat it, 'cause it stunk so much.

board (2): dining table. *Furze* (3): a man's name.

Even on the unpleasant subject of bad breath, Herrick sounds like his usual pleasant and fanciful self. It is his way of writing—his style—that is identifiable, rather than the subject he chooses. Another in this vein:

Upon Blanche

Blanche swears her husband's lovely, when a scald
Has bleared his eyes. Besides, his head is bald.
Next, his wild ears, like leathern wings full spread,
Flutter to fly, and bear away his head.

scald (1): scabby infection.

Exercise 55

Among the twenty-two short poems that follow, six are by Robert Herrick, eleven are by Emily Dickinson (1830–1886), and five are by Stephen Crane (1871–1900). First try to sort out the poems by Herrick, and then in the remaining poems try to distinguish Crane's work from Emily Dickinson's. For the purposes of this exercise, Dickinson's poems have been "normalized." Her characteristic dashes, which are a dead giveaway, have been for the most part replaced by more conventional punctuation, and many of her capitals have been reduced to small letters.

Single Life Most Secure

Suspicion, discontent, and strife
Come in for dowry with a wife.

Much Madness Is Divinest Sense

Much madness is divinest sense
To a discerning eye;
Much sense, the starkest madness.
'Tis the majority
In this, as all, prevail.
Assent—and you are sane;
Demur—you're straightway dangerous
And handled with a chain.

The Tongue of Wood

There was a man with tongue of wood
Who essayed to sing.
And in truth it was lamentable.
But there was one who heard
The clip-clapper of this tongue of wood
And knew what the man
Wished to sing,
And with that the singer was content.

The Sea

To the maiden
The sea was blue meadow
Alive with little froth-people
Singing.

To the sailor, wrecked,
The sea was dead grey walls
Superlative in vacancy,
Upon which, nevertheless, at fateful time
Was written
The grim hatred of nature.

After Great Pain

After great pain a formal feeling comes;
The nerves sit ceremonious, like tombs.
The stiff heart questions, "Was it he that bore,
And yesterday, or centuries before?"

The feet, mechanical, go round,
Of ground, or air, or ought,
A wooden way,
Regardless grown;
A quartz contentment like a stone.

This is the hour of lead:
Remembered, if outlived,
As freezing persons recollect the snow,
First chill, then stupor, then the letting go.

Because I Could Not Stop for Death

Because I could not stop for Death,
He kindly stopped for me;
The carriage held but just ourselves
And immortality.

We slowly drove. He knew no haste,
And I had put away
My labor and my leisure too
For his civility.

We passed the school, where children strove
At recess in the ring;
We passed the fields of gazing grain,
We passed the setting sun,

Or rather, he passed us.
The dews drew quivering and chill:
For only gossamer, my gown;
My tippet, only tulle.

We paused before a house that seemed
A swelling in the ground.
The roof was scarcely visible;
The cornice, in the ground.

Since then 'tis centuries, and yet
Feels shorter than the day
I first surmised the horses' heads
Were toward Eternity.

gossamer (15) : light, delicate fabric. *tippet* (16) : cape. *tulle* (16) : netlike fabric.

Apparently with No Surprise

Apparently with no surprise
To any happy flower,
The frost beheads it at its play,
In accidental power.

The blonde assassin passes on;
The sun proceeds unmoved
To measure off another day
For an approving God.

My Life Closed Twice

My life closed twice before its close.
It yet remains to see
If Immortality unveil
A third event to me

So huge, so hopeless to conceive
As these that twice befell.
Parting is all we know of heaven
And all we need of hell.

If I Should Cast Off

If I should cast off this tattered coat,
And go free into the mighty sky;
If I should find nothing there
But a vast blue,
Echoless, ignorant—
What then?

I Walked in a Desert

I walked in a desert.
And I cried:
"Ah, God, take me from this place!"
A voice said: "It is no desert."
I cried: "Well, but—
The sand, the heat, the vacant horizon."
A voice said: "It is no desert."

I Never Lost as Much

I never lost as much but twice,
And that was in the sod.
Twice have I stood a beggar
Before the door of God!

Angels, twice descending,
Reimbursed my store.
Burglar! Banker! Father!
I am poor once more.

Upon a Maid That Died the Day She Was Married

That morn which saw me made a bride,
The evening witnessed that I died.
Those Holy lights, wherewith they guide
Unto the bed the bashful bride
Served but as tapers for to burn,
And light my relics to their urn.
The epitaph, which here you see,
Supplied the epithalamie.

epithalamie (8): wedding song.

Putrefaction

Putrefaction is the end
Of all that nature doth intend.

Presentiment

Presentiment is that long shadow on the lawn
Indicative that suns go down:

The notice to the startled grass
That darkness is about to pass.

Grace for a Child

Here a little child I stand,
Heaving up my either hand;
Cold as Paddocks though they be,
Here I lift them up to Thee,
For a Benison to fall
On our meat and on us all. Amen.

Paddocks (3): toads. *Benison* (5): blessing. *meat* (6): food.

Success Is Counted Sweetest

Success is counted sweetest
By those who ne'er succeed.
To comprehend a nectar
Requires sorest need.

Not one of all the purple host
Who took the flag today
Can tell the definition
So clear of victory

As he defeated, dying,
On whose forbidden ear
The distant strains of triumph
Burst agonized and clear!

There's a Certain Slant of Light

There's a certain slant of light,
Winter afternoons,
That oppresses like the heft
Of cathedral tunes.

Heavenly hurt it gives us;
We can find no scar,
But eternal difference
Where the meanings are.

None may teach it any;
'Tis the seal despair,
An imperial affliction
Sent us of the air.

When it comes, the landscape listens;
Shadows hold their breath.
When it goes, 'tis like the distance
On the look of death.

Hope Is the Thing

Hope is the thing with feathers
That perches in the soul,
And sings the tune without the words,
And never stops at all,

And sweetest in the gale is heard,
And sore must be the storm
That could abash the little bird
That kept so many warm.

I've heard it in the chillest land
And on the strangest sea;
Yet never, in extremity,
It asked a crumb of me.

Think As I Think

"Think as I think," said a man,
"Or you are abominably wicked;
You are a toad."

And after I had thought of it,
I said, "I will, then, be a toad."

Upon a Child That Died

Here she lies, a pretty bud
Lately made of flesh and blood,
Who as soon fell fast asleep
As her little eyes did peep.
Give her strewings, but not stir
The earth that lightly covers her.

strewings (5): flowers strewn on the grave.

I Heard a Fly Buzz

I heard a fly buzz when I died.
The stillness in the room
Was like the stillness in the air
Between the heaves of storm.

The eyes around had wrung them dry,
And breaths were gathering firm
For that last onset, when the king
Be witnessed in the room.

I willed my keepsakes, signed away
What portion of me be
Assignable, and then it was
There interposed a fly

With blue, uncertain, stumbling buzz
Between the light and me;
And then the windows failed, and then
I could not see to see.

I Fear No Earthly Powers

I fear no earthly powers,
But care for crowns of flowers,
And love to have my beard
With wine and oil besmeared.
This day I'll drown all sorrow.
Who knows to live tomorrow?

10. Judging a Poem

We can not only like whatever we like to like but we can like it for any reason we choose.

T. S. Eliot

Judging a poem, like judging anything else, is attempting to evaluate it: to say whether it is any good, or not, and in what way it is good and in what way bad. To some extent all readers are judges of the poems they read. A reader coming to the end of a poem will make an almost automatic judgment of it. If he likes the poem, he will judge it to be a good one; if he dislikes it, he will be inclined to feel that the fault must be in the poem rather than in himself. Such a reaction is only human, and in behaving this way inexperienced readers are exactly like famous literary critics and scholars: they approve of what they like. One chief difference between the experienced critic and the beginning reader is that the former can give convincing reasons for his judgment, while the latter ordinarily cannot. And the process of finding convincing reasons to defend a literary judgment often serves to modify the judgment. Thus, an experienced critic who is also open-minded may start by hating a poem but end by admiring it—after he has fully explored the poem and his own relationship to it.

Although there are no universally agreed-upon standards or criteria by which all poems are judged, there are certain habits and attitudes that most experienced judges cultivate. An experienced judge reserves his opinion until he is sure that he understands just what a poet is doing in a given poem. For example, he avoids damning a poet for not expressing a deep and heart-felt emotion, when all the poet intended to write was a pleasant piece of light verse. Thus, "What is the poet trying to do?" is the first question that an open-minded critic asks. Then he asks, "How well has the poet realized or fulfilled his apparent purposes?" This question guides one toward measuring the poem by itself, rather than measuring it by criteria or standards imposed on it from outside the poem.

Finally, a critic may ask, "Is what the poet has done worth doing?" The answer that an individual reader gives to the last question is determined by his own set of values—that is, by whatever he considers worthy, significant, interesting, excellent, and rewarding in poetry. The purpose of this chapter is not to impose someone else's values on you as a reader of poems but to help you establish your own.

"Good" and "Bad" Poems

There are no absolutely good or absolutely bad poems. Instead, poems are "good for" something, or "bad for" something. A poem that is suitable for a Mother's Day greeting card would be totally unsuitable for printing in a highbrow quarterly read only by the literary intelligentsia. A complex poem that would provide enough good materials for an hour's discussion in a literature course would not necessarily be good for using as the lyrics of a folk song. A poem that is good enough to win a literary contest in a local newspaper may not impress the poetry editor of a national magazine as being good for his publication.

What Does Little Birdie Say

What does little birdie say
In her nest at peep of day?
Let me fly, says little birdie,
Mother, let me fly away.
Birdie, rest a little longer,
Till the little wings are stronger.
So she rests a little longer,
Then she flies away.

What does little baby say,
In her bed at peep of day?
Baby says, like little birdie,

Let me rise and fly away.
Baby, sleep a little longer,
Till the little limbs are stronger.
If she sleeps a little longer,
Baby too shall fly away.

Alfred, Lord Tennyson
(1809–1892)

One wrong way to judge this poem would be to look at the signature and exclaim, "Ah, Tennyson! This must be a great poem because it's by a famous poet." A judgment founded merely on an author's name is no judgment at all, because it is a truism of literary history that even the greatest authors are not great all the time. If Homer sometimes nods and Shakespeare occasionally sleeps, Dryden, Wordsworth, and Shelley frequently snore. An author's name is not necessarily a hallmark.

Another procedure would be to look up the opinions of well-known literary critics and teachers and to accept their judgment as final. But this, too, is a wrong approach to the problem because critics and teachers are not infallible. Moreover, the sheeplike student who always accepts established opinions may earn good grades in certain kinds of literature courses, but he will never develop his own powers of discrimination.

Tennyson's poem itself must be examined to discover whether it actually is what it purports to be. A mother appears to be speaking, or perhaps singing, these words to a very small child. She is describing the experience of growing up by comparing the child to a little bird, which she calls a *birdie* because such baby talk is appropriate to the occasion. The simple diction and strictly regular meter are also appropriate because the listening child will understand the former and enjoy the latter. As a poem for a small child, this is probably a good one; if it were intended for adults, it would be insufferably bad because it oversimplifies and sentimentalizes the experience of growing up. But all the evidence suggests that Tennyson did not write the poem for adults, and therefore he was not trying to communicate an experience that would satisfy or delight them.

"Little Birdie" is of course not characteristic of Tennyson's poetry as a whole; a poem like *In Memoriam* is much more representative of his serious, mature work. Too long to reprint here in its entirety, *In Memoriam,* is a somber and impressive poem in memory of Tennyson's dead friend Arthur Hallam. The following lines, in the form of a prayer, come from section fifty.

Be near me when my light is low,
  When the blood creeps, and the nerves prick
  And tingle; and the heart is sick,
And all the wheels of being slow.

Be near me when the sensuous frame
  Is racked with pangs that conquer trust;
  And Time, a maniac scattering dust,
And Life, a Fury slinging flame.

Be near me when my faith is dry,
  And men the flies of latter spring,
  That lay their eggs, and sting and sing
And weave their petty cells and die.

Be near me when I fade away,
  To point the term of human strife,
  And on the low dark verge of life
The twilight of eternal day.

In Memoriam and "Little Birdie" are poles apart, and so it's not very hard to judge what each is "good for" or "bad for." For most poems, judgment is a much more demanding task:

The Night Has a Thousand Eyes

The night has a thousand eyes,
  And the day but one;
Yet the light of the bright world dies
  With the dying sun.

The mind has a thousand eyes,
 And the heart but one;
Yet the light of a whole life dies
 When love is done.

Francis William Bourdillon
(1852–1921)

Most literature teachers and most other people who take the art and craft of poetry seriously would judge "The Night Has a Thousand Eyes" to be a bad poem. A defense of this adverse judgment might go something like this:

Although a reader can never know for certain what a poet's intentions were when he wrote a given poem, it seems likely that Bourdillon intended this poem for adults because it is about an adult experience: the end of a love affair. The questions to ask about this poem, then, are these: Does the poem communicate this experience? Does it tell, as exactly as words can tell, what falling out of love feels like? When love is done, the poet says, all light dies in a person's life. One could hardly object to this metaphorical overstatement except, perhaps, to say that it is trite. To support the metaphor, however, the poet develops an elaborate parallel between the way love goes out of a life and the way the sun goes out of the sky, leaving it dark for the stars. Look closely at this parallel. If seeing thousands of stars is a pleasant experience—and most people would find it so—the parallel is inappropriate because it contributes nothing to the unhappy experience that the poem is attempting to communicate. If the parallel is specious, the poem is a failure because it contains nothing except the parallel. Moreover, lines 5 and 6 seem to have no other function in the poem than to keep the parallel intact. Most readers, indeed, would prefer not to visualize a heart with an eye in it, even though the eye is about to go blind. This grotesquely anatomical image was apparently forced on the poet because he was determined to find something to correspond with the cliché *mind's eye*. When the devices of a poem assume control, as they do here, the result is invariably disastrous. This poem is bad because it does not do what it was designed to do; it fails to communicate an experience in such a way that the reader also has the experience.

However damaging this attack might seem to some readers, there are undoubtedly others who would not accept it as the final word on this poem and who would question the assumptions and values that underlie the attack. For instance, some readers may value vagueness over precision; they may not seek a sharply defined experience when they read and may prefer their poems to be impressive-sounding in a cloudy way, tinged with indefinite sadness. And so this poem would seem to be a good one to such a reader, who is certainly entitled to his opinion.

There is, however, one sort of opinion on a poem of this kind that does not seem justified. Suppose that a reader were to defend his high opinion of "The Night Has a Thousand Eyes" by saying "This poem may be bad, according to the strict standards of critical judgment, but it is so much better than any I could write that I admire it. Besides, I understand it." The first part of this remark confuses making and judging. Writing a good poem is indeed very difficult for most people, but this fact does not justify a refusal to pass judgment. Only a very mad, or a very poor, or a very stingy man would say, "This egg may be rotten, but it's a better egg than I could lay, so I'll eat it and like it." Further, the reader who thinks that he understands the poem has been deluded by its simple language. The individual words are clear enough, but they have been put together in such a way that they cannot be understood. An obscure poem is not necessarily profound; it may be merely confused.

Exercise 56

In what ways are these poems "good" or "bad?"

I Have a Rendezvous with Death

I have a rendezvous with Death
At some disputed barricade,
When Spring comes back with rustling shade
And apple-blossoms fill the air—
I have a rendezvous with Death
When Spring brings back blue days and fair.

It may be he shall take my hand
And lead me into his dark land

And close my eyes and quench my breath—
It may be I shall pass him still.
I have a rendezvous with Death
On some scarred slope of battered hill,
When Spring comes round again this year
And the first meadow-flowers appear.

God knows 'twere better to be deep
Pillowed in silk and scented down,
Where Love throbs out in blissful sleep,
Pulse nigh to pulse, and breath to breath,
Where hushed awakenings are dear . . .
But I've a rendezvous with Death
At midnight in some flaming town,
When Spring trips north again this year,
And I to my pledged word am true,
I shall not fail that rendezvous.

Alan Seeger
(1888–1916)

1. Identify the experience that the poet apparently is attempting to communicate.
2. How well does he communicate that experience? Do all the elements of the poem contribute to it? Specifically, what contribution is made by the descriptions of spring? By the scene in bed?
3. Are the details organized in such a way that the important parts of the experience are emphasized?
4. Is the fact that Seeger was killed in action in 1916 relevant to our judgment of the poem?

Dulce Et Decorum Est

Bent double, like old beggars under sacks,
Knock-kneed, coughing like hags, we cursed through sludge,
Till on the haunting flares we turned our backs,
And towards our distant rest began to trudge.
Men marched asleep. Many had lost their boots,
But limped on, blood-shod. All went lame, all blind;
Drunk with fatigue; deaf even to the hoots
Of gas-shells dropping softly behind.

Gas! GAS! Quick, boys!—An ecstasy of fumbling,
Fitting the clumsy helmets just in time,
But someone still was yelling out and stumbling
And flound'ring like a man in fire or lime.—
Dim through the misty panes and thick green light,
As under a green sea, I saw him drowning.

In all my dreams before my helpless sight
He plunges at me, guttering, choking, drowning.

If in some smothering dreams, you too could pace
Behind the wagon that we flung him in,
And watch the white eyes writhing in his face,
His hanging face, like a devil's sick of sin,
If you could hear, at every jolt, the blood
Come gargling from the froth-corrupted lungs
Bitter as the cud
Of vile, incurable sores or innocent tongues,—
My friend, you would not tell with such high zest
To children ardent for some desperate glory,
The old lie: *Dulce et decorum est*
Pro patria mori.

Wilfred Owen
(1893–1918)

Dulce . . . mori (title and 27–28) : "It is sweet and fitting to die for one's native land" (Horace) . *Gas* (9) : poisonous gas contains chlorine, used against infantry by both sides in World War I. *children* (25) : schoolchildren, who in Owen's day were required to study such Latin writers as Horace.

1. What experience is the poet attempting to communicate? How well does he do so?
2. Discuss the effectiveness of the images, similes, and metaphors. In what ways do they help the poet carry out his intentions?
3. In the fact that Wilfred Owen was killed in action in 1918 relevant to our judgment of the poem?
4. Compare this poem with Seeger's "I Have a Rendezvous." Which seems to you the better poem? Defend your judgment.

Before Disaster

Evening traffic homeward burns,
Swift and even on the turns,
Drifting weight in triple rows,
Fixed relation and repose.
This one edges out and by,
Inch by inch with steady eye.
But should error be increased,
Mass and moment are released;
Matter loosens, flooding blind,
Levels drivers to its kind.
  Ranks of nations thus descend,
Watchful to a stormy end.
By a moment's calm beguiled,
I have got a wife and child.
Fool and scoundrel guide the State.
Peace is whore to Greed and Hate.
Nowhere may I turn to flee:
Action is security.
Treading change with savage heel,
We must live or die by steel.

Yvor Winters
(1900–1968)

1. If you read this poem aloud, you will discover that it has an almost perfectly regular meter. Why is such a meter more appropriate to the theme of this poem than an irregular rhythm or free verse (see Appendix, page 000) would be?
2. What does the word *thus* (line 11) tell the reader about the relationship between the first verse paragraph and the second?
3. Paraphrase line 16 and explain the personifications.
4. What is suggested by the word *steel* (line 20)? Does it mean only the steel in cars, or does it also carry other connotations?

The Prophet Speaks of Love

When love beckons to you, follow him,
Though his ways are hard and steep.
And when his wings enfold you yield to him,
Though the sword hidden among his pinions may wound you.
And when he speaks to you believe in him,
Though his voice may shatter your dreams as the north
wind lays waste the garden.
For even as love crowns you so shall he crucify you. Even
as he is for your growth so is he for your pruning.
Even as he ascends to your height and caresses your
tenderest branches that quiver in the sun,
So shall he descend to your roots and shake them in their
clinging to the earth.
Like sheaves of corn he gathers you unto himself.
He threshes you to make you naked.
He sifts you to free you from your husks.
He grinds you to whiteness.
He kneads you until you are pliant;
And then he assigns you to his sacred fire, that you may
become sacred bread for God's sacred feast.

Kahlil Gibran
(1883–1931)

The Voyeur

While walking in a lonely wood
I saw a big man fall a tree
his muscles bulging in the sun
he never said hello to me.

Once in a gray-green meadowland
I saw a girl with yellow hair
she didn't pause to speak my name
or even know that I was there.

Some children playing in the street
and bouncing balls against the wall
went right on playing in the street
and never noticed me at all.

I've been a stranger all my life
to everything and everyone
just passing through this lonely world
until my journeying is done.

Rod McKuen
(1933–)

Clear, Easy, Noncontroversial Poems

There are readers who think well of a poem only if it meets three tests: (1) Everything in the poem must be perfectly understandable on a first reading. (2) Nothing in the poem can contradict any of the reader's cherished beliefs or opinions. (3) Nothing in the poem can be left uncertain or unresolved. While these expectations are common enough, they do interfere badly with the proper exercise of literary judgment.

The first expectation results from intellectual laziness. While there are many admirable poems that are also easy, many others are subtle and difficult, and it is just as unreasonable to demand that all poems be easy as to demand that life itself be easy. Every adult reader knows that there are some human attitudes, experiences, and problems that cannot be reduced to simple formulas.

The second expectation is harder to deal with; we all like to have our opinions confirmed and reinforced, and we think well of whatever reading matter gives us this sort of confirming experience. But a good poem is not necessarily one that agrees with the reader's own ideas, nor a bad poem one that conflicts with them. In judging a poem, it is well to ignore one question at the outset: "Do I agree with the ideas?" By answering this question too early, the reader is likely to ignore the poem and concentrate on himself and his own ideas. Later, when he has fully considered the poem as a poem—rather than as an expression of ideas—he may find himself agreeing with it and liking it. On the other hand, further inspection may confirm his dislike. In this case, a student should never pretend to like a poem simply because his teacher or some other authority expects him to. Hypocritical admiration has no place in the study of poems or anything else; it circumvents the aim of all study, which is to cultivate genuine admiration of excellence.

The third expectation also comes from a very ordinary human desire: most of us want to know where we are most of the time. We become irritable when confronted with uncertainties; we long for a world of facts, definite names and clear labels on everything. But again, mature people know that life is always full of doubt and uncertainty, and so must poetry be if it is to reflect life's uncertainties.

Exercise 57

Try to judge the following poems as poems. Which ones confirm your own outlook on life? Do you regard a poem that expresses a version of your outlook as a better poem than one which expresses a different philosophy?

Dover Beach

The sea is calm to-night.
The tide is full, the moon lies fair
Upon the straits;—on the French coast the light
Gleams and is gone; the cliffs of England stand,
Glimmering and vast, out in the tranquil bay.
Come to the window, sweet is the night-air!
Only, from the long line of spray
Where the sea meets the moon-blanch'd land,
Listen! you hear the grating roar
Of pebbles which the waves draw back, and fling,
At their return, up the high strand,
Begin, and cease, and then again begin,
With tremulous cadence slow, and bring
The eternal note of sadness in.

Sophocles long ago
Heard it on the Ægean, and it brought
Into his mind the turbid ebb and flow
Of human misery; we
Find also in the sound a thought,
Hearing it by this distant northern sea.
The Sea of Faith
Was once, too, at the full, and round earth's shore
Lay like the folds of a bright girdle furl'd.

But now I only hear
Its melancholy, long, withdrawing roar,
Retreating, to the breath
Of the night-wind, down the vast edges drear
And naked shingles of the world.

Ah, love, let us be true
To one another! for the world, which seems
To lie before us like a land of dreams,
So various, so beautiful, so new,
Hath really neither joy, nor love, nor light,
Nor certitude, nor peace, nor help for pain;
And we are here as on a darkling plain
Swept with confused alarms of struggle and flight,
Where ignorant armies clash by night.

Matthew Arnold
(1822–1888)

shingles (28) : pebbly beaches.

The Dover Bitch

A Criticism of Life
for Andrews Wanning

So there stood Matthew Arnold and this girl
With the cliffs of England crumbling away behind them,
And he said to her, "Try to be true to me,
And I'll do the same for you, for things are bad
All over, etc., etc."
Well now, I knew this girl. It's true she had read
Sophocles in a fairly good translation
And caught that bitter allusion to the sea,
But all the time he was talking she had in mind
The notion of what his whiskers would feel like
On the back of her neck. She told me later on
That after a while she got to looking out
At the lights across the channel, and really felt sad,
Thinking of all the wine and enormous beds
And blandishments in French and the perfumes.
And then she got really angry. To have been brought
All the way down from London, and then be addressed

As a sort of mournful cosmic last resort
Is really tough on a girl, and she was pretty.
Anyway, she watched him pace the room
And finger his watch-chain and seem to sweat a bit,
And then she said one or two unprintable things.
But you mustn't judge her by that. What I mean to say is,
She's really all right. I still see her once in a while
And she always treats me right. We have a drink
And I give her a good time, and perhaps it's a year
Before I see her again, but there she is,
Running to fat, but dependable as they come.
And sometimes I bring her a bottle of *Nuit d'Amour*.

Anthony Hecht
(1923–   )

Nuit d'Amour (29): apparently a brand of perfume, "Night of Love."

Say Not the Struggle Nought Availeth

Say not the struggle nought availeth,
  The labour and the wounds are vain,
The enemy faints not, nor faileth,
  And as things have been, things remain.

If hopes were dupes, fears may be liars;
  It may be, in yon smoke concealed,
Your comrades chase e'en now the fliers,
  And, but for you, possess the field.

For while the tired waves, vainly breaking,
  Seem here no painful inch to gain,
Far back through creeks and inlets making
  Comes, silent, flooding in, the main,

And not by eastern windows only,
  When daylight comes, comes in the light,
In front the sun climbs slow, how slowly,
  But westward, look, the land is bright.

Arthur Hugh Clough
(1819–1861)

Dust of Snow

The way a crow
Shook down on me
The dust of snow
From a hemlock tree

Has given my heart
A change of mood
And saved some part
Of a day I had rued.

Robert Frost
(1875–1963)

After Death Nothing Is

After death nothing is, and nothing death:
The utmost limits of a gasp of breath.
Let the ambitious zealot lay aside
His hopes of heaven, where faith is but his pride;
Let slavish souls lay by their fear,
Nor be concerned which way or where
After this life they shall be hurled.
Dead, we become the lumber of the world;
And to that mass of matter shall be swept,
Where things destroyed with things unborn are kept.
Devouring time swallows us whole;
Impartial death confounds body and soul.
For hell and the foul fiend that rules
God's everlasting fiery jails,
Devised by rogues, dreaded by fools
(With his grim, grisly dog that keeps the door),
Are senseless stories, idle tales,
Dreams, whimseys, and no more.

Seneca
(*c.* 54 B..C.–A.D. 39)
(*translated by John Wilmot, Earl of Rochester*)

dog (16): Cerberus, who guards the Underworld.

If—

IF YOU can keep your head when all about you
  Are losing theirs and blaming it on you,
If you can trust yourself when all men doubt you,
  But make allowance for their doubting too;
If you can wait and not be tired by waiting,
  Or being lied about, don't deal in lies,
Or being hated, don't give way to hating,
  And yet don't look too good, nor talk too wise:

If you can dream—and not make dreams your master;
  If you can think—and not make thoughts your aim;
If you can meet with Triumph and Disaster
  And treat those two impostors just the same;
If you can bear to hear the truth you've spoken
  Twisted by knaves to make a trap for fools,
Or watch the things you gave your life to, broken,
  And stoop and build 'em up with worn-out tools:

If you can make one heap of all your winnings
  And risk it on one turn of pitch-and-toss,
And lose, and start again at your beginnings
  And never breathe a word about your loss;
If you can force your heart and nerve and sinew
  To serve your turn long after they are gone,
And so hold on when there is nothing in you
  Except the Will which says to them: "Hold on!"

If you can talk with crowds and keep your virtue,
  Or walk with Kings—nor lose the common touch,
If neither foes nor loving friends can hurt you,
  If all men count with you, but none too much;
If you can fill the unforgiving minute
  With sixty seconds' worth of distance run,
Yours is the Earth and everything that's in it,
  And—which is more—you'll be a Man, my son!

Rudyard Kipling
(1865–1936)

One Poet's Values

A twentieth-century poet, Archibald MacLeish, has expressed his sense of what the values of a good poem are in the following lyric.

Ars Poetica

A poem should be palpable and mute
As a globed fruit,

Dumb
As old medallions to the thumb,

Silent as the sleeve-worn stone
Of casement ledges where the moss has grown—

A poem should be wordless
As the flight of birds.

*

A poem should be motionless in time
As the moon climbs,

Leaving, as the moon releases
Twig by twig the night-entangled trees,

Leaving, as the moon behind the winter leaves,
Memory by memory the mind—

A poem should be motionless in time
As the moon climbs.

*

A poem should be equal to:
Not true.

For all the history of grief
An empty doorway and a maple leaf.

For love
The leaning grasses and two lights above the sea—

A poem should not mean
But be.

Archibald MacLeish
(1892–)

Title: "Poetic Art."

The repeated use of *should* (lines 1, 7, 9, 15, 17, 23) indicates that this poem is concerned with literary judgments. MacLeish would presumably value more highly a poem that did what he says poems should do than one that did not. *Palpable* (line 1) implies that a good poem is concrete; like such real things as fruit, medallions, and ledges, it makes an appeal to the senses. A good poem must therefore contain precise images. But what of *mute, dumb, silent,* and *wordless?* It is paradoxical to apply these adjectives to a poem, a structure of words. The truth behind the paradox is the special way that good poems use language. Although made of words, a poem does not use words to communicate factual information, but to communicate experience. Poems are also wordless in the sense that their words cannot be translated. Every word in a good poem seems to be the inevitably right one, in the inevitably right place. Although the words are organized into an organic unity, like fruit, a poem is also something made, like a medallion. The words in a good poem are rich in connotation, as old objects are rich in associations. Finally, the words move toward a destination or end, as birds fly.

In the second section, MacLeish is concerned with the relationship between a poem and time. This relationship is also paradoxical. Although poetry is a temporal art, and although a particular poem is the product of a particular time, a good poem will seem independent of time. Like the moon, which is always "climbing" yet always appears static in the heavens, a poem at a given moment will be both static and dynamic—that is, moving yet standing still in such a way as to illuminate the mind.

Section three contains two paradoxes. First, it asserts that a poem is "not true," but, rather, is "equal to": that is, it is an equivalent of an experience that may or may not have actually happened.

The statement that a poem is not true does not deny the validity of its experience but merely emphasizes the element of make-believe in all imaginative literature. The very language of a good poem is figurative, and therefore not literally true. Poems present concrete images as if they were "all the history of grief" or "love." By convention, the reader accepts the object for the idea, the image for the emotion. Finally, in the most famous lines of the poem, MacLeish claims that a poem "should not mean/But be." Here he is not necessarily saying that good poems lack meaning; his own poem is very meaningful. Rather, he is insisting that a poem exists in such a way that it has more meaning than can be set down in any verbal statement about it. The amount of meaning in a good poem is inexhaustible because the poem is what it is.

These, then, are among the values that MacLeish seems to admire: concreteness, concentration, exactness and inevitability in diction, structure, memorability, imaginative figures, and meaning coextensive with the poem itself.

Exercise 58

To what degree, and in what respects, do these poems exemplify the values set forth in "Ars Poetica"? Think about these poems, and about others that you have read, and then consider this question: Are there good poems that do not exemplify the values of "Ars Poetica," but some other values?

Ozymandias

I met a traveller from an antique land
Who said: Two vast and trunkless legs of stone
Stand in the desert. Near them, on the sand,
Half sunk, a shattered visage lies, whose frown,
And wrinkled lip, and sneer of cold command,
Tell that its sculptor well those passions read
Which yet survive, stamped on these lifeless things,
The hand that mocked them, and the heart that fed:
And on the pedestal these words appear:
"My name is Ozymandias, king of kings:
Look on my works, ye Mighty, and despair!"

Nothing beside remains. Round the decay
Of that colossal wreck, boundless and bare
The lone and level sands stretch far away.

Percy Bysshe Shelley
(1792–1822)

Title: a Pharaoh. *survive* (7): live longer than. *hand* (8): the sculptor's. *heart* (8): the pharaoh's heart, which fed those passions.

In a Station of the Metro

The apparition of these faces in the crowd;
Petals on a wet, black bough.

Ezra Pound
(1884–1972)

Title: the Paris subway system.

To—

Music, when soft voices die,
Vibrates in the memory—
Odours, when sweet violets sicken,
Live within the sense they quicken.

Rose leaves, when the rose is dead,
Are heaped for the belovèd's bed;
And so thy thoughts, when thou art gone,
Love itself shall slumber on.

Percy Bysshe Shelley
(1792–1822)

Once by the Pacific

The shattered water made a misty din.
Great waves looked over others coming in,
And thought of doing something to the shore
That water never did to land before.

The clouds were low and hairy in the skies,
Like locks blown forward in the gleam of eyes.
You could not tell, and yet it looked as if
The shore was lucky in being backed by cliff,
The cliff in being backed by continent;
It looked as if a night of dark intent
Was coming, and not only a night, an age.
Someone had better be prepared for rage.
There would be more than ocean water broken
Before God's last *Put out the Light* was spoken.

Robert Frost
(1875–1963)

Amateurish Poems

An amateurish poem is one in which the various elements—rhythm, sound, diction, figurative language—fail to work together to present an experience. One or more of the elements either does not make its appropriate contribution to the experience or actively detracts from the experience. It is not surprising that there are so many amateurish poems in the world, since anyone who has attempted to write a poem soom becomes aware of the difficulties of harmonizing all the elements. To evade some of these difficulties, many amateur poets elect to write nothing but free verse (see page 465); in this kind of poetry, they mistakenly suppose, anything will do.

Another kind of amateurishness results when a poet relies too much on another poet to furnish him with his subject matter or with his words, images, and structures. Poems written in this way are said to be derivative, and they are bad because they are second-hand. They inevitably dilute the experience of the original poem. Every age has a large number of imitators, a fact that is brought about because inferior writers cannot resist the masterly influence of a few great writers.

A third type of amateur poem simply fails to communicate any experience at all. It may suffer from trite ideas, or it may simply be overly didactic or prosaic. In short, many amateurish poems result more from the overwhelming desire of the amateur to write a poem—to be known as a person who has written a poem—than from any desire to use language in an interesting way, or from any real need to say something in a poem.

Love virtue; avoid all temptations;
  Be humble and meek and sincere;
Walk upright in all situations;
  To God then you'll always be dear.

This quatrain is too platitudinous and too general to convey any experience. However much a reader may agree with the advice it gives, he must call it a bad poem because advice of this sort is much better given in prose, in a sermon or an inspirational talk. A poem will also not communicate an experience if all or most of its images and figures are intelligible only to the poet himself and perhaps to a few of his friends and admirers.

Exercise 59

Among the following, distinguish the poorer from the better poems. What is it that makes the poorer poems seem amateurish to you?

Virtue

Sweet day, so cool, so calm, so bright,
The bridal of the earth and sky:
The dew shall weep thy fall tonight,
    For thou must die.

Sweet rose, whose hue, angry and brave,
Bids the rash gazer wipe his eye:
Thy root is ever in its grave,
    And thou must die.

Sweet spring, full of sweet days and roses,
A box where sweets compacted lie;
My music shows ye have your closes,
    And all must die

Only a sweet and virtuous soul,
Like seasoned timber, never gives;
But though the whole world turn to coal,
    Then chiefly lives.

George Herbert
(1593–1633)

closes (11): cadences.

Thus Passeth

Oh Nature! World! Oh Life! Oh Time!
Why aren't you always in your prime?
Why doesn't summer always stay?
Why aren't the flowers always gay?
Why is love's song so short a tune?
Why isn't January June?
I sigh to see all young girls grow
Older and older, their hair like snow.
All things on earth thus pass away:
Nothing save virtue lasts for aye.

Anonymous
(Twentieth Century)

Simple Nature

Be it not mine to steal the cultured flower
  From any garden of the rich and great,
Nor seek with care, through many a weary hour,
  Some novel form of wonder to create.
Enough for me the leafy woods to rove,
  And gather simple cups of morning dew,
Or, in the fields and meadows that I love,
  Find beauty in their bells of every hue.
Thus round my cottage floats a fragrant air,
  And though the rustic plot be humbly laid,
Yet, like the lilies gladly growing there,

I have not toil'd, but take what God has made.
My Lord Ambition pass'd, and smiled in scorn;
I plucked a rose, and lo! it had no thorn.

George John Romanes
(1848–1894)

The World Is Too Much with Us

The world is too much with us; late and soon,
Getting and spending, we lay waste our powers:
Little we see in Nature that is ours;
We have given our hearts away, a sordid boon!
This Sea that bares her bosom to the moon;
The winds that will be howling at all hours,
And are up-gathered now like sleeping flowers;
For this, for everything, we are out of tune;
It moves us not.—Great God! I'd rather be
A Pagan suckled in a creed outworn;
So might I, standing on this pleasant lea,
Have glimpses that would make me less forlorn;
Have sight of Proteus rising from the sea;
Or hear old Triton blow his wreathèd horn.

William Wordsworth
(1770–1850)

God's World

O world, I cannot hold thee close enough!
Thy winds, thy wide grey skies!
Thy mists, that roll and rise!
Thy woods, this autumn day, that ache and sag
And all but cry with colour! That gaunt crag
To crush! To lift the lean of that black bluff!
World, World, I cannot get thee close enough!
Long have I known a glory in it all,
But never knew I this:
Here such a passion is
As stretcheth me apart,—Lord, I do fear
Thou'st made the world too beautiful this year;

My soul is all but out of me,—let fall
No burning leaf; prithee, let no bird call.

Edna St. Vincent Millay
(1892–1950)

On a Faded Violet

The odour from the flower is gone
  Which like thy kisses breathed on me;
The colour from the flower is flown
  Which glowed on thee and only thee!

A shrivelled, lifeless, vacant form,
  It lies on my abandoned breast,
And mocks the heart which yet is warm,
  With cold and silent rest.

I weep,—my tears revive it not!
  I sigh,—it breathes no more on me;
Its mute and uncomplaining lot
  Is such as mine should be.

Percy Bysshe Shelley
(1792–1822)

To a Firefly

Hail, scintillate flasher, thou jewel in the dark,
Thou inconstant being, thou glittering spark!
Thou hang'st on each twig, a molten green light,
And bring'st forth the darkness to sparkeling night.
Thy tiny lamp filters through mould-covered leaves,
Or thy short wingèd body hangs poised in the air;
Thou glitterest and darkenest until one believes
Thy beam was fantastic, thy form never there.
Forever live thou, bright glimmering mark;
Thine ember doth fade, gay faery sprite.
But my heart is still glad having seen thee at dark,
And my cup brimming o'er in ascending delight.

Anonymous
(Twentieth Century)

Poets Judging Their Own Work

A real poet is born and not made. This is axiomatic, since nobody by sheer will power ever became a real poet, just as nobody ever became a great composer of music or a great high jumper without some innate ability. But many good poets have become better poets by hard work, by acting as severe judges of their own poems and improving them before showing them to the world. One of the differences between an amateur and a professional poet is the latter's determination to write as well as he possibly can.

We are fortunate in having the working papers of many nineteenth- and twentieth-century poets, preserved in the manuscript collections of libraries. These papers show us how carefully some poets have revised and polished their poems. For instance, the following poems are two versions of a sonnet by Keats. The first is a draft preserved in manuscript and dated in the spring of 1819; the second is the version that Keats had printed in the autumn of 1820. In this text the italicized words in the second version represent changes that Keats made in the sonnet during the months between the draft and the publication.

Bright Star

Bright Star! would I were steadfast as thou art!
  Not in lone splendour hung amid the night;
Not watching, with eternal lids apart
  Like Nature's devout sleepless Eremite
The morning waters at their priestlike task
  Of pure ablution round earth's human shores;
Or gazing on the new soft fallen mask
  Of snow upon the mountains and the moors:—
No:—yet still steadfast, still unchangeable
  Cheek-pillow'd on my Love's white ripening breast,
To touch, for ever, its warm sink and swell,
  Awake, for ever, in a sweet unrest;
To hear, to feel her tender-taken breath,
  Half-passionless, and so swoon on to death.

John Keats
(1795–1821)

Bright Star

Bright star, would I were stedfast as thou art—
  Not in lone splendour hung *aloft* the night
And watching, with eternal lids apart,
  Like nature's *patient,* sleepless Eremite,
The *moving* waters at their priestlike task
  Of pure ablution round earth's human shores,
Or gazing on the new soft fallen mask
  Of snow upon the mountains and the moors—
No—yet still stedfast, still unchangeable,
  Pillow'd upon my *fair* love's ripening breast,
To *feel* for ever its *soft fall* and swell,
  Awake for ever in a sweet unrest,
Still, still to hear her tender-taken breath,
And so live ever—or else swoon to death.

It is impossible to be certain of Keats's precise motives for making the changes he did, but they have immeasurably improved the poem. *Aloft* for *amid* (line 2) sharpens the visual image of the star that hangs in the sky far above the speaker; *and* for *not* (line 3) improves the logic of the octave; the star is hung high in the night sky and is watching ceaselessly the waters of the oceans cleansing the shores and the new snow fallen on mountains and moors. *Patient* for *devout* (line 4) smooths out the meter and makes the line perfectly regular. The change of *morning* to *moving* (line 5) is a major one. In the full light of day the star would not be visible; moreover, it is not only in the morning that the oceans wash the continents. *Morning waters* and *ablution,* by an unfortunate association, suggests plumbing fixtures running rather than the grand cosmic image Keats sought of the tidal ebb and flow laving the world's shores. Finally, *moving* reinforces the parallel with the beloved's breast (line 10), which rises and falls under the speaker's head as the tides do under the influence of sun, moon, and stars. The two spondees in line 10 of the original version are metrically awkward, and the revisions get rid of at least one of them. The changes *feel* for *touch* and *soft fall* for *warm sink* (line 11) are improvements of diction and imagery: they soften the rather graphic sensual imagery of the sestet. The phase *warm sink and swell* (line 11) is rather harshly alliterative, and the substituted words *soft fall and swell* echoes the *soft fallen mask/Of snow* (lines 7 and 8).

The repeated *Still, still* (line 13) reinforces the notion of steadfastness that the lover seeks (lines 1 and 9). *Half-passionless* (line 14 of the first version) is a needless quibble; and if the lover can be united with his mistress, why would he want to *swoon on to death?* In the revision the alternative is made perfectly clear: either he will *so live ever,* or else die.

The point of this comparison for a reader of poems—as opposed to the writer of poems—is obvious: if a poet can take such care to improve the minute details of his poem, he deserves the sort of reader who will make a similar effort to understand what those details signify.

Exercise 60

Compare the final versions of the following lines of poetry with the earlier versions below, and try to explain why the poets made the revisions they did.

1. Keats, "On First Looking into Chapman's Homer" (page 133).
   Line 7: "Yet never could I judge what men could mean"
   Line 11: "Or like stout Cortez when with wondering eyes"

2. Blake, "The Sick Rose" (page 184).
   Lines 7–8: "A dark-secret love
   Doth life destroy."

3. Wordsworth, "Strange Fits of Passion Have I Known" (page 178). In 1798–99 the original version contained a final stanza, later cancelled:

   "I told her this; her laughter light
   Is ringing in my ears;
   And when I think upon that night
   My eyes are dim with tears."

4. Yeats, "The Sorrow of Love," 1891 version:

   "The quarrel of the sparrows in the eaves,
   The full round moon and the star-laden sky,
   The song of the ever-singing leaves,
   Had hushed away earth's old and weary cry.

   And then you came with those red mournful lips,
   And with you came the whole of the world's tears,
   And all the sorrows of her labouring ships,
   And all the burden of her million years.

And now the angry sparrows in the eaves,
The withered moon, the white stars in the sky,
The wearisome loud chanting of the leaves,
Are shaken with earth's old and weary cry."

Final version:

"The brawling of a sparrow in the eaves,
The brilliant moon and all the milky sky,
And all that famous harmony of leaves,
Had blotted out man's image and his cry.

A girl arose that had red mournful lips
And seemed the greatness of the world in tears,
Doomed like Odysseus and the labouring ships
As proud as Priam murdered with his peers;
Arose, and on the instant clamorous eaves,

A climbing moon upon an empty sky,
And all that lamentation of the leaves,
Could but compose man's image and his cry."

you (5): apparently a reference to Maud Gonne, whom Yeats loved, but who did not requite his affection. *girl* (17): an allusion to Helen of Troy as an archetype of women who motivate men to make war. *Odysseus* (19): a Greek leader, and hero of the *Odyssey*. *Priam* (20): King of Troy, killed by Pyrrhus when the city fell to the Greeks. *labouring ships* (19): Odysseus' fleet wandered the seas for ten years after the fall of Troy, only the leader surviving the various perils encountered.

Enduring Poems

Every age produces a large number of poems, most of which perish. Books of poetry wear out, their paper turns brown and brittle, they gather dust on library shelves, and they are not reprinted because the taste of one generation differs from that of the next. A living poet will take care to see that his poems remain in print and available to the public; when he is dead, his poems must stand on their own feet. If succeeding generations find merit in them, they will continue to be reprinted and read; if not, they will be forgotten.

Time, then, is the final judge of which poems are the good ones. A good poem lasts in two ways: for the individual reader, and for the whole reading public. The individual cannot exhaust it in one reading, or even in many readings. Throughout his life he can return to the poem and find new things in it. The echoes that it sets up in his mind will reverberate at the most unlikely times and places. It will change his way of looking at the world, because it will give him an experience that he might otherwise never have had. A good poem also outlives an individual reader, to go on providing wisdom and pleasure to many generations of readers. A good poem will last as long as its language is known, as Auden points out in his famous elegy on Yeats (p. 360).

Certain poems endure because they are "relevant"—because they focus on what is permanent in human life, regardless of their age. Such poems are likely to be somewhat complex, for they treat the most complex matter in the world: men and women, as spiritual, physical, moral, and intellectual beings. These poems embody a kind of wisdom about the whole human being that differs from the specialized information and knowledge found in books on psychology, religion, ethics, sociology, medicine, government, and so on. Since poets and other creators of literature look at man as a whole, they have one of the most important functions in life. By defining our experiences, they give us a sense of who we are.

Exercise 61

Many discriminating readers have admired these poems. Analyze them to see whether you can discover why.

Song

Go, lovely rose!
Tell her that wastes her time and me
That now she knows,
When I resemble her to thee
How sweet and fair she seems to be.

Tell her that's young
And shuns to have her graces spied,
That hadst thou sprung
In deserts where no men abide,
Thou must have uncommended died.

Small is the worth
Of beauty from the light retired;
Bid her come forth,
Suffer herself to be desired,
And not blush so to be admired.

Then die, that she
The common fate of all things rare
May read in thee;
How small a part of time they share
That are so wondrous sweet and fair!

Edmund Waller
(1606–1687)

resemble (4) compare.

A Prayer for my Daughter

Once more the storm is howling, and half hid
Under this cradle-hood and coverlid
My child sleeps on. There is no obstacle
But Gregory's wood and one bare hill
Whereby the haystack- and roof-levelling wind,
Bred on the Atlantic, can be stayed;
And for an hour I have walked and prayed
Because of the great gloom that is in my mind.

I have walked and prayed for this young child an hour
And heard the sea-wind scream upon the tower,
And under the arches of the bridge, and scream
In the elms above the flooded stream;
Imagining in excited reverie
That the future years had come,
Dancing to a frenzied drum,
Out of the murderous innocence of the sea.

May she be granted beauty and yet not
Beauty to make a stranger's eye distraught,
Or hers before a looking-glass, for such,
Being made beautiful overmuch,
Consider beauty a sufficient end,

Lose natural kindness and maybe
The heart-revealing intimacy
That chooses right, and never find a friend.

Helen being chosen found life flat and dull
And later had much trouble from a fool,
While that great Queen, that rose out of the spray,
Being fatherless could have her way
Yet chose a bandy-leggèd smith for man.
It's certain that fine women eat
A crazy salad with their meat
Whereby the Horn of Plenty is undone.

In courtesy I'd have her chiefly learned;
Hearts are not had as a gift but hearts are earned
By those that are not entirely beautiful;
Yet many, that have played the fool
For beauty's very self, has charm made wise,
And many a poor man that has roved,
Loved and thought himself beloved,
From a glad kindness cannot take his eyes.

May she become a flourishing hidden tree
That all her thoughts may like the linnet be,
And have no business but dispensing round
Their magnanimities of sound,
Nor but in merriment begin a chase,
Nor but in merriment a quarrel.
O may she live like some green laurel
Rooted in one dear perpetual place.

My mind, because the minds that I have loved,
The sort of beauty that I have approved,
Prosper but little, has dried up of late,
Yet knows that to be choked with hate
May well be of all evil chances chief.
If there's no hatred in a mind
Assault and battery of the wind
Can never tear the linnet from the leaf.

An intellectual hatred is the worst,
So let her think opinions are accursed.
Have I not seen the loveliest woman born
Out of the mouth of Plenty's horn,

Because of her opinionated mind
Barter that horn and every good
By quiet natures understood
For an old bellows full of angry wind?

Considering that, all hatred driven hence,
The soul recovers radical innocence
And learns at last that it is self-delighting,
Self-appeasing, self-affrighting,
And that its own sweet will is Heaven's will;
She can, though every face should scowl
And every windy quarter howl
Or every bellows burst, be happy still.

Any may her bridegroom bring her to a house
Where all's accustomed, ceremonious;
For arrogance and hatred are the wares
Peddled in the thoroughfares.
How but in custom and in ceremony
Are innocence and beauty born?
Ceremony's a name for the rich horn,
And custom for the spreading laurel tree.

William Butler Yeats
(1865–1939)

Daughter (title) : Anne Butler Yeats, newborn when the poem was written. *Gregory's wood* (4) : a forest belonging to Yeats's friend Lady Gregory. *tower* (10) : Yeats's home Thoor Ballylee in Western Ireland. *Helen* (25) : of Troy. *Queen* (27) : Aphrodite or Venus, Goddess of Love. *smith* (29) : Hephaestus or Vulcan. *Horn of Plenty* (32) : a cornucopia, which is supposed to make every wish or desire of its possessor come true. *woman* (59) : probably Maude Gonne, who was imprisoned for her political views. *horn* (60) : cf. line 32.

Methought I Saw

Methought I saw my late espoused Saint
Brought to me like *Alcestis* from the grave,
Whom *Jove's* great Son to her glad Husband gave,
Rescu'd from death by force though pale and faint.

Mine as whom washt from spot of child-bed taint,
  Purification in the old Law did save,
  And such, as yet once more I trust to have
  Full sight of her in Heaven without restraint,
Came vested all in white, pure as her mind:
  Her face was veil'd, yet to my fancied sight,
  Love, sweetness, goodness, in her person shin'd
So clear, as in no face with more delight.
  But O, as to embrace me she inclin'd,
  I wak'd, she fled, and day brought back my night.

John Milton
(1608–1674)

Methought (1): I dreamed. *Alcestis* (2): in Greek mythology, the wife of Admetus, who agreed to die for her husband to procure him a longer life. She was brought back from death and restored to her husband by Hercules, "Jove's great Son." *old Law* (6): Leviticus xii:1–8. *vested . . . white* (9): Revelations vii:13–17. *night* (14): Milton had become blind by the time he wrote this poem.

Ode to a Nightingale

My heart aches, and a drowsy numbness pains
  My sense, as though of hemlock I had drunk,
Or emptied some dull opiate to the drains
  One minute past, and Lethe-wards had sunk:
'Tis not through envy of thy happy lot,
  But being too happy in thine happiness,—
    That thou, light-winged Dryad of the trees,
      In some melodious plot
  Of beechen green, and shadows numberless,
    Singest of summer in full-throated ease.

O, for a draught of vintage! that hath been
  Cool'd a long age in the deep-delved earth,
Tasting of Flora and the country green,
  Dance, and Provençal song, and sunburnt mirth!
O for a beaker full of the warm South,
  Full of the true, the blushful Hippocrene,
    With beaded bubbles winking at the brim,
      And purple-stained mouth;
  That I might drink, and leave the world unseen,
    And with thee fade away into the forest dim:

Fade far away, dissolve, and quite forget
What thou among the leaves hast never known,
The weariness, the fever, and the fret
Here, where men sit and hear each other groan;
Where palsy shakes a few, sad, last gray hairs,
Where youth grows pale, and spectre-thin, and dies;
Where but to think is to be full of sorrow
And leaden-eyed despairs,
Where Beauty cannot keep her lustrous eyes,
Or new Love pine at them beyond to-morrow.

Away! away! for I will fly to thee,
Not charioted by Bacchus and his pards,
But on the viewless wings of Poesy,
Though the dull brain perplexes and retards:
Already with thee! tender is the night,
And haply the Queen-Moon is on her throne,
Cluster'd around by all her starry Fays;
But here there is no light,
Save what from heaven is with the breezes blown
Through verdurous glooms and winding mossy ways.

I cannot see what flowers are at my feet,
Nor what soft incense hangs upon the boughs,
But, in embalmèd darkness, guess each sweet
Wherewith the seasonable month endows
The grass, the thicket, and the fruit-tree wild;
White hawthorn, and the pastoral eglantine;
Fast fading violets cover'd up in leaves;
And mid-May's eldest child,
The coming musk-rose, full of dewy wine,
The murmurous haunt of flies on summer eves.

Darkling I listen; and for many a time
I have been half in love with easeful Death,
Call'd him soft names in many a mused rhyme,
To take into the air my quiet breath;
Now more than ever seems it rich to die,
To cease upon the midnight with no pain,
While thou art pouring forth thy soul abroad
In such an ecstasy!
Still wouldst thou sing, and I have ears in vain—
To thy high requiem become a sod.

Thou wast not born for death, immortal Bird!
  No hungry generations tread thee down;
The voice I hear this passing night was heard
  In ancient days by emperor and clown:
Perhaps the self-same song that found a path
  Through the sad heart of Ruth, when, sick for home,
    She stood in tears amid the alien corn;
      The same that oft-times hath
  Charm'd magic casements, opening on the foam
    Of perilous seas, in faery lands forlorn.

Forlorn! the very word is like a bell
  To toll me back from thee to my sole self!
Adieu! the fancy cannot cheat so well
  As she is fam'd to do, deceiving elf.
Adieu! adieu! thy plaintive anthem fades
  Past the near meadows, over the still stream,
    Up the hill-side; and now 'tis buried deep
      In the next valley-glades:
  Was it a vision, or a waking dream?
    Fled is that music:—Do I wake or sleep?

John Keats
(1795–1821)

hemlock (2): poisonous European plant. *Lethe-wards* (4): toward the river of forgetfulness in Hades. *Dryad* (7): a wood nymph. *Flora* (13): Roman goddess of flowers. *Provençal* (14): late medieval language of love poets in Southern France. *Hippocrene* (16): fountain of the Muses in Mt. Helicon; its waters inspire poets. *charioted . . . pards* (32): "not by getting drunk." The god of wine was charioted by leopards. *Fays* (37): fairies. *embalmed* (43): perfumed. *eglantine* (46): honeysuckle. *Ruth* (66): Old Testament heroine.

Sonnet 116

Let me not to the marriage of true minds
Admit impediments. Love is not love
Which alters when it alteration finds,
Or bends with the remover to remove.
O, no! it is an ever-fixèd mark,
That looks on tempests and is never shaken;
It is the star to every wandering bark,
Whose worth's unknown, although his height be taken.

Love's not Time's fool, though rosy lips and cheeks
Within his bending sickle's compass come;
Love alters not with his brief hours and weeks,
But bears it out even to the edge of doom.
  If this be error and upon me proved,
  I never writ, nor no man ever loved.

William Shakespeare
(1564–1616)

mark (5): beacon. *unknown* (8): unknowable. *height* (8): altitude. *bears it out* (12): endures.

The Onset

Always the same, when on a fated night
At last the gathered snow lets down as white
As may be in dark woods, and with a song
It shall not make again all winter long
Of hissing on the yet uncovered ground,
I almost stumble looking up and round,
As one who overtaken by the end
Gives up his errand, and lets death descend
Upon him where he is, with nothing done
To evil, no important triumph won,
More than if life had never been begun.

Yet all the precedent is on my side:
I know that winter death has never tried
The earth but it has failed: the snow may heap
In long storms an undrifted four feet deep
As measured against maple, birch, and oak,
It cannot check the peeper's silver croak;
And I shall see the snow all go down hill
In water of a slender April rill
That flashes tail through last year's withered brake
And dead weeds, like a disappearing snake.
Nothing will be left white but here a birch,
And there a clump of houses with a church.

Robert Frost
(1874–1963)

In Memory of W. B. Yeats

(d. Jan. 1939)

I

He disappeared in the dead of winter:
The brooks were frozen, the airports almost deserted,
And snow disfigured the public statues;
The mercury sank in the mouth of the dying day.
O all the instruments agree
The day of his death was a dark cold day.

Far from his illness
The wolves ran on through the evergreen forests,
The peasant river was untempted by the fashionable quays;
By mourning tongues
The death of the poet was kept from his poems.

But for him it was his last afternoon as himself,
An afternoon of nurses and rumours;
The provinces of his body revolted,
The squares of his mind were empty,
Silence invaded the suburbs,
The current of his feeling failed: he became his admirers.

Now he is scattered among a hundred cities
And wholly given over to unfamiliar affections;
To find his happiness in another kind of wood
And be punished under a foreign code of conscience.
The words of a dead man
Are modified in the guts of the living.

But in the importance and noise of tomorrow
When the brokers are roaring like beasts on the floor of the Bourse,
And the poor have the sufferings to which they are fairly accustomed,
And each in the cell of himself is almost convinced of his freedom;
A few thousand will think of this day
As one thinks of a day when one did something slightly unusual.
O all the instruments agree
The day of his death was a dark cold day.

II

You were silly like us: your gift survived it all;
The parish of rich women, physical decay,
Yourself; mad Ireland hurt you into poetry.
Now Ireland has her madness and her weather still,
For poetry makes nothing happen: it survives
In the valley of its saying where executives
Would never want to tamper; it flows south
From ranches of isolation and the busy griefs,
Raw towns that we believe and die in; it survives,
A way of happening, a mouth.

III

Earth, receive an honoured guest;
William Yeats is laid to rest:
Let the Irish vessel lie
Emptied of its poetry.

Time that is intolerant
Of the brave and innocent,
And indifferent in a week
To a beautiful physique,

Worships language and forgives
Everyone by whom it lives;
Pardons cowardice, conceit,
Lay its honours at their feet.

Time that with this strange excuse
Pardoned Kipling and his views,
And will pardon Paul Claudel,
Pardons him for writing well.

In the nightmare of the dark
All the dogs of Europe bark,
And the living nations wait,
Each sequestered in its hate;

Intellectual disgrace
Stares from every human face,
And the seas of pity lie
Locked and frozen in each eye.

Follow, poet, follow right
To the bottom of the night,
With your unconstraining voice
Still persuade us to rejoice;

With the farming of a verse
Make a vineyard of the curse,
Sing of human unsuccess
In a rapture of distress;

In the deserts of the heart
Let the healing fountain start,
In the prison of his days
Teach the free man how to praise.

W. H. Auden
(1907–1973)

Bourse (25): a stock exchange. *Kipling* (55): Rudyard Kipling (1865–1938), whose colonialist and imperialist views were notorious in his lifetime. *Claudel* (56): French poet and playwright whom the liberals disliked for his conservative views. *him* (57): Yeats: see line 32. *nightmare* (58): World War II has broken out on September 1, 1939.

When I Heard the Learn'd Astronomer

When I heard the learn'd astronomer,
When the proofs, the figures, were ranged in columns before me,
When I was shown the charts and diagrams, to add, divide, and
    measure them,
When I sitting heard the astronomer where he lectured with much
    applause in the lecture-room,
How soon unaccountable I became tired and sick,
Till rising and gliding out I wander'd off by myself,

In the mystical moist night-air, and from time to time,
Look'd up in perfect silence at the stars.

Walt Whitman
(1819–1892)

The Love Song of J. Alfred Prufrock

S'io credesse che mia risposta fosse
A persona che mai tornasse al mondo,
Questa fiamma staria senza piu scosse.
Ma perciocche giammai di questo fondo
Non torno vivo alcun, s'i'odo il vero,
Senza tema d'infamia ti rispondo.

Let us go then, you and I,
When the evening is spread out against the sky
Like a patient etherized upon a table;
Let us go, through certain half-deserted streets,
The muttering retreats
Of restless nights in one-night cheap hotels
And sawdust restaurants with oyster-shells:
Streets that follow like a tedious argument
Of insidious intent
To lead you to an overwhelming question . . .
Oh, do not ask, 'What is it?'
Let us go and make our visit.

In the room the women come and go
Talking of Michelangelo.

The yellow fog that rubs its back upon the window-panes,
The yellow smoke that rubs its muzzle on the window-panes
Licked its tongue into the corners of the evening,
Lingered upon the pools that stand in drains,
Let fall upon its back the soot that falls from chimneys,
Slipped by the terrace, made a sudden leap,
And seeing that it was a soft October night,
Curled once about the house, and fell asleep.

And indeed there will be time
For the yellow smoke that slides along the street,

Rubbing its back upon the window-panes;
There will be time, there will be time
To prepare a face to meet the faces that you meet;
There will be time to murder and create,
And time for all the works and days of hands
That lift and drop a question on your plate;
Time for you and time for me,
And time yet for a hundred indecisions,
And for a hundred visions and revisions,
Before the taking of a toast and tea.

In the room the women come and go
Talking of Michelangelo.

And indeed there will be time
To wonder, 'Do I dare?' and, 'Do I dare?'
Time to turn back and descend the stair,
With a bald spot in the middle of my hair—
(They will say: 'How his hair is growing thin!')
My morning coat, my collar mounting firmly to the chin,
My necktie rich and modest, but asserted by a simple pin—
(They will say: 'But how his arms and legs are thin!')
Do I dare
Disturb the universe?
In a minute there is time
For decisions and revisions which a minute will reverse.

For I have known them all already, known them all:—
Have known the evenings, mornings, afternoons,
I have measured out my life with coffee spoons;
I know the voices dying with a dying fall
Beneath the music from a farther room.
  So how should I presume?

And I have known the eyes already, known them all—
The eyes that fix you in a formulated phrase,
And when I am formulated, sprawling on a pin,
When I am pinned and wriggling on the wall,
Then how should I begin
To spit out all the butt-ends of my days and ways?
  And how should I presume?

And I have known the arms already, known them all—
Arms that are braceleted and white and bare
(But in the lamplight, downed with light brown hair!)

Is it perfume from a dress
That makes me so digress?
Arms that lie along a table, or wrap about a shawl.
  And should I then presume?
  And how should I begin?

. . . . .

Shall I say, I have gone at dusk through narrow streets
And watched the smoke that rises from the pipes
Of lonely men in shirt-sleeves, leaning out of windows? . . .

I should have been a pair of ragged claws
Scuttling across the floors of silent seas.

. . . . .

And the afternoon, the evening, sleeps so peacefully!
Smoothed by long fingers,
Asleep . . . tired . . . or it malingers,
Stretched on the floor, here beside you and me.
Should I, after tea and cakes and ices,
Have the strength to force the moment to its crisis?
But though I have wept and fasted, wept and prayed,
Though I have seen my head (grown slightly bald) brought in upon a
    platter,
I am no prophet—and here's no great matter;
I have seen the moment of my greatness flicker,
And I have seen the eternal Footman hold my coat, and snicker,
And in short, I was afraid.

And would it have been worth it, after all,
After the cups, the marmalade, the tea,
Among the porcelain, among some talk of you and me,
Would it have been worth while,
To have bitten off the matter with a smile,
To have squeezed the universe into a ball
To roll it toward some overwhelming question,
To say: 'I am Lazarus, come from the dead,
Come back to tell you all, I shall tell you all'—
If one, settling a pillow by her head,
  Should say: 'That is not what I meant at all.
  That is not it, at all.'

. . . . .

And would it have been worth it, after all,
Would it have been worth while,
After the sunsets and the dooryards and the sprinkled streets,
After the novels, after the teacups, after the skirts that trail along the
    floor—

And this, and so much more?—
It is impossible to say just what I mean!
But as if a magic lantern threw the nerves in patterns on a screen:
Would it have been worth while
If one, settling a pillow or throwing off a shawl,
And turning toward the window, should say:
'That is not it at all.
That is not what I meant, at all.'

. . . . .

No! I am not Prince Hamlet, nor was meant to be;
Am an attendant lord, one that will do
To swell a progress, start a scene or two,
Advise the prince; no doubt, an easy tool,
Deferential, glad to be of use,
Politic, cautious, and meticulous;
Full of high sentence, but a bit obtuse;
At times, indeed, almost ridiculous—
Almost, at times, the Fool.

I grow old . . . I grow old . . .
I shall wear the bottoms of my trousers rolled.

Shall I part my hair behind? Do I dare to eat a peach?
I shall wear white flannel trousers, and walk upon the beach.
I have heard the mermaids singing, each to each.

I do not think that they will sing to me.

I have seen them riding seaward on the waves
Combing the white hair of the waves blown back
When the wind blows the water white and black.

We have lingered in the chambers of the sea
By sea-girls wreathed with seaweed red and brown
Till human voices wake us, and we drown.

T. S. Eliot
(1888–1965)

Epigraph: Dante's *Inferno*, Canto 27, lines 61–66. "If I believed that my answer would be to a person who could return to the world, this flame would shake no more; but since no one ever did return alive from this depth, if I hear true, without fear of infamy I answer you." *head . . . prophet* (82–83): Matthew xiv: 1–12. *Lazarus* (94): John xi:1–44. *rolled* (121): cuffed.

2
Poems for Comparison

Group 1

The Three Ravens

There were three ravens sat on a tree,
  Downe a downe, hay downe, hay downe.
There were three ravens sat on a tree,
  With a downe.
There were three ravens sat on a tree,
They were as blacke as they might be.
  With a downe derrie, derrie, derrie,
    downe, downe.

The one of them said to his mate,
"Where shall we our breakfast take?"

"Downe in yonder greene field,
There lies a knight slain under his shield.

"His hounds they lie downe at his feete,
So well they can their master keepe.

"His haukes they flie so eagerly,
There's no fowle dare him come nie."

Downe there comes a fallow doe,
As great with yong as she might goe.

She lift up his bloudy hed,
And kist his wounds that were so red.

She got him up upon her backe,
And carried him to earthen lake.

She buried him before the prime,
She was dead herselfe ere even-song time.

God send every gentleman
Such haukes, such hounds, and such a leman.

Anonymous
(Seventeenth Century)

Downe, etc. (2): refrain, to be repeated in each stanza. *Nie* (15): nigh. *yong* (17): young. *lake* (21): pit. *prime* (22): 6 A.M. *leman* (25): beloved lady.

The Twa Corbies

As I was walking all alane,
I heard twa corbies making a mane;
The tane unto the t'other say,
"Where sall we gang and dine to-day?"

"In behint yon auld fail dyke,
I wot there lies a new slain knight;
And naebody kens that he lies there,
But his hawk, his hound, and lady fair.

"His hound is to the hunting gane,
His hawk to fetch the wild-fowl hame,
His lady's ta'en another mate,
So we may mak our dinner sweet.

"Ye'll sit on his white hause-bane,
And I'll pike out his bonny blue een;
With ae lock o his gowden hair
We'll theek our nest when it grows bare.

"Mony a one for him makes mane,
But nane sall ken where he is gane;
O'er his white banes, when they are bare,
The wind sall blaw for evermair."

Anonymous
(Seventeenth Century)

Title: "The Two Ravens." *alane* (1): alone. *mane* (2): moan. *tane* (3): one. *sall* (4): shall. *gang* (4): go. *auld fail dyke* (5): old turf wall. *hause-bane* (13): neck bone. *pike* (14): pick. *een* (14): eyes. *ae* (15): one. *gowden* (15): golden. *theek* (16): thatch.

Group 2

Stopping by Woods on a Snowy Evening

Whose woods these are I think I know.
His house is in the village, though;
He will not see me stopping here
To watch his woods fill up with snow.

My little horse must think it queer
To stop without a farmhouse near
Between the woods and frozen lake
The darkest evening of the year.

He gives his harness bells a shake
To ask if there is some mistake.
The only other sound's the sweep
Of easy wind and downy flake.

The woods are lovely, dark, and deep,
But I have promises to keep,
And miles to go before I sleep,
And miles to go before I sleep.

Robert Frost
(1875–1963)

Loveliest of Trees

Loveliest of trees, the cherry now
Is hung with bloom along the bough,
And stands about the woodland ride
Wearing white for Eastertide.

Now, of my threescore years and ten,
Twenty will not come again,
And take from seventy springs a score,
It only leaves me fifty more.

And since to look at things in bloom
Fifty springs are little room,
About the woodlands I will go
To see the cherry hung with snow.

A. E. Housman
(1859–1936)

Trees

I think that I shall never see
A poem lovely as a tree.

A tree whose hungry mouth is pressed
Against the earth's sweet flowing breast;

A tree that looks to God all day,
And lifts her leafy arms to pray;

A tree that may in summer wear
A nest of robins in her hair;

Upon whose bosom snow has lain;
Who intimately lives with rain.

Poems are made by fools like me,
But only God can make a tree.

Joyce Kilmer
(1886–1918)

Group 3

The Passionate Shepherd to His Love

Come live with me and be my love,
And we will all the pleasures prove
That valleys, groves, hills, and fields,
Woods, or steepy mountain yields.

And we will sit upon the rocks,
Seeing the shepherds feed their flocks
By shallow rivers, to whose falls
Melodious birds sing madrigals.

And I will make thee beds of roses
And a thousand fragrant posies,
A cap of flowers and a kirtle
Embroidered all with leaves of myrtle;

A gown made of the finest wool
Which from our pretty lambs we pull;
Fair-linèd slippers for the cold,
With buckles of the purest gold;

A belt of straw and ivy buds,
With coral clasps and amber studs.
And if these pleasures may thee move,
Come live with me and be my love.

The shepherd swains shall dance and sing
For thy delight each May morning.
If these delights thy mind may move,
Then live with me and be my love.

Christopher Marlowe
(1564–1593)

prove (2) : experience

The Nymph's Reply to the Shepherd

If all the world and love were young,
And truth in every shepherd's tongue,
These pretty pleasures might me move
To live with thee and be thy love.

Time drives the flocks from field to fold,
When rivers rage and rocks grow cold,
And Philomel becometh dumb;
The rest complains of cares to come.

The flowers do fade, and wanton fields
To wayward winter reckoning yields.
A honey tongue, a heart of gall,
Is fancy's spring, but sorrow's fall.

Thy gowns, thy shoes, thy beds of roses,
Thy cap, thy kirtle, and thy posies
Soon break, soon wither, soon forgotten:
In folly ripe, in reason rotten.

Thy belt of straw and ivy buds,
Thy coral clasps and amber studs,
All these in me no means can move
To come to thee and be thy love.

But could youth last and love still breed,
Had joys no date nor age no need,
Then these delights my mind might move
To live with thee and be thy love.

Sir Walter Ralegh
(*c.* 1552–1618)

Philomel (7): Philomela, the nightingale.

The Bait

Come live with me and be my love,
And we will some new pleasures prove,
Of golden sands and crystal brooks,
With silken lines and silver hooks.

There will the river whispering run,
Warmed by thy eyes more than the sun;
And there the enamored fish will stay,
Begging themselves they may betray.

When thou wilt swim in that live bath,
Each fish, which every channel hath,
Will amorously to thee swim,
Gladder to catch thee, than thou him.

If thou to be so seen beest loath,
By sun or moon, thou darkenest both;
And if myself have leave to see,
I need not their light, having thee.

Let others freeze with angling reeds,
And cut their legs with shells and weeds,
Or treacherously poor fish beset
With strangling snare or windowy net.

Let coarse bold hands from slimy nest
The bedded fish in banks out-wrest,
Or curious traitors, sleave-silk flies,
Bewitch poor fishes' wandering eyes.

For thee, thou need'st no such deceit,
For thou thyself art thine own bait;
That fish that is not catched thereby,
Alas, is wiser far than I.

John Donne
(1572–1631)

sleave-silk (23) : very fine thread.

The Passionate Shepherd to His Love

Come live with me and be my wife,
We'll seek the peaks and pits of life
And run the gauntlet of the heart
On mountains or the depths of art.
We'll do the most that thinking can
Against emotion's Ghengis Khan.
And we will play on Hallowe'en
Like all souls on the silver screen,
Or at a masked ball ask for fun
Dancing dressed as monk and nun.
We'll ride a solemn music's boat
When humours cough in breast and throat.
When snow comes like a sailing fleet
We'll skate a ballet in the street,
Though poor as saints or rocks, immense
Our chatter's rich irreverence.
And sometimes speak of endless death
To quicken every conscious breath.
If one becomes too serious,
The other can bring down the house
With jokes which seem hilarious
About the self's pretentious Ows.
I'll be your room-mate and your hoax,
The scapeghost of your gentle jokes.
Like Molière's bourgeois gentleman,
You may discover you have been
Speaking blank verse all your life,
And hence you must become my wife.
For you will know of metaphors,
If I say aeroplanes are bores.
If these excursions seem to you
Interesting as a rendezvous,
Rich as cake and revenue,
Handsome as hope and as untrue,
And full of travel's points of view,
Vivid as red and fresh as dew,
Come live with me and try my life,
And be my night, my warmth, my wife.

Delmore Schwartz
(1913–1966)

Ghengis Khan (6): Mongol conqueror (1162–1227); his name means "very mighty ruler." *Molière's . . . gentlemen* (25): M. Jourdain, in Molière's comedy, is surprised when he is told that he has been speaking prose all his life.

Group 4

La Belle Dame sans Merci

O what can ail thee, knight-at-arms,
  Alone and palely loitering?
The sedge has wither'd from the lake,
  And no birds sing.

O what can ail thee, knight-at-arms,
  So haggard and so woe-begone
The squirrel's granary is full,
  And the harvest's done.

I see a lilly on thy brow,
  With anguish moist and fever dew,
And on thy cheeks a fading rose
  Fast withereth too.

I met a lady in the meads,
  Full beautiful—a faery's child,
Her hair was long, her foot was light,
  And her eyes were wild.

I made a garland for her head,
  And bracelets too, and fragrant zone;
She look'd at me as she did love,
  And made sweet moan.

I set her on my pacing steed,
  And nothing else saw all day long,
For sidelong would she bend, and sing
  A faery's song.

She found me roots of relish sweet,
  And honey wild, and manna dew,
And sure in language strange she said—
  'I love thee true.'

She took me to her elfin grot,
  And there she wept, and sigh'd full sore,
And there I shut her wild wild eyes
  With kisses four.

And there she lulled me asleep,
  And there I dream'd—Ah! woe betide!
The latest dream I ever dream'd
  On the cold hill side.

I saw pale kings and princes too,
  Pale warriors, death-pale were they all;
They cried—'La Belle Dame sans Merci
  Hath thee in thrall!'

I saw their starved lips in the gloam,
  With horrid warning gaped wide,
And I awoke and found me here,
  On the cold hill's side.

And this is why I sojourn here,
  Alone and palely loitering,
Though the sedge has wither'd from the lake,
  And no birds sing.

John Keats
(1795–1821)

Title: "The Beautiful, Pitiless Lady."

The Harlot's House

We caught the tread of dancing feet,
We loitered down the moonlit street,
And stopped beneath the harlot's house.

Inside, above the din and fray,
We heard the loud musicians play
The 'Treues Liebes Herz' of Strauss.

Like strange mechanical grotesques,
Making fantastic arabesques,
The shadows raced across the blind.

We watched the ghostly dancers spin
To sound of horn and violin,
Like black leaves wheeling in the wind.

Like wire-pulled automatons,
Slim silhouetted skeletons
Went sidling through the slow quadrille.

They took each other by the hand,
And danced a stately saraband;
Their laughter echoed thin and shrill.

Sometimes a clockwork puppet pressed
A phantom lover to her breast,
Sometimes they seemed to try to sing.

Sometimes a horrible marionette
Came out, and smoked its cigarette
Upon the steps like a live thing.

Then, turning to my love, I said,
"The dead are dancing with the dead,
The dust is whirling with the dust."

But she—she heard the violin,
And left my side, and entered in:
Love passed into the house of lust.

Then suddenly the tune went false,
The dancers wearied of the waltz,
The shadows ceased to wheel and whirl.

And down the long and silent street,
The dawn, with silver-sandalled feet,
Crept like a frightened girl.

Oscar Wilde
(1854–1900)

Treues Liebes Herz (6): "True Love's Heart"

Group 5

To an Athlete Dying Young

The time you won your town the race
We chaired you through the market-place;
Man and boy stood cheering by,
And home we brought you shoulder-high.

To-day, the road all runners come,
Shoulder-high we bring you home,
And set you at your threshold down,
Townsman of a stiller town.

Smart lad, to slip betimes away
From fields where glory does not stay
And early though the laurel grows
It withers quicker than the rose.

Eyes the shady night has shut
Cannot see the record cut,
And silence sounds no worse than cheers
After earth has stopped the ears:

Now you will not swell the rout
Of lads that wore their honours out,
Runners whom renown outran
And the name died before the man.

So set, before its echoes fade,
The fleet foot on the sill of shade,
And hold to the low lintel up
The still-defended challenge-cup.

And round that early-laurelled head
Will flock to gaze the strengthless dead.
And find unwithered on its curls
The garland briefer than a girl's.

A. E. Housman
(1859–1936)

On My First Son

Farewell, thou child of my right hand, and joy;
My sin was too much hope of thee, loved boy:
Seven years thou wert lent to me, and I thee pay,
Exacted by thy fate, on the just day.
O could I lose all father now! for why
Will man lament the state he should envy,
To have so soon scaped world's and flesh's rage,
And, if no other misery, yet age?
Rest in soft peace, and asked, say, "Here doth lie
Ben Jonson his best piece of poetry."
For whose sake henceforth all his vows be such
As what he loves may never like too much.

Ben Jonson
(1573–1637)

child . . . hand (1) : Benjamin—the boy's name—means "child of the right hand" in Hebrew. *lent* (3) : by God. *pay* (3) : pay back. *just day* (4) : some kinds of bills came due in seven years, which was the boy's age when he died. *father* (5) : fatherly feeling. *Jonson his* (10) : old form of the possessive Jonson's. *like* (12) : please—that is, please fate.

Group 6

The Two Deserts

Not greatly moved with awe am I
To learn that we may spy
Five thousand firmaments beyond our own.
The best that's known
Of the heavenly bodies does them credit small.
View'd close, the Moon's fair ball
Is of ill objects worst,
A corpse in Night's highway, naked, fire-scarr'd, accurst;
And now they tell
That the Sun is plainly seen to boil and burst
Too horribly for hell.
So, judging from these two,
As we must do,
The Universe, outside our living Earth,
Was all conceiv'd in the Creator's mirth,
Forecasting at the time Man's spirit deep,
To make dirt cheap.

Put by the Telescope!
Better without it man may see,
Stretch'd awful in the hush'd midnight,
The ghost of his eternity.
Give me the nobler glass that swells to the eye
The things which near us lie,
Till Science rapturously hails,
In the minutest water-drop,
A torment of innumerable tails.
These at the least do live.
But rather give
A mind not much to pry
Beyond our royal-fair estate
Betwixt these deserts blank of small and great.
Wonder and beauty our own courtiers are,
Pressing to catch our gaze,
And out of obvious ways
Ne'er wandering far.

Coventry Patmore
(1823–1896)

Desert Places

Snow falling and night falling fast oh fast
In a field I looked into going past,
And the ground almost covered smooth in snow,
But a few weeds and stubble showing last,

The woods around it have it—it is theirs.
All animals are smothered in their lairs.
I am too absent-spirited to count;
The loneliness includes me unawares.

And lonely as it is that loneliness
Will be more lonely ere it will be less—
A blanker whiteness of benighted snow
With no expression, nothing to express.

They cannot scare me with their empty spaces
Between stars—on stars where no human race is.
I have it in me so much nearer home
To scare myself with my own desert places.

Robert Frost
(1875–1963)

Group 7

Days

Daughters of Time, the hypocritic Days,
Muffled and dumb like barefoot dervishes,
And marching single in an endless file,
Bring diadems and fagots in their hands.
To each they offer gifts after his will,
Bread, kingdoms, stars, and sky that holds them all.
I, in my pleached garden, watched the pomp,
Forgot my morning wishes, hastily
Took a few herbs and apples, and the Day
Turned and departed silent. I, too late,
Under her solemn fillet saw the scorn.

Ralph Waldo Emerson
(1803–1882)

hypocritic (1): playing a part. *pleached* (7): with boughs intertwined.

Today

So here hath been dawning
Another blue Day:
Think wilt thou let it
Slip useless away.

Out of Eternity
This new Day is born;
Into Eternity,
At night, will return.

Behold it aforetime
No eye ever did:
So soon it forever
From all eyes is hid.

Here hath been dawning
Another blue Day:
Think wilt thou let it
Slip useless away.

Thomas Carlyle
(1795–1881)

Group 8

During Wind and Rain

They sing their dearest songs—
He, she, all of them—yea,
Treble and tenor and bass,
And one to play;
With the candles mooning each face. . . .
Ah, no; the years O!
How the sick leaves reel down in throngs!

They clear the creeping moss—
Elders and juniors—aye,
Making the pathways neat
And the garden gay;
And they build a shady seat. . . .
Ah, no; the years, the years;
See, the white storm-birds wing across!

They are blithely breakfasting all —
Men and maidens—yea,
Under the summer tree,
With a glimpse of the bay,
While pet fowl come to the knee. . . .
Ah, no; the years O!
And the rotten rose is ript from the wall.

They change to a high new house,
He, she, all of them—aye,
Clocks and carpets and chairs
On the lawn all day,
And brightest things that are theirs. . . .
Ah, no; the years, the years;
Down their carved names the rain-drop ploughs.

Thomas Hardy
(1840–1928)

The Tide Rises, the Tide Falls

The tide rises, the tide falls,
The twilight darkens, the curlew calls;
Along the sea-sands damp and brown
The traveller hastens toward the town,
And the tide rises, the tide falls.

Darkness settles on roofs and walls,
But the sea, the sea in the darkness calls;
The little waves, with their soft, white hands,
Efface the footprints in the sands,
  And the tide rises, the tide falls.

The morning breaks; the steeds in their stalls
Stamp and neigh, as the hostler calls;
The day returns, but nevermore
Returns the traveller to the shore,
  And the tide rises, the tide falls.

Henry Wadsworth Longfellow
(1807–1882)

curlew (2): a bird.

Group 9

An Elegy for Five

When I lay sick and like to die
five chosen friends came out to call;
for each I put my bottles by
and arched my back against the wall.
The live man visiting the sick
within him finds his own death quick.

Each was embarrassed, and the first,
who could not give his hand the most;
he kept ten fingers tightly pursed
to clasp his own half-given ghost.
His whitened knuckles more than mine
showed how death climbs live veins, a vine.

My friend believe me, even you
for whom all friendship is caress,
no hand can ever touch the blue
background of others' nothingness.
As night horizons close the sea,
in you death closes death in me.

The second brought a singing voice
as if, such was her rising fear,
she might by heaping noise on noise
delude a little her inward ear.
Hot with the longing in her brain
her pink shells reddened in refrain.

And now my friend believe me, death
that ends voice, has none of its own;
no slightest sibilance of breath
can ever give to silence tone,—
nor friendship ever in a word
escape separate silence heard.

The third kept taking from the air
half-savoured morsels of disease,
the hope that garnishes despair;
and tasting swallowed all his ease.
Upon his purpling lips I saw
death rise ruminant from his maw.

Believe now, friend, this is the gist
of old friendship and all its savour:
the unpredictable last tryst
when neither feeds on other's favour,
but each can in his salt blood taste
the sea that rising lays us waste.

The fourth put lilies in a vase
to mix the scent of their distress
with mine, and prayed the two bouquets
might fuse themselves, and coalesce.
Immovable, her nostrils meant
she smelt herself, intent.

Believe, now more than ever, friend,
odours are omens on the air,
signals that interchange and blend
solitudes they cannot impair.
Death, as it signals us, perfumes
the ecstasy the flesh resumes.

The fifth, by grace, came late at night
when I was thoughtful, and his eyes
absorbing mine absorbed their light
and the dark image that in them lies.
Across his naked face he wore
the long shudder of one death more.

Wherefore, my bitter friend, believe
friendship that wears to nakedness,
like life, like hope, leaves least to grieve
and most, O sweet unknown, to bless:
the sight that proves each man alone—
unknowable death, as such, made known.

Richard P. Blackmur
(1904–1965)

Five O'Clock Shadow

This is the time of day when we in the Men's Ward
Think "One more surge of the pain and I give up the fight,"
When he who struggles for breath can struggle less strongly;
This is the time of day which is worse than night.

A haze of thunder hangs on the hospital rose-beds,
  A doctors' foursome out on the links is played,
Safe in her sitting-room Sister is putting her feet up:
  This is the time of day when we feel betrayed.

Below the windows, loads of loving relations
  Rev in the car park, changing gear at the bend,
Making for home and a nice big tea and the telly:
  "Well, we've done what we can. It can't be long till the end."

This is the time of day when the weight of bedclothes
  Is harder to bear than a sharp incision of steel.
The endless anonymous croak of a cheap transistor
  Intensifies the lonely terror I feel.

Sir John Betjeman
(1906–   )

Sister (7): a nurse, not necessarily a nun.

In the Hospital

Here everything is white and clean
as driftwood. Pain is localized
and suffering, strictly routine,
goes on behind a modest screen.

Softly the nurses glide on wheels,
crackle like windy sails, smelling of soap.
I am needled and the whole room reels.
The Fury asks me how I feel

and, grinning, turns to the brisk care
of an old man's need, he who awake
is silent, at the window stares,
sleeping, like drowning, cries for air.

And finally the fever like a spell
my years cast off. I notice now
nurse's plump buttocks, the ripe swell
of her breasts. It seems I will get well.

Next visitors with magazines;
they come whispering as in church.
The old man looks away and leans
toward light. Dying, too, is a routine.

I pack my bag and say goodbyes.
So long to nurse and this Sargasso Sea.
I nod to him and in his eyes
read, fiercely, the seabird's lonely cry.

George Garrett
(1929–)

Sargasso Sea (22): see note, p. 269.

The Hospital Window

I have just come down from my father.
Higher and higher he lies
Above me in a blue light
Shed by a tinted window.
I drop through six white floors
And then step out onto pavement.

Still feeling my father ascend,
I start to cross the firm street,
My shoulder blades shining with all
The glass the huge building can raise.
Now I must turn round and face it,
And know his one pane from the others.

Each window possesses the sun
As though it burned there on a wick.
I wave, like a man catching fire.
All the deep-dyed windowpanes flash,
And, behind them, all the white rooms
They turn to the color of Heaven.

Ceremoniously, gravely, and weakly,
Dozens of pale hands are waving
Back, from inside their flames.
Yet one pure pane among these
Is the bright, erased blankness of nothing.
I know that my father is there,

In the shape of his death still living.
The traffic increases around me
Like a madness called down on my head.

The horns blast at me like shotguns,
And drivers lean out, driven crazy—
But now my propped-up father

Lifts his arm out of stillness at last.
The light from the window strikes me
And I turn as blue as a soul,
As the moment when I was born.
I am not afraid for my father—
Look! He is grinning; he is not

Afraid for my life, either,
As the wild engines stand at my knees
Shredding their gears and roaring,
And I hold each car in its place
For miles, inciting its horn
To blow down the walls of the world

That the dying may float without fear
In the bold blue gaze of my father.
Slowly I move to the sidewalk
With my pin-tingling hand half dead
At the end of my bloodless arm.
I carry it off in amazement,

High, still higher, still waving,
My recognized face fully mortal,
Yet not; not at all, in the pale,
Drained, otherworldly, stricken,
Created hue of stained glass.
I have just come down from my father.

James Dickey
(1923–   )

Group 10

Psalm 23

The Lord is my shepherd;
I shall not want.
He maketh me to lie down in green pastures;
He leadeth me beside the still waters;
He restoreth my soul.
He leadeth me in the paths of righteousness for his name's sake.
Yea, though I walk through the valley of the shadow of death,
I will fear no evil, for thou art with me.
Thy rod and thy staff they comfort me.
Thou preparest a table before me in the presence of mine enemies;
Thou anointest my head with oil;
My cup runneth over.
Surely goodness and mercy shall follow me all the days of my life,
And I will dwell in the house of the Lord for ever.

The Bible, King James Version
(1611)

A Psalm of David

The Lord to me a shepherd is; want therefore shall not I.
He in the folds of tender grass doth cause me down to lie.
To waters calm me gently leads, restore my soul doth he;
He doth in paths of righteousness for his name's sake lead me.
Yea, though in valley of death's shade I walk, none ill I'll fear
Because thou art with me; thy rod and staff my comfort are.
For me a table thou hast spread in presence of my foes;
Thou dost anoint my head with oil; my cup it overflows.
Goodness and mercy surely shall all my days follow me,
And in the Lord's house I shall dwell so long as days shall be.

The Whole Book of Psalms Faithfully Translated
into English Meter (the "Bay Psalm-Book")
(1640)

Group 11

The End of the World

Quite unexpectedly as Vasserot
The armless ambidextrian was lighting
A match between his great and second toe
And Ralph the lion was engaged in biting
The neck of Madame Sossman while the drum
Pointed, and Teeny was about to cough
In waltz-time swinging Jocko by the thumb—
Quite unexpectedly the top blew off:

And there, there overhead, there, there, hung over
Those thousands of white faces, those dazed eyes,
There in the starless dark the poise, the hover,
There with vast wings across the canceled skies,
There in the sudden blackness the black pall
Of nothing, nothing, nothing—nothing at all.

Archibald MacLeish
(1892–   )

Vasserot (1): a fictitious circus performer, like the other people mentioned in the poem.

Warhead Wakes

I

"To prevent surprise destruction an undisclosed number of the planes of any strategic command must today be always airborne, fuelled and equipped for action," the spokesman said.

Over East Anglia
No bluer skies could be
Illumined so with fear
Illimitably.

So over Novgorod
Or elsewhere, where you will,
Calligraphy of God
Suspends the Kill.

The circuits of our hopes as well
Depend—on a common hell.

II

The flash of nuclear explosions set off at very great altitudes last year blinded rabbits up to 300 miles away, the Atomic Energy Commission disclosed today.—*The Times,* June 16, 1959

Was this carefulness
Beyond excess,
Or just carelessness
Or couldn't care less?

You'd think
This'd make us blink!
It did. The sentence was so bleak
We rabbits have said nothing for a week.

Blink-reflex times are slow: too slow, it's clear,
Think-reflex times far slower; so we fear.

I. A. Richards
(1893–)

First epigraph: apparently quoted from a newspaper, like the second epigraph. *East Anglia* (1): Eastern England. *Novgorod* (4): city in the U.S.S.R.

When It Comes

I hope to feel some pity when it comes,
Before the burning instant that devours,
Before the final flash when terror numbs.

Time to seek out a field with grass and flowers
And minutes eat like cherries, one by one,
Will be my single prayer to those grim Powers.

Much that I loved will have already gone—
Shapes, places, people, words—but there will be
Regret for nothing that has once been done,

Because completeness needs no sympathy.
If there are tears in that last hour of life
Keep them for toilers cheated of their fee.

I hope to feel some pity when the knife
Plunges at last into the world's sick heart
And stills its pounding and its seething strife:

Mainly for those who never got a start;
The painter with his colours in his head,
The actor hoping for a speaking part,

The young who leave their proper words unsaid.
When all the mountains crash like kettledrums,
The hour before my world and I are dead,

I hope to feel some pity, when it comes.

John Wain
(1925–)

Group 12

Plot Improbable, Character Unsympathetic

I was born in a bad slum
Where no one had to die
To show his skeleton.
The wind came through the walls,
A three-legged rat and I
Fought all day for swill.
My father was crazed, my mother cruel
My brothers chopped the stairs for fuel,
I tumbled my sisters in a broken bed
And jiggled them till all were dead.
Then I ran away and lived with my lice
On my wits, a knife, and a pair of dice,
Slept like a rat in the river reeds,
Got converted fifty times
To fifty different creeds
For bowls of mission broth,
Till I killed the grocer and his wife
With a stove-poker and a butcher-knife.
The mayor said, Hang him high,
The merchants said, He won't buy or sell,
The bishop said, He won't pay to pray.
They flung me into a jail,
But I, I broke out,
Beat my bars to a bell,
Ran all around the town
Dingling my sweet bell,
And the mayor wanted it for his hall,
The merchants wanted to buy it,
The bishop wanted it for his church,
But I broke my bell in two,
Of one half a huge bullet made,
Of the other an enormous gun,
Took all the people of all the world
And rolled them into one,
And when the World went by
With a monocle in his eye,
With a silk hat on his head,
Took aim and shot him dead.

Elder Olson
(1909–)

Infant Sorrow

My mother groan'd, my father wept;
Into the dangerous world I leapt,
Helpless, naked, piping loud,
Like a fiend hid in a cloud.

Struggling in my father's hands
Striving against my swaddling bands,
Bound & weary, I thought best
To sulk upon my mother's breast.

When I saw that rage was vain,
And to sulk would nothing gain,
Turning many a trick & wile,
I began to soothe & smile.

And I sooth'd day after day
Till upon the ground I stray;
And I smil'd night after night,
Seeking only for delight.

And I saw before me shine
Clusters of the wand'ring vine,
And many a lovely flower & tree
Stretch'd their blossoms out to me.

My father then with holy look,
In his hand a holy book,
Pronounc'd curses on my head
And bound me in a mirtle shade.

Why should I be bound to thee,
O my lovely mirtle tree?
Love, free love, cannot be bound
To any tree that grows on ground.

O, how sick & weary I
Underneath my mirtle lie,
Like to dung upon the ground
Underneath my mirtle bound.

Oft my mirtle sigh'd in vain
To behold my heavy chain;
Oft my father saw us sigh,
And laugh'd at our simplicity.

So I smote him & his gore
Stained the roots my mirtle bore.
But the time of youth is fled,
And grey hairs are on my head.

William Blake
(1757–1827)

mirtle (24): The myrtle, sacred to Venus, is a symbol of love.

Group 13

Sonnet 129

The expense of spirit in a waste of shame
Is lust in action; and, till action, lust
Is perjured, murderous, bloody, full of blame,
Savage, extreme, rude, cruel, not to trust;
Enjoyed no sooner but despisèd straight;
Past reason hunted, and no sooner had,
Past reason hated, as a swallowed bait
On purpose laid to make the taker mad;
Mad in pursuit, and in possession so;
Had, having, and in quest to have, extreme;
A bliss in proof—and proved, a very woe;
Before, a joy proposed; behind, a dream.
All this the world well knows; yet none knows well
To shun the heaven that leads men to this hell.

William Shakespeare
(1564–1616)

spirit (1): vitality. *to trust* (4): to be trusted.

Abstinence Sows Sand All Over

Abstinence sows sand all over
The ruddy limbs and flaming hair,
But Desire Gratified
Plants fruits of life and beauty there.

William Blake
(1757–1827)

Doing a Filthy Pleasure Is

Doing a filthy pleasure is, and short;
And done, we straight repent us of the sport.
Let us not, then, rush blindly on unto it
Like lustful beasts, that only know to do it,
For lust will languish, and that heat decay.

But thus, thus, keeping endless holiday,
Let us together closely lie, and kiss;
There is no labor, nor no shame in this.
This hath pleased, doth please, and long will please; never
Can this decay, but is beginning ever.

Ben Jonson
(1572–1637)

Two Songs

1.

Sex, as they harshly call it,
I fell into this morning
at ten o'clock, a drizzling hour
of traffic and wet newspapers.
I thought of him who yesterday
clearly didn't
turn me to a hot field
ready for plowing,
and longing for that young man
piercéd me to the roots
bathing every vein, etc.
All day he appears to me
touchingly desirable,
a prize one could wreck one's peace for.
I'd call it love if love
didn't take so many years
but lust too is a jewel
a sweet flower and what
pure happiness to know
all our high-toned questions
breed in a lively animal.

2.

That "old last act"!
And yet sometimes
all seems post coitum triste
and I a mere bystander.
Somebody else is going off,
getting shot to the moon.

Or, a moon-race!
Split seconds after
my opposite number lands
I make it—
we lie fainting together
at a crater-edge
heavy as mercury in our moonsuits
till he speaks—
in a different language
yet one I've picked up
through cultural exchanges . . .
we murmur the first moonwords:
Spasibo. Thanks. O.K.

Adrienne Rich
(1929–)

longing . . . vein (9–11) : an allusion to the opening lines of Chaucer's *Canterbury Tales*. *post coitum triste* (24) : feeling of sadness after intercourse. *Spasibo* (40) : thanks.

Group 14

The Berg

(A Dream)

I saw a ship of martial build
(Her standards set, her brave apparel on)
Directed as by madness mere
Against a stolid iceberg steer,
Nor budge it, though the infatuate ship went down.
The impact made huge ice-cubes fall
Sullen, in tons that crashed the deck;
But that one avalanche was all—
No other movement save the foundering wreck.

Along the spurs of ridges pale,
Not any slenderest shaft and frail,
A prism over glass-green gorges lone,
Toppled; or lace of traceries fine,
Nor pendant drops in grot or mine
Were jarred, when the stunned ship went down.
Nor sole the gulls in cloud that wheeled
Circling one snow-flanked peak afar,
But nearer fowl the floes that skimmed
And crystal beaches, felt no jar.
No thrill transmitted stirred the lock
Of jack-straw needle-ice at base;
towers undermined by waves—the block
Atilt impending—kept their place.
Seals, dozing sleek on sliddery ledges
Slipt never, when by loftier edges
Through very inertia overthrown,
The impetuous ship in bafflement went down.

Hard Berg (methought), so cold, so vast,
With mortal damps self-overcast;
Exhaling still thy dankish breath—
Adrift dissolving, bound for death;
Though lumpish thou, a lumbering one—
A lumbering lubbard loitering slow,
Impingers rue thee and go down,
Sounding thy precipice below,

Nor stir the slimy slug that sprawls
Along thy dead indifference of walls.

Herman Melville
(1819–1891)

sliddery (24): slippery.

The Convergence of the Twain

(*Lines on the loss of the* Titanic)

In a solitude of the sea
Deep from human vanity,
And the Pride of Life that planned her, stilly couches she.

Steel chambers, late the pyres
Of her salamandrine fires,
Cold currents thrid, and turn to rhythmic tidal lyres.

Over the mirrors meant
To glass the opulent
The sea-worm crawls—grotesque, slimed, dumb, indifferent.

Jewels in joy designed
To ravish the sensuous mind
Lie lightless, all their sparkles bleared and black and blind.

Dim moon-eyed fishes near
Gaze at the gilded gear
And query: "What does this vaingloriousness down here?" . . .

Well: while was fashioning
This creature of cleaving wing,
The Immanent Will that stirs and urges everything.

Prepared a sinister mate
For her—so gaily great—
A Shape of Ice, for the time far and dissociate.

And as the smart ship grew,
In stature, grace, and hue,
In shadowy silent distance grew the Iceberg too.

Alien they seemed to be:
No mortal eye could see
The intimate welding of their later history.

Or sign that they were bent
By paths coincident
On being anon twin halves of one august event.

Till the Spinner of the Years
Said "Now!" And each one hears,
And consummation comes, and jars two hemispheres.

Thomas Hardy
(1840–1928)

thrid (6): thread.

RMS Lusitania

Down under green,
under blown gray, white creaming
indigo across the collapse of slipping waterhills, thin
with wind hollowed through spray, gulls screaming,

under the cold still pool
of crosslit green that slabs the giant fidgeting skin of the
world's ocean,
where water stilled, jelled, is nothing like water except to be cool,
and wears no color but color of silence after commotion;

there on the blind floor she has been lying
since the iron fish exploded in the heart,
since her short drama of dying,
sloped boats, hopeless swimmers, flame water steam shrieking
her apart.

Big broken and black
she bulks there still in the gloom
with enormities of red keel, girded bridge and stack;
hulled gold (they said); paintings decor silver china;
grace-ghosts of the stateroom, the dining room.

Lost? Saved? Sealed for judgment? Did you find
your islands there, your harbor and berth, green down
these miles, promised that day, that moment above in the sun,
when your blind
and dying swimmers watched you drown?

Richmond Lattimore
(1906–)

The Imaginary Iceberg

We'd rather have the iceberg than the ship,
although it meant the end of travel.
Although it stood stock-still like cloudy rock
and all the sea were moving marble.
We'd rather have the iceberg than the ship;
we'd rather own this breathing plain of snow
though the ships' sails were laid upon the sea
as the snow lies undissolved upon the water.
O solemn, floating field,
are you aware an iceberg takes repose
with you, and when it wakes may pasture on your snows?

This is a scene a sailor'd give his eyes for.
The ship's ignored. The iceberg rises
and sinks again; its glassy pinnacles
correct elliptics in the sky.
This is a scene where he who treads the boards
is artlessly rhetorical. The curtain
is light enough to rise on finest ropes
that airy twists of snow provide.
The wits of these white peaks
spar with the sun. Its weight the iceberg dares
upon a shifting stage and stands and stares.

The iceberg cuts its facets from within.
Like jewelry from a grave
it saves itself perpetually and adorns
only itself, perhaps the snows
which so surprise us lying on the sea.
Good-bye, we say, good-bye, the ship steers off
where waves give in to one another's waves

and clouds run in a warmer sky.
Icebergs behoove the soul
(Both being self-made from elements least visible)
to see them so: fleshed, fair, erected indivisible.

Elizabeth Bishop
(1911–   )

Group 15

Musée des Beaux Arts

About suffering they were never wrong,
The Old Masters: how well they understood
Its human position; how it takes place
While someone else is eating or opening a window or just walking
    dully along;
How, when the aged are reverently, passionately waiting
For the miraculous birth, there always must be
Children who did not specially want it to happen, skating
On a pond at the edge of the wood:
They never forgot
That even the dreadful martyrdom must run its course
Anyhow in a corner, some untidy spot
Where the dogs go on with their doggy life and the torturer's horse
Scratches its innocent behind on a tree.
In Brueghel's *Icarus,* for instance: how everything turns away
Quite leisurely from the disaster; the ploughman may
Have heard the splash, the forsaken cry,
But for him it was not an important failure; the sun shone
As it had to on the white legs disappearing into the green
Water; and the expensive delicate ship that must have seen
Something amazing, a boy falling out of the sky,
Had somewhere to get to and sailed calmly on.

W. H. Auden
(1907–1973)

Title: "Fine-Arts Museum." *Icarus* (14): painting by Pieter Brueghel the Elder (1520?–69).

Fall of Icarus: Brueghel

Flashing through falling sunlight
A frantic leg late plunging from its strange
Communicating moment
Flutters in shadowy waves.

Close by those shattered waters—
The spray, no doubt, struck shore—
One dreamless shepherd and his old sheep dog
Define outrageous patience
Propped on staff and haunches,
Intent on nothing, backs bowed against the sea,
While the slow flocks of sheep gnaw on the grass-thin coast.
Crouched in crimson homespun an indifferent peasant
Guides his blunt plow through gravelled ground,
Cutting flat furrows hugging this hump of land.
One partridge sits immobile on its bough
Watching a Flemish fisherman pursue
Fish in the darkening bay;
Their stillness mocks rude ripples rising and circling in.

Yet that was a stunning greeting
For any old angler, peasant, or the grand ship's captain,
Though sent by a mere boy
Bewildered in the gravitational air,
Flashing his wild white arms at the impassive sea-drowned sun.

Now only coastal winds
Ruffle the partridge feathers,
Muting the soft ripping of sheep cropping,
The heavy whisper
Of furrows falling, ship cleaving,
Water lapping.

Lulled in the loose furl and hum of infamous folly,
Darkly, how silently, the cold sea suckles him.

Joseph Langland
(1917-)

To a Friend Whose Work Has Come to Triumph

Consider Icarus, pasting those sticky wings on,
testing that strange little tug at his shoulder blade,
and think of that first flawless moment over the lawn
of the labyrinth. Think of the difference it made!
There below are the trees, as awkward as camels;
and here are the shocked starlings pumping past

and think of innocent Icarus who is doing quite well:
larger than a sail, over the fog and the blast
of the plushy ocean, he goes. Admire his wings!
Feel the fire at his neck and see how casually
he glances up and is caught, wondrously tunneling
into that hot eye. Who cares that he fell back to the sea?
See him acclaiming the sun and come plunging down
while his sensible daddy goes straight into town.

Anne Sexton
(1928–1974)

Icarus

Only the feathers floating around the hat
Showed that anything more spectacular had occurred
Than the usual drowning. The police preferred to ignore
The confusing aspects of the case,
And the witnesses ran off to a gang war.
So the report filed and forgotten in the archives read simply
"Drowned," but it was wrong: Icarus
Had swum away, coming at last to the city
Where he rented a house and tended the garden.

"That nice Mr. Hicks" the neighbors called him,
Never dreaming that the gray, respectable suit
Concealed arms that had controlled huge wings
Nor that those sad, defeated eyes had once
Compelled the sun. And had he told them
They would have answered with a shocked, uncomprehending stare.
No, he could not disturb their neat front yards;
Yet all his books insisted that this was a horrible mistake:
What was he doing aging in a suburb?
Can the genius of the hero fall
To the middling stature of the merely talented?

And nightly Icarus probes his wound
And daily in his workshop, curtains carefully drawn,
Constructs small wings and tries to fly
To the lighting fixture on the ceiling:
Fails every time and hates himself for trying.

He had thought himself a hero, had acted heroically,
And dreamt of his fall, the tragic fall of the hero;
But now rides commuter trains,
Serves on various committees,
And wishes he had drowned.

Edward Field
(1924–)

Group 16

Song

Come, my Celia, let us prove,
While we can, the sports of love;
Time will not be ours forever:
He at length our good will sever.
Spend not, then, his gifts in vain;
Suns that set may rise again,
But if once we lose this light,
'Tis with us perpetual night.
Why should we defer our joys?
Fame and rumor are but toys.
Cannot we delude the eyes
Of a few poor household spies?
Or his easier ears beguile,
Thus removed by our wile?
'Tis no sin love's fruits to steal;
But the sweet thefts to reveal,
To be taken, to be seen,
These have crimes accounted been.

Ben Jonson
(1572–1637)

Come, Lesbia, Let Us Live and Love

Come, Lesbia, let us live and love,
nor give a damn what sour old men say.
The sun that sets may rise again
but when our light has sunk into the earth,
it is gone forever.
        Give me a thousand kisses,
then a hundred, another thousand,
another hundred
        and in one breath
still kiss another thousand,
another hundred.
        O then with lips and bodies joined
many deep thousands;
        confuse

their number,
so that poor fools and cuckolds (envious
even now) shall never
learn our wealth and curse us
with their evil eyes.

Catullus
(*c.* 84–54 B.C.)
(*translated by Horace Gregory*)

To the Virgins, to Make Much of Time *

Gather ye rosebuds while ye may:
Old Time is still a-flying,
And this same flower that smiles today
Tomorrow will be dying.

The glorious lamp of heaven, the sun,
The higher he's a-getting,
The sooner will his race be run,
And nearer he's to setting.

That age is best which is the first,
When youth and blood are warmer;
But being spent, the worse and worst
Times still succeed the former.

Then be not coy, but use your time;
And while ye may, go marry:
For having lost but once your prime,
You may forever tarry.

Robert Herrick
(1591–1674)

To His Coy Mistress

Had we but world enough and time,
This coyness, lady, were no crime.
We would sit down and think which way
To walk, and pass our long love's day;
Thou by the Indian Ganges' side
Shouldst rubies find; I by the tide
Of Humber would complain. I would
Love you ten years before the Flood;

And you should, if you please, refuse
Till the conversion of the Jews.
My vegetable love should grow
Vaster than empires, and more slow.
An hundred years should go to praise
Thine eyes, and on thy forehead gaze;
Two hundred to adore each breast,
But thirty thousand to the rest;
An age at least to every part,
And the last age should show your heart.
For, lady, you deserve this state,
Nor would I love at lower rate.
  But at my back I always hear
Time's winged chariot hurrying near;
And yonder all before us lie
Deserts of vast eternity.
Thy beauty shall no more be found,
Nor in thy marble vault shall sound
My echoing song; then worms shall try
That long preserved virginity,
And your quaint honor turn to dust,
And into ashes all my lust.
The grave's a fine and private place,
But none, I think, do there embrace.
  Now therefore, while the youthful hue
Sits on thy skin like morning dew,
And while thy willing soul transpires
At every pore with instant fires,
Now let us sport us while we may;
And now, like amorous birds of prey,
Rather at once our time devour,
Than languish in his slow-chapped power.
Let us roll all our strength, and all
Our sweetness, up into one ball;
And tear our pleasures with rough strife
Thorough the iron gates of life.
Thus, though we cannot make our sun
Stand still, yet we will make him run.

Andrew Marvell
(1621–1678)

Coy (title): cold, disdainful. *Mistress* (title): lady, without the modern connotation. *conversion of the Jews* (10): symbol of the end of the world. *vegetable* (11): having great powers of growth. *chapped* (40): devouring. *thorough* (44): through.

Group 17

Bermudas

Where the remote Bermudas ride
In th' ocean's bosom unespied,
From a small boat that rowed along,
The list'ning winds received this song:
What should we do but sing his praise
That led us through the wat'ry maze
Unto an isle so long unknown,
And yet far kinder than our own?
Where he the huge sea-monsters wracks,
That lift the deep upon their backs,
He lands us on a grassy stage,
Safe from the storms and prelates' rage.
He gave us this eternal spring
Which here enamels everything,
And sends the fowls to us in care,
On daily visits through the air.
He hangs in shades the orange bright,
Like golden lamps in a green night;
And does in the pomegranates close.
Jewels more rich than Ormus shows.
He makes the figs our mouths to meet
And throws the melons at our feet,
But apples plants of such a price,
No tree could ever bear them twice.
With cedars, chosen by his hand,
From Lebanon, he stores the land,
And makes the hollow seas that roar
Proclaim the ambergris on shore.
He cast, of which we rather boast,
The Gospel's pearl upon our coast,
And in these rocks for us did frame
A temple, where to sound his name.
Oh, let our voice his praise exalt,
Till it arrive at heaven's vault;
Which thence, perhaps, rebounding, may
Echo beyond the Mexic Bay.
Thus sung they in the English boat
An holy and a cheerful note,

And all the way, to guide their chime,
With falling oars they kept the time.

Andrew Marvell
(1621–1678)

Title: Some of the early settlers of these islands in the West Indies left England in the seventeenth century to escape religious persecution. *Ormus* (20): town on the strait connecting the Persian Gulf and the Gulf of Oman. *apples* (23): pineapples. *pearl* (30): see Matthew xiii:46.

In a Green Night

The orange tree, in various light,
Proclaims perfected fables now
That her last season's summer height
Bends from each over-burdened bough.

She has her winters and her spring,
Her moult of leaves, which in their fall
Reveal, as with each living thing,
Zones truer than the tropical.

For if by night each golden sun
Burns in a comfortable creed,
By noon harsh fires have begun
To quail those splendours which they feed.

Or mixtures of the dew and dust
That early shone her orbs of brass,
Mottle her splendours with the rust
She sought all summer to surpass.

By such strange, cyclic chemistry
That dooms and glories her at once
As green yet ageing orange tree,
The mind enspheres all circumstance.

No Florida loud with citron leaves
With crystal falls to heal this age
Shall calm the darkening fear that grieves
The loss of visionary rage.

Or if Time's fires seem to blight
The nature ripening into art,
Not the fierce noon or lampless night
Can quail the comprehending heart.

The orange tree, in various light
Proclaims that fable perfect now
That her last season's summer height
Bends from each over-burdened bough.

Derek Walcott
(1930–)

Group 18

Leda and the Swan

Though her Mother told her
  Not to go a-bathing,
Leda loved the river
  And she could not keep away;
Wading in its freshets
  When the noon was heavy;
Walking by the water
  At the close of day.

Where between its waterfalls,
  Underneath the beeches,
Gently flows a broader
  Hardly moving stream,
And the balanced trout lie
  In the quiet reaches;
Taking all her clothes off,
  Leda went to swim.

There was not a flag-leaf
  By the river's margin
That might be a shelter
  From a passer-by;
And a sudden whiteness
  In the quiet darkness,
Let alone the splashing,
  Was enough to catch an eye.

But the place was lonely,
  And her clothes were hidden;
Even cattle walking
  In the ford had gone away;
Every single farm-hand
  Sleeping after dinner,—
What's the use of talking?
  There was no one in the way.

In, without a stitch on,
  Peaty water yielded,
Till her head was lifted
  With its ropes of hair;

It was more surprising
  Than a lily gilded
Just to see how golden
  Was her body there:

Lolling in the water,
  Lazily uplifting
Limbs that on the surface
  Whitened into snow;
Leaning on the water,
  Indolently drifting,
Hardly any faster
  Then the foamy bubbles go.

You would say to see her
  Swimming in the lonely
Pool, or after, dryer,
  Putting on her clothes:
"O but she is lovely,
  Not a soul to see her,
And how lovely only
  Leda's Mother knows!"

Under moving branches
  Leisurely she dresses,
And the leafy sunlight
  Made you wonder were
All its woven shadows
  But her golden tresses,
Or a smock of sunlight
  For her body bare.

When on earth great beauty
  Goes exempt from danger,
It will be endangered
  From a source on high;
When unearthly stillness
  Falls on leaves, the ranger,
In his wood-lore anxious,
  Gazes at the sky.

While her hair was drying,
  Came a gentle languor,
Whether from the bathing
  Or the breeze she didn't know.

Anyway she lay there,
  And her Mother's anger
(Worse if she had wet hair)
  Could not make her dress and go.

Whitest of all earthly
  Things, the white that's rarest,
Is the snow on mountains
  Standing in the sun;
Next the clouds above them,
  Then the down is fairest
On the breast and pinions
  Of a proudly sailing swan.

And she saw him sailing
  On the pool where lately
She had stretched unnoticed,
  As she thought, and swum;
And she never wondered
  Why, erect and stately,
Where no river weed was
Such a bird had come.

What was it she called him:
  Goosey-goosey gander?
For she knew no better
  Way to call a swan;
And the bird responding
  Seemed to understand her,
For he left his sailing
  For the bank to waddle on.

Apple blossoms under
  Hills of Lacedæmon,
With the snow beyond them
  In the still blue air,
To the swan who hid them
  With his wings asunder,
Than the breasts of Leda,
  Were not lovelier!

Of the tales that daughters
  Tell their poor old mothers,

Which by all accounts are
  Often very odd;
Leda's was a story
  Stranger than all others.
What was there to say but:
  Glory be to God?

And she half-believed her,
  For she knew her daughter;
And she saw the swan-down
  Tangled in her hair.
Though she knew how deeply
  Runs the stillest water;
How could she protect her
  From the wingèd air?

Why is it effects are
  Greater than their causes?
Why should causes often
  Differ from effects?
Why should what is lovely
  Fill the world with harness?
And the most deceived be
  She who least suspects?

When the hyacinthine
  Eggs were in the basket,—
Blue as at the whiteness
  Where a cloud begins;
Who would dream there lay there
  All that Trojan brightness;
Agamemnon murdered;
  And the mighty Twins?

Oliver St. John Gogarty
(1878–1957)

Title: Disguised as a swan, Zeus made love to Leda, who, in the myth is grown-up, the wife of Tyndareus, king of Sparta. *harness* (134) : strife. *Eggs* (138) : From the eggs came Castor and Clytemnestra (children of Tyndareus) and Pollux and Helen of Troy (children of Zeus) . *Agamemnon* (143) : killed by his wife Clytemnestra. *Twins* (144) : Castor and Pollux.

Leda and the Swan

A sudden blow: the great wings beating still
Above the staggering girl, her thighs caressed
By the dark webs, her nape caught in his bill,
He holds her helpless breast upon his breast.

How can those terrified vague fingers push
The feathered glory from her loosening thighs?
And how can body, laid in that white rush,
But feel the strange heart beating where it lies?

A shudder in the loins engenders there
The broken wall, the burning roof and tower
And Agamemnon dead.
                                        Being so caught up,
So mastered by the brute blood of the air,
Did she put on his knowledge with his power
Before the indifferent beak could let her drop?

William Butler Yeats
(1865–1939)

broken wall (10): breached to admit the wooden horse.

Leda

Heart, with what lonely fears you ached,
  How lecherously mused upon
That horror with which Leda quaked
  Under the spread wings of the swan.

Then soon your mad religious smile
  Made taut the belly, arched the breast,
And there beneath your god awhile
  You strained and gulped your beastliest.

Pregnant you are, as Leda was,
  Of bawdry, murder and deceit;
Perpetuating night because
  The after-languors hang so sweet.

Robert Graves
(1895–   )

A Sunbather in Late October

On the bank of the river
covered by a haze as if
there hung a bird—
its head deep in the sky
its wings so immense
they are always there—
a young sunbather lay
in the dry grass reclined
as on a bed
waiting to submit
to the power of
the autumn sun whose rays
could scarcely penetrate
the veils of thick white air.

From time to time
behind the haze
a ship appeared
whose bulk looked vague
in the diffusing
manner of the day.
No one could say
if men hung in its masts
dead or alive
intent on
spotting the bird
kept out of sight
by the pervasive glare.

In such anticipation
the young sunbather lay
his legs apart
like a woman enraptured by
the whir of wings
waiting for mysterious heat
to sting his bones,
for haze to wipe his body out,
for unexperienced magic in the air
like a bird with giant beak

to pick his flesh,
eager to recognize his disembodied self
in the mirror blazing in the air!
Why else was he there?

Arthur Gregor
(1923–   )

Group 19

Leda and the Swan

Now can the swooping godhead have his will
Yet hovers, though her helpless thighs are pressed
By the webbed toes; and that all powerful bill
Has suddenly bowed her face upon his breast.

How can those terrified vague fingers push
The feathered glory from her loosening thighs?
All the stretched body's laid in that white rush
And feels the strange heart beating where it lies.
A shudder in the loins engenders there
The broken wall, the burning roof and Tower
And Agamemnon dead. . . .
Being so caught up
Did nothing pass before her in the air?
Did she put on his knowledge with his power
Before the indifferent beak could let her drop?

William Butler Yeats
(1865–1939)

Note: This early version of the poem is from a manuscript dated 1923.

Leda and the Swan

A rush, a sudden wheel, and hovering still
The bird descends, and her frail thighs are pressed
By the webbed toes, and that all-powerful bill
Has laid her helpless face upon his breast.
How can those terrified vague fingers push
The feathered glory from her loosening thighs!
All the stretched body's laid on the white rush
And feels the strange heart beating where it lies;
A shudder in the loins engenders there
The broken wall, the burning roof and tower
And Agamemnon dead.

Being so caught up,
So mastered by the brute blood of the air,
Did she put on his knowledge with his power
Before the indifferent beak could let her drop?

Note: This version was published in a magazine in 1924.

Leda and the Swan

A sudden blow: the great wings beating still
Above the staggering girl, her thighs caressed
By the dark webs, her nape caught in his bill,
He holds her helpless breast upon his breast.

How can those terrified vague fingers push
The feathered glory from her loosening thighs?
And how can body, laid in that white rush,
But feel the strange heart beating where it lies?

A shudder in the loins engenders there
The broken wall, the burning roof and tower
And Agamemnon dead.
Being so caught up,
So mastered by the brute blood of the air,
Did she put on his knowledge with his power
Before the indifferent beak could let her drop?

Note: This is the final version of the poem, which Yeats first published in 1928.

Group 20

Come In

As I came to the edge of the woods,
Thrush music—hark!
Now if it was dusk outside
Inside it was dark.

Too dark in the woods for a bird
By sleight of wing
To better its perch for the night,
Though it still could sing.

The last of the light of the sun
That had died in the west
Still lived for one song more
In a thrush's breast.

Far in the pillared dark
Thrush music went—
Almost like a call to come in
To the dark and lament.

But no, I was out for stars:
I would not come in.
I meant not even if asked,
And I hadn't been.

Robert Frost
(1875–1963)

The Darkling Thrush

I leant upon a coppice gate
  When Frost was spectre-gray,
And Winter's dregs made desolate
  The weakening eye of day.
The tangled bine-stems scored the sky
  Like strings of broken lyres,
And all mankind that haunted nigh
  Had sought their household fires.

The land's sharp features seemed to be
  The Century's corpse outleant,
His crypt the cloudy canopy,
  The wind his death-lament.
The ancient pulse of germ and birth
  Was shrunken hard and dry,
And every spirit upon earth
  Seemed fervourless as I.

At once a voice arose among
  The bleak twigs overhead
In a full-hearted evensong
  Of joy illimited;
An aged thrush, frail, gaunt, and small,
  In blast-beruffled plume,
Had chosen thus to fling his soul
  Upon the growing gloom.

So little cause for carolings
  Of such ecstatic sound
Was written on terrestrial things
  Afar or nigh around,
That I could think there trembled through
  His happy good-night air
Some blessed Hope, whereof he knew
  And I was unaware.

Thomas Hardy
(1840–1928)

Group 21

The Snake's Destiny

In between mud pies and the cultivated gardens
There crept a sudden snake.
Fangs darting harmless, it wriggled on its fertilizing way
But fear ran me toward a croquet mallet
And I swung and swung
My venom purging itself on its non-venomed head.
When I returned to find my spoils
Her mate's body lay matched above
As it was made to match, curve pressed on curve.
Its hissing innocence mourned the unwieldy death
In language tone of whimpering,
Dragged him into the deepest grass to suffer then
Such interment as only snakes can bear.

Now on my walks
I come upon my barren work
And face this grazing image.
With the grass grown black to shelter shadows
The croquet mallet like a conquerer's mace
Reminds my dreams that every tyrant's stroke I struck
Erased their trace of coil
And left a poet's rage
And all my guilt unpurged.

Hy Sobiloff
(1912–)

Snakecharmer

As the gods began one world, and man another,
So the snakecharmer begins a snaky sphere
With moon-eye, mouth-pipe. He pipes. Pipes green. Pipes water.

Pipes water green until green waters waver
With reedy lengths and necks and undulatings.
And as his notes twine green, the green river

Shapes its images around his songs.
He pipes a place to stand on, but no rocks,
No floor: a wave of flickering grass tongues

Supports his foot. He pipes a world of snakes,
Of sways and coilings, from the snake-rooted bottom
Of his mind. And now nothing but snakes

Is visible. The snake-scales have become
Leaf, become eyelid; snake-bodies, bough, breast
Of tree and human. And he within this snakedom

Rules the writhings which make manifest
His snakehood and his might with pliant tunes
From his thin pipe. Out of this green nest

As out of Eden's navel twist the lines
Of snaky generations: let there be snakes!
And snakes there were, are, will be—till yawns

Consume this piper and he tires of music
And pipes the world back to the simple fabric
Of snake-warp, snake-weft. Pipes the cloth of snakes

To a melting of green waters, till no snake
Shows its head, and those green waters back to
Water, to green, to nothing like a snake.
Puts up his pipe, and lids his moony eye.

Sylvia Plath
(1932–1963)

The Death of a Toad

A toad the power mower caught,
Chewed and clipped of a leg, with a hobbling hop has got
To the garden verge, and sanctuaried him
Under the cineraria leaves, in the shade
Of the ashen heartshaped leaves, in a dim,
Low, and a final glade.

The rare original heartsblood goes,
Spends on the earthen hide, in the folds and wizenings, flows
In the gutters of the banked and staring eyes. He lies

As still as if he would return to stone,
  And soundlessly attending, dies
    Toward some deep monotone,

  Toward misted and ebullient seas
And cooling shores, toward lost Amphibia's emperies.
 Day dwindles, drowning, and at length is gone
 In the wide and antique eyes, which still appear
  To watch, across the castrate lawn,
    The haggard daylight steer.

Richard Wilbur
(1921–   )

Group 22

A Slumber Did My Spirit Seal

A slumber did my spirit seal;
  I had no human fears:
She seemed a thing that could not feel
  The touch of earthly years.

No motion has she now, no force;
  She neither hears nor sees;
Rolled round in earth's diurnal course
  With rocks, and stones, and trees.

William Wordsworth
(1770–1850)

The Night Is Freezing Fast

The night is freezing fast,
  To-morrow comes December;
    And winterfalls of old
Are with me from the past;
  And chiefly I remember
    How Dick would hate the cold.

Fall, winter, fall; for he
  Prompt hand and headpiece clever,
    Has woven a winter robe,
And made of earth and sea
  His overcoat for ever,
    And wears the turning globe.

A. E. Housman
(1859–1936)

Immortal Helix

Hereunder Jacob Schmidt who, man and bones,
Has been his hundred times around the sun.

His chronicle is endless—the great curve
Inscribed in nothing by a point upon
The spinning surface of a circling sphere.

Dead bones roll on.

Archibald MacLeish
(1892–   )

Group 23

Ode on a Grecian Urn

Thou still unravish'd bride of quietness,
Thou foster-child of silence and slow time,
Sylvan historian, who canst thus express
A flowery tale more sweetly than our rhyme:
What leaf-fring'd legend haunts about thy shape
Of deities or mortals, or of both,
In Tempe or the dales of Arcady?
What men or gods are these? What maidens loth?
What mad pursuit? What struggle to escape?
What pipes and timbrels? What wild ecstasy?

Heard melodies are sweet, but those unheard
Are sweeter; therefore, ye soft pipes, play on;
Not to the sensual ear, but, more endear'd,
Pipe to the spirit ditties of no tone:
Fair youth, beneath the trees, thou canst not leave
Thy song, nor ever can those trees be bare;
Bold Lover, never, never canst thou kiss,
Though winning near the goal—yet, do not grieve;
She cannot fade, though thou has not thy bliss,
For ever wilt thou love, and she be fair!

Ah, happy, happy boughs! that cannot shed
Your leaves, nor ever bid the Spring adieu;
And, happy melodist, unwearied,
For ever piping songs for ever new;
More happy love! more happy, happy love!
For ever warm and still to be enjoy'd,
For ever panting, and for ever young;
All breathing human passion far above,
That leaves a heart high-sorrowful and cloy'd,
A burning forehead, and a parching tongue.

Who are these coming to the sacrifice?
To what green altar, O mysterious priest,
Lead'st thou that heifer lowing at the skies,
And all her silken flanks with garlands drest?
What little town by river or sea shore,
Or mountain-built with peaceful citadel,

Is emptied of this folk, this pious morn?
And, little town, thy streets for evermore
Will silent be; and not a soul to tell
Why thou art desolate, can e'er return.

O Attic shape! Fair attitude! with brede
Of marble men and maidens overwrought,
With forest branches and the trodden weed;
Thou, silent form, dost tease us out of thought
As doth eternity: Cold Pastoral!
When old age shall this generation waste,
Thou shalt remain, in midst of other woe
Than ours, a friend to man, to whom thou say'st,
Beauty is truth, truth beauty,—that is all
Ye know on earth, and all ye need to know.

John Keats
(1795–1821)

Tempe (7): a beautiful valley in Thessaly praised by the Greek poets. *Arcady* (7): Arcadia.

The Progress of Beauty

When first Diana leaves her Bed
Vapors and Steams her Looks digrace,
A frouzy dirty colour'd red
Sits on her cloudy wrinckled Face.

But by degrees when mounted high
Her artificiall Face appears
Down from her Window in the Sky,
Her Spots are gone, her Visage clears.

'Twixt earthly Femals and the Moon
All Parallells exactly run;
If Celia should appear too soon
Alas, the Nymph would be undone.

To see her from her Pillow rise
All reeking in a cloudy Steam,
Crackt Lips, foul Teeth, and gummy Eyes,
Poor Strephon, how would he blaspheme!

The Soot or Powder which was wont
To make her Hair look black as Jet,
Falls from her Tresses on her Front
A mingled Mass of Dirt and Sweat.

Three Colours, Black, and Red, and White,
So gracefull in their proper Place,
Remove them to a diff'rent Light
They form a frightfull hideous Face,

For instance; when the Lilly slipps
Into the Precincts of the Rose,
And takes Possession of the Lips,
Leaving the Purple to the Nose.

So Celia went entire to bed,
All her Complexions safe and sound,
But when she rose, the black and red
Though still in Sight, had chang'd their Ground.

The Black, which would not be confin'd
A more inferior Station seeks
Leaving the fiery red behind,
And mingles in her muddy Cheeks.

The Paint by Perspiration cracks,
And falls in Rivulets of Sweat,
On either Side you see the Tracks,
While at her Chin the Conflu'ents met.

A Skillfull Houswife thus her Thumb
With Spittle while she spins, anoints,
And thus the brown Meanders come
In trickling Streams betwixt her Joynts.

But Celia can with ease reduce
By help of Pencil, Paint and Brush
Each Colour to its Place and Use,
And teach her Cheeks again to blush.

She knows her Early self no more,
But fill'd with Admiration, stands,
As Other Painters oft adore
The Workmanship of their own Hands.

Thus after four important Hours
Celia's the Wonder of her Sex;
Say, which among the Heav'nly Pow'rs
Could cause such wonderfull Effects.

Venus, indulgent to her Kind
Gave Women all their Hearts could wish
When first she taught them where to find
White lead, and Lusitanian Dish.

Love with White lead cements his Wings,
White lead was sent us to repair
Two brightest, brittlest earthly Things
A Lady's Face, and China ware.

She ventures now to lift the Sash,
The Window is her proper Sphear;
Ah Lovely Nymph be not too rash,
Nor let the Beaux approach too near.

Take Pattern by your Sister Star,
Delude at once and Bless our Sight,
When you are seen, be seen from far,
And chiefly chuse to shine by Night.

In the Pell-mell when passing by,
Keep up the Glasses of your Chair,
Then each transported Fop will cry,
G--d d--m me Jack, she's wondrous fair.

But, Art no longer can prevayl
When the Materialls all are gone,
The best Mechanick Hand must fayl
Where Nothing's left to work upon.

Matter, as wise Logicians say,
Cannot without a Form subsist,
And Form, say I, as well as They,
Must fayl if Matter brings no Grist.

And this is fair Diana's Case
For, all Astrologers maintain
Each Night a Bit drops off her Face
When Mortals say she's in her Wain.

While Partridge wisely shews the Cause
Efficient of the Moon's Decay,
That Cancer with his pois'nous Claws
Attacks her in the milky Way:

But Gadbury in Art profound
From her pale Cheeks pretends to show
That Swain Endymion is not sound,
Or else, that Mercury's her Foe.

But, let the Cause be what it will,
In half a Month she looks so thin
That Flamstead can with all his Skill
See but her Forehead and her Chin.

Yet as she wasts, she grows discreet,
Till Midnight never shows her Head;
So rotting Celia stroles the Street
When sober Folks are all a-bed.

For sure if this be Luna's Fate,
Poor Celia, but of mortall Race
In vain expects a longer Date
To the Materialls of Her Face.

When Mercury her Tresses mows
To think of Oyl and Soot, is vain,
No Painting can restore a Nose,
Nor will her Teeth return again.

Two Balls of Glass may serve for Eyes,
White Lead can plaister up a Cleft,
But these alas, are poor Supplyes
If neither Cheeks, nor Lips be left.

Ye Pow'rs who over Love preside,
Since mortal Beautyes drop so soon,
If you would have us well supply'd,
Send us new Nymphs with each new Moon.

Jonathan Swift
(1667–1745)

the Pell-Mell (73): Pall Mall. *Wain* (88): wane. *Partridge* (89), *Gadbury* (93): astrologers. *Endymion* (95): in Greek myth, a beautiful sleeping youth kissed by the moon. *Mercury* (96): a medicine for venereal disease. *Flamstead* (99): an astronomer.

Group 24

Ulysses

It little profits that an idle king,
By this still hearth, among these barren crags,
Match'd with an aged wife, I mete and dole
Unequal laws unto a savage race,
That hoard, and sleep, and feed, and know not me.
I cannot rest from travel: I will drink
Life to the lees: all times I have enjoy'd
Greatly, have suffer'd greatly, both with those
That loved me, and alone; on shore, and when
Thro' scudding drifts the rainy Hyades
Vext the dim sea: I am become a name;
For always roaming with a hungry heart
Much have I seen and known; cities of men
And manners, climates, councils, governments,
Myself not least, but honour'd of them all;
And drunk delight of battle with my peers,
Far on the ringing plains of windy Troy.
I am a part of all that I have met;
Yet all experience is an arch wherethro'
Gleams that untravell'd world, whose margin fades
For ever and for ever when I move.
How dull it is to pause, to make an end,
To rust unburnish'd, not to shine in use!
As tho' to breathe were life. Life piled on life
Were all too little, and of one to me
Little remains: but every hour is saved
From that eternal silence, something more,
A bringer of new things; and vile it were
For some three suns to store and hoard myself,
And this gray spirit yearning in desire
To follow knowledge like a sinking star,
Beyond the utmost bound of human thought.

This is my son, mine own Telemachus,
To whom I leave the sceptre and the isle—
Well-loved of me, discerning to fulfil
This labour, by slow prudence to make mild
A rugged people, and thro' soft degrees
Subdue them to the useful and the good.

Most blameless is he, centred in the sphere
Of common duties, decent not to fail
In offices of tenderness, and pay
Meet adoration to my household gods,
When I am gone. He works his work, I mine.

There lies the port; the vessel puffs her sail:
There gloom the dark broad seas. My mariners,
Souls that have toil'd, and wrought, and thought with me—
That ever with a frolic welcome took
The thunder and the sunshine, and opposed
Free hearts, free foreheads—you and I are old;
Old age hath yet his honour and his toil;
Death closes all: but something ere the end,
Some work of noble note, may yet be done,
Not unbecoming men that strove with Gods.
The lights begin to twinkle from the rocks:
The long day wanes: the slow moon climbs: the deep
Moans round with many voices. Come, my friends,
'Tis not too late to seek a newer world.
Push off, and sitting well in order smite
The sounding furrows; for my purpose holds
To sail beyond the sunset, and the baths
Of all the western stars, until I die.
It may be that the gulfs will wash us down:
It may be we shall touch the Happy Isles,
And see the great Achilles, whom we knew.
Tho' much is taken, much abides; and tho'
We are not now that strength which in old days
Moved earth and heaven; that which we are, we are;
One equal temper of heroic hearts,
Made weak by time and fate, but strong in will
To strive, to seek, to find, and not to yield.

Alfred, Lord Tennyson
(1809–1892)

Title: the Latin name for Odysseus, Greek chieftain at the Trojan War, and hero of Homer's *Odyssey*. *race* (4): the people of Ithaca, to whom King Ulysses has returned after ten years' wandering. *Hyades* (10): a constellation that portended rainy weather. *Happy Isles* (63): Elysium. *Achilles* (64): Greek hero in the Trojan War.

Ulysses

Sixty was hardly the age for such youthful excesses!—
Colleagues would primly suggest: all those trips and weekends,
Lighthearted postcards that came from outlandish addresses,
Walking or sailing with *most* unaccountable friends,
Painters, and poets, and women in bright skimpy dresses.

What was bizarre and abnormal could not be respected:
Those sentimentally sly diagnosed some deep grief
(Well, after all, he was ageing . . . and surely, neglected?)
Right at the core of the man—quite surpassing belief.
Others just said it was some new drug he'd had injected.

One and all wanted to be at some intimate session
Late at a party, you know, sitting out on the stairs,
Big slow tears trundling over his wine-dark expression,
When he would tell them of meetings, the press of affairs,
Loneliness, unwanted love . . . what a yearned-for confession!

All those kind people agreed it would be such a pity
Not to be there—just to help. But it never occurred.
No matter what, he just smiled, or he gave them some witty
Answer, or whistled with glee like a mischievous bird,
Hummed an odd snatch of a tune, or an old-fashioned ditty.

Dante imagined that Ulysses (much-travelled hero)
Spread sail again in old age. But when he came to die,
Fell to the eighth ring of Hell: one, perhaps, up from Nero.
Was he, though, just an old man with a light in his eye,
Quick jerky movements, a grin—just an elderly pierrot?

John Holloway
(1920–)

pierrot (25): a clown in the old French pantomime comedy.

Group 25

Elegy Written in a Country Church-Yard

The Curfew tolls the knell of parting day,
The lowing herd wind slowly o'er the lea,
The plowman homeward plods his weary way,
And leaves the world to darkness and to me.

Now fades the glimmering landscape on the sight,
And all the air a solemn stillness holds,
Save where the beetle wheels his droning flight,
And drowsy tinklings lull the distant folds;

Save that from yonder ivy-mantled tow'r
The mopeing owl does to the moon complain
Of such, as wand'ring near her secret bow'r,
Molest her ancient solitary reign.

Beneath those rugged elms, that yew-tree's shade,
Where heaves the turf in many a mould'ring heap,
Each in his narrow cell for ever laid,
The rude Forefathers of the hamlet sleep.

The breezy call of incense-breathing Morn,
The swallow twitt'ring from the straw-built shed,
The cock's shrill clarion, or the echoing horn,
No more shall rouse them from their lowly bed.

For them no more the blazing hearth shall burn,
Or busy housewife ply her evening care:
No children run to lisp their sire's return,
Or climb his knees the envied kiss to share.

Oft did the harvest to their sickle yield,
Their furrow oft the stubborn glebe has broke;
How jocund did they drive their team afield!
How bow'd the woods beneath their sturdy stroke!

Let not Ambition mock their useful toil,
Their homely joys, and destiny obscure;
Nor Grandeur hear with a disdainful smile,
The short and simple annals of the poor.

The boast of heraldry, the pomp of pow'r,
And all that beauty, all that wealth e'er gave,
Awaits alike th' inevitable hour.
The paths of glory lead but to the grave.

Nor you, ye Proud, impute to These the fault,
If Mem'ry o'er their Tomb no Trophies raise,
Where thro' the long-drawn isle and fretted vault
The pealing anthem swells the note of praise.

Can storied urn or animated bust
Back to its mansion call the fleeting breath?
Can Honour's voice provoke the silent dust,
Or Flatt'ry sooth the dull cold ear of Death?

Perhaps in this neglected spot is laid
Some heart once pregnant with celestial fire;
Hands, that the rod of empire might have sway'd,
Or wak'd to extasy the living lyre.

But Knowledge to their eyes her ample page
Rich with the spoils of time did ne'er unroll;
Chill Penury repress'd their noble rage,
And froze the genial current of the soul.

Full many a gem of purest ray serene,
The dark unfathom'd caves of ocean bear:
Full many a flower is born to blush unseen,
And waste its sweetness on the desert air.

Some village-Hampden, that with dauntless breast
The little Tyrant of his fields withstood;
Some mute inglorious Milton here may rest,
Some Cromwell guiltless of his country's blood.

Th' applause of list'ning senates to command,
The threats of pain and ruin to despise,
To scatter plenty o'er a smiling land,
And read their hist'ry in a nation's eyes,

Their lot forbad: nor circumscrib'd alone
Their growing virtues, but their crimes confin'd;
Forbad to wade through slaughter to a throne,
And shut the gates of mercy on mankind,

The struggling pangs of conscious truth to hide,
To quench the blushes of ingenuous shame,
Or heap the shrine of Luxury and Pride
With incense kindled at the Muse's flame.

Far from the madding crowd's ignoble strife,
Their sober wishes never learn'd to stray;
Along the cool sequester'd vale of life
They kept the noiseless tenor of their way.

Yet ev'n these bones from insult to protect
Some frail memorial still erected nigh,
With uncouth rhimes and shapeless sculpture deck'd,
Implores the passing tribute of a sigh.

Their name, their years, spelt by th' unletter'd muse,
The place of fame and elegy supply:
And many a holy text around she strews,
That teach the rustic moralist to die.

For who to dumb Forgetfulness a prey,
This pleasing anxious being e'er resign'd,
Left the warm precincts of the chearfúl day,
Nor cast one longing ling'ring look behind?

On some fond breast the parting soul relies,
Some pious drops the closing eye requires;
Ev'n from the tomb the voice of nature cries,
Ev'n in our Ashes live their wonted Fires.

For thee, who mindful of th' unhonour'd Dead
Dost in these lines their artless tale relate;
If chance, by lonely contemplation led,
Some kindred Spirit shall inquire thy fate,

Haply some hoary-headed Swain may say,
"Oft have we seen him at the peep of dawn
Brushing with hasty steps the dews away
To meet the sun upon the upland lawn.

There at the foot of yonder nodding beech
That wreathes its old fantastic roots so high,
His listless length at moontide would be stretch,
And pore upon the brook that babbles by.

Hard by yon wood, now smiling as in scorn,
Mutt'ring his wayward fancies he would rove,
Now drooping, woeful wan, like one forlorn,
Or craz'd with care, or cross'd in hopeless love.

One morn I miss'd him on the custom'd hill,
Along the heath and near his fav'rite tree;
Another came; nor yet beside the rill,
Nor up the lawn, nor at the wood was he;

The next with dirges due in sad array
Slow thro' the church-way path we saw him born.
Approach and read (for thou can'st read) the lay,
Grav'd on the stone beneath yon aged thorn."

The Epitaph.

Here rests his head upon the lap of Earth
A Youth to Fortune and to Fame unknown.
Fair Science frown'd not on his humble birth,
And Melancholy mark'd him for her own.

Large was his bounty, and his soul sincere,
Heav'n did a recompence as largely send:
He gave to Mis'ry all he had, a tear,
He gain'd from Heav'n ('twas all he wish'd) a friend.

No farther seek his merits to disclose,
Or draw his frailties from their dread abode,
(There they alike in trembling hope repose,)
The bosom of his Father and his God.

Thomas Gray
(1716–1771)

mopeing (10): melancholy. *glebe* (26): soil. *isle* (39): aisle of a church. *fretted* (39): ornamented. *village-Hampden* (57): an obscure person who, given the opportunity, might have become another John Hampden (1594–1643), an important statesman who resisted Charles I. *Cromwell* (60): Oliver the Protector, who ruled England after Charles was beheaded. *Swain* (97): inhabitant of a rural area.

Lycidas

In this monody the author bewails a learned friend, unfortunately drowned in his passage from Chester on the Irish Seas, 1637. And by occasion foretells the ruin of our corrupted clergy then in their height.

Yet once more, O ye laurels, and once more
Ye myrtles brown, with ivy never sere,
I come to pluck your berries harsh and crude,
And with forced fingers rude,
Shatter your leaves before the mellowing year.
Bitter constraint, and sad occasion dear,
Compels me to disturb your season due:
For Lycidas is dead, dead ere his prime,
Young Lycidas, and hath not left his peer.
Who would not sing for Lycidas? He knew
Himself to sing, and build the lofty rhyme.
He must not float upon his watery bier
Unwept, and welter to the parching wind,
Without the meed of some melodious tear.
  Begin then, sisters of the sacred well,
That from beneath the seat of Jove doth spring,
Begin, and somewhat loudly sweep the string.
Hence with denial vain and coy excuse;
So may some gentle muse
With lucky words favor my destined urn,
And as he passes turn,
And bid fair peace be to my sable shroud.
For we were nursed upon the self-same hill,
Fed the same flock, by fountain, shade, and rill.
  Together both, ere the high lawns appeared
Under the opening eyelids of the morn,
We drove afield, and both together heard
What time the gray-fly winds her sultry horn,
Battening our flocks with the fresh dews of night,
Oft till the star that rose, at evening, bright,
Toward heaven's descent had sloped his westering wheel.
Meanwhile the rural ditties were not mute,
Tempered to the oaten flute,
Rough satyrs danced, and fauns with cloven heel,
From the glad sound would not be absent long,

And old Damaetas loved to hear our song.
  But O the heavy change, now thou art gone,
Now thou art gone, and never must return!
Thee, shepherd, thee the woods and desert caves,
With wild thyme and the gadding vine o'ergrown,
And all their echoes mourn.
The willows and the hazel copses green
Shall now no more be seen,
Fanning their joyous leaves to thy soft lays.
As killing as the canker to the rose,
Or taint-worm to the weanling herds that graze,
Or frost to flowers, that their gay wardrobe wear,
When first the white-thorn blows:
Such, Lycidas, thy loss to shepherd's ear.
  Where were ye, nymphs, when the remorseless deep
Closed o'er the head of your loved Lycidas?
For neither were ye playing on the steep,
Where your old bards, the famous druids, lie,
Nor on the shaggy top of Mona high,
Nor yet where Deva spreads her wizard stream:
Ay me, I fondly dream!
"Had ye been there"—for what could that have done?
What could the Muse herself that Orpheus bore,
The Muse herself for her enchanting son
Whom universal nature did lament,
When by the rout that made the hideous roar,
His gory visage down the stream was sent,
Down the swift Hebrus to the Lesbian shore?
  Alas! What boots it with uncessant care
To tend the homely slighted shepherd's trade,
And strictly meditate the thankless Muse?
Were it not better done, as others use,
To sport with Amaryllis in the shade,
Or with the tangles of Neaera's hair?
Fame is the spur that the clear spirit doth raise
(That last infirmity of noble mind)
To scorn delights, and live laborious days;
But the fair guerdon when we hope to find,
And think to burst out into sudden blaze,
Comes the blind Fury with the abhorrèd shears,
And slits the thin-spun life. "But not the praise,"
Phoebus replied, and touched my trembling ears:
"Fame is no plant that grows on mortal soil,
Nor in the glistering foil

Set off to the world, nor in broad rumor lies,
But lives and spreads aloft by those pure eyes
And perfect witness of all-judging Jove;
As he pronounces lastly on each deed,
Of so much fame in heaven expect thy meed."
  O fountain Arethuse, and thou honored flood,
Smooth-sliding Mincius, crowned with vocal reeds,
That strain I heard was of a higher mood.
But now my oat proceeds,
And listens to the herald of the sea,
That came in Neptune's plea.
He asked the waves and asked the felon-winds,
What hard mishap hath doomed this gentle swain,
And questioned every gust of rugged wings
That blows from off each beakèd promontory.
They knew not of his story,
And sage Hippotades their answer brings:
That not a blast was from his dungeon strayed;
The air was calm, and on the level brine,
Sleek Panopë with all her sisters played.
It was that fatal and perfidious bark
Built in the eclipse, and rigged with curses dark,
That sunk so low that sacred head of thine.
  Next Camus, reverend sire, went footing slow,
His mantle hairy, and his bonnet sedge,
Inwrought with figures dim, and on the edge
Like to that sanguine flower inscribed with woe.
"Ah, who hath reft," quoth he, "my dearest pledge?"
Last came, and last did go,
The pilot of the Galilean Lake;
Two massy keys he bore of metals twain
(The golden opes, the iron shuts amain).
He shook his mitered locks, and stern bespake:
"How well could I have spared for thee, young swain,
Enow of such as for their bellies' sake
Creep, and intrude, and climb into the fold!
Of other care they little reckoning make,
Than how to scramble at the shearers' feast,
And shove away the worthy bidden guest.
Blind mouths, that scarce themselves know how to hold
A sheep hook, or have learned aught else the least
That to the faithful herdman's art belongs!
What recks it them? What need they? They are sped,
And when they list, their lean and flashy songs

Grate on their scrannel pipes of wretched straw.
The hungry sheep look up and are not fed,
But swollen with wind, and the rank mist they draw,
Rot inwardly, and foul contagion spread;
Besides what the grim wolf with privy paw
Daily devours apace, and nothing said;
But that two-handed engine at the door
Stands ready to smite once, and smite no more."
  Return, Alpheus, the dread voice is past,
That shrunk thy streams; return, Sicilian Muse,
And call the vales, and bid them hither cast
Their bells and flowerets of a thousand hues.
Ye valleys low, where the mild whispers use
Of shades and wanton winds and gushing brooks,
On whose fresh lap the swart star sparely looks,
Throw hither all your quaint enameled eyes,
That on the green turf suck the honeyed showers,
And purple all the ground with vernal flowers.
Bring the rathe primrose that forsaken dies,
The tufted crow-toe, and pale jessamine,
The white pink, and the pansy freaked with jet,
The glowing violet,
The musk-rose, and the well-attired woodbine,
With cowslips wan that hang the pensive head,
And every flower that sad embroidery wears.
Bid amaranthus all his beauty shed,
And daffodillies fill their cups with tears,
To strew the laureate hearse where Lycid lies.
For so to interpose a little ease,
Let our frail thoughts dally with false surmise.
Ay me! Whilst thee the shores and sounding seas
Wash far away, where'er thy bones are hurled,
Whether beyond the stormy Hebrides,
Where thou perhaps under the whelming tide
Visitest the bottom of the monstrous world;
Or whether thou to our moist vows denied,
Sleepest by the fable of Bellerus old,
Where the great vision of the guarded mount
Looks toward Namancos and Bayona's hold;
Look homeward, Angel, now, and melt with ruth.
And, O ye dolphins, waft the hapless youth.
  Weep no more, woeful shepherds, weep no more,
For Lycidas your sorrow is not dead,
Sunk though he be beneath the watery floor,

So sinks the day-star in the ocean bed,
And yet anon repairs his drooping head,
And tricks his beams, and with new-spangled ore
Flames in the forehead of the morning sky:
So Lycidas sunk low, but mounted high,
Through the dear might of him that walked the waves
Where, other groves and other streams along,
With nectar pure his oozy locks he laves,
And hears the unexpressive nuptial song,
In the blest kingdoms meek of joy and love.
There entertain him all the saints above
In solemn troops and sweet societies
That sing, and singing in their glory move,
And wipe the tears forever from his eyes.
Now, Lycidas, the shepherds weep no more;
Henceforth thou art the genius of the shore,
In thy large recompense, and shalt be good
To all that wander in that perilous flood.
  Thus sang the uncouth swain to the oaks and rills,
While the still morn went out with sandals gray;
He touched the tender stops of various quills,
With eager thought warbling his Doric lay.
And now the sun had stretched out all the hills,
And now was dropped into the western bay.
At last he rose, and twitched his mantle blue:
Tomorrow to fresh woods, and pastures new.

John Milton
(1608–1674)

Title: a lute-player and shepherd in ancient pastorals whose name Milton gives to his dead fellow-student at Cambridge, Edward King. *dear* (6): dire. *sisters* (15): Muses. *Damaetas* (36): conventional pastoral name, perhaps designating someone at Cambridge. *taint-worm* (46): parasitic worm. *white-thorn* (48): hawthorn. *Mona* (54): Anglesey, and *Deva* (55): the River Dee—both areas near where King was drowned. *Muse* (59): Calliope, mother of Orpheus. *rout* (61): Thracian women who tore Orpheus to pieces. The Hebrus River carried his head down to the sea, which washed it up on Lesbos. *use* (67): do. *Amaryllis* (68) and *Neaera* (69): any pretty girl. *Fury* (75): a Fate. *shears* (75): for cutting life's thread. *Phoebus* (77): The god of poetry interrupts the speaker. *Arethuse* (85) and *Mincius* (86): Water from these sources, a fountain and a river, inspired pastoral poets in antiquity. *strain* (87): Phoebus's interruption. *herald* (89): Triton. *Hippotades* (96): Aeolus. *Panopë* (99): a sea nymph. *eclipse* (101): an unlucky omen. *Camus* (103): spirit of the River Cam and symbol of Cambridge

University. *flower* (106): the hyacinth, whose markings supposedly resemble a Greek word meaning "alas." *pilot* (109): St. Peter, originally a fisherman on the Sea of Galilee; traditionally first Bishop of Rome. *keys* (110): See Matthew xvi:19. *engine* (130): variously explained as the sword of divine justice, the English Parliament, the common people. *Alpheus* (132): Sicilian river-god, symbolizing pastoral poetry. *star* (138): the dog star. *fable of Bellerus* (160): Land's End, Cornwall; Latin *Bellerium,* after the giant Bellerus. *mount* (161): Mount St. Michael, Cornwall. *Namancos* and *Bayona* (162): on the Spanish coast. *Angel* (163): St. Michael. *day-star* (168): sun. *him* (173): Christ. *unexpressive nuptial song* (176): inexpressible heavenly music, celebrating the soul's union with God. *Doric* (189): pastoral.

Appendix

The Rhythm and Meter of a Poem

There are virtually but two meters, strict iambic and loose iambic.

Robert Frost

Poetry, according to Coleridge, is "the best words in their best order." Although this remark hardly satisfies the requirements of formal definition, it does assert an important fact: the order of the words in a poem is as material as the words themselves. Consider this stanza from Coleridge's "Rime of the Ancient Mariner."

He prayeth best, who loveth best
All things both great and small;
For the dear God who loveth us,
He made and loveth all.

To demonstrate the importance of word order, one has only to rearrange the first two lines:

He who loves all things both great
And small prayeth best.

Tampered with in this way, the words still make sense, but they neither please the ear nor slip easily off the tongue. They obviously lack something that the original had. That something is measurable rhythm.

Rhythm and Meter

Rhythm implies alternation: something is here, then it is replaced by something else, then the first thing returns. People speak of the rhythm of the tides, of the seasons, of the heavenly bodies. All human utterances are rhythmical: the voice rises, falls, then rises again; stressed syllables precede and follow unstressed syllables; words said hastily alternate with words said slowly. The rewritten lines from the "Ancient Mariner" are rhythmical when read aloud, because all speech is rhythmical. But, unlike the original lines, they are not metrical. **Meter** is rhythm that can be measured in poems.

Scansion

Since meter is to a poem approximately what beat is to music, any literate person who has ever tapped his foot in time with a march or a waltz can learn to scan a poem—that is, to mark it in such a way that its meter is made evident. **Scansion** is the art of marking a poem to show the metrical units of which it is composed.

The smallest of these metrical units is the syllable. English syllables are of two kinds: accented or stressed, and unaccented or unstressed. An **accented syllable** requires more wind and push behind it than an **unaccented;** it also may be pitched slightly higher or held for a slightly longer time. In the following words the two kinds of syllables have been marked according to a widely used system of scansion:

/ ◡   ◡ /   / ◡ ◡   / ◡   / ◡ / ◡
learned   until   flattery   forceps   alabaster

Observe that the first word in the list could just as well have been treated as a monosyllable and marked *leárned.* This word must be seen in a context before the number of syllables it contains can be determined. Notice also that the last word has two accented syllables. The fact that one of these is a secondary accent has been ignored; both have been marked as having equal stress. In actual speech there are many degrees of accent that any system of scansion must ignore if it is to remain manageable. The first step in learning to scan, then, is learning to recognize syllables and to determine whether they are accented or unaccented.

Feet

The next largest metrical unit is the **foot,** which is a group of two or more syllables. The six most common kinds of feet in English metrics have names derived from Greek:

1. The **iambic** foot, or **iamb**, consists of an unaccented syllable followed by an accented. It is marked like this: ˘ ′
2. The **trochaic** foot, or **trochee**, consists of an accented syllable followed by an unaccented. It is marked like this: ′ ˘
3. The **dactylic** foot, or **dactyl**, consists of an accented syllable followed by two unaccented syllables. It is marked like this: ′ ˘ ˘
4. The **anapestic** foot, or **anapest**, consists of two unaccented syllables followed by an accented syllable. It is marked like this: ˘ ˘ ′
5. The **spondaic** foot, or **spondee**, consists of two accented syllables. It is marked like this: ′′
6. The **pyrrhic** foot, or **pyrrhic**, consists of two unaccented syllables. It is marked like this: ˘ ˘

The iambic foot is by far the most common foot in poems written in the English language. Trochaic or anapestic feet often occur as variations in predominantly iambic lines, and the other kinds of poetic feet occur less frequently. There are no poems written entirely in spondees or pyrrhics.

Lines

The next largest metrical unit is the line. A **line** is a regular succession of feet, and, though it is not necessarily a sentence, it customarily begins with a capital letter. These lines from four different poems illustrate the four kinds of meter:

1. Iambic: With loads | of lear | ned lum | ber in | his head.
2. Trochaic: Pleasant | was the | landscape | round him.
3. Dactylic: One more un | fortunate.
4. Anapestic: With his nos | trils like pits | full of blood | to the brim.

Lines consisting entirely of spondaic feet are extremely rare, and those consisting entirely of pyrrhic feet are nonexistent because of the accentual nature of our language. A line containing only one foot is called a **monometer** line; one with two feet, a **dimeter** line; and so on through **trimeter, tetrameter, pentameter, hexameter,**

heptameter, and **octameter.** Since each of these eight lengths may be composed of any of the four kinds of feet, thirty-two different varieties of line are theoretically possible. In practice, however, lines containing more than six feet are rare because they are too long to strike the ear as a unit. When read aloud, the heptameter line

O, rest ye, brother mariners, we will not wander more

sounds as though it were written

O, rest ye, brother mariners,
We will not wander more.

Similarly, iambic octameter usually splits into two iambic tetrameter lines. Dactylic lines, of whatever length, are the rarest of the four kinds in English, perhaps because their movement is not suitable to many subjects, as Coleridge observed:

This is a | galloping | measure, | | a | hop and a | trot and a | gallop.

The bulk of traditional English poetry is in iambic pentameter or tetrameter. A line of iambic hexameter is called an **alexandrine.**

A need | less A | lexan | drine ends | the song,
That like | a woun | ded snake | drags its | slow length | along.

The second of these two lines is, of course, the alexandrine. In the passage quoted from Coleridge iambic tetrameter alternates with iambic trimeter:

He pray | eth best, | | who lov | eth best
All things | | both great | and small;
For the | dear God | | who lov | eth us,
He made | | and lov | eth all.

How does one go about scanning a poem as these lines have been scanned? The procedure is much simpler than, say, that of bidding a hand of contract bridge.

Steps in Scansion

1. Mark the syllables in the line to be scanned. A student beginning the study of scansion should pronounce the words aloud because the ear rather than the eye determines the number of syllables. Avoid distortion; a word should be pronounced in poetry as in prose. Remember that accent and lack of accent are relative rather than absolute. Notice the words *but, to, their, how, they,* and *of* in the following scansion:

˘ ´ | ˘ ´ | ˘ ´ | ˘ ´ | ˘ ´
But when | to mis | chief mor | tals bend | their will

´ ´ | ˘ ´ | ´ ´ | ˘ ´ | ˘ ´
How soon | they find | fit in | struments | of ill.

2. Examine the marks over the syllables to discover which of the four main kinds of feet predominates. One kind of foot *will* predominate, but do not expect every foot in a line—let alone in a whole poem—to be like every other foot. Having determined the dominant kind of foot (and to be perfectly certain you should mark the syllables in more than one line), you are ready to put in the vertical marks that indicate the end of one foot and the beginning of another. Notice, in the examples already given, that the vertical marks do not necessarily come before or after a word, but that they may, and frequently do, divide a word, especially in lines containing polysyllabic words. Here, with scansion, is such a line from *Paradise Lost:*

˘ ´ | ˘ ˘ | ˘ ´ | ˘ | ´ | ˘ ˘
Immu | table, | | immor | tal, | | in | finite.

Since iambic is the predominant foot in English, you might first try to read the line or lines as iambic. If that doesn't work, try the other meters. And if none of them works, you apparently have an example of free verse before you. Free verse cannot be scanned. (See below, p. 465.)

3. Discover, by reading the line aloud, whether there is a pause in it. A natural pause within a line of poetry is called a **caesura,** and its position is indicated by a double vertical line (or another single vertical line if the pause coincides with the end of a foot). The line just quoted from *Paradise Lost* has two caesuras: one after the second foot, and one in the middle of the fourth foot.

Caesuras always coincide with punctuational pauses within lines, but they can also occur in places not marked by punctuation. In these latter cases, the caesura (if there is one) is determined by the sense, phrasing, or rhetoric (how the line is read). One way in which a poet achieves variety in his metrics is to shift the position of the caesura from line to line (look back at the quotation from the "Ancient Mariner"). In addition to achieving variety, the skillful poet will make his caesuras coincide with his units of thought. Another pause may occur at the end of a line. A line with a pause at the end is said to be **end-stopped.**

> Sigh no more, ladies, sigh no more!
>   Men were deceivers ever;
> One foot in sea, and one on shore,
>   To one thing constant never.
>
> *William Shakespeare*
> (1564–1616)

In contrast, a line without a pause at the end is called a **run-on** line. The practice of running on the line to the next line is sometimes called **enjambment.**

> Roll on, thou deep and dark blue Ocean—roll!
> Ten thousand fleets sweep over thee in vain;
> Man marks the earth with ruin—his control
> Stops with the shore. . . .
>
> *George Gordon, Lord Byron*
> (1788–1824)

The effect of the run-on third line is quite different from that of the end-stopped first.

4. Count the number of feet to determine the appropriate label for the line. Frequently one kind of line will alternate with another, as in the "Ancient Mariner."

5. It is a gross error to suppose that if the feet are not all alike, the poet must have made a mistake. Meter is not a straitjacket into which a poet must force his words. If it were, poets would be so limited in choosing their words that they would almost never be able to say what they wanted to. Meter is made for the poem, not

the poem for meter. Another good reason why meter is seldom strictly "regular" is that poems in which the kind of foot is never varied are likely to become as monotonous as the ticking of a watch. Once the poet has established his meter, he will vary it according to the effects he wishes to create. These lines, for instance, occur in an iambic context:

This a | ged Prince, | | now flour | ishing | in peace,
And blest | with is | sue | | of | a large | increase,
Worn out | with bus | iness, | | did | at length | debate
To set | tle the | succes | sion of | the state.

John Dryden
(1631–1700)

Lines 1 and 3 have six accented syllables rather than the expected five. Consequently they move somewhat more slowly than the second, and much more slowly than the fourth, which contains two pyrrhic feet substituted for the expected iambs. An anapest substituted in a context that is primarily iambic also tends to hasten the movement, as in the fourth foot of this line:

Keen fit | ful gusts | | are whis | pering here | and there.

In practice almost any foot may be substituted for another. The most common substitutions are trochee or spondee for iamb (especially at the beginning of a line or directly after the caesura), iamb for anapest, and anapest for iamb.

Another way in which a poet can vary the meter of a line is to drop an unaccented syllable or two. Carets are inserted to replace the missing syllables:

Take her up | tenderly,
Lift her with | care; ^ ^
Fashion'd so | slenderly,
Young, and so | fair! ^ ^

Thomas Hood
(1798–1845)

The omitted syllables create moments of silence.

6. Try to discover the meter in the poem instead of imposing on the poem your own notion of what the metrical pattern should be. Before putting in the foot marks, decide whether the poem is in **rising meter** (iambic and anapestic) or **falling meter** (trochaic and dactylic). In falling meter the voice is first up, and then it goes down:

Greedy | hawk must | gorge its | prey. ^
Pious | priest must | have his | pay. ^

In rising meter the voice is first down, and then it goes up:

With hon | or and glo | ry through trou | ble and dan | ger.

The extra unaccented syllable at the end is called a **feminine ending.**

7. Avoid scansions that may be mechanically "correct" but that do not show how the voice moves in reading:

^ ^ With | honor and | glory through | trouble and | danger.

Here a falling meter has been imposed on a rising meter.

8. Since you must rely on your own ear, and since no two ears are exactly alike, there may be legitimate—but usually slight—differences between your scansion and another person's. The thing to avoid is a scansion that, like the following, could satisfy *nobody's* ear:

With hon | or and | glory | through trou | ble and | danger.

To read the line in this fashion is to mangle English pronunciation beyond recognition.

Here is a summary of the steps to take in scanning a poem:

1. Mark the syllables. (Read the poem at this and each succeeding step.)
2. Mark the feet.
3. Mark the caesuras.
4. Expect to encounter variations, but do not consider them in naming the basic meter.
5. Check your scansion to make sure that it reflects the poem rather than a preconceived notion of your own.

Meter and Meaning

Some people regard scansion as a dull, mechanical sort of activity, having no usefulness to anyone except perhaps to the professional student or to poets. This view would be correct if scansion were an end in itself. But it is not. Scansion is, rather, a means whereby the reader understands and appreciates a poem more fully than he would if he had not scanned it. Marking the syllables and the feet and identifying the kind of meter present are useless activities unless they are followed by an analytical discussion. Discussions of meter usually contain answers to questions like these:

1. *Is the meter appropriate to the poem?* This question has to be asked about each poem, for none of the kinds of meter has built-in features that make it uniquely and automatically appropriate for a given subject. Occasionally a poem seems to be in a very inappropriate meter. In these lines from Christina Rossetti's "Next of Kin," an elderly person is addressing a younger one and telling him that he too will die eventually.

> Yet when your day is over, as mine is nearly done,
> And when your race is finished, as mine is almost run,
> You, like me, shall cross your hands and bow your graceful head:
> Yea, we twain shall sleep together in an equal bed.

The rapid, jogging effect of this meter is certainly inappropriate to such a doleful subject.

2. *Is the meter monotonous and unvaried?* If so, is there a discoverable reason for the monotony other than the poet's lack of skill?

3. *What does the meter contribute to the total effect of the poem?* In some poems the meter makes no easily definable contribution; in others, it does. The meter of Browning's "How They Brought the Good News from Ghent to Aix," for instance, reinforces the words in such a way that rapid and vigorous action is suggested. The poem begins like this:

> I sprang to the stirrup, and Joris, and he;
> I galloped, Dirck galloped, we galloped all three;
> "Good speed!" cried the watch, as the gate-bolts undrew;
> "Speed!" echoed the wall to us galloping through.

The meter, of course, does not gallop, but working with the words of the poem it creates the effect of galloping.

4. *Why has the poet varied his basic meter in certain places?* This is the most important question that arises in discussions of meter. Pay special attention to omitted syllables and substituted feet. They deserve comment because they control emphasis by accelerating or retarding a line. Try to discover why the poet apparently wished to change the speed of the line. The poet also varies his meter to call attention to important words. Take these two lines, for example:

> The drunkard now supinely snores,
> His load of ale sweats through his pores.

The meter is basically iambic. Yet in the third foot of the second line the poet has substituted a trochee for an expected iamb, has thereby singled out the word *sweats* for special attention, and can rely on the connotation of *sweats* to create the desired feeling of disgust in the reader.

A more savory example showing how a poet can use metrical variation to reinforce his meaning and direct his reader's response occurs in these lines from John Donne's sixteenth elegy, a poem in which a man is saying farewell to a girl with whom he is having a secret love affair and telling her how to behave while he is away traveling on the Continent.

> When I am gone, dream me some happiness,
> Nor let thy looks our long-hid love confess;
> Nor praise nor dispraise me; nor bless nor curse
> Openly love's force; nor in bed fright thy nurse
> With midnight startings, crying out, "Oh! Oh!
> Nurse, oh my love is slain! I saw him go
> O'er the white Alps alone, I saw him, I,
> Assailed, fight, taken, stabbed, bleed, fall, and die!"

The first four lines of this passage are dominantly iambic. Two of them are run-on to give the effect of talk. Then, at the end of line five, when the poet arrives at a moment of emotional stress, the meter becomes wildly different from the basic meter. A climax is reached with the loud spondees in the last line. They imitate the cries of the girl, frightened by a nightmare in which she sees her lover cut down by bandits. Notice, too, that the substituted spondee of *white Alps* in the seventh line emphasizes *white* and helps the reader picture the cold and desolate place where the bloody deed occurs.

5. *Is there more than one defensible way of scanning a line or a foot?* A discussion of the scansion of a poem should always avoid dogmatism. Defend the scansion that you have made, but by all means mention the possibility of alternative scansions. Even the most carefully worked-out scansion can show only approximately the metrical phenomena in a poem. At its best, scansion is merely a compromise between the strictly regular meter that is, so to speak, at the back of the poet's mind as he writes and the reader's as he reads, and the many subtle variations on the basic meter that the poet incorporates for the skillful reader to discover.

Free Verse

Granted that much more than meter is needed for a poem—and what that "much more" consists of is the subject of this book—does it follow that a poem must have meter? A large number of poets, especially in the twentieth century, have answered this question negatively. Their poems, written in rhythmical language but not in the traditional meters, are called **free verse.** Nonmetrical poetry is called "free" because the poet has freed himself from conforming to the set metrical patterns.

Once I Pass'd through a Populous City

Once I pass'd through a populous city imprinting my brain for future use with its shows, architecture, customs, traditions,
Yet now of all that city I remember only a woman I casually met there who detain'd me for love of me,
Day by day and night by night we were together—all else has long been forgotten by me,
I remember I say only that woman who passionately clung to me,
Again we wander, we love, we separate again,
Again she holds me by the hand, I must not go,
I see her close beside me with silent lips sad and tremulous.

Walt Whitman
(1819–1892)

This piece of writing resembles metrical poetry in having capitals at the start of each line; but unlike metrical lines, these are not composed of recurring feet of the same kind and number. Whitman has relied on other devices (which we have discussed in previous chapters) to organize his poem. These devices would not be found in such number and frequency in ordinary prose. It might be well to look at the whole matter like this: prose is rhythmical; free verse is more rhythmical than prose; metered poetry is so highly rhythmical that the rhythm conforms to a measurable pattern.

A poet who chooses to write free rather than metered verse sacrifices certain things and gains others. One thing that he gives up is the primitive appeal to the nervous system that meter makes. Thus, his poems will probably not reach so deeply into his audience's minds, and they will be somewhat difficult to memorize. An advantage of free verse is that the poet owes no allegiance to a metrical pattern that may take over the actual composition and force him to write like his predecessors who used that meter.

Blank Verse

Free verse must not be confused with **blank verse,** which is the customary label for iambic pentameter without rhyme (see page 207). Unlike free verse, blank verse has a regular metrical pattern. The characters in Shakespeare's plays sometimes speak in prose, but more often in unrhymed iambic pentameter verse. For instance, the Duke in *As You Like It* makes this comment on having to live in a forest:

> Sweet are the uses of adversity,
> Which, like the toad, ugly and venomous,
> Wears yet a precious jewel in his head;
> And this our life, exempt from public haunt,
> Finds tongues in trees, books in the running brooks,
> Sermons in stones, and good in everything.

The ideas in these lines are not made more "poetic" by the addition of rhyme:

The man to solitude accustom'd long
Perceives in ev'ry thing that lives a tongue;
Not animals alone, but shrubs and trees,
Have speech for him, and understood with ease.

William Cowper
(1731–1800)

The greatest dramatic (*Hamlet, King Lear*) and epic (*Paradise Lost*) poems in English are in blank verse.

The Functions of Meter and Rhythm

Meter and rhythm have two main functions. First, they make a poem pleasurable because they themselves are intrinsically delightful. Like dancing and playing games, reading and writing poems are among the rhythmical activities of mankind. These activities are everywhere apparent: children chant rhythmically, as do some insane people; boys enjoy passing a ball regularly back and forth; a smoothly running automobile motor is music to many an adult ear. Just why rhythm should affect people so powerfully and in so many different ways is far from clear; perhaps it has something to do with the in and out of their breathing, the come and go of their pulses.

In addition to making a poem enjoyable, meter and rhythm make it more meaningful. They are a part of the total meaning—a part that cannot always be described in words but can always be felt and is always lost when a poem is paraphrased or when it is translated from one language to another.

The Hourglass

Do but consider this small dust,
Here running in the glass,
  By atoms moved;
Could you believe that this
The body was
  Of one that loved?

And in his Mistress' flame, playing like a fly,
Turned to cinders by her eye?
Yes; and in death, as life, unblest,
To have't expressed,
Even ashes of lovers find no rest.

Ben Jonson
(1572–1637)

Here the meter is very much a part of the meaning. The poem moves somewhat unsteadily, by fits and starts, as though the speaker were thinking of what he should say as he goes along. Spondees make line 1 slow and thoughtful:

Do but | consid | er | | this | small dust,

Line 2, in contrast, is fast, its unaccented syllables and shorter length reinforcing the action of the running sand:

Here run | ning | | in | the glass,

Line 3, a parenthesis, is appropriately shorter still. Then line 4, which marks the next step in the argument, is like line 1, the first step, except that it is a foot shorter—perhaps because the speaker is becoming more and more unwilling to give out information:

Could you | believe | | that this

Lines 4 and 5 are run-on; yet there is bound to be a slight pause at the end of each, a pause that would be lessened if the lines were printed continuously. The pause seems to be functional. The speaker is in no hurry to give away the surprise in line 6; the sand in the glass is a man's ashes. Having divulged this much, as though reluctantly, he blurts out his next surprising question in two lines that resemble metrically no others in the poem:

And in | his Mist | ress' flame, | | playing | like a fly,
Turned to | cinders | | by her | eye? ^

To emphasize this surprise, he shifts from the expected iambs to quite unexpected trochees. Although his rhetorical questions require no answer, he gives a resounding affirmative:

Yés; | | ănd | ĭn déath, | | ăs lífe, | | ŭnblést,

The omitted syllable at the end of line 8 and the strong caesura after the semicolon isolate the *yes*. The speaker now has a third point to make, and he makes it by means of another new metrical arrangement:

Tŏ háve't | ĕxpréssed,
Évĕn | áshĕs | ŏf lóv | ĕrs | | fínd | nó rést.

Shifting from iambs to trochees and then back to iambs forces the voice to linger on *lovers*. Thus the final point is made emphatically and at the same time reluctantly—as though the speaker knew that nobody would take his remarks for literal truth.

The meter enables the reader to participate in the sequence of thoughts, to experience the surprises in the poem. Since the experience of any poem is a large part of its meaning, the poem has a different meaning when put into a different meter, because it then conveys a different experience.

The Hour-Glass

O think, fair maid! these sands that pass
In slender threads adown this glass,
Were once the body of some swain,
Who lov'd too well and lov'd in vain,
And let one soft sigh heave thy breast,
That not in life alone unblest
E'en lovers' ashes find no rest.

Samuel Taylor Coleridge
(1772–1834)

Coleridge omits the part about the lover who burns in the flames of his mistress' eye; he is not interested in such macabre details. Instead, his speaker wishes to emphasize the pathos of the situation and to communicate that pathos to a girl. The meter therefore moves with stately regularity throughout. It is notably varied only in line 5:

And lét | óne sóft | sígh | | héave | thy bréast,

Coleridge has not only added the idea in this line, but he has emphasized it because it is an important part of his meaning. His poem seems to be a more finished performance than Jonson's; actually it is not, because Jonson distorted his meter intentionally. Coleridge avoided surprise and drama: these would be incompatible with tender feelings. His easy smoothness is as much a part of his meaning as Jonson's contrived roughness is part of *his.*

Index of Terms

Index of Authors, First Lines, and Titles

All titles are listed under their authors, but when a title is identical with the opening words of the first line, only the first line is given a separate entry. An asterisk following a title indicates an excerpt.